A FINE CHEST OF MEDALS

By the same author:
Seeds of Trouble: Government Policy and Land Rights in Nyasaland, 1946-1964
Development Governor: A Biography of Sir Geoffrey Colby
State of Emergency: Crisis in Central Africa, Nyasaland 1959-1960
Retreat From Empire: Sir Robert Armitage in Africa and Cyprus
Sir Glyn Jones: A Proconsul in Africa
Revolt of the Ministers: The Malawi Cabinet Crisis, 1964-1965
Wild Goose: the Life and Death of Hugh van Oppen
Johnston's Administration: A History of the British Central Africa Administration, 1891-1897
The Evolution of Local Government in Malawi
Education and Research in Public Administration in Africa (with A. Adedeji)
Ife Essays in Public Administration (with M. J. Balogun)

A FINE CHEST OF MEDALS

THE LIFE OF JACK ARCHER

'You will have a fine chest of medals after this show, Archer'.

General Snow, August 1914.

Colin Baker

Mpemba Books
Cardiff

Published in 2003 by Mpemba Books
55A Lon y Deri, Cardiff
CF14 6JP

Copublished in Malawi by Kachere Series as Kachere Book No. 15

Copyright © Colin Baker, 2003

All rights reserved. Except for brief quotations in a review, this book, or any part thereof, may not be reproduced, stored in or introduced into a retrieval system, or transmitted, in any form or by any means, electronic, mechanical, photocopying, recording or otherwise, without the prior written permission of the publisher.

ISBN 0 9542020 1 5 in the United Kingdom
      99908 16 56 5 in Malawi

Photoset in 10 Times New Roman by Mpemba Books, Cardiff
Printed and bound by Antony Rowe Ltd, Chippenham

For our Children,
Christopher, Daryll and Lynette

CONTENTS

Maps		ix-xiv
Preface		xv
Chapter One	Early Years - 1871-1889	1
Chapter Two	The Rifle Brigade – England and Ireland: 1889-1896	6
Chapter Three	The Mounted Infantry - Mashonaland: 1896-1897	26
Chapter Four	The Rifle Brigade - Malta, Egypt and Crete: 1897-1899	63
Chapter Five	The Rifle Brigade – South Africa: 1899-1902	82
Chapter Six	The Rifle Brigade - Egypt, the Sudan and India: 1902-1908	125
Chapter Seven	The King's African Rifles - Nyasaland and Somaliland: 1908-1914	140
Chapter Eight	The First World War: 1914-1918	171
Chapter Nine	The Nyasaland Prison Service: 1919-1939	193
Chapter Ten	The Second World War and Retirement: 1939-1954	225
Chapter Eleven	A Man Among Men	231
Notes		243

MAP ONE: MASHONALAND: BEIRA-SALISBURY ROUTE

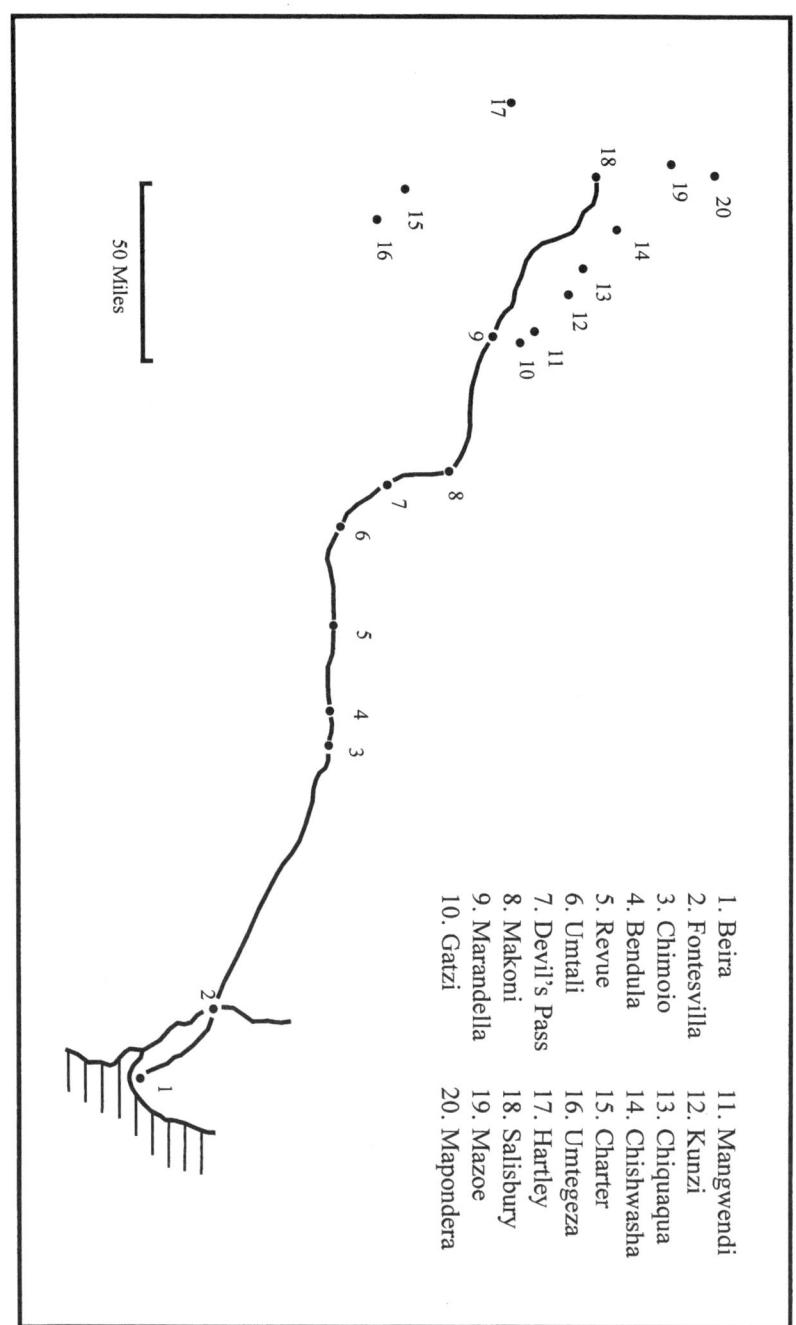

1. Beira
2. Fontesvilla
3. Chimoio
4. Bendula
5. Revue
6. Umtali
7. Devil's Pass
8. Makoni
9. Marandella
10. Gatzi
11. Mangwendi
12. Kunzi
13. Chiquaqua
14. Chishwasha
15. Charter
16. Umtegeza
17. Hartley
18. Salisbury
19. Mazoe
20. Mapondera

MAP TWO: THE NILE

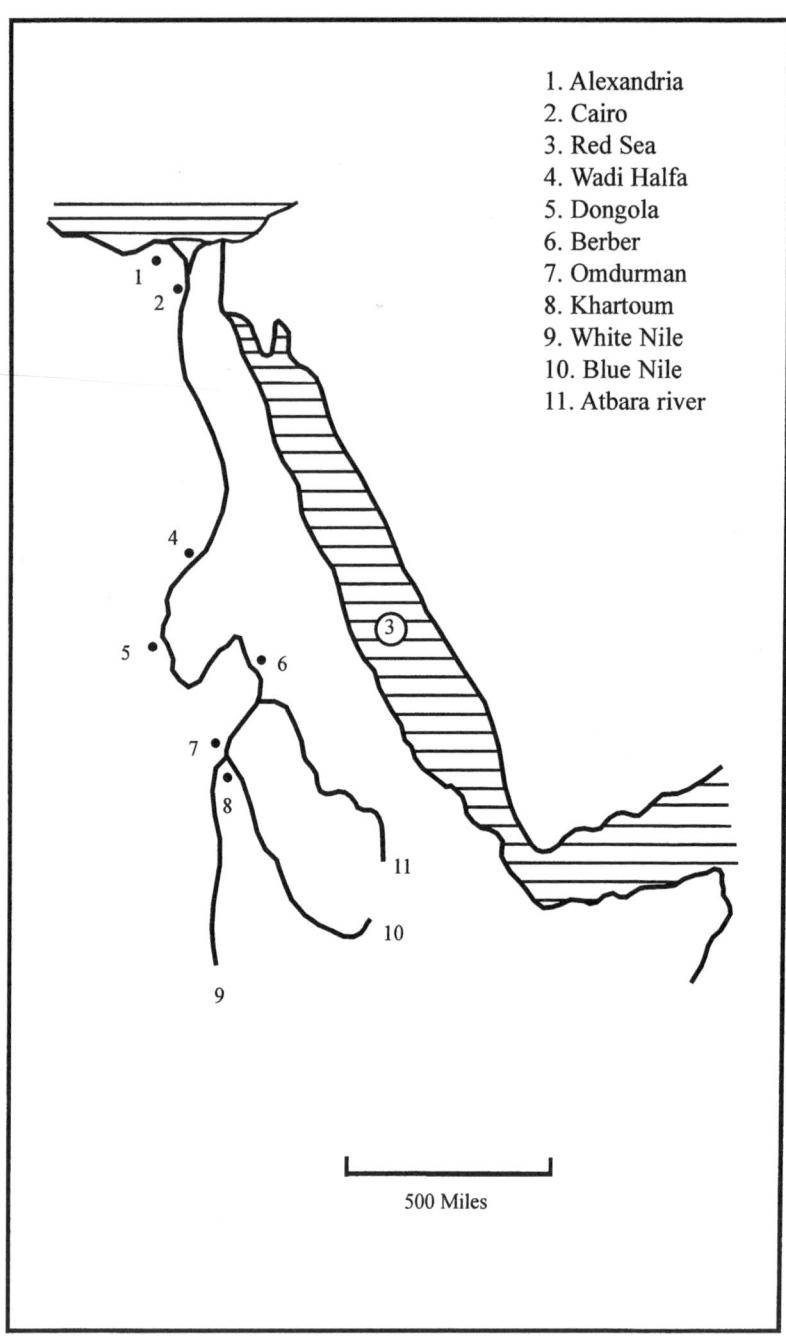

MAP THREE: LADYSMITH

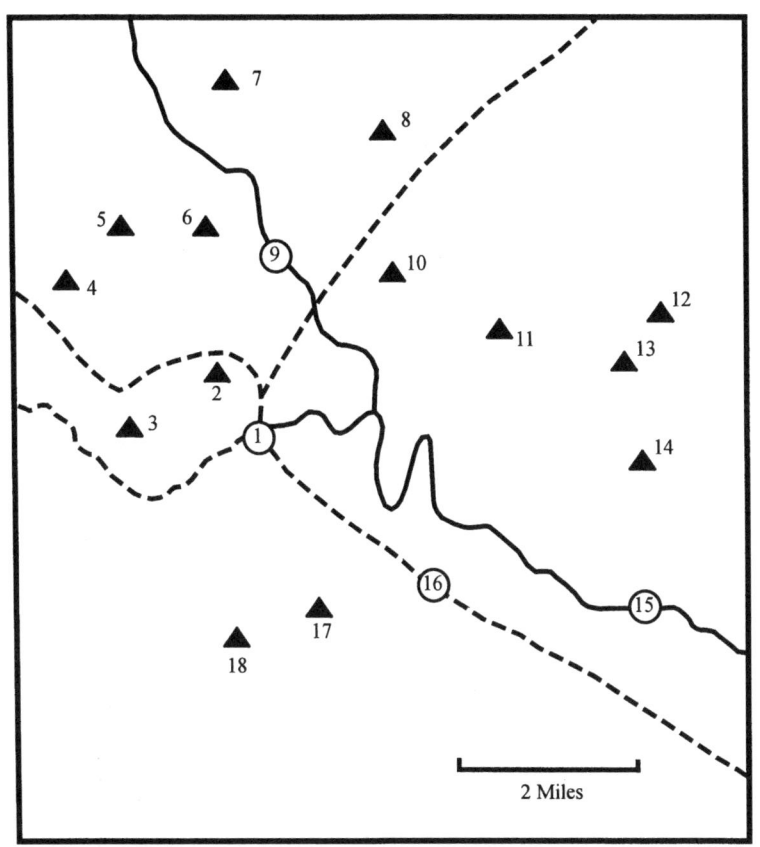

1. Ladysmith
2. Observation Hill
3. King's Post
4. Thornhill's Kopje
5. Surprise Hill
6. Bell's Kopje
7. Nicholson's Nek
8. Pepworth Hill
9. Modder Spruit
10. Limit Hill
11. Flag Hill
12. Lombard's Kop
13. Gun Hill
14. Bulwana
15. Klip River
16. Railway
17. Caesar's Camp
18. Wagon Hill

MAP FOUR: NATAL AND TRANSVAAL

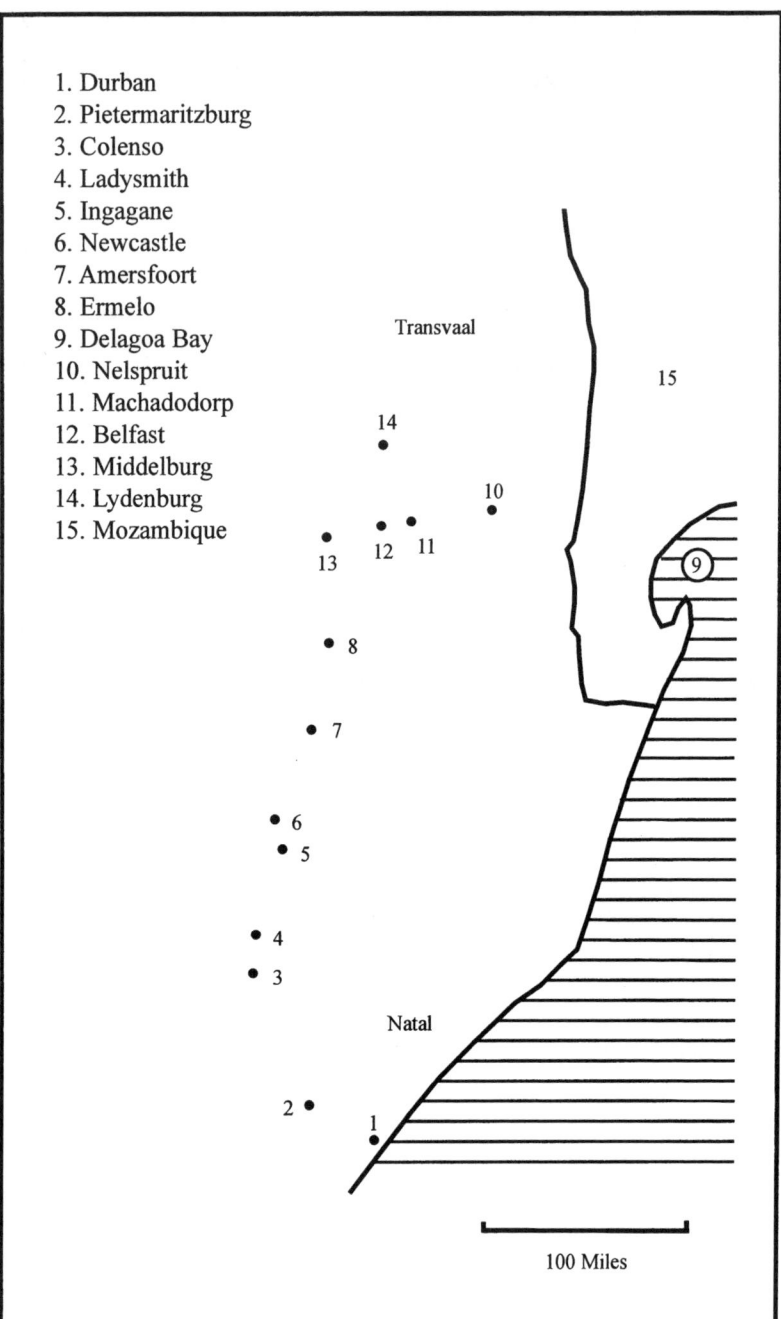

MAP FIVE: SOMALILAND

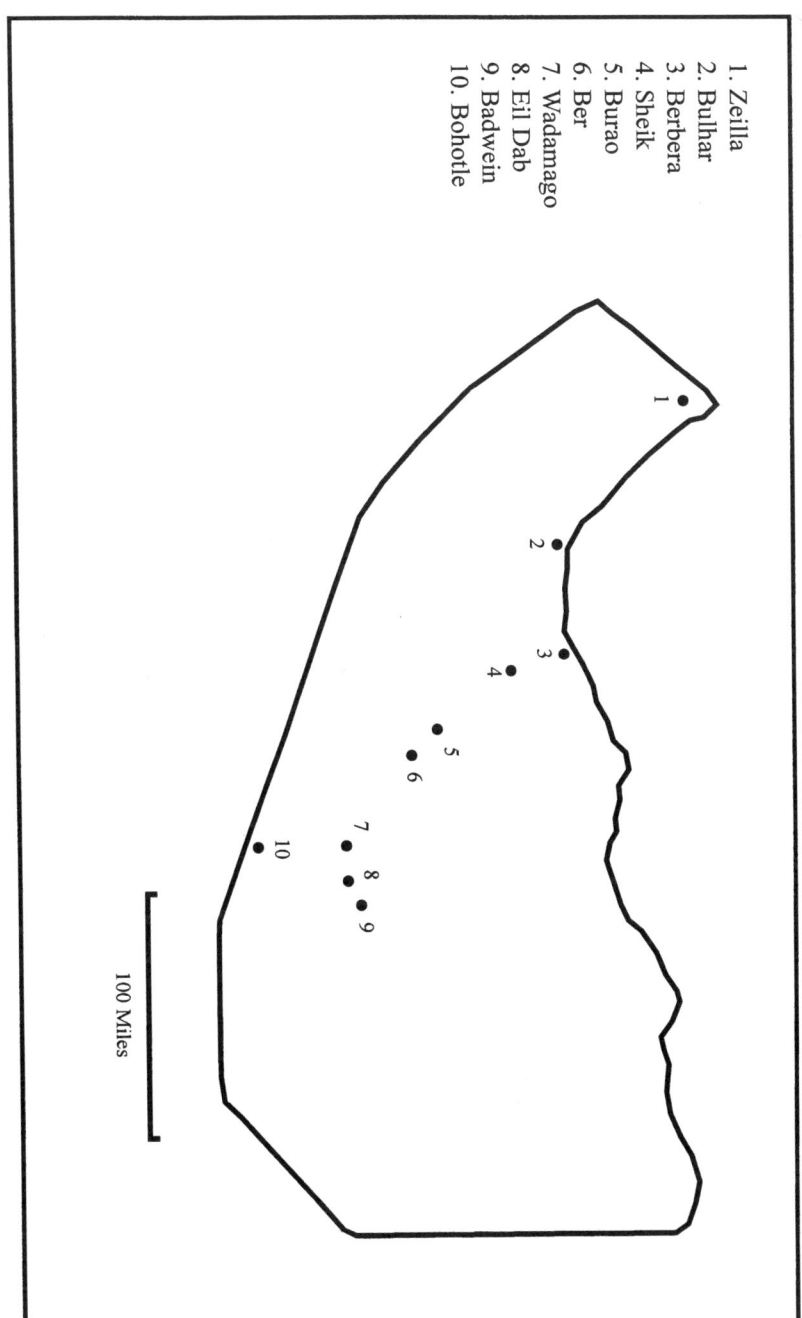

MAP SIX: SOUTHERN NYASALAND

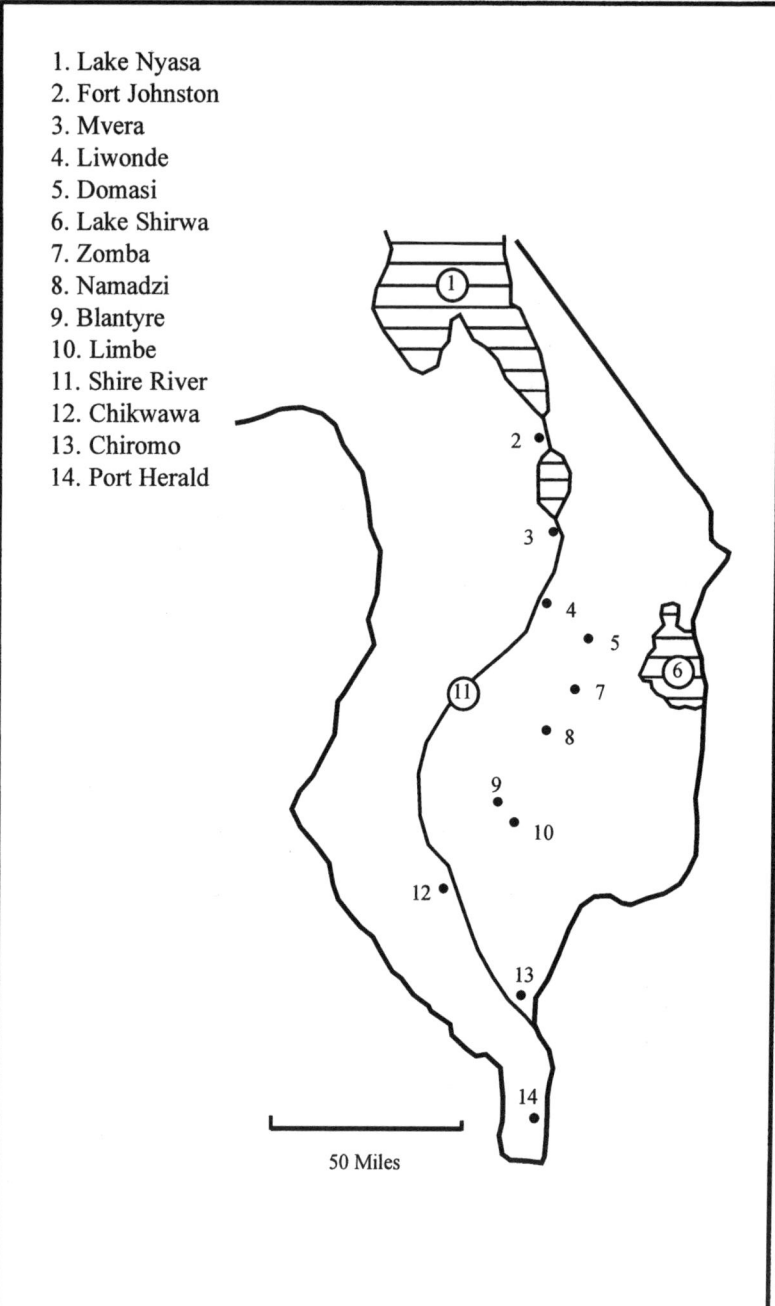

1. Lake Nyasa
2. Fort Johnston
3. Mvera
4. Liwonde
5. Domasi
6. Lake Shirwa
7. Zomba
8. Namadzi
9. Blantyre
10. Limbe
11. Shire River
12. Chikwawa
13. Chiromo
14. Port Herald

50 Miles

PREFACE

A few years ago, my wife and I were returning by sea on a small ship from a holiday in South Africa. There were only half a dozen of us at the dining room table: the Chief Officer, three other passengers and ourselves. One of these passengers was a rather quiet lady and it was difficult to engage her in conversation. My wife felt that I was not making as full an effort as I might to be sociable, and after a few days at sea, and in order to tempt me into conversation, she told me that the lady in question had visited Nyasaland. She knew, of course, that Nyasaland was a country about which I could listen endlessly - we had been married there, our children had been born there, we had lived there for many years and it had long been the main focus of my research and writing. She knew, too, that it would not now be long before I would ask the lady about her Nyasaland visits. She was, and not for the first – or last – time, absolutely right.

Shortly, I spoke with this lady and learned that some fifty odd years previously she had on a number of occasions visited her cousins in Zomba, Nyasaland, where their father worked in the civil service. I asked what her uncle's name was and learned that it was Jack Archer. She knew little more about him, and whilst the name rang a faint bell in my mind, I could not recall anything of him. However, when we arrived back in Britain, I looked up the name Archer in my card index of former Nyasaland civil servants and discovered that from 1919 to 1939 he had been Superintendent of the Central Prison, the Lunatic Asylum and the Leprosarium in Zomba. The bizarre splendour and scope of his title was sufficient for me to dig a little further, and the records told me that he had been appointed at the age of 48 years and had retired at the age of 68. I dismissed these entries as errors, because most expatriate civil servants at that time retired when they reached or approached the age of 50, and I knew of none who had stayed on into their 60s, still less nearly 70s, even when temporarily recalled during the Second World War. I was wrong to dismiss the entries so quickly, though I was not to learn this until later.

None the less, I was intrigued and wrote to our shy shipboard companion and asked if any of her cousins happened still to be alive and, if they were, could she let me have their addresses. She kindly did so, and I wrote to Dr Elizabeth Saunder in the USA, Rosemary Page in South

Africa and Dr Beryl Groves in Zimbabwe. They all kindly wrote back to me, answered my questions about their father and confirmed that he indeed had been appointed at the age of 48 and retired when he was 68. What was more, they said, his appointment to Nyasaland followed an army career lasting 30 years and was followed by a further seven years in the army in Nyasaland, mainly during the Second World War.

In one of the letters I received from Dr Groves she said that she was coming to Britain for a short holiday, and if I were really interested in writing about her father she would bring some of his papers for me to see. The papers were, she told me, in a suitcase weighing eleven kilograms but she would bring them to me if we could arrange a convenient meeting place. I lived in Cardiff and the nearest she would be to that city was Radlett in Hertfordshire, where she would be staying for a day or so with friends. Luck was on my side because my son lived in Radlett. Even more extraordinary was the fact that when she told me the address of her friends, we discovered that their house was only a hundred or so yards from my son's!

So it was that one sunny morning, my daughter-in-law, Catherine, and I walked round the corner for coffee and to meet Dr Groves. After a delightful couple of hours we left – carrying the heavy suitcase that we soon found was packed full of letters, diaries, newspaper cuttings and photographs. Jack Archer - splendid man - had been a hoarder of his personal papers. I had a number of other pieces of writing that I had to complete before I could turn my attention more fully to Jack Archer, but what I found in that suitcase was so tempting that I began to write about him in parallel with my other writing. The result has been a fascinating journey, following his life from Hertfordshire, where he was born, through his Rifle Brigade army days in England, Ireland, the Mashonaland Rebellion, the Boer War, Kitchener's Nile Expedition and Omdurman, Crete, Malta, India, the King's African Rifles in Nyasaland and the Fourth Somaliland Expedition, France, German Prisoner of War camps, the Nyasaland Prison Service, the King's African Rifles again in the Second World War and retirement in Nyasaland.

In his, probably unparalleled, long military and civil career Jack Archer was awarded sixteen campaign and other medals that are now on display at the Royal Green Jackets Museum in Winchester. His was a true and richly deserved 'fine chest of medals'.

CHAPTER ONE

EARLY DAYS
1871-1889

When her baby was born on New Year's Day 1871, young Eliza Archer must have wondered into what sort of world she was bringing him. Internationally, Bismark's Prussian Army had advanced on Paris and was besieging and bombarding its inhabitants so as to force the French Republic into peace talks. Closer to where she was living, with her husband and first son - at Eastwick in Hertfordshire, between Harlow and Hertford, just inside the county border with Essex - events were also worrying. The local *Hertford Mercury* reported a 'terrible rail crash at Hatfield', killing eight people, and the burning of Watford's Masonic Hall in which the building had been 'totally destroyed by a serious fire.' There were, too, numerous crimes reported that Eliza, with a young family, would have read with alarm: an indecent assault on a fourteen-year-old girl, a 'murderous assault on a gamekeeper', together with many related offences such as trespassing by poachers, possessing snares and using traps to take game. Cases of theft were numerous: stealing fowls, game, apples, oats and clothing. Many of these were the consequence of poverty and were committed by tramps, some of whom occupied the usually full tramp ward in the Hatfield Union Workhouse.[1]

Yet, Eliza would have been amused by some of these reports. There was the case of a tramp who was charged with stealing 'one bottle of currant jelly, one bottle of anchovy paste, and a pound of pork sausages.' Having stolen them, he had persuaded a local woman to cook the sausages, which she very kindly did, and he went off to a nearby hostelry to eat them. Unfortunately for him, the local constable, to whom the theft had been reported, walked into the tap room and found him in *flagrante delicto,* eating the sausages. The tramp then compounded his offence by telling the chairman of the bench, the Mayor, for reasons he did not explain: 'I am King John of England and all I want is your ------- head off your shoulders. I refer you to the Prince of Wales, my brother-in-law.' It is little wonder that the Mayor immediately committed him for trial at the assizes.

Mrs Archer would have been amused, too, to read of the man who, at half past ten at night on Christmas Eve, in the main road of a nearby town, had thrown snowballs at everyone within his reach, including those on the top of passing omnibuses. A constable approached him and cautioned him, whereupon the man threw a well-compacted snowball at the officer. Presumably miffed by this flagrant flouting of his authority, the constable arrested him, and the local bench fined him three shillings.[2] Eliza, and the miscreant, may well have thought this not an unreasonable sum for the fun he must have had.

None the less, the sources of amusement were few, and the general picture was depressing, both internationally and locally. Contemplating 1871 and its prospects in a leading article, the pessimistic editor of the *Hertford Mercury* penned the gloomy view that:

> The new year opens on a scene of desolation and bloodshed unparalleled in modern times, and with the prospect of confusion, gloom and uncertainty.

It was against this unpromising background that Eliza's second child was born on the first day of the new year, 1871. Christened John, he was known throughout his life by his family, friends and acquaintances as Jack, though at least in her letters, his mother invariably continued to call him John. He personally preferred 'Jack' as in his view it was less staid.

His parents, Thomas Archer and Eliza Thurlow, had been married at Great Parndon some four years earlier, when Eliza was 21. The family, including Jack's elder brother, Harry William, two years his senior, moved shortly after his birth the small distance to Walnut Tree House, Netteswell Cross, near Harlow.[3]

One of Jack's earliest memories was learning to ride a horse, bare back, while at Netteswell Cross. He was quite young, because the top of his head did not come up to his pony's withers. He recalled how his father would tell him to get ready to mount and then, on the count of three, he would bring his crop down across the pony's rump, and the animal would set off apace with his diminutive rider clinging on for all he was worth. Sometimes Jack fell off but he was always made to keep hold of the reins - a lesson he was to value later in life. He long remembered, too, coursing, at an early age, with greyhounds on Hill Farm, land belonging to his Aunt Ricketts, accompanied by his cousin Fred:

> We put up a half grown fox. The greyhounds were bowling him over when there was a shout and, spotting my father, Fred Ricketts and I

bolted. Fred managed to reach a ditch with a quick hedge and escaped, but I got several lashes with a hunting whip before I reached a hedge and ditch. The fox got away but not before he had been well winded.

He was brought up in a stern fashion by his father - though not unusually so for the time - as the riding instruction and the lashing indicate. It was part of a generally toughening process that was to stand him in good stead throughout his life.

He recalled, as well, an occasion on which he climbed with another youngster up the inside of a barn to the roof apex where they discovered that an owl had nested in the thatch. He was dropping the young owls down onto a pile of straw to his companion when the adult owl flew out of the thatch and struck him in the face. Startled, he let go his hold and fell onto the pile of straw below. In doing so, however, he hit his head on a 56-pound weight that was concealed in the straw, and split his skull over the right eye. Even months later he could not look straight down, so if he wanted to pick up something from the floor he had to feel for it with his feet and hands. The doctor believed he had had a lucky escape, and fortunately his vision was not permanently impaired, though he carried the scar for the rest of his life. This was the first of many serious knocks he was to suffer - and recover from - during his life.

He went to school at Harlow but, as he recalled many years later, he 'didn't learn much', a matter on which he was subsequently to express regret.

When he was about nine years old the family moved again, this time to Waltham Cross. It was here that his father died, the day after Jack's twelfth birthday. This brought about another family move. Harry was sent to Hatfield Heath, apprenticed to a butcher, and the rest of the family moved to Lewisham in southeast London. Here, Jack was employed in the wine and spirit trade. The hours were long: from 8.0 a.m. till 9.0 p.m. except on Saturday when he worked to 11.0 p.m. or even later. After a while there was another move as Mrs Archer took over the management of 8 St James Place, St James Street, London.

His aunt, the wife of his mother's brother, William Thurlow, of Brockles Farm, Great Parndon, died, leaving her husband with four daughters and a son. Jack's mother left London and moved to Great Parndon, to look after her brother and his five children while Jack moved into lodgings. At least two evenings a week after he left work at 9.0 p.m. he learned to box, and in order to improve his breathing for boxing he did a good deal of running. He reached the final of a six rounds competition, and in the second round got his nose broken, but fought on. Mainly because he was guarding his nose, he lost on points. The boxing and running were early steps in physical activities, especially running, that he was to pursue enthusiastically in the years ahead of him - and with considerable distinction.

Not keen on making his living in the wine and spirit trade, but preferring to see the world, he tried to join the navy, probably the merchant navy, but his mother wrote to the Naval Department at the West India Docks on the Isle of Dogs, to say that she did not give her consent. Her letter had the effect that she desired, for when he attended for inspection he was turned down as being flat footed! None the less, he left his job in the wine and spirit trade and went to stay, on an extended holiday, with an uncle at Thruston Downs Farm near Andover in Hampshire.[4] Here he showed an early interest in shooting - and an innovative approach to economizing on the use of ammunition. Many years later he recalled:

> I got some pigeon shooting but was restricted for cartridges. I dug a pit near one of the Downs sheep ponds and fixed up a hurdle covered with grass and boughs and left it until the pigeons got used to it. Then I hid there until the pigeons came down for water. I found that by putting my foot on a dry twig and breaking it I could get the pigeons that were sitting on the sheep rail just as they opened their wings. The result was more cartridges for flying shots.

Shooting, too, was to become a pastime he pursued enthusiastically and with distinction in the years ahead.

He was still hankering after seeing the world, and, having failed to get into the navy, he thought the next best thing was the army. His mother contacted Captain F E Lawrence[5] of the Rifle Brigade who had rooms at 8 St James Place, about her son's prospects. Lawrence's private letter of advice was helpful:

> I imagine that he will not be able to go to India until he is 20 in whatever branch of the army he enlists. If he is bent on the Cavalry he should try for the 7th Hussars, now in India, in which case he would go to the Canterbury depot until he is old enough to join. The Royal Dragoons, now at Aldershot, is another cavalry regiment but they never serve in India or abroad except for war service. *It is of the utmost importance to enter a good regiment.* If he is not bent on smart clothes and riding a horse, he should enlist in the *Rifle*

Brigade. There the promotion is quick, chances of active and foreign service frequent. If he enlists in the Rifle Brigade he will be sent at first to the Depot at Winchester, then to the 2nd Battalion at Woolwich and afterwards to India or possibly on active service to Burma. If he makes a good soldier I could help him. Cavalry regiments I would recommend are 7th Hussars, 16th Lancers (in India), 12th Lancers (Aldershot), Royal Dragoons (Aldershot). This letter is only for his assistance and should not be shown about.

It seems that initially the young Archer, still anxious to see the world, was keen to serve overseas, preferably in India, and - possibly because of his early training in riding horses - favoured joining the Cavalry. He saw the Captain and, as he had not selected a regiment, Lawrence arranged for him to spend a week at Aldershot to look around. Although 'very struck by the uniform of the 16th Lancers', the prospects of frequent active and foreign service and of rapid promotion attracted him more, and he finally decided on the Rifle Brigade, Lawrence's regiment. He left home on his eighteenth birthday and formally enlisted, at Winchester, on 12 January 1889.

CHAPTER TWO

THE RIFLE BRIGADE - ENGLAND AND IRELAND: 1889-1896

When he first joined the army, Archer's daily pay was a shilling. From this he paid three pence a day for messing, half a penny a day for laundry, about six pence a month for 'barrack damages', and another six pence a month for 'clubs'. 'So', as he remarked, 'one got very little pay to spend.' Indeed, after two years in the Rifle Brigade he was in debt to the tune of one shilling and four and a half pence.[1]

He could recall many years later precisely what the clothing issue was when he joined the Rifle Brigade: a pair of boots; a cap; a great coat; a cape; two 'frocks' or long tunics - one undress for recruit drill and fatigues and the other tartan for dress parades; a haversack and a haversack pocket; a pair of woollen mittens; a pair of trousers, issued bi-annually for ceremonies; a pair of undress trousers; a pair of trousers and a waistcoat; a tunic; a helmet; and a pair of leggings. Some of these items did not last long and wore out quickly: 'One was constantly having to buy a shirt, socks or to replace one's uniform.'

Food was much less of a problem. He received free rations of a daily issue of a pound of bread and a pound of meat, including bone. Vegetables were bought out of the three pence a day that he paid for messing. 'Things were certainly cheap in the Dry Canteen. One could get a fair supper for two pence.'

His bedding was far from lavish: a straw mattress, two blankets, two sheets, a straw pillow and a pillowslip.

> Everything was very damp when I drew my bedding and I was soon in hospital with bronchitis.[2] One night in getting into bed I found a lot of damp salt in it. Whilst remaking my bed amongst laughter I said, 'If I knew who put salt in my bed I would punch him on the nose.' A man named Harford put his face close to mine and said, 'Punch me on the nose.' I could not resist the temptation and hit him on his nose as hard as I could, knocking him down, and in falling he

hit the back of his head on an iron cot, splitting it open. There was lots of blood from nose and wound and he was taken to the hospital. The other recruits said I would be 'for it' in the morning.

True enough, the following morning Archer was marched before his company commander, Captain Rokeby, by Colour Sergeant Horsman. However, much to his surprise, rather than reprimanding him, Horsman told the Captain, 'Sir, this is the recruit I recommend for Lance Corporal.' Rokeby agreed and Archer was appointed Temporary Lance Corporal and put in charge of a room of 'bad recruits'. 'I was put in charge of a room of drunken recruits as I was a fair boxer.' Horsman told these men that 'if they didn't keep clean and behave, Archer was to knock the spots off them, and if Archer couldn't do it, he would.' Jack's early training in boxing was beginning to pay dividends, and his retaliation against Harford added to his prestige as a tough fighter.

On his recruits course, there was a good deal of musketry training with 450 bore Martin Henry rifles, and he badly bruised his shoulder using this heavy weapon, despite - like so many others before and after him - having discreetly padded his shoulder with socks. Scoring 223 points, he tied first place and was awarded a prize of seven shillings and six pence - a week's pay - which he found 'most welcome'. 149 points were needed to become a First Class shot, and 165 to become a Marksman. He greatly exceeded both these levels and was made a Marksman, proud to wear the crossed rifles badge on the lower sleeve of his uniform.

At the end of his initial training course, he left the Depot at Winchester and joined F Company, under Captain Arthur Somerset[3], in the Second Battalion of the Rifle Brigade. This battalion was stationed, not at Woolwich as Captain Lawrence had indicated, but at Citadel Barracks in Dover. Here it was under the command of Colonel Leopold Swaine[4], whom Archer much admired, particularly for his skill on the parade ground:

> Colonel Swaine was a splendid drill. He could manoeuvre the Battalion at the double on the South Front Barracks parade ground, which was very small, very easily. Whenever a Company Commander was slow or made mistakes he was on it at once, gave instructions what should be done and saw it carried out. At a Brigade drill under the General, as soon as the Bugler sounded the 'G' we moved into place at the double, so had completed the movement before the other Battalions. Soon other Regiments began to move before the 'G' was sounded, and completed the move ordered, with

the Second Battalion still waiting for the 'G'. Up rode an ADC or Staff Officer to say the General was waiting for us to move. Colonel Swaine said we were waiting for the 'G' to sound. No love lost between the General and our CO.

Already, clearly, he was taking great pride in the precision and discipline of parade ground drill and in the unit to which he belonged - and its commander.

He was made a temporary Corporal during this second part of his recruits training. Though all temporary NCOs reverted to their normal rank at the end of this part, as soon as his draft completed it he was appointed Chosen Man - called by the troops, 'P T Major' - an appointment known only in the Rifle Brigade, with the duties of an Orderly Corporal. In this position he was excused fatigues and coal carrying, and in the absence of a substantive NCO he took charge. During this period he had 'plenty of boxing'. On 26 November 1889 he was awarded a Musketry Drill Certificate, and two weeks later, having been in the army less than eleven months, he was promoted to be Unpaid Acting Corporal in A Company, under Captain Hon. D Lawless, and moved to the South Front Barracks at Dover.

When he joined A Company and took over as Orderly Corporal, he again met up with Harford whose nose he had punched at the Depot. One of the other Acting Corporals, unaware that he had encountered Harford previously, and trying to be helpful, advised Archer, 'Don't warn Harford to draw spuds' - an unpleasant duty which soldiers tried to avoid. Archer made it clear, however, that he intended to do precisely this, and two others accompanied him to see if he was as good as his word. On entering Harford's room, he simply but firmly said, 'Harford. Draw spuds' and received the compliant reply, 'All right Corporal', despite his 'reputation of turning nasty and structures butting when ordered to do something by a young junior NCO'. No doubt he recalled the earlier punch on the nose and the serious damage to his head as he fell. Perhaps, too, he had learned of the 'plenty of boxing' that this particular young junior NCO had been undertaking. The other NCOs were both astonished by Harford's reply and impressed by Archer's boldness and authority. His reputation was growing.

At the end of December 1889 he moved to Fort Burgoyne and attended school at the nearby Castle to be coached for the Third Class Certificate in Education, which he successfully achieved.

A few months into 1890 he left Dover by train for Lydd on the south Kent coast, some twenty miles away. He went with an advance party to prepare the camp for A and C Companies, who arrived there on 30 April and 1 May. At Lydd he continued to do a good deal of shooting and to do it well. In May, for example, he fired the Dutyman's Course of Musketry, made 182 points, came fifth in the Company and won a prize of ten shillings. They used the Martin Henry rifle, which he still found had 'plenty of kick', though, it seems, he no longer padded his shoulder with socks. Shortly, the Battalion was issued with the new Mark I Lee Metford rifle, which they used only for drills while continuing all musketry practices with the Martin Henry rifle. He recalled that during a field firing exercise:

> We had a big attack with ball ammunition on a fort. On parade the CO said 'Fall out all marksmen'. We were formed into a [separate] Company and with the artillery opened the attack. Although casualties were told to fall out, none of the marksmen seemed to be selected so I continued right up to the final charge. Shoulder very much bruised.

At Lydd, too, he spent time on athletics, again successfully. In the Company sports he came first in the high jump, second in the 120 yards hurdles and the long jump, and third in the 440 yards flat race, winning money prizes totalling one pound and three shillings. These were early successes in an athletics career that was to last a long time.

While at Lydd the Battalion undertook regular bathing parades in the sea. On one of these several men ventured round the seaward side of an old wreck and got into difficulties as the water became rough and the tide began to run strongly. The men clung to the wreck and were badly scratched with mussel shells. It was difficult to get them ashore. Archer was swimming on the seaward side of the wreck and got 'a wigging' for doing so until he explained that he was waiting in case any of his men got washed out to sea. Whether or not this was an 'old soldier's' excuse, he did in fact help several of the men who were in danger to reach the shore. Already a strong swimmer, he was to develop this sport, too, and his prowess in it still further, in the years ahead.

It was when he was at Lydd that the Battalion was issued with the new 'Rifle Cap' to replace the helmet they had previously worn. He found the new cap 'not so comfortable, especially in the rain,' as the old helmet, but certainly much smarter and different from the other regiments' headgear. 'The officers one evening burnt the CO's old helmet and had quite a ceremony to do it.' His pride in his regiment and its differentiation from others was considerable.

In June, the Battalion was moved from Lydd to Aldershot. This was a substantial operation and involved setting up camps en route at Rushmoor Bottom - where they held manoeuvres - Burley Bottom, Normandy, Putenham Common, Stanford Common, Staples Hill, Chobham Common, Deer Rock Hills and Yateley Common. Despite it being early summer, the weather was bad and it rained almost continuously. The ground was boggy and often flooded. Sometimes they were able to gather heather to put on the floor of their tents to keep a little drier and warmer, and they found their clothes dried quicker on than off, 'if one can stand it'. At Rushmoor Bottom, the Prince of Wales inspected the Battalion and congratulated them: 'Splendid Battalion, Swaine.' At another point the Battalion was paraded by the Duke of Connaught, and at Chobham Common the officers organised a three quarters of a mile race which Archer - continuing the athletics successes he had at Lydd - won, together with a prize of four shillings. Much to his satisfaction, Stockman, the Army's 1891 quarter mile champion, came second.

In July he started a three months mounted infantry course at Aldershot, with two officers - Lieutenant Ramsay, Archer's section officer, and Lieutenant Harry Wilson[5] - and 63 NCOs and Riflemen. He was to spend later parts of his army career in mounted infantry units, and this was important early training for that role. He had, of course, learned to ride as a young boy. The members started their course under canvas on the square of the West Cavalry Barracks, taking over the horses from the 11th Hussars, and later moved into the West Cavalry block itself. Drill, of which there was a great deal, was at the riding school, under Colonel Hutton.

They began cavalry manoeuvres early in September and marched to Crookham Common where they stopped to feed and water the horses before going on to Straightfieldsaye and the Duke of Wellington's Park. Two days later they marched to Effingham via Newbury and camped in a field with 1st and 2nd Life Guards, 2nd Dragoons, The Blues, 5th Dragoons and 8th Hussars. Here they 'turned up lots of hares every day'; more, Archer reminisced, 'than at Thruston Down Farm.' Here, too, they had an exercise against the Cavalry that he long remembered with pride. They put all their horses in a farm building and its yards, under escort, and then went off and lined the hedges and ditches nearby. The result was 'a proper slaughter of the Cavalry.' At the end of the course he was awarded 'one of the best certificates.' On 12 September there was a march past of all the mounted troops before the Prince of Wales and the Duke of Connaught. Two days later they started their four days' return to Aldershot, camping at Crookham in wet and windy weather during which some of the horses got loose and the men did not get much rest. The poor weather and loose horses were not his only problems. On the last day he recorded: 'My horse got kicked about eight miles from Aldershot so I had to walk. Horse laid up so took over Rifleman Godwin's.' A week later they were on the move again, this time for Ireland:

> 25 September 1890. Started with horses for Shorncliffe [just west of Folkestone], billeted at Dorking where inhabitants gave us tea and afterwards got up a Concert.
> 26 September. Marched to Sevenoaks, billeted at Underriver. Harry Turner gave me a good supper and took me round the Town.
> 27 September. Marched to Cranbrook. Stopped there 28th.
> 29 September. Marched to Shorncliffe and handed over horses to 17th Lancers.
> 1 October. Train to Portsmouth, put up by Yorkshire Regiment. Barracks very dirty. Some of the Yorks stole some M I [Mounted Infantry] kit.

The day after he arrived at Portsmouth, he embarked on HMS *Assistance* for Dublin to rejoin his Battalion. The voyage started well and he enjoyed the good view from the ship of the Isle of Wight and the south coast of England and, early the following morning, of Lands End. Here his luck ran out, for the weather then changed and 'it began to blow what the sailors called half a gale.' The ship rolled badly, his stomach rolled even more badly and he was very seasick. Unable to tolerate the idea of going down below - as many of his fellows did - because 'one could cut the atmosphere with a knife,' he instead tucked himself away on deck in a horsebox, and survived the ordeal. This was his first experience of the seasickness that was to plague him for many years.

At eight in the morning on 4 October, the *Assistance* anchored in Dublin Bay. Archer had a much needed wash and brush up and was congratulated by a naval lieutenant on the work of the 'swobbers' who had been placed under his command soon after they sailed from Portsmouth. Fortunately his swobbers were old soldiers and had not been sick and unable to 'swob' the decks. He was pleased to receive the congratulations, and wisely did not reveal that he himself had been very sick and had done nothing after leaving Lands End. The ship entered the dock during the afternoon and, with a sigh of relief and a still queasy stomach, he hoped he would never again have to travel on the *Assistance*, which, a sailor told him, 'was so old that she was not allowed out of sight of land!' No doubt he felt that she should not be let in sight of the sea!

The next day he disembarked and went by train to Belfast. 'The mail train was very slow although we had Lord Wolseley on it. Left Dublin at 8.30 a m., arrived Belfast 1.15 p.m. and this is supposed to be the best railway in Ireland.'

The Battalion was stationed at Victoria Barracks in Belfast, and his Company was housed in huts at Willow Bank. He spent the first month there on a gymnastics course and played football nearly every afternoon. He played in a six a side football tournament and his team won five shillings each. On 5 November he passed the written examination for promotion to Corporal and a fortnight later 'passed on Square for Corporal'. Two months later he was awarded his first Good Conduct Badge, and his pay rose to a shilling and a penny a day. He had been in the army two years.

From mid January to late February 1891 he was granted six weeks furlough, which he took in England, and drew advance pay of three pounds, fifteen shillings, four and a half pence. In addition, as Acting Corporal he was paid an allowance of three pence a day. On leave he spent a good deal of time at Great Parndon with his mother, and frequently rode his Uncle Willie's hunter, Squire Todhunter's horse, which he broke in to stand for train and other noises – putting to good use his mounted infantry training.

On his return from furlough he became a drill instructor and was shortly drilling recruits in musketry. In April he was promoted to full Corporal in his own A Company, commanded by Captain Lawless, and moved into Victoria Barracks, where he found the conditions more comfortable: 'What a pleasure to get a bunk to oneself.' A bunk was a small, individually occupied, room and provided a great deal more privacy than did barrack rooms. Furthermore, he was now 'rich enough to have a batman.' This was Bugler Cole, who was 'dagging mad and always cleaning.' Every week he cleaned out Archer's bunk and scrubbed the floor with hot soap suds and water from the women's wash house. He was an 'old soldier with Egyptian Medal and Star,' and was the Army Champion Bugler.[6] Archer's ability to afford a batman derived only partly from his pay, and mainly from the monetary prizes he was winning at athletics, sports and rifle shooting.

Although no doubt he had to undertake a good deal of military work, much of the remainder of 1891 and the whole of 1892 and 1893 seems to have been taken up with athletics and swimming.

Late in July, at the Company athletic sports held at Crumlin Road, the Royal Irish Constabulary ground, he came first in the one mile flat, the high jump and the long jump, but since the regulations allowed a competitor to take only one first prize, two second prizes and 'as many third prizes as one can get', he did not collect as many prizes as his performance otherwise merited. In a sports meeting against the Lancashire Fusiliers, he came second to Sergeant Wallison of the Fusiliers in the one mile open to the garrison, and was awarded a bronze medal and ten shillings. A few days later, in the 880 yards open to the garrison, the tables were turned and Archer came first, receiving a prize of one pound ten shillings, while Wallison came second. He became friendly with Police Sergeant Forbes who trained the Royal Irish Constabulary and who offered to give him tips and to get permission for him to train at Crumlin Road. After this, he did practically all his training there. Among his prizes at this time were a tea urn, a travelling clock, a claret jug, a cruet, a marble clock, a hot water kettle and a good deal of prize money.

He was one of only two soldiers - the other was Corporal Webb, champion swimmer of Dover - to become members of the Ormean Amateur Swimming Club, 'a very good club'. In December 1890 he won three swimming prizes at the club's baths. A year later he won a senior swimming handicap and a prize for those who had never won a first prize before, and the rightly suspicious Mayor of Belfast, in handing him the prize, remarked, 'You are a queer novice!' He also played a good deal of water polo and football - being in the winning team of a six a side final - trained regularly at running and swimming and frequently boxed.

Naturally, sports did not take up all his time and he had a number of interesting formal assignments. For example, in May 1891 he travelled to Dublin on 'conducting duty', returning the following day. Of this trip he remarked that 'the country looked lovely, greener than anywhere I have ever seen before.' A little later he 'drove married families to Helens Bay', and in July 1891 he went to Downpatrick on Judges Guard. He was billeted in this 'very dirty town.' 'We had a guard on his house, mounted police escorted him from house to court where we received him and did guard while court was sitting.'

That same month he took temporary charge of the regiment and garrison transport and received an extra duty allowance of four pence a day. Two sergeants in succession had got into trouble when in charge of the transport and were removed from their duties. Some months later, at the tram stables, with a detachment of the 9th Lancers, something frightened the pair of horses pulling an ambulance and they bolted. Archer ran after them, caught up with them and jumped on to the ambulance. As he tried to pull up the horses a rein broke, so he jumped on the pole and with his feet against the pole chains he was able to get hold of the bridle and pull the horses up. He was putting to good use his father's early tuition in mounting horses and hanging on to the reins, and his own athletics training. At about this time, too, he was asked to ride Captain Lawrence's polo pony as scout as far as Dumbridge. When Lawrence's groom heard that Archer was to ride one of the ponies, he stopped taking them out for exercise because he thought Archer would probably be thrown and that would stop the ponies being taken for military service. The result was that the groom had more mud and sweat to clean off the unexercised horses when Archer had finished riding them - without being thrown - and he made no more objections. While in charge of the transport Archer regularly drove the regimental brake to races and football matches. He was also involved in training men for mounted infantry work with the Regimental Transport Battalion. When the men were confined to barracks two or three times a week, Archer was exempted because he still took the ambulance to detachments at Willow Bank and at the Tram Stables.

During 1891 he and his colleagues had their first shoot with the Lee Martin Mark 1 rifle, which until then had been used only for drills. They found that the sights on this new rifle were disconcertingly different from those they previously used. The fore-sight was a small rectangular block with a slot down its centre that had to be aligned with a similar slot below a rectangular cut-out in the rear sight. To their dismay and chagrin, all the best shots in the Battalion, including Archer, secured poorer results than they had previously, and they attributed this to the sights. When Archer experimented with his rifle a little later, he discovered that if he fixed a pinhead in the slot of the fore-sight he could shoot 'exceptionally well'. In the annual course at Hollywood Camp, without his pinhead, he shot very badly, and lamented, 'Wish I could have used my pinhead fore-sight.' A year later, when the Battalion was issued with a new rifle, he said he was glad to get rid of the Mark 1 rifle and its 'barleycorn fore-sight.'

At the beginning of January 1892, Archer's company commander, Captain Lawrence, was seconded to the Cape Mounted Rifles. Archer was sorry to see him go, but was both proud and pleased when, as he left, Lawrence shook hands and said, 'I hope you will be a sergeant major when I return.'

On 10 October 1892, at his own request, he left his duties with the regimental and garrison transport in order to undertake military training, and on 7 November he was promoted Acting Sergeant. This was not an unmixed blessing because Acting Sergeants were unpaid and drew the same pay as a Corporal, a shilling and eight pence a day. Yet he had to pay six pence instead of three pence a day for messing, and there were other sergeants' mess charges. Additionally, he had to pay for the sergeants' chevron braiding on his tunic and jacket, and for his pill box forage cap for walking out and parades.

Early in December 1892 he again went on six weeks furlough, leaving Ireland via Larne and spending most of his time in England with his mother. Soon after he returned to Belfast in January 1893, he embarked on the *Assistance* for Kingston Harbour, Dublin, to relieve the Gloucestershire Regiment. He would have viewed sailing on the *Assistance* with a degree of trepidation, but since it was a short voyage, not across the open Irish Sea and 'not out of the sight of land', he was not seasick, though others were. When he arrived at Dublin he helped the Quarter Master Sergeant to collect the men's blankets: 'a filthy job as several were covered in vomit. Made me sick.' He then marched to the Ship Stree Barracks. It was a 'rotten march over wet muddy cobbles, especially when marching to bagpipes as one had difficulty in keeping step'. He spent several days cleaning the barracks, scraping off years of whitewash from the walls. A little later he took a party of recruits to the Curragh Camp to put them through a musketry course, and here again he found the huts - which had been put up for the army returning from the Crimean War - very dirty, with soaking wet straw beds, blankets and sheets.

At the end of a six weeks garrison course on military topography he passed first in the practical examination and third in the written, and his sketch was sufficiently good for it to be sent to the General Officer Commanding. Later in his military career he showed considerable skill in observing the landscape through which he happened to be passing, in drawing sketch maps of the topography and in describing it. It was a skill, too, which he later put to good practical effect, especially when in a tight corner.

He was also engaged on a number of 'social' duties in 1893. In February he spent two days on duty at a levee at Dublin Castle and in the Drawing Room there, noting 'Some very smart dresses and uniforms with decorations.' In April he went to the Puncherstown Races to assist in the officers' mess and to guard the plate at night.

He played a good deal of football during 1893. On one occasion, when playing against the gym staff, 'after about ten minutes I had my shoulder put out. Medical staff pulled it in. Played on again in second half but took good care no one touched me.' Just as when his nose had been broken in a boxing match when he was working in the wine and spirit trade before joining the army, he carried on but was careful to avoid further injury.

In a letter to his mother in the middle of June, he told her that he might come over to England sometime during the next month for the Army Championships Athletics Meeting. 'If I do I shall be able to come and see you. I am not certain they will send me yet as it is expensive and Captain Lawrence has gone away or he would pay the money out of his own pocket.'[7] This was the Captain Lawrence, Archer's company commander, who had advised his mother and him about his joining the army, and it appears that he continued to take a practical interest in Archer after he joined, at least until he, Lawrence, was seconded to the Cape Mounted Rifles in January 1892. For example, on 9 October 1891, after his men had marched from Hollywood Camp to Victoria Barracks, Lawrence got together twelve starters to try and equal or beat a record made by some Italian soldiers who had 'done six miles in 47 minutes', dressed in drill order with leggings and Rifle Cap.

> The run was nine times round the Barracks, fairly steep. All the others fell out after the third round. I did six times and was told I could not do the distance in the time so fell out. Mr Lawrence gave me four shillings.

In June Archer was made Caterer of the sergeants' mess, a job he would have preferred to avoid because it curtailed his athletics training. In July he went to Aldershot for the Army Championships Athletics meeting that he had mentioned to his mother, and again was very seasick during the 'rotten journey'. Although the grass track was heavy and he felt 'rotten' during the meeting - the result of inadequate recent training and of seasickness - he came second in the 440 yards heat and in the final, first in the NCOs' mile, and second in the 880 yards Championship of the Army. The 880 yards race was won by Lieutenant T T Pitman, the Amateur Champion of England. Part of the incentive for the team to do well was their being threatened - probably not genuinely - before they left Ireland that if they did not do well they would have to refund their fares out of their own pockets. During the evening following the meeting, he went to see his brother, Harry, and then spent a few days, as he had said he would, with his mother at Brockles Farm. He returned to Ireland on 27 July, feeling done in and resolving that there would be 'no more going to Army Championships from being Caterer.'

In July, too, he won the 440 yards flat race at the Worcestershire Regiment sports; the 880 yards at the Army Service Corps sports; the mile - in 4 minutes 45 seconds - at the Lancashire Fusiliers Minden sports; the mile, the 880 yards and the 440 yards at the All Ireland Army Athletics

Meeting at the Curragh; and the mile at the Royal Engineers' sports. He thought this last meeting, at the Curragh, was quite 'the worst arranged sports [that he had] ever seen and [with a] badly laid out ground.' It is possible that he was still not feeling entirely fit, despite his remarkable successes.

He again took six weeks furlough in December and January, and once more was very seasick on the crossings. On leave he did a good deal of rabbit and pigeon shooting and rode Squire Todhunter's young hunters. He also played football for Burnt Hill, beating Waltham Abbey 8-0 and Hoddesden 9-0.

In February and May 1894 he had two unfortunate injuries. As he told his mother:

> Four of us (Sergeants) have a hut to ourselves. We have plenty of ventilation but have lined the hut with blankets. The iron stove goes well and we stoke it up at night. Trying to move the stove a little one day, the top piping, which had evidently not been fastened, came down on my head. Several stitches and head very sore.
>
> Put on milk diet for two days to get down swollen knee [he had sprained his left knee cap and had to wear an elastic stocking to support it] then on hospital diet. Fortunately the married sergeants sent me some extra food. Practically no medical treatment. I told my OC Company (Capt. Hon. St. Aubyn) about this and he arranged for me to see a specialist at the Royal College of Surgeons. Rest.

Between these accidents to his head and to his knee, in March 1894, there was an outbreak of scarlet fever and all the recruits were placed in quarantine. With the cancellation of parades, Archer was able to take things easy - though he was not inactive - and walked to the Hill of Allen, from where he had 'a splendid view', and then walked across the Bog of Allen.

He was promoted Acting Sergeant on 22 April 1894. This time it was a paid promotion and his pay was increased by four pence a day.

By this time his reputation as an athlete was high, as an aborted bet of well over a month's pay by a colleague illustrates. Private A H Preece, of the Medical Staff Corps, who had done a good deal of running in England, let it be known that he could beat Archer easily at the half mile.

> Arrangements were made to run the half mile for £5 a side. I paid £1 first instalment and £2 second instalment. Preece paid only first instalment of £1 and then cried off, forfeiting his £1.

Betting on the outcome of races, and especially accepting monetary prizes, was a dangerous practice and got him into trouble. The Irish Amateur Athletics Association ruled that since he was running for money prizes, his entry to amateur athletics events would not be accepted in future. He had indeed been accepting money prizes for some considerable time. Naturally, he was very unhappy about being banned from amateur athletics and tried to get himself reinstated. The decision was reiterated: 'A soldier competing in military sports for money or against those who have taken money prizes cannot enter for amateur sports.' He tried again in May 1894, writing to the secretary of the Irish Amateur Athletics Association, asking him to bring his name before the next meeting of the Association. The reply was encouraging and indicated that the recommendation of his officers would help. His Commanding Officer and his Company Commander both gave helpful recommendations and he was reinstated on 14 June 1894.

The day after his reinstatement as an amateur, he joined the Elysian Harriers and started training with them at Balls Bridge. During the following months he had a very full and successful time in competitive athletics. At the Balls Bridge Horse Show on 26 June he came second in the steeplechase and received a fruit bowl as a prize. His knee still troubled him, and for a while he had to give up training and competing, as his 'legs were very hard' and his knee was swollen. He was pleased when the June Military Tournament was over, for while it lasted he never got to bed until after midnight and had to be up early in the mornings for military training. Several of his men got drunk and had to be disciplined, and this involved him in extra work. He was fit enough by mid July to compete in the All Ireland Army Athletics Meeting at the Curragh and came first in the 440 yards heat and final, over 'rough and hilly ground', winning the Army Challenge Cup and another cup valued at £5. A week later he came third in the 440 yards at the Grocers Assistants Sports and won a Gladstone Bag. Six days later still he competed at the Army Athletic Meeting at Aldershot, and in the Championship of the Army 880 yards he 'won easily by five yards' in 2 minutes 3.4 seconds. He was awarded the Army Challenge Cup and a cup for the winner. He was particularly pleased with how well the Second Battalion of the Rifle Brigade performed at this meeting, because his colleagues came first in the long jump, second in the gymnastics and third in the obstacle race. And two weeks after that he ran at the Dublin Metropolitan Police Sports at Balls Bridge and came second in the steeplechase, winning a pair of field glasses. At the Dunshaughlin Sports on 26 August he won the 220 yards final, winning a biscuit box. He won the heat but came third in the final of the 440 yards, none the less winning a silver mounted walking stick. Although he was unplaced in the 100 yards final, the 880 yards and the mile, he still considered the meeting 'excellent practice'. At the Drumdrum Sports on 1 September he won the mile race: 'Archer gradually got up and, after lying handy for the last quarter, came out a hundred yards from home and won by three yards.' For this race he won a lamp with shade. The next day at the Garrison Sports he won the 100 yards and a cup, and came second in the mile, winning a butter cooler. He exchanged the cup and cooler with the tradesman who supplied the prizes, for a set of razors, a leather writing case and a pocket knife. Next, on 12 September at the Bacon and Mullen Match at Balls Bridge he came second, by just one foot, in the 440 yards and won a cruet set. Four days later at the Dunleary Sports he won the mile race and with it a Gladstone dressing bag. In this race he showed his skill as a tactician as well as a fast runner, possibly benefiting from the tips given to him by Sergeant Forbes of the Constabulary:

> A grand race, the first three being covered by one and a half yards. Won in the last two strides, the mile was one of the best races which we have seen this season. J J Butler, 48 yards [handicap] was virtual scratch, his nearest opponent being Sergeant Archer 60 yards, and out of 14 starters there were some very warm ones on the 100, 110 and 120 yards mark including Chadwick (100) who started favourite. Butler ran poorly and failed to make any impression on Archer who was moving with the greatest freedom and ease. Two laps from home Chadwick had the limit man caught and a ding dong race for a lap and a half ensued between himself, Cahill, Duffy and Conroy. At this point Duffy and Chadwick drew away from the field and disputing every inch of the ground up to the straight it looked as if it would be a question of inches between the pair. Archer, however, finished the last 100 yards at a terrific bat and before he was noticed by the spectators had taken the tape by inches from Duffy who beat Chadwick by a foot.

Archer recorded his vital statistics at this time, when he was in full training and aged 23 years: weight 10 stone 4.5 pounds; height 5 feet 9.25 inches; thighs 20 inches; waist 30.25 inches; hips 31.5 inches; leg length 35.25 inches; arm length 29.6 inches; chest lowered 34.4 inches; chest expanded 37.2 inches; calf, right 15 inches, left 14.2 inches; upper arm 12.5 inches; fore arm 10.5 inches; wrist 7 inches. Clearly, he was in top physical condition.

With the closing of the track athletics season Archer turned to other sporting activities in his off duty hours: shooting, football, hockey, cross-country running and steeplechasing. He came second on 29 September in the shoot for the Battalion best shot and won a £2 prize - it was only athletics, and not shooting, to which the Irish Amateur Athletics Association took exception. The best shots in the Battalion were doing a great deal of practice for the Queen's Cup and other competitions at this time. Earlier in the year, soon after he returned to Ireland from leave, he had bought a .22 rook and rabbit rifle with a falling block for £1.17.6. Now, as a leisure pursuit he did a good deal of shooting with it, placing a penny on a post and shooting at it from fifteen yards, a pastime at which he also won money.

On 1 October he returned from the Curragh to Richmond Barracks and took over as Regimental Postman. This post was a subterfuge that enabled him to train the regimental football team. He found them 'a bad lot to train: lazy, too light weight and not fast enough.' He did his best to get them fit, but it was very hard work because they did not like training. He played a lot of Company football and in one game he 'got badly kicked on [his] game knee'. He was glad his team was beaten in this match, and out of the competition, because he recognized that 'rough football is not good for training for running.' Of all his sports it was running to which he gave priority. At hockey he played half or full back, right or left, for the Rifle Brigade Sergeants against Trinity College in a 'rough but fast game' in which he got hit on the head, hand and instep; and against the Sherwood Foresters Sergeants in which he 'got kicked in calf of right leg'. He also played hockey against the Coldstream Guards Sergeants, the Corinthians, Palmerston, and Officers and Sergeants of the North Staffordshire Regiment, in all of which matches he seems to have escaped injury. The matches were usually followed by a smoking concert in the evening, and on at least one occasion 'several tried to get [him] drunk by putting whiskey in [his] sherry' - a soldierly but not comradely thing to do.

Cross-country races started about the middle of November and steeplechase races a month later. In a seven mile race at Milltown, Mullen came first and Archer second. Between them, they 'ran the others off their feet.' At the Haddington Harriers' invitation race on 1 December Mullen again won and Archer came second, for which he was awarded a silver medal with gold centre. He trained at cross-country running at the back of Richmond Barracks almost daily. Two races in particular serve as examples of his gluttony for punishment. The first was on 24 November when, having just completed a four mile cross-country run from Ashtown

Clonkseagh, he and his colleagues immediately formed up at Goatstown for the Elysian Harriers invitation run of about one and three quarter miles. There were 65 starters and again Mullen came first and Archer second, winning a silver medal. The second involved not only a steeplechase race on Boxing Day but also a boxing match the previous evening, Christmas Day:

> At the Battalion evening entertainment the final for the NCOs' boxing cup was to take place. Sergeant Hodder, the holder, who weighs over 13 stones, is a pretty good handful. The NCO who got into the final with Hodder backed out. So I was asked to box three exhibition rounds. I didn't want to as I was running in Belfast the next day. I saw Hodder and arranged for no slogging. At the end of the first round I had him puffing. In the second round he became vicious and I got some very hard blows, so I retaliated and it became a slogging match. Luckily for me he was well winded so missed a lot. I had him groggy at the end of the third round. Later in the evening Mrs Hodder gave me a wigging saying that he (Hodder) knew he would not have to box so had some stouts (Guinness) and then my volunteering to box upset everything.

The next morning Archer left by the early train for Belfast for the inter-club six miles steeplechase between the County Down, Elysian, Dublin and Belfast Harriers. He came first, and the Elysian Harriers came second in the club race. The course had hurdles and water jumps on each lap, a total of 54 jumps. 'McGuirk of the Elysian Harriers cut out the pace for three laps then Campbell of the County Down Harriers led for seven laps. Archer, who had been lying handy until then, went to the front and, never being headed, won easily.' He won the gold medal, despite being very stiff from the boxing of the previous day and a cold uncomfortable train journey. He could not turn his head as Hodder had hit him several times on the neck with his forearm.

At this time he was winning a fair amount of money at cards - probably poker[8] - at dances in the Sergeants' mess. In this, too, he showed his ability as a tactician:

> I used to go to bed at about 7.0 p.m. and get my batman to wake me about 11.0 p.m., then go to the dance. By that time several players would be slightly fuddled. After playing a little while one could tell by the way the players looked at their cards fairly well what they held.

It appears from this and a number of other events that he, whilst not a teetotaller, certainly recognised and took advantage of the benefits of abstinence. He spent some of the prize money that he won playing cards, on clothing, for example, 3 shirts at 7/6, 2 pairs of drawers at 2/- each, a pair of braces at 4/6, three pairs of socks for 2/- each and a dozen handkerchiefs for sixpence.

He was promoted full Sergeant on 1 November 1894 and moved from Captain Wilson's company to Captain Wenman Coke's company.[9]

1895 was another full year for athletics, although his performance was marred by a further injury to his knee, which he strained during training in February. Although the favourite to win, he was unable to compete in the Irish Cross-country Championships at the end of that month, much to his disappointment. Early in March he travelled to England for the National Cross-country Championships, and was sea sick, as usual, during the crossing. He spent a few days at Parndon, shooting rabbits and doing a little training on the frozen ground. His knee was still 'groggy'. While he personally felt that he ran worse than he had ever run before and recognized that three weeks without training, and a bad knee, together with the sea sickness, did not improve his running, others saw that

> Archer was the trump card of the pack and after his recent illness surprised everyone by his forward running. Morris of Salford passed him in the straight for home but the Elysian was not to be denied even one place and sprinting strongly secured 49th place [out of 149 starters].

He paid the price for his exertions in these National Championships. After the race there was a smoking concert before he left to return to Dublin. There was a delay at Birmingham railway station and his knee was very swollen. The sea passage was as bad as ever. It was a miserable journey and he was 'done up, with a bad cold and very stiff.' The Senior Cross-country Championship of Ireland over six miles took place three weeks later, on 30 March, and although he did not want to run he was persuaded to do so because the Elysian Harriers stood a good chance of winning. His knee was 'still groggy' but he came fifth and won a bronze medal. The Elysian harriers came second as a team.

By early April 1895 he seems to have recovered, and in the County Dublin Harriers ten miles open cross-country race for the Carr Cup he came first, and won the Cup and the gold medal. A week later at the Irish Cycling Association Sports at Balls Bridge he won the three-quarters of a mile invitation steeplechase: 'Archer who jumped in beautiful style went away with a clear lead and, never being headed, he won easily by 40 yards.' He exchanged the fish carvers and trowel that he won for a gold Albert chain. During May, too, he came first in the half mile handicap, winning a case of silver mounted carvers, and second in the mile race at the Irene Sports. Of the half mile it was reported: 'This was an exciting race and perhaps the fastest decided over the Royal Dublin Society's course for some years, and although gruelling no one could overtake Archer [who got] home easily by a yard.' After these races his knee was again 'groggy' and he had to interrupt his training to rest it. Early in June he was fit enough to compete in the Irish Amateur Athletics Association sports at Balls Bridge, though his knee was still stiff. He came second in the half mile championship of Ireland, winning the silver medal, and first in the mile steeplechase, winning the gold medal: 'Archer went ahead at the very start and, jumping in his usual faultless style, soon gained a substantial lead and ultimately finished alone amidst loud applause.' Three weeks later, on 22 June, in the one mile Championship of Leinster he came first, winning by ten yards in 4 minutes 37 seconds, and was awarded the gold medal. At the end of June he travelled to England, again spent a short time at Parndon and then attended the Army Athletics Meeting at Aldershot. Here he won the 880 yards Championship of the Army by ten yards. 'A very slow race up to 200 yards from home when Second Lieutenant King sprinted but never passed me.' Archer was awarded the Army Challenge Cup and a silver cigarette box. On 7 July at the Tradesmen's Sports he came second in the mile, winning a meerschaum pipe and cigar case; and third in the 440 yards - 'a desperate final with inches separating the first three' - and won a pair of hand made boots to measure. Five days later at the All Ireland Army Athletics Meeting 440 yards Championship of the Army he came second, having got a very bad start, but won a silver cup presented by Mappin and Webb. Two days after that, at the Purveyors Association Sports at Jones Road, he came third in the 880 yards race and won a pair of field glasses which he exchanged for a case of razors and a pocket book. On 18 July, having travelled from Dublin to Glasgow, in the International Athletics Contest between Scotland and Ireland at Celtic Park, running for Ireland, he won the half mile 'easily by eight yards' in the pouring rain and with the ground covered with water. He won the gold international medal for this race. In the four miles race, Mullen got permission for Archer, who was a reserve, to run. He made the pace for the first three miles and then, when Mullen said he was fit, Archer dropped out. At this meeting he found 'the most fair lot of spectators [he had] ever seen at a sports meeting.' The Scottish Amateur Athletics Association entertained the competitors to a dinner at the Alexandra Hotel where they were accommodated, and treated them 'splendidly all the time'. Not unusually, he was seasick on the return journey to Dublin. On 28 July at the Navan Sports in the Gaelic Athletics Championship of Ireland 440 yards race he came first, winning the gold medal, and came first also in the 880 yards and in an 880 yards trial race. On 2 August he travelled to Manchester to take part in the Blackley Sports and came third in the one mile handicap. It rained all day and this was 'one of the worst courses [he had ever] run on. Very sharp corners, plenty of bumping and [he] got spiked.' He returned to Dublin the same night, and the next day took part in the Grocers Assistants Sports, being unplaced in the mile race. Then at the Royal Irish Constabulary meeting the following day he was unplaced in the 220, 440 and 880 races. It seems that he was feeling the ill effects of a great deal of concentrated competitive running, in a variety of events, and of uncomfortable travelling. On 15 August, however, at the Gaelic Athletic Association Championships he came second and won silver medals in the 880 yards and one mile races. Two days later, at the Dublin Metropolitan Police Sports at Balls Bridge, he came first in the 600 yards steeplechase and was awarded a silver tea and coffee set. Of another race he later wrote: 'One of my best performances was at Jones Road trotting track, Dublin – ten miles flat in 53 minutes 36 seconds. One did not specialise in those days.' All this was accomplished in four and a half months!

From mid August to mid September 1895 he attended the annual course of musketry at Curragh: 'My course lasts 6 weeks, got to cram 6 months work into that time.' He received a prize of £3 for being the best shot in the Battalion and then he made the top score in the Queen's Cup team. On 7 October he left for Hythe to qualify for a School of Musketry Certificate. Here he was the second best shot in the School. He felt he should have been the best but failed because of three misses at 800 yards when there was 'fifteen feet of wind.' He beat the next best by 24 points, securing 194 himself. Here, too, he qualified as Sergeant Instructor of Musketry and Machine Guns. While at Hythe, he played a good deal of football, unusually playing at outside left. He rejoined his Battalion at Aldershot on 19 November.

He took his annual furlough during December and again spent most of his time at Brockles Farm, where he 'did a lot of rabbit shooting with Squire Todhunter and also rode his young hunter several times to hounds.' He was deeply saddened to learn of the death of Captain Lawrence 'who had done so much for [him] before and during the first years of [his] service.' He had been killed in East Africa near Mombasa.

'A very fine soldier and keen on everything to do with the Rifle Brigade.'[10]

By the end of 1895, Archer was twenty-five years of age. He had been in the army seven years. He had risen by fairly rapid stages from the rank of Rifleman to that of Acting Sergeant. He had his own batman. He had served at Winchester, Dover, Lydd, Hythe and Aldershot, and for a lengthy period in Ireland. His military training had been thorough, he had undergone long marches on manoeuvres and he had done well in topography, mounted infantry work and particularly musketry in which he had become a marksman and a trainer of others. He devoted a great deal of his time to sports: athletics, swimming, football, shooting and boxing, and in all of these - particularly athletics - he excelled. He won many prizes, and the injuries that he sustained did not seem to deter or for very long hamper him. He was a popular and extremely fit man. But, save for nearby Ireland, his desire to see the world outside Britain was as yet unfulfilled. Nor had he seen any active service.

CHAPTER THREE

THE MOUNTED INFANTRY - MASHONALAND: 1896-1897

The authorities at the School of Musketry had wanted Archer to stay on as an instructor. In the normal course of events he would have snapped up this opportunity, but, far away in West Africa, a more exciting opportunity beckoned him. He wrote to the School Commandant to say he wanted to return to his Battalion and not stay at the School, since he was 'Waiting Sergeant for the Ashanti Expedition.' There was considerable general excitement at the beginning of January 1896 about the prospects of going to Ashanti, fighting and winning medals: 'The soldiers are all rubbing their hands - Ashanti War going on, row in South Africa, and another one with America, expect to find ourselves packed off to one of the above places some morning in a hurry.' Initially disappointed that he did not go, six weeks later he was able to tell his mother with some comfort: 'The men that went to Ashanti get back here next week. They get no medal as they did not have to fight.' Instead, it was the 'row in South Africa', or rather in Rhodesia to the north, that provided the opportunity for active service - and medals - that he was seeking.[1]

Until the end of 1895 Cecil Rhodes's British South Africa Company had seemed successful. In reality, however, it had come close to disaster on a number of occasions. Rhodes knew the true and inadequate potential of the gold mines and he thought he might avoid financial disaster in the conquest of the Transvaal, but the failure of the Jameson Raid early in 1896 not only ended his plans for extending his sphere of influence, it endangered the control of his existing possessions. The most serious result of Jameson's raid was the reaction of the African people. By withdrawing almost all the police force from Matabeleland, Jameson had given the people there the opportunity they had been waiting for. In March 1896 they rose against the European settlers. 'Two hundred and sixty four Europeans were killed at the outbreak of these risings, and in the fighting that followed the Company was forced to spend considerable amounts, including the humiliating price of paying for the Imperial troops that were required.'[2]

Towards the end of March 1896, to handle the Matabele insurrection, Rhodes ordered that 800 men should be recruited through his offices in Kimberley and Mafeking - the terminus of the railway - in South Africa to reinforce the local volunteer units in Rhodesia. This new force, the Matabeleland Relief Force, commanded by Major Plumer, left by road for Bulawayo in Matabeleland at the end of April. In addition, the British Government agreed to reinforce them and the local Rhodesia Volunteers by Imperial troops, by transferring from Pietermaritzburg to Matabeleland 300 men of the British cavalry - the 7th Hussars - and 200 of the Mounted Infantry - the West Riding and Yorkshire and the Lancashire Regiments. Furthermore, and of particular importance to Archer, the British government ordered that four specially trained companies of Mounted Infantry should be sent from England to South Africa ready to move to Rhodesia if needed.[3]

On 26 April 1896 Lieutenant-Colonel Edwin Alderson, of the Royal West Kent Regiment, was told that he 'was to command the four companies of Mounted Infantry that were being sent out to Cape Town, in case they might be wanted in Rhodesia.' Each of the four companies was comprised of four detachments, called sections, of about 30 men and an officer, all 'specially selected by their own battalion commanding officers for the Mounted Infantry work.' 'The conditions for the selection of the men [were] that they should be marksmen or first-class shots, of good character and physique, and not above a certain weight.'[4]

Alderson had an enlightened and innovative approach to organizing his men at the lowest level of command:

> The principle ... is one of decentralization ... The men in each section are told to form themselves into permanent 'subsections' i.e. groups of four. These groups have their beds together in the barrack room, lie down side by side in the bivouac, have their horses picketed together, form up on parade together, and do their work together. The group selects its own leader who is responsible for it in every way ... The Mounted Infantry are essentially an active service corps. They are not cavalry and do not fight on horses.[5]

The opportunity that now presented itself for active service in Rhodesia was one that Archer seized enthusiastically, and on 27 April 1896 – twenty-four hours after Alderson had been appointed to command it - he joined the newly recruited Mounted Infantry. He fitted the requirements admirably: he was an outstanding marksman of several years' standing, he possessed a good conduct badge, he was of splendid physique and he was not a heavy man - the result of his intense sporting and athletic activities. It must have given him considerable satisfaction to be specially selected by his battalion commander, particularly since there was 'a good deal of picking and choosing' of those who volunteered to join what was seen as an elite unit.[6] His departure was, however, regretted by others in the Battalion:

> The departure of Sergt Archer, the famous Army half mile champion, is deeply regretted, not only by the battalion but by all who know him. He is a fine all-round sportsman, and beside being a high-class runner, he is a fine shot and can also hold his own at football, cricket, billiards etc. Apart from this he is a thorough good fellow, and seldom does a NCO acquire such popularity as he has done.[7]

His section, from the 2nd Battalion of the Rifle Brigade, numbering 31, was commanded by Lieutenant Reginald Stephens[8] and was one of the four sections in the Rifle Company, commanded by Captain Albert Jenner[9] of the 4th Battalion of the Rifle Brigade. Archer was appointed Armourer Sergeant to the Mounted Infantry. As a Section Sergeant, also, he had under him Corporals Morgan and Warless, Acting Corporals Back and Bryan; Bugler Mead and 24 Riflemen.[10] Of the other three sections in the Rifle Company, one came from the 4th Battalion of the Rifle Brigade, under Lieutenant Hubert Vernon;[11] one from the 3rd Battalion of the King's Royal Rifle Corps, under Lieutenant G St Aubyn; and another from the 4th Battalion of the King's Royal Rifle Corps, under Lieutenant C Eustace. Archer was, therefore, in a Rifle Brigade section, commanded by a Rifle Brigade Lieutenant, Stephens, in a company having another Rifle Brigade section, commanded by a Rifle Brigade Captain, Jenner. The Rifle Brigade sections left headquarters on 28 April for South Africa, only two days after Alderson was appointed.[12]

The clothing for the expedition was sent from Pimlico to Aldershot and the members were fitted out there. Several of them were 'surprised at the time to find that the only Khaki issued was one suit of drill for "sea-kit".' The saddlery was taken out to South Africa in bulk. The companies assembled at Aldershot on 29 April.[13] They embarked on the RMS *Tantallon Castle*[14] at Southampton on 2 May after being seen off at the North Camp Station by the Duke of Connaught, commanding the Aldershot district.[15] They sailed the same day. Four days later they called at Madeira, where the ship took on mail and coal. They left at half past eleven in the morning and subsequently understood that a telegram arrived only twenty minutes after their departure, recalling them to Britain.[16] Archer and all his colleagues would have been bitterly disappointed to be recalled.

There followed two days of rough weather and it was 'as hot as a Turkish Bath which made nearly everyone sea sick', including, not surprisingly, Archer. 'It was so hot that the thermometer had to be iced every hour'.[17] They crossed the line, the equator, on 11 May,[18] when 'everyone was well lathered and shaved' in the traditional ceremony. That night one of Archer's two Acting Corporals, Bryan, had a 'most painful accident': he fell out of his hammock and broke his jaw badly when the hammock rope broke. Another of his men slipped down some steps and fell to the deck below, cutting his hand and arm severely. Fortunately, after a few days both were recovering satisfactorily. The following day, a saloon passenger,[19] an ex-Army captain, died and was buried at sea. During the voyage Archer helped to arrange several concerts with Lieutenant Vernon as Chairman: the Rifle Brigade was clearly playing a leading part on the voyage. Everything went well, though Archer was disappointed that they did not have enough time to finish the full programmes. 'Colonel Baden-Powell could keep one entertained himself for a full evening.' They had sports nearly every day for small prizes but, since he was the judge, Archer did not compete.

> The voyage was a very pleasant, if an uneventful one; we did our best to keep the men fit by arranging for regular exercise for them, getting up athletics, tugs of war, and concerts, Baden-Powell invariably bringing down the house at the latter.[20]
> The usual sports and exercises were carried on - running, jumping, *tableaux vivants*, tug-of-war, obstacle races, etc.[21]

On 19 May, seventeen days after sailing, they arrived at Cape Town, in Archer's view 'a very rising place but very dirty [though] they appear to be making great improvements.'[22] They anchored in the dark at about four in the morning and went alongside the wharf five hours later.[23] Although on the whole it had been a pleasant voyage - Jenner said 'We had a cheery party going out, and the quarters were as comfortable as could be expected'[24] - everyone was pleased to get on land again. When they arrived in Cape Town they were sent by train to Wynberg Castle, about nine miles away, much to their disappointment because they were keen to move forward to the battlefield and not be detained on the way.

Jenner described this delay as being 'as big a "sell" as it was possible to imagine, as none of us had doubted when we hurried away from Aldershot that we should go straight up-country.'[25] Archer understood that the British South Africa Company and the War Office were at loggerheads over who should pay for the imperial troops on the expedition. This sort of problem still existed over a hundred years later: the Ministry of Defence and the Department for International Development were at loggerheads in 1999 over who should pay for helicopters to assist Mozambique at the time of very severe floods. The poor interdepartmental relations may have been the reason for the aborted recall from Madeira. The British South Africa Company was refusing to pay, though they were eventually made to do so. They paid then, apparently, with good grace: 'The Company was paying the bill, and certainly they stinted us for nothing it was in their power to provide.'[26]

> The Chartered Company throughout behaved very liberally to the Imperial Troops engaged [in the Mashonaland campaign]. Necessities were of course not plentiful, and food cost £200 a ton to reach Salisbury, but whatever necessaries were procurable, were generally at our service, and the Chartered Company paid allowances to all ranks on a generous scale.[27]

Though he was as keen as his fellows to be in action, Archer looked on the bright side of things and felt that the delay at Wynberg would at least enable them 'to get to know what sort of officers and men the other Regiments have sent and also to be trained together.' On arrival, they were inspected by Lieutenant-General Goodenough, the officer commanding troops in South Africa. During the inspection, the General stopped in front of Archer who was introduced to him as the champion runner of the Army - much to his pleasure. Goodenough jocularly 'wanted to know how much start I would require to give the Dragoons a good run.' We do not know what his reply was but it was doubtless both diplomatic and pointed. Alderson, from the perspective of a senior officer, recalled:

> At Wynberg we ... learnt, much to our disgust, that there was no immediate prospect of our being wanted in Rhodesia, and [we also learnt] that there were no horses being bought for [our use in Rhodesia]. It *was* a damper! For a month we remained at Wynberg, having a very good time it is true; but this was not what we had come out for, and we all felt as if we had had cold water thrown over us.

We spent the time in teaching the men to work, and fight, through the bush on Cape Town flats, having many little field days of our own ... By the middle of June we had fairly settled down, had bought ponies, started polo, and been out with the Cape Hounds, which I [Alderson] had taken over.[28]

Archer found the living conditions at Wynberg poor: 'The huts are full of bugs. If one breaks off a piece of whitewash there are bugs.' However, there were compensations: the huts were in a healthy spot, built in the middle of a wood, and he found Wynberg itself 'a pretty place with splendid views - weather like home in August but colder at nights.' One day he climbed Table Mountain and enjoyed both the climb and the 'splendid views from the top.'[29] Others arriving in South Africa for the first time also admired the beauty of Wynberg: 'At Wynberg the scenery is enchanting: vineyards clothe the ground, creeping far up the slopes of the mountain, while acres of arum lilies grow wild.'[30] 'Wynberg ... is a very pretty place.'[31]

Writing home about the cost of living, he said that he found the fruit very cheap: grapes were a penny a bunch of about a pound, pineapples a penny each, while peaches were 'lovely' and cost three a penny. All the other food seemed to him expensive, with butter at a shilling and sixpence a pound, potatoes at two shillings a stone and a tin of salmon at just over a shilling. Eggs, surprisingly, were five pence each. Everything got dearer the further one went upcountry. Horses on the other hand were inexpensive and he asked his mother to tell his uncle that he could get a horse for £5 that would cost £25 to £30 in England. A mixture of beer and wine at three pence a pint, called 'Tickie', was in great favour with the men. Whether the word 'tickie' referred at that time to the mixture or, as later, to the three pence, is unclear. In any case, some of it was very strong and a temptation to the soldiers: 'I shall be glad when we get a move on as it's a job to keep the men in order. Some sections have a lot of crime.'

With the fascination of a newcomer to Africa, he described the inhabitants of Cape Town in a letter to his mother:

> They are every colour from jet black with lips that nearly cover their nose to yellow with thin lips, and in Cape Town you can see people of nearly every nationality under the sun, some of the men dressed like women with sun shades (don't know what they want them for as they have faces the same colour as if they had been black-leaded) some are great toffs with no boots on and some have only a loin cloth on.

The Queen's official birthday was a special occasion, and he accompanied the troops to Cape Town by train for the march past. They fired a *feu-de-joie,* marched past on the Market Square, and then walked back the nine miles to Wynberg Castle, in very hot weather.[32]

A good deal of time was occupied in shooting, both for practice - to remain in top condition for active service - and in competitions. Unused to the rapidly changing strength of the wind, Archer was greatly irritated by the conditions when shooting in a competition against the Leicestershire Regiment:

> One of the worst days I have ever seen for shooting. Regulation sights and targets. At 500 yards aim varied from 6 feet off right edge to 1 foot off right edge of target. At 600 yards changed so quickly that it was impossible to keep on the target.

He had just started a musketry course and was doing well when two companies of the Mounted Infantry, including his unit, were ordered to move up to Mashonaland via the east coast. This order was received quite suddenly, and was the result of the Mashona people following the Matabele example, mounting a rebellion and murdering Europeans.

> The 'gentle' Mashonas, goaded to desperation by the fact that the police had been withdrawn from the country (they had all gone on furlough to take part in the Jameson Raid), had risen and murdered all the white men, women, and children they could lay hands on - cut the telegraph wires and closed the roads.[33]

As soon as the rising began, on 18 June 1896,[34] the Europeans in the districts affected retired into laagers at Salisbury, Charter, Enkeldoorn, Victoria and Umtali. Then a relief patrol went from Salisbury down the Umtali road to pick up the settlers in the Marandellas, Headlands and Lesapi districts and escorted them to Umtali. Thereafter, until the end of August, no post remained occupied by Europeans on the main line of communications between Salisbury and Umtali. The road to the east coast was therefore completely closed, and it was impossible for any supplies to come from that direction until it could be reopened. The road to Bulawayo was also closed for the transport of supplies, and could only be used safely by a strong force.[35]

On 23 June, a week after the rising began, Archer wrote from Wynberg to tell his mother that they had just received orders to proceed to Fort Salisbury, Mashonaland, where they all expected 'plenty of service.'

Everyone very glad to get a move from this place, no one more pleased than myself as we (the sergeants) have had our work cut out keeping the men in order. They are all right now they are under orders for the front.[36]

Alderson recorded that on 19 June he received a telegram saying the British South Africa Company had asked for two companies of Mounted Infantry - two hundred men in all - to proceed to Salisbury, via Beira, in order to assist the local forces in suppressing the Mashona rising, 'which had by this time began to assume serious proportions.'

> The rising had commenced on the 16th June when the first whites were murdered at the Beatrice Mine ... This was quickly followed by other murders at Hartley and at Norton's farm on the Hunyani River ... Apparently no one in Mashonaland had dreamt it was possible that the Mashona might rise ... There was no doubt that at the commencement of the rising, Salisbury was in an awkward position. It then had no police, these having been taken for the Jameson raid; the bulk of its available fighting men, and of the horses, were in Matabeleland ... some three hundred miles away: what was worse was that arms were none too plentiful.[37]

The officers had agreed that the companies of the Mounted Infantry should go on detachment in order of seniority of the company commanders. Since, however, the headquarters of the corps was moving to Mashonaland, the two senior companies remained behind because *they* were now the detachment. This was how the Rifle Company, commanded by Captain Jenner, and the Irish Company, commanded by Captain Horace McMahon,[38] the two junior commanders, went to Mashonaland - much to Archer's delight. He would have hated to be left behind in South Africa.[39]

The order for these two companies to go to Salisbury was received on the night of 19 June and they were to sail on 26 June, a week later, so, in Alderson's view, there was plenty of time to draw equipment.[40] It is unlikely that the endangered Europeans in Mashonaland would have shared his view. Nor was it the case that there was plenty of time to acquire horses - essential to a mounted infantry unit. As Alderson recalled:

> Now that we were wanted, horses were necessary, and these of course had to be bought in a hurry; the result was that the numbers were

difficult to make up, and the quality was not so good as it would have been had they been bought gradually, and properly fed, during the last month, in which we had been doing comparatively nothing. For some time prior to the purchase of the horses, forage, especially in and around Cape Town, had been very scarce and expensive; consequently the majority of the horses were in bad condition, some of them being extremely low. One hundred and forty five horses were bought in and near Cape Town and were put on board the ... steamer *Arab*, which had been hastily fitted up, on 25th June.[41]

Members of the Rifle Company found the ability of Cape Town to fit out their 'small military expedition' extremely limited. None the less, they acquired two Maxims, 'two old 7-pounders were dug out from somewhere', a whole variety of ponies were hurriedly bought and the saddlery was altered to fit them. They put 'everything likely to be useful, and a good many other things' on board the *Arab* and set off late in the morning of 26 June.[42] The ship was far from being a robust vessel, suitable for transporting so many men and horses, and she had to be hastily - and inadequately - converted:

> The *Arab* had for some time been employed in carrying mules and cargo coastwise, and she was a mere shell, her bulkheads having been taken down to make room. The only cabin accommodation was on the upper deck and that was very rough and very limited. The men were put on the fore part of the main deck, which was roughly fitted up and partitioned off from the after part, which was full of horses. When we got out of the Bay and began to round Cape Agulhas, the swell, consequent on the previous day's gale, made the ship, light as she was, roll considerably, and many of the horse fittings [were] carried away. [Jenner explained that 'the hastily-constructed horse partitions in the hold went like match-wood soon after starting; the horses could not keep their legs and but for the very great exertions of officers and men, the consequences might have been disastrous.'[43]] This gave us all plenty of [work], and ... little time to be seasick.[44]

Other soldiers, including those of the West Riding Regiment, and some civilian doctors and nurses, travelled from Cape Town by rail to East London before boarding ships and going on by sea to Beira and thence inland, with Alderson's troops.[45]

Archer wrote to his mother from the *Arab* – which he described as 'a proper old tug' - at Beira on the coast of Portuguese East Africa on 4 July and gave her details of the eventful voyage from Cape Town, where they loaded 137 horses, a few having already died soon after Alderson bought them.

> We arrived here quite safe on the 2nd after a rather eventful passage from Cape Town. We ran into a pier at Cape Town carrying part of it away. Then we encountered a gale. Luckily it blew behind us. Made a record passage to Durban Natal. [In the rough seas, the horses, and Archer, were very seasick and he and his men had great difficulty in getting the horses to their feet after they had fallen down, and in repairing their stalls. He was 'on guard all night keeping the horses on their feet'.[46]] Ran aground in Durban Harbour and had to stop there about 36 hours.[47] Shipped 140 horses [which were ready there waiting for them,[48] 80 of them had never had a bridle on. Regular wild ones. Worked all night getting them on board. [Having completed this task he went ashore and had a good walk.] [They left the following morning[49].] One of them broke his leg the first day out from Durban and had to be shot; another died of fever the day we arrived here. Had to wait six hours for the tide when we arrived outside the harbour here and when we got in found that the tug [the *Kimberley*] had broken down that had to tow the lighters up the Pungwe River as far as Fontes Villa so we are still waiting here. Our Engineers and the Engineers of HMS *Widgeon* are working day and night repairing the tug and expect to finish her tonight so that the first lot can start tomorrow ... I had another turn at the sea sickness but soon got over it. The horses were very bad for a day or two until they got their sea legs. We have two hundred and seventy eight on board. The ones on the lower deck have had rather a hot time of it and will be glad of a roll and to stretch their legs. Some of them are covered with ticks (South African bugs) but as soon as we land we will be able to groom them and get them all right again. We had a good view of the coast nearly all the voyage, especially Zululand. Could see the surf breaking on the cliffs, and [understand] it is about three miles. It looked grand ... Beira lays very low, cannot see a hill anywhere. Does not look much of a place from the harbour. Will not let anyone but officers land so I can't tell much about this place ... We get no more pay until we get back again so we shall have a good lot to draw.[50]

Alderson's account of their departure from Cape Town, their voyage to Beira and their arrival there helps to fill out some of the details. He said that at Cape Town the *Arab* was 'stuck fast in the harbour, while 140 odd horses were waiting on the wharf to be shipped, and the daylight was fast going.'

> Just as it was getting dark the ship got alongside, and we at once began with the horses, and a rare game we had with some of them. The ship's side being high above the wharf, all had to be put in slings, hoisted up to the upper deck, and then lowered down on to the main deck. Some of the horses were only partially broken, and several appeared to have been scarcely handled at all, while a few had to be cast and their legs tied before they could be slung ... As each horse was put into his place down below, the bar to keep him there was fixed up; several times we had to suspend operations till extra fittings were hastily put up by the ship's carpenters. All this delayed us, and it was 3.30 a.m. before we had got the whole of the horses on board ... We left Durban at 6.30 the next morning, the 30th June. The sea being still somewhat rough, more trouble ensued with the horse fittings, many of them carrying away and a few horses getting down. [Jenner says the sea was 'rougher than ever.'[51]] Next day one of the horses taken on board at Durban developed symptoms of farcy of which there had been cases at Maritzburg, where the horses had been purchased. We had no veterinary surgeon with us, and, rather than run risk of infection in the crowded ship, I had the horse shot at once ... On the evening of July 2nd, we were in sight of the one solitary tree, on the low flat coast to the north of Beira, which serves as a landmark to ships. The tide not serving, we anchored near the outer buoy, some twenty miles from Beira, which is approached by a shallow tortuous channel. The next morning we upped anchor at daybreak, and dropped it again in the Pungwe River, off Beira, about 10.0 a.m.[52]

Another account of the arrival at Beira of those going to Mashonaland at this time was given by a nurse, Elsa Green:

> Next day we entered the wide mouth of the Pungwe River. Soon Beira lay before us in the brilliant sunshine ... It is the starting-point for the shortest and, in some ways, the best route to Mashonaland. The railway is progressing rapidly, thus conveying travellers much more quickly through deadly fever swamps and the districts haunted by the tsetse fly. From the sea Beira presents to the eye a collection of low houses built on the strand. Many of them are painted in gay

colours. An erection of brilliant green and vermilion colour, bearing the Portuguese flag, is the most conspicuous.[53]

Having arrived at Beira, the Rifle Company stayed on board for the next six days. They could not land, because the lighters had rotten bottoms and the steam tug that would have helped them was being repaired by the Engineers and this took time. This defect was serious because the horses would be in danger of putting their feet through the boards. Other vessels at anchor included HMS *Widgeon,* commanded by Lieutenant-Commander Hunt,[54] and SS *Garth Castle,* the latter with 91 members of the Royal Engineers and other drafts on board on their way to Mauritius. Alderson took off 111 officers and men from the *Garth* to help him and to protect Beira if this turned out to be necessary. The others went on to Mauritius. To lessen the risk of catching malaria the men were given 'a dose of quinine followed by a tot of rum, as fever preventives, and then [they] all turned in, every man getting under cover of some sort, so that he should not sleep in the mist.'[55] The true manner in which malaria is contracted - via the *anopheles* mosquito - was not yet discovered and was attributed to the exhalations of *mala aria* - bad air - in mist rising nocturnally from marshes.

Elsa Green, too, wrote of the malaria and other serious dangers to health in Portuguese East Africa through which Archer and she passed at this time:

> During our journeyings in Portuguese territory we met many victims of the terrible fever. Men who looked as if they had not a drop of red blood in their bodies, with skin like yellow parchment, shaking hands and wasted strength. It is a pity that the country has so many drawbacks to the health of men and beasts. Fever, horse sickness, the fatalities arising from the bite of the tsetse fly, fowl sickness etc.[56]

While they were waiting on board the *Arab,* Archer and his men unpacked their kit ready to disembark, and the carpenters from the *Widgeon* put boards in the bottom of the lighters so that the horses would not fall through. The small Portuguese garrison had about 50 men, including Africans. Soon after they arrived in Beira, two of his senior NCO colleagues went ashore and visited the Portuguese barracks sergeants' mess. They reported, with admiration and a touch of envy, that in their mess the sergeants had table napkins and a bottle of wine for each person. Impressed by this report, Archer decided to pay a courtesy visit to the mess himself:

Went ashore one day and visited Portuguese barracks, Serjeants' mess *à la* officers, bottle of wine, table napkins, glasses, fruit, etc on the table, got in tow with the Commandant who treated us to as much wine as we could drink.[57]

At Beira Alderson discovered that the railway company, boat company and officials generally were not expecting them and many seemed indifferent to helping them.[58] He learned, too, first, that the telegraph wire was cut north of Umtali and no communication was possible with Cape Town or anywhere else. Repairing this link became an urgent priority once the Mounted Infantry got into Mashonaland. Second, he learned that the Africans in Portuguese territory were restless and might revolt, and the troops available in Beira were insufficient to cope with a rising, which would cut Salisbury's and the Mounted Infantry's lines of supply: hence, in part, his taking the officers and men from the *Garth* so that they could, if necessary, protect the town. As the point of entry on the shortest route to Mashonaland from South Africa, it was essential that it remain in friendly hands. Third,

> the one steam tug available for towing lighters up the Pungwe had a hole in her boiler, and the Beira-Fontesvilla section of the railway was still four miles short of Fontesvilla, and there were no horse trucks on it. Even if that piece of line could be used, local opinion differed as to whether it was possible to get horses across the river at Fontesvilla.

Fourth, 'Local labour available to repair the tug, to improvise horse trucks, and to construct a landing stage and a pontoon at Fontesvilla was nil.' This meant that the work on the tug, trucks, landing stage and pontoon had to be done by the army themselves. Fortunately, they were well up to the tasks, though a great deal of hard work and improvisation was involved. Fifth, 'The local officials and the representatives of the Boating Company, who were supposed to be responsible for the river transport, were supine and lethargic to the last degree.' Again the Mounted Infantry had to manage by themselves, largely without other help. Sixth, since the people at Salisbury by this time must have become very short of food, speed was essential. Seventh, and for a while the most exasperating of all the troubles, at a meeting with Colonel Machado, the Governor at Beira, the Governor said that whilst his Government had given permission for three hundred troops to pass through the country, they had said nothing about arms, though he suggested these could be packed in boxes and follow the troops. Alderson, sensibly unwilling to part his men from their arms - especially if there was the danger of local insurrection - would not agree to this. In the end they amicably decided that soldiers without arms could not be considered to be troops, and the arms could therefore be allowed to pass. It is more likely that Colonel Alderson than Governor Machado suggested this type of solution, though Major-General Carrington, Commander of the forces in Rhodesia, officially commended Machado for affording 'every facility and kindness to the Imperial troops passing through Portuguese territory to Mashonaland.'[59] A certain amount of difficulty over transporting troops and firearms through Beira may well have been anticipated. Some of the ships leaving South Africa had been delayed:

> Everything now seemed ready, and yet we did not start. Then it leaked out that we awaited a telegram from Beira giving permission to land troops in Portuguese territory. The next report stated that we could not start without a message from England.[60]

By the time Archer reached Beira, the Portuguese telegram and the message from England had arrived, but the details of the agreement between the two governments had not been made fully clear. Clarifying them on the ground fell to Alderson and Machado.

The Mashonaland Field Force which Alderson now had at his command at Beira consisted of 22 officers, 46 NCOs, 312 men and 284 horses.[61] On 6 July, three days after they landed at Beira, he sent an advance party up the Pungwe River on lighters pulled by the tug, *Kimberley* - its boiler now repaired - to Fontesvilla and Chimoio. He sent 66 horses and equipment and a detachment of Engineers to Fontesvilla to improvise a pontoon there, and he sent a second detachment of Engineers on to Chimoio to arrange accommodation, water and supplies.[62]

Alderson and Elsa Green, separately, have given us a description of the Pungwe, its attractions and its difficulties:

> The Pungwe River near its mouth is certainly very pretty. Perhaps two miles wide, its banks are fringed with green, and it is studded with numerous islands, covered with vegetation. As a navigable river, however ... it is shallow and its channel changes with almost every tide - with crocodiles, hippos and, on the land, other game.[63]
>
> The hippopotamus, rhinoceros and crocodile, are still frequently seen on the banks and in the waters of the Pungwe River. The shores at one time abounded with elephants and other large game; buffalo,

wildebeest, hartebeest and quagga, are still found in the neighbourhood of Beira. The climate is not very healthy during summer, malaria is present more or less. Fever trees with their yellow weird-looking branches abound in the swamps. The sandbanks in the river make navigation very tedious at times - as the traveller who is unfortunate to get stuck on one finds to his discomfort ... The flowers, ferns and tropical foliage were magnificent, shining in the damp thickets as one steamed somewhat slowly through the country. Beautiful orchids hung from the trees. We passed a herd of buffalo in the jungle grass near the [railway] line, and saw some zebra grazing quietly in the far distance.[64]

On 7 July Alderson left for Chimoio by rail, and the next day Archer and his men disembarked from the *Arab*. They loaded another 29 horses, and he and four of his men set off for Fontesvilla in railway trucks. The country through which they were to pass was a dangerous tsetse fly area. Consequently, the trucks carrying the horses had to be adapted at Beira by covering them with wire gauze to prevent the tsetse fly biting them, and the horses had to be taken through the area as quickly as possible. As Archer explained: 'a horse that gets bitten by the Tsetse Fly nearly always dies. The horse gets wet then it begins to get thinner and thinner until finally it dies of poverty ... Still eats after being bitten, in fact up to the time it dies.'[65] Elsa Green also wrote of the dangers to horses and added: 'Perhaps worse than the fly is the disease known as horse sickness. He is liable to this during and after the rains. Should he have it and recover, he is termed a salted horse, and commands a much higher price in consequence, for he is unlikely to have a second attack, though this occasionally happens.'[66]

In addition to the tsetse fly and horse sickness, Archer experienced other dangers: one of his horses fell out of the truck in which it was being carried, but, with considerable difficulty, he managed to get it back into the truck again - 'minus pieces of skin and hair.' Nor was this the end of his troubles. The railway was 'a tiny one, the gauge being only two feet and the carriages overhanging the wheels about the same distance on each side.'[67] They used three troop trains. Alderson went on the first. The second train - that on which Archer travelled - consisting of five horse and one baggage truck, 'upset about the 57th or 58th mile peg, and ... all the horses not hurt were loose in the bush ... among the tsetse flies and lions!' After a while, the engine of Archer's train continued on its journey, to bring help to the upset trucks. At the same time, Alderson, who was now on his way back from Chimoio, decided to take his engine and an empty truck with tools down to help. When he got to the place where Archer's train had toppled over, he

> found a pretty mess; the whole of the second troop train except the engine, had, in rounding the curve, gone over a three foot embankment, the result being that the trucks were turned almost upside down, all their upper works were smashed, two horses killed outright, two so badly hurt that they had to be shot, and four had galloped off into the forest ... Luckily no men, there had been about five [that is, Archer and four of his men] with the horses, were hurt ... The turned out horses were led along the line up to Sixty-two, where they remained for the night in charge of St Aubyn [who] was by no means pleased at having his men and horses turned out of the train.[68]

But even in getting to the site of the accident, Alderson had a good deal of trouble. He described what happened on his way down from Chimoio by rail:

> About the 56th mile peg, just as we were rounding a sharp curve at a fair pace, we heard a whistle and at the same time saw an engine [that of the second train] coming up on the other end of the curve and not a hundred yards from us. Both drivers shut off steam, put on the brake and then jumped, as did [everyone else]. Crash we went down a rather steep embankment all among the bushes and boulders, and bang went the two engines together, breaking up, and entangling their cow catchers, but luckily doing no other damage and both remaining on the line. [They sorted out the crash and then] went on to the scene of the [other] accident.[69]

It may be that in their anxiety to move the horses safely through the tsetse fly area and get up country as soon as possible, it was a case of more haste, less speed.

Archer described the country through which he passed on his way to Fontesvilla from Beira as being very flat, with the grass about six feet tall, all of it, he understood, under water in the rainy season. He described, too, the difficult work they had to undertake once they got to Fontesvilla itself:

> On arrival at Fontes Villa, [a distance of] about 40 miles, we had a job to get the horses across the river on a small pontoon boat. [The]

right bank was very steep, the left bank sloping and shallow. River deep. I had to swim several horses that we could not get on to the pontoon, across the river. Got treated by railway people to a bottle of champagne, which cost £1. I had refused whisky. I was told I would soon be down with fever over swimming horses across the Pungwe. [The next day we] stopped at Fontes Villa to help No. 4 Section, 4th Battalion Rifle Brigade [commanded by Lieutenant Vernon] over the river with their horses. More swimming. Got treated to more champagne.[70]

Alderson, who had already moved on to Chimoio, painted a somewhat less troubled picture of getting the horses across the river at Fontesvilla: the Engineers 'improvised a pontoon, by lashing two small lighters together and building a platform on them, and ... also made a landing stage. By means of these the horses of the scouts had been easily got across the river ten to twelve at a time.'[71] He wrote of Fontesvilla and the country inland between it and Chimoio:

Fontesvilla is certainly about the most feverish looking spot that can be imagined, and from all accounts, and judging by the two nearly full cemeteries, it is as bad as it looks. Nearly all of the few houses are built on piles, as it is often flooded during the rainy season, and we were told that when the burials take place the coffins have to be weighted to make them sink, as the graves fill with water as soon as they are dug. Truly a man should be well paid to work in such a place! ... For the first twenty miles the line goes as straight as an arrow from Fontesvilla, through a perfectly flat and most gamey-looking country - long grass, with here and there patches of thick scrub, or of trees about twenty feet high, of various sorts including borassus palms. I do not think I have ever enjoyed a railway journey more ... zebra, buffalo, and innumerable sorts of buck ... At Forty Mile Station ... we began to enter the forest country, which extends from there up to and some distance beyond Chimoio.[72]

Elsa Green, too, enjoyed the scenery through which they passed after Fontesvilla, and she waxed lyrically in describing it:

The line passes through some lovely scenery. In the neighbourhood of seventy-seven-mile-spruit it is beautifully wooded like an English park, allowing of course for the difference in tint, the trees being entirely unlike the oak, elm and beech. The sombre laurel-like tint of evergreens is enlivened by trees such as kaffirboom, with its brilliant coral blossoms, and others bearing glorious fruit. Fern-trees abound in some parts and beautiful creepers trail from the tree tops to the ground. At some seasons of the year an ever-changing panorama of colour is presented to the eye of the traveller ... Next we passed through country having much shorter jungle grass. Tall palms lifted their feathery tops high into the blue ether, which was now melting into the emerald and gold of sunset.[73]

At six in the morning on 10 July Archer and his men moved on from Fontesvilla for Chimoio, the railhead. They stopped for the night after about eighty miles, sleeping in the trucks. There was no marked stop and they just stopped when and where they felt like it. The narrow track ran through very thick forest made up of 'splendid trees'. The next day, they arrived at Chimoio, 120 miles from Beira, and took over 21 horses and 29 sets of saddlery. There had been alarming reports in the South African newspapers of lions roaming the streets of Chimoio:

They were said to be so hungry that they walked the streets in daylight. The rinderpest was depleting the country of game as well as transport oxen and milch cows, while the carnivorous animals were not affected by it, except that their food-supply ran short ... All along the route we saw dead or dying oxen, victims of the terrible rinderpest which was depleting the land of its most valuable means of transport.[74]

Archer recorded how at Chimoio they nearly lost their rations: 'five lions had a walk around the hut where our meat had been put, but got hustled off by some scouts.'[75]

Elsa Green travelled - far more comfortably than did any of the soldiers - from Fontesvilla to Chimoio: 'in a cattle truck ... furnished comfortably with a garden seat on either side. A case of medicines and surgical appliances placed in the centre served as a dining table'. She wrote of Chimoio that the 'cold of night was intense when contrasted with the heat of the day, [and the] smell of the swamp lying in the vicinity was most objectionable, though not as bad as at Fontesvilla.'[76] Here Archer and his colleagues took all the horses off the train for exercise. Some of them had never had a saddle on them before. Mitchell - Archer's recently appointed batman - was thrown by one of these horses while Archer was holding its head. The muscles and sinews of Archer's left arm were strained as Mitchell pitched onto him. He rode several of these untrained horses that others were unable to ride, but even he was unable to ride two of them. The next day involved more mounted work and Archer with CSM H Worthing, of the 4th Battalion of the Rifle Brigade - who arrived with No. 4 Section the previous evening - rode the two horses that they had been unable to mount the previous day, and gave them 'a good doing'. In the course of this Archer received more dangerous blows:

> They were rare bulkers. I nearly got my head smashed as I dismounted. He got me in the back with both front hoofs ... That evening someone gave me some Absinthe to drink, made me drunk. Fortunately I was afterwards very sick.[77]

Several days later he had 'still got a very bad head', whether from the kick of the horse or from the liquor he did not say.

It took six days to get all the 380 men and 284 horses away from Beira and take them via Fontesvilla as far as Chimoio. Archer stopped at Chimoio from 11 to 18 July, 'breaking in horses and getting stores ready for the march.' During this time he was made Acting Sergeant Major. 'From the 14th until the 20th, men, horses or stores, were arriving at Chimoio daily,' and the last of them moved forward on 20 July. In such short supply was the ox and mule transport that some of them had to use donkey wagons and took nine and a half hours to cover 3 miles.[78]

Archer must have been relieved to get away from Chimoio. He found it hot by day and cold at night, lions roamed the streets looking for food, the nearby swamp was foul-smelling, the horses were difficult and he had injured his arm and back trying to break them. He none the less remained in good spirits.

Before he left Portuguese East Africa to move westwards into Rhodesia, he wrote a note to his mother. The regular mail service had been gravely disrupted by the revolt and it was difficult while on the march to find either time or materials to write proper letters. His note was written on a small scrap of paper and gave neither the date nor the place.

> If everything goes all right we expect to reach Salisbury in about 15 days time. They say here (the Portuguese) that there are 30,000 Mashonas under arms but not together. We are 12 officers, 230 NCOs and men, Mounted Infantry. Two Doctors, one NCO and four men Medical Staff. 97 men of the 43rd Company Royal Engineers. One officer, two Sergeants, six men Royal Artillery with two seven pound field guns, and about 20 officers and men of the Chartered Company. We shall get about 100 natives to act as drivers for the

waggons when we get up country. We have two Maxim guns with plenty of ammunition so we shall be able to give a good account of ourselves.[79]

On 14 July, while all the other men and horses were being brought up to Chimoio, the first party, comprised of Sections 1, 2 and 4 of the Rifle Company - about 100 of all ranks - under Captain Jenner, marched from Chimoio for Umtali.[80] They took Archer's horses with them, leaving him and the others of Section 3 at Chimoio.[81] It took Jenner's Rifle Company six arduous marches to travel uphill from Chimoio to Umtali, where they arrived on 19 July. They used 'enormous waggons, drawn by spans of from ten to twenty oxen or mules [through] hills, woods, ravines and rough roads.' Their mobility depended entirely on the number of mules available, and they had only a quarter of those they required. Umtali was the furthest point inland to which the road, a rough one, was open. The Mashona east of Umtali had not risen, so they encountered no trouble against them.[82]

On 18 July, Alderson and the remainder of his force, including Archer - still Acting Sergeant Major - followed Jenner's party and set out for Umtali. They started very early each morning, before it was daylight, so as to begin while it was still cool, and they travelled by the light of the moon. Their daily routine was: 'reveille at 4 and 4.30 a.m., march till about 10.0 a.m., halt about three or four hours, and then march to place appointed, but [it was] nearly always dark when we arrived at our camping place.' It took them from 18 to 24 July to reach Umtali, where they camped until 28 July.[83] 'The road between Chimoio and Umtali was in a very bad state, and the veldt dried up and poor.'[84] Consequently, the journey was far from easy, and involved taking the men, guns, animals and vehicles

> down *donga*s (steep hills where a river is crossed) almost as steep as the roof of a house, across rivers, and up the opposite bank at a like speed, unless the [vehicle] sticks in the river drift, which is not an uncommon experience. In that case it frequently necessitates waiting until a fresh span of mules can be got to help them out of their difficulties. Then on again ... over stones, tree stumps, and water-courses.[85]

In the evening they reached the Revue River where they found Lieutenant French, who was in command of No. 1 Section, the Irish Company, and Lieutenant Stephens, who was in command of No.3

Section, the Rifle Company - Archer's section - with their Mounted Infantry sections which had marched from Chimoio earlier. Alderson remarked that 'they appeared very comfortable and ... had the horses picketed in a very ship-shape manner.'[86] Revue was a very small settlement and Elsa Green described it as a 'little compound with its mud huts ... encircled with dense thicket and jungle grass; inside the enclosure grow tree-ferns and tall bananas.'[87]

The next day Alderson's Column moved on to Umtali. On the way, Elsa Green, going in the same direction in a 'coach' pulled by fourteen mules, passed them:

> We had only proceeded a short distance when we saw waggons with mule spans, long trains of [eighteen or twenty] donkeys drawing guns on carriages, mounted men and foot soldiers, with all the paraphernalia of a column of Her Majesty's troops on the march. We learned that they were the Mounted Infantry Regiment.[88]

Five hundred mules and twenty-five wagons had arrived at Beira - presumably from South Africa - on 16 June, intended to be used for transporting food to the civilian population of the Umtali area, but they had to be used almost entirely to transport Alderson's armaments, stores and equipment.[89] It was these mules and wagons that Elsa Green saw *en route*.

Umtali at this time was a settlement in which only the Masonic Hotel had two storeys rather than one, and only a few others were made of brick: the bank, courthouse and prison. The private dwellings were built of three or four mud huts roofed with grass thatch.

> When we first saw Umtali, all places of any size were in a laager formed of sacks of earth, branches of trees and thorn-bushes, with ox waggons to further strengthen it. Thus a stockade was made as a defence against an attack ... A very strong laager, with the addition of a barbed wire entanglement, was constructed round the courthouse and the gaol in the market square. A seven-pound gun further defended it. The firing of this gun was the signal for every one to fly to the laager in the prison. Umtali was full of refugees from outlying districts, which were not considered safe, since brutal murders had been perpetrated by natives upon the white settlers in lonely out-of-the-way places in Mashonaland. These had taken place only a short time before. It was feared at this time that several of the powerful native chiefs were only waiting a fitting opportunity to rebel.[90]

Alderson and his men were now ready to tackle these Mashona chiefs - six weeks after they had started the rebellion. Initially he had intended to take a small group of nurses and a doctor to Salisbury to help there, but on reflection thought this was too dangerous, because the road, which ran through Chief Makoni's country, was 'swarming with hostile natives.' Instead he decided first to attack Makoni's kraal, about forty miles away, dispose of the threat that the chief presented and *then* go on to Salisbury. Makoni, one of the most powerful chiefs, 'had been giving much trouble to the country. Several murders in the Salisbury and Umtali districts had been distinctly traced to his people.'[91] Tackling him was not a straightforward task for those versed only in Western and European warfare:

> [The Shona] tactics were of the most baffling kind ... they soon abandoned all pretence of fighting in the open and, on the approach of white troops, withdrew to their stockaded villages, which were usually situated in close proximity to clusters of granite *kopjes*, constituting an almost impenetrable second line of defence ... Ensconced in inaccessible crevices and crannies, they were able, without exposing themselves, to use their Tower muskets, flint-locks and antiquated blunderbusses at close range with deadly effect. Military science could devise no means of dealing expeditiously with such methods, and it seemed that only a wearing down process would reduce the rebels to submission.[92]

Makoni's kraal was composed of about three hundred huts. The caves into which he and his people retired are of considerable dimensions and almost impregnable. Makoni is reported to have said that he had sufficient food stored to last a year or two, and that he had no intention of surrendering ... The kraal was defended by high stone walls ... There were a number of rifle-pits about eight hundred yards from it. These were circular in form, having earth thrown up in front and brushwood piled upon it. These pits were unoccupied at the time of the attack, as Makoni's people were taken completely by surprise. The natives were armed with Lee-Metford and Martini rifles as well as a miscellaneous collection of muzzle-loading guns.[93]

No one, I think, had any idea beforehand of how enormously strong the Mashonas could make their kraals. These are built amongst huge boulders on the top of rocky hills, and are natural fastnesses, generally very difficult of access even when entirely deserted, but when occupied by an enemy concealed behind thick loopholed walls, or in caves commanding every approach, the difficulties are considerably increased. The caves, though often of fine proportions inside, are entered as a rule by small fissures, or by holes from above. There is generally nothing to show where they are as there are numberless cracks in the rocks, and it is impossible to tell which of them are cave entrances or holes out of which the cave inhabitants can fire.[94]

The whole of Alderson's force left Umtali on 27 July[95] to attack Makoni. In order to deal with the chief in a single engagement, Alderson avoided the Devil's Pass, 'a very bad place on the main road some twenty miles from Odzi', where they camped the night after leaving Umtali.[96] The rebels had fortified the pass and were assembled in force there. His deployment consisted of Honey's scouts two to four miles ahead of the advance party. They were followed by the advance guard under Jenner, comprised of two sections of the Rifle Company. These were followed by the main body, led by the other two sections of the Rifle Company with one machine gun, the main body of the Royal Engineers, and the detachment of the Royal Artillery with two seven pounders. Behind them came 23 wagons, then a detachment of the West Riding Regiment and the unmounted portion of the Umtali Rifles, who were in turn followed by 22 wagons and a party of the Royal Engineers and two sections of the Irish Company. The Engineers carried tools likely to be useful in repairing damaged wagons. The Rear Guard, under Captain McMahon, was made up of the other two sections of the Irish Company and the mounted portion of the Umtali Rifles.

Archer was in the advance guard and was 'put in charge of ten picked men to act as scouts.' On 30 July, while out with these scouts, he

> Got lost for about six hours, just arrived in camp as search parties were being sent out to find me ... Went out scouting again within half an hour of arriving in camp (fresh horse), came across about 200 of the enemy in a pass that I had come down by myself in the morning (good job for me that they were not there earlier), they tried to cut us off from the main body, but the firing brought up the other scouts, so we drove them into the bush, don't know how many we killed as they carry their dead and wounded away with them, but think about fifty. [The following day we] attacked a kraal, nearly got hit with pieces of rock that they threw at us, got some chickens, goats, monkey nuts etc. I received orders to place myself under Mr Ross, Native Commissioner, with two men as escort, to visit kraals and find out if they were friendly or not, a rather risky job.[97]

On 1 and 2 August Archer recorded that they 'burnt more kraals [though the] natives had deserted them.'[98] On 2 August they halted on the main road to Salisbury, about ten miles from Umtali and eight miles from Makoni's kraal, and laagered there on the farther side of the Odzi river. Here, Alderson issued his operation orders for the following day:

> The two companies Mounted Infantry [the Rifle Company and the Irish Company] with one Maxim, two officers [Jenner and McMahon] and twenty non-commissioned officers and men Royal Engineers, all the detachment Royal Artillery, with the two seven-pounder guns, Mr Honey's scouts, forty of the Umtali Rifles, all the Native Contingent, and a portion of the Medical Staff Corps, will parade at 1.45 a.m., tomorrow. All will be dismounted except the scouts. The Mounted Infantry will carry 140 rounds of ammunition per rifle, the remainder 100 rounds. The day's rations will be carried in haversacks, and water bottles will be filled with cold tea. Reveille tomorrow will be at 5.30 a.m. Breakfast at 6.0 a.m.[99]

These last two sentences were a subterfuge: the late reveille and breakfast times, which would have been accompanied by bugle calls, were given so as not to reveal to spies any unusual steps. No bugles were blown at 1.45 a.m., and the men got up and fell in silently. They set off a little after 2.0 a.m., arrived at daybreak and immediately engaged Makoni's rebels - about 4000 of them.[100]

Alderson's force was divided into two parties. The Irish Company, Engineers and Artillery under Alderson himself made the frontal attack from the north. The Rifle Company, including Archer and his section, the Umtali Volunteers, and Scouts under Jenner, attacked the enemy on the right, south, flank.[101] Archer recorded his personal experiences of what then happened at Makoni's kraal on Monday 3 August, which, as he pointed out, was 'a bank holiday'!

> 3rd (Bank Holiday). Paraded at 1.30 a.m., to attack Makoni's fortress at daybreak; the Irish company and RA taking the north, the RE volunteers the east, Rifle Company and Scouts the south (Mr Ross acted as guide). Distance there about ten miles on foot. The RA opened the ball, Makoni being taken completely by surprise; several of his people tried to escape our way and ran nearly into us. After about two and a half hours of this kind of work, and putting in volleys at 800 yards, we received orders to cease fire and advance as close up as we could; we got up to about 150 yards by creeping alone,

the Irish Company bullets and RA shells going over our heads all the time, and the first they knew of us was by seeing our swords [bayonets] fixed. Captain Jenner gave the order to charge, and you may be sure we lost no time in getting in. Directly we started to charge they fired at us as hard as they could, all the bullets going over our heads. I made for the place in the wall where there was no loophole, and started pushing the bushes off the top of the wall [which] was about ten feet high. Captain Jenner and Captain [Alfred Ernest] Haynes, RE, and myself scrambled through the gap that I had made, Captain Haynes being shot through the head directly afterwards. Mitchell [Archer's batman] shot the [African] that shot him. I soon got into a good position for shooting, which commanded the entrance to one of the caves, and put in some good shooting at [Africans] going in it, distance twenty yards. I don't know how many I killed, as they pulled them in as quickly as I hit them, but I fired thirty-four rounds. Private Broad was shot through the leg, taken off at the knee next day; we left him at the old Police Barracks, now called Fort Haynes. Others killed were Private Vickers, 3rd KRR; Private Wickham, Royal Irish; there were about two dozen wounded. Acting Corporal Wide got hit on the water bottle with a spear; expect we killed about 200 of them, but could not tell, as they fled to their caves, from which it is impossible to get them out. [The whole force then occupied the kraal, which was burnt. They also captured 355 cattle and 210 sheep and goats.[102]] Every one completely knocked up when we arrived in camp, Mr Stephens and [Private] Mitchell down with fever, Mitchell all right again in two days, Mr Stephens in a week.[103]

With Stephens down with fever, No. 3 section of the Rifle Company was without a commissioned officer, and Archer, the senior NCO, was given temporary charge of the section, directly responsible to Captain Jenner who was in charge of the Rifle Company.

Alderson, like Archer, estimated the enemy's loss to be 200 killed[104] and many wounded. On his own side, in addition to the deaths of Captain Haynes, Private Wickham and Private Vickers, four men - Privates W M Mackay,[105] R Broad,[106] D D Young[107] and 'a coloured boy' - were wounded.[108] Jenkins, Alderson's servant, was accidentally shot through the thigh by one of the medical staff regulars, with Jenkins's own revolver, early in the morning before they set out to attack Makoni.[109] He was taken to the temporary laager hospital in the Umtali prison, looked after by Nurse Green, but died a few days later.[110] Dr Lovell attended the wounded until they could be taken to Umtali.¹¹¹ Alderson established Fort Haynes on the road near Makoni's kraal, naming it in honour of his deceased colleague, with a garrison of 50 troops to guard the Devil's Pass.

> The forces returned to laager at 2 o'clock on the morning of the 4th, Colonel Alderson left laager at 7.0 a.m. with one hundred men, and made reconnaissance in force in the Devil's Pass, where the enemy was supposed to be in force. The pass was found fortified but deserted, Makoni having recalled his men prior to our attack on his kraal. We also repaired the telegraph line, which was found cut on the pass, connecting us with Umtali. On return to laager, we burnt one of the enemy's kraals, which was deserted.[112]

Repairing the telegraph line was important. Within a few days of the outbreak of the rebellion, the wires connecting Salisbury with Umtali, to the south-east, and Charter, to the south-west towards Bulawayo, had been slashed. Except for a few days in the middle of July when the line was temporarily linked with Bulawayo, Salisbury was in this way completely cut off until permanent communication was restored on 5 August. The telegraph line south-eastwards to Umtali was not restored until it was repaired by Alderson's column on 4 August.[113] Until the beginning of August, therefore, no arrangements about the vital questions of supplies and transport could be made from, or in consultation with, Salisbury. Furthermore, no telegraphic communication had been established between Delagoa Bay and Beira, where Alderson could have been contacted. It followed that even after telegraphic communications with Bulawayo had been restored, and until the Umtali link was re-established, it was impossible to communicate rapidly with Alderson and allow him to make decisions based on knowledge of what was happening in the interior.[114]

Reporting the attack on Makoni, *The Rhodesia Herald* announced,

> This action practically smashed up Makoni ... at least 200 men including a witch doctor and ten chief councillors were killed. In the engagement all our men acted with the greatest gallantry, and the plan of attack was excellently conceived and smartly delivered.[115]

In another note to his mother, also written on a small scrap of paper, two days before the attack on Makoni's kraal, Archer had told her:

> Since writing the others I find out that we are going to Fort Charter for about a month. Don't know how much longer we shall be kept

out here. The Mashonas are giving in daily but we don't expect to get back before next summer. I am escorting this and other letters as far as Marandellas and the Royal Engineers escort them from there to Beira and we go to Charter from Marandellas.[116]

He made no mention of the forthcoming attack on Makoni. Alderson had kept his intentions to himself and his staff officers, and revealed them - carefully and clearly - to the men only once they had gathered 'some little distance from the laager'.[117]

On 5 August, after the attack on Makoni's kraal and the following day's reconnaissance, Alderson and virtually the whole of his force, including Archer's section, spent five days travelling to Gatzi's kraal, north of Marandellas, which they reached at sunset on 9 August. The next six days were spent attacking and destroying Gatzi's, Mangwendi's and numerous other kraals. One European and a few rebels were killed.[118]

Destroying the power of the rebels was, however, only part of the problem facing the Europeans in Mashonaland. They were gravely short of food, especially flour, and of other supplies, and they looked to Alderson to help solve this acute difficulty. At the beginning of August the people in Salisbury were daily expecting news of, and then the arrival of, his column. They anticipated that he would bring with it large supplies of food and other essential goods, and they hoped that after a few weeks all danger would be over and they could begin to live a more secure and peaceful life again. 'These expectations were, however, doomed to disappointment.' Alderson's ability to help was severely limited by

> the difficulty of moving a large number of animals over the Beira Railway, the necessity of fighting at Makonis and other points along the road so as to ensure the future safety of transport, and the impossibility of immediately getting together sufficient wagons at the railhead to serve both for the conveyance of troops and of large supplies. [It] was out of Lieutenant-Colonel Alderson's power to do more than at once despatch some five ox-wagons forward ... These, owing to rinderpest, barely succeeded in reaching Salisbury, and their contents, though sufficiently welcome, only relieved, without terminating, the strain. Towards the middle of August, apart from Lieutenant-Colonel Alderson's forces, there were 978 white people in Salisbury, beside a large number of friendly natives of various classes. Fresh meat was nearly exhausted, and the future outlook was becoming most serious. With the exception of a few salted spans, ox-

wagon transport on the Umtali road had been completely swept off by rinderpest, and the mules then available in the country barely sufficed for the conveyance of the necessary forces.

As regard the other centres in Mashonaland, Enkeldoorn and Charter were in even worse plight than Salisbury, as at neither place were any large stocks stored before the commencement of the rising. [Thus] the problem pressing for immediate solution in August and September principally related to the supply of rations for both men and animals in the Salisbury and Charter districts, and along the line of communication with Umtali. The white population at these points, inclusive of the Imperial troops and volunteers, numbered at this time upwards of 2000, and the quantity of grain required for horses and mules engaged in military operations, apart from transport, was very considerable.[119]

Two days after the attack on Gatzi's kraal, on 13 August, Alderson left for Salisbury to see what he could do to help. He took with him Lieutenant St Aubyn, in charge of No.1 Section of the Rifle Company, and Lieutenant King-Harman, in charge of No. 4 Section of the Irish Company. He left Captain Jenner in charge of the remainder of the Rifle and Irish Companies, including Archer's section, to carry out punitive expeditions against Marandella and other chiefs, destroying their kraals and collecting large quantities of grain and oat hay before moving on to Salisbury. On 17 August Jenner and his men took Ushewekunzi's kraal without suffering any loss. The column reached Law's store on the main road on 21 August and found its ashes still warm. It had not been burned when Alderson passed it a week earlier, so it was clear that rebel activity was continuing. The following day the column swung off the road into Chiquaqua's country, found all the kraals deserted, and 'got but little grain.' They then moved on to Salisbury, which they reached on 25 August.[120]

At Salisbury they were joined by Lieutenant St Aubyn and Lieutenant King-Harman at the Nursery Farm. The Natal Troop did not accompany Jenner but went straight to Charter to await his arrival there.

Nine spans of mules, which it was intended to use for the transport of grain, accompanied Captain Jenner's column to Charter from Salisbury on 31st August. Of these, however ... five would be required for military purposes, and of the remaining four two were constantly employed on military duty up to the middle of November.[121]

They started out for Umtegeza's kraal on 1 September. Since there was not nearly enough food in Salisbury to ration the column, instead of going direct to Umtegeza's, they went back via Marandellas, where they hoped to meet a convoy with the supplies that they needed. The food shortage gravely hampered the Mashonaland Field Force's operations because it was impossible to gather sufficient stocks to allow the force as a whole to take the field with a full month's rations, as they would normally. Fodder for their animals also restricted their ability to move *en masse*, fast and far.

> It certainly was a bit disheartening for all of us. Instead of being able to push rapidly about the country with scouting parties some miles out on either flank, we had to plod slowly along a few miles at a time, saving our horses as much as possible, and letting them graze for hours in the middle of the day. Grazing at night was supposed to bring on a deadly disease known as 'horse-sickness', so at sunset they were picketed in the laager with nosebags on - well-named nosebags, being bags that contained their noses, and nothing else.[122]

The British South Africa Company claimed that despite the grave food shortages, it proved possible to keep the troops, both Imperial and Volunteer, on full rations throughout the whole period of operations, unlike the civilians who were severely rationed.[123] But this seems not to have been true, because Jenner reported that the middle of October 'was our shortest time as regards rations, a three-quarter allowance of flour or biscuit being all that we could run to.'[124]

Jenner - now a Brevet Major - and his column marched to Marandellas, following the telegraph line. The purpose of this march was to enable them to acquire whatever grain they could find for their 'half-starved horses and mules.'

> We collected what grain we could near the route. A village situated between the telegraph line and the main road gave considerable resistance before it was burned and depleted of grain ... On arrival at Marandellas we found that the expected convoy had not arrived; but we had not long to wait, and then began a great off-loading and sorting and rearranging and reloading of stores. There was a good deal of difficulty about the mules too, but we managed to make a start the next morning, and very glad we were. The road between Marandellas and Charter was not quite so well watered in some parts as most of the roads, and the grass was very extensively burnt; we

then had finished all our 'collected' grain, and the horses and mules were very weak in consequence.[125]

When they reached Charter they were joined by the Natal Troop. They started south on 13 September in the afternoon, working south and east, and bivouacked the following night at 'Shaw's'. They left the road there at five o'clock the next morning and headed south and east into Umtegeza's country, 'with orders to get hold of this gentleman, break up his gang, and return to Charter as soon as possible, to take part in a fresh expedition in another direction.'[126]

Major Jenner, who, with the bulk of the Imperial troops, had been patrolling the Charter Marandella district, attacked and completely destroyed the kraal of Umtegeza, the paramount chief in the Charter district. Umtegeza surrendered on condition of his life being spared, but most of his followers escaped ... The patrol went on to destroy kraals and clear the district, and were successful in capturing large quantities of the grain and cattle so urgently needed in Salisbury.[127]

We got back to Charter on the 25th, bringing 'Mtegeza with us, having killed a good lot of his men, taken about 30 prisoners, captured 80 head of cattle, and destroyed his three principal strongholds [Zabi, Gona and Mzimilima's]. In this expedition we were joined by a large number of 'friendlies' from the Victoria District. They were of great use to us in various ways, especially in finding hidden stores of grain etc and destroying what could not be carried away. They were champion devastators, and spread out all over the country - about 2000 of them - running at a good pace for miles.[128]

When they arrived back at Charter they immediately set about making arrangements for co-operating with Alderson's column against the rebels in the Hartley Hills. They left Charter on the 6 October and travelled via Beatrice Mine - where the rebellion had started three months earlier - 'destroying deserted kraals and seizing the grain.' They joined Alderson's column at Matshangombi's kraal on 10th October.[129]

The next day, 11 October, the two columns - Alderson's and Jenner's - worked in 'such a manner as to thoroughly scour the whole district' around Hartley. They continued their attacks for the next fortnight, sometimes the two columns working together, sometimes separately. Working together between 11 and 24 October, they destroyed

Matshangombi's, Chena's, Zimba's and 'a very large number' of other kraals. Working separately from 25 October to 10 November, Jenner's column - of 170 troops and 1000 friendlies from Victoria - burned Mapondera's and other kraals, and built a new fort at Mazoe. At Mapondera's the Africans fled as soon as they heard Jenner's column approaching.[130] They then returned to Salisbury.

By this time, the middle of October, the soldiers' boots were falling apart - most of the men were dismounted and walked long distances over rough ground. Their clothing was wearing very thin and they were suffering from the folly of the only khaki drill issued to them before leaving Britain being a single suit for 'sea-kit'. They were reduced to three-quarter rations, and their horses and mules were on the point of starvation, the old grass having been burned off and the new grass not yet having sprung up. Indeed, as early as August Archer wrote to a friend and told him:

> Four biscuits and one pound of bully don't make us very fat, but I keep about the same. All we can get to help the bully down with are occasional chickens and a few pumpkins ... Everybody walking on the uppers of their boots; we only brought one pair with us. I am all right as I got a pair of top-boots from Captain Hully. I look a trophy now, top boots, trousers out at the knee, khaki serge the worse for wear, equipment bandolier fifty rounds, fifty more rounds in the wallets, revolver and pouch on the left side, and I wear a slouch hat and pugaree, and nearly as black as [an African]; we sometimes go two or three days without washing ... All our transport bullocks have died of rinderpest; have seen hundreds on each side of the road coming up here, a splendid smell about; fifty vultures sitting on each bullock (get fined £1 for shooting one of them). They say we shall not have fifty of our horses live through the rainy season, and that nearly everyone will get a touch of fever; a nice lookout for us. There is a rumour that we are going to get extra pay from the Chartered Company; I hope so, as we shall want a new rig-out when we get back.[131]

From Salisbury Jenner made one more expedition, this time a peaceful one. On 15 November he had a 'successful parley with Chiquaqua and Kunzi', petty chiefs with whom he settled peace terms.[132]

During November Rhodes and Earl Grey visited Umtali on an 'historic visit' and Archer was their escort from Salisbury to Umtali, an event he long remembered with pride.[133]

Archer had not expected to leave Mashonaland before the summer of 1897. Indeed, it had been intended that the punitive operations in which he and his colleagues were engaged should continue so as thoroughly to pacify a much larger part of the country, but the serious shortage of food, livestock feed and other supplies forced a curtailment.

> For almost four months the Mounted Infantry, with the local forces [were] hindered by shortage of supplies, which prevented them from undertaking more extensive operations. Eventually it was admitted that further pacification would be better left to the new Police Force, the organisation of which was now proceeding apace, and that it was important to get as many as possible of the Imperial troops out of the country quickly because if they stayed during the rainy season they would be forced to remain inactive and would be exposed to the risks of malaria.[134]

Although it was not said, they would also cost Rhodes a great deal more money in paying for their services and their maintenance if they remained in the country.

There was still a grave shortage of food; uniforms and boots were almost worn out; and horses and mules continued to die of starvation. Consequently, on Monday 28 November Major-General Sir Frederick Carrington, officer commanding the forces in Matabeleland and Mashonaland, issued orders for 150 members of the Mounted Infantry, with the detachment of the Royal Artillery, to move down to Umtali, so as to be ready to move to the rail head - now at Bendula[135] - and onwards to Beira, for re-embarkation. 'The ponies or what was left of them, were handed over to the Chartered Company.'[136] The next day, after the General had inspected the Imperial troops in the afternoon, the Rifle Company, including Archer's section, the half English Company and a convoy of the sick, marched for Umtali 'in a tremendous thunder and rain storm.' When Alderson passed them he said they were 'plodding along in the mud, drenched to the skin, but all as merry as crickets.'[137] No doubt they put on a brave face in front of their commanding officer, but it is unlikely that they genuinely felt merry. On 2 December Carrington and his staff followed them. Six days later the Irish Company and the remaining Imperial troops also marched to Umtali and then to Bendula, where they arrived on Christmas day, tired and soaking wet.

> After dragging starving ponies behind one for some months, the idea of being whirled along in a train is decidedly pleasing. The poor

train appeared however to be starving too, and we all had to get out and push it a good part of the way. It was, however, very good going downhill, which, of course, most of our journey fortunately was ... and the amount of game on the line was really marvellous. Waterbuck, harte-beests, zebras, etc, trotted and walked by the side of the train, as it dashed at its greatest speed along the Beira Flats. Sergeant Archer got out of the train, ran after one buck, cut its throat, put it on the engine, and got into the train again, all in one motion. But it ought, perhaps, to be mentioned that the train was standing still, and that Vernon had shot the buck [but had not killed it.][138]

Bearing in mind the way in which a few years earlier, in Ireland, he had handled a team of bolting horses and saved the ambulance they were pulling, even if the train on the Beira flats had been moving, there is no doubt that he would have leapt out of it to retrieve the wounded buck – though possibly not all in one motion.

Apart from 36 NCOs and men - 15 from the Rifle Brigade, including eight from Archer's section - who transferred to the service of the British South Africa Company to join their police force,[139] everyone had arrived at Beira by the evening of 28 December, and they sailed on the *Pembroke Castle* on the last day of the year.

Looking back on the military action, the Company reported of Alderson's force that:

> The result of their five months campaign in Mashonaland had been to relieve the towns and free them from any apprehension of an attack from the rebels, and to open up all lines of communication between the chief centres. They had, however, been seriously hampered by the shortness of supplies, and had been prevented thereby from undertaking any extensive operations; no thorough punishment had been inflicted on the natives; none of the murderers of white men had been captured, nor had the power of any important chief, with the exception of Makoni and the chiefs in the Charter District, been broken. It was considered that this work might be left to the new police ... who were gradually replacing the troops as they left the country.[140]

It is unlikely that Archer or any other member of Alderson's force would have agreed that they had not undertaken any extensive operations and had inflicted no thorough punishment on the Mashona. Still less would the Mashona themselves have agreed.

Alderson recorded that the sea journey from Beira to Durban was 'very smooth and comfortable'. They arrived on 2 January 1897 and immediately went up to Pietermaritzburg by train. Here, as Alderson and Jenner reported,

> All the barracks being full, we had to go under canvas; this at a time of year when one day there was heavy rain and the next a hot sun. This, no doubt, brought out the fever which had been contracted when marching down to Beira in the rains and, in ten days, we had nearly fifty per cent. of both officers and men in hospital.[141]
>
> As is so often the case, as soon as the hard work was over, the effects of climate, exposure, and indifferent food became apparent in the form of malarial fever of a severe type, which placed most of the officers and a very large number of the men in hospital on our arrival at Pietermaritzburg, Natal, where we were quartered about four months before coming home.[142]

Archer accompanied his colleagues to Pietermaritzburg. By the end of January he and two of his men were in hospital, they with fever and he recovering from a broken left leg that he had fractured just above the ankle while playing football. It was extremely painful for the first few days but he was soon feeling much better - partly because he was 'getting plenty to eat and two pints of lemonade to drink daily.' He still did not know when he would be returning to England - where, he told his mother, he would enjoy a day's rabbit shooting - and expected that they would be kept in South Africa until after the rainy season, possibly in May, to see if the Africans 'are going to break out again. If everything is quiet then there is nothing to stop us coming home.' Captain Jenner, Lieutenant St Aubyn and a number of other officers had already left for England on leave.[143]

In the middle of February he was still in hospital, his leg was in plaster but giving him no pain, he was able to get up, sit outside his ward and walk a little. He was relieved to learn from his doctor that the injury should not interfere with his running and other sports, provided he rested it well when he left hospital. He had plenty of books and papers to read, partly due to the Quartermaster Sergeant - the Chief Clerk in the General's office there - being a former Sergeant in the Second Battalion of the Rifle Brigade. One of the wives sent him fruit and eggs, and if anything special was sent to the hospital he got his share. All his men were now out of hospital though there were many from other sections still there. Lieutenant Stephens was in the civilian hospital with a very severe attack of fever, his third since leaving England. He had gone down with 'a touch of fever' at Chimoio and other, more serious, attacks followed.[144] Alderson had been invalided home after a bad attack of fever and with an abscess on the liver. He had very much wanted to stay in South Africa with his men but the General would not hear of it. Archer much preferred a broken leg to having fever - which he seems to have escaped. He was pleased with the state of his personal finances. He had received £44.18.0 from the British South Africa Company and £36 under-drawn on his Army pay. He had been Armourer Sergeant to the Mounted Infantry for the whole of his time on the expedition and this gave him an extra six pence a day.[145]

A month later he was still in hospital but almost fit again. He was expecting to return to England in May when the Suffolk Regiment relieved them. He did not think he would stay in England long because his battalion was due to go to Malta at the end of the year. He had kept a diary and sent it to his mother in instalments.[146]

He was still in hospital the following month on 10 April but expected to be let out the following week:

> Shall be very glad to get out of Hospital. I walked about two miles round the grounds last night with the aid of a stick. My leg is set all right only the ankle is very stiff through being bandaged up so long in plaster of Paris.[147]

He now expected to be relieved by the Royal Irish Rifles and be home late May or early June. He looked forward to playing cricket for Parndon but would need a good deal of practice. At his request his mother had sent a number of rabbits shot on the farm to his battalion sergeants' mess.

On 15 May he wrote a last letter from South Africa, saying he was out of hospital and progressing well. He would embark at Durban on 23 May on the hired transport *Dunera* and expected to be in Southampton on 24 June.[148] On the Eve of Queen Victoria's Jubilee Day, they arrived in the Solent. Alderson was there to meet and welcome them.

> On 22 June the Mounted Infantry under Stephens came back, almost all the men seemed pretty fit. Out of the thirty who went out eight remained with the Chartered Company and two were invalided, including Private Broad, who lost a leg at Makoni's kraal.[149]

When the Mashonaland campaign was over Alderson wrote to Archer's Rifle Brigade Commanding Officer and commended him, saying he was 'very cool under fire, was of great assistance to the officers and that he (Colonel Alderson) could trust him with the most important duties at any time.'

> The section under Lieutenant Stephens did their work and behaved excellently in every way and this was specially noticed when they were on active service in Mashonaland. They were always ready and willing to work, cool and handy under fire, and gave no trouble when in town, and proving themselves at all times thoroughly good soldiers. Of the NCOs I would specially bring to your notice the following: Sergeant Archer and Corporal Morgan.[150]

Archer was awarded the British South Africa Company Mashonaland Medal for his services there in 1896. Major-General Frederick Carrington, Commander of the forces in Matabeleland and Mashonaland wrote of 'the good work done by the Mounted Infantry and other detachments of Imperial Troops, comprised in Lieutenant-Colonel Alderson's command in Mashonaland, whose steadiness and discipline under all circumstances was unvarying and highly satisfactory.'[151]

From a military point of view, the Mashonaland Field Force campaign was conducted under a number of difficulties not usually encountered. Its members had to be recruited and equipped in considerable haste. Having got to South Africa by sea, they had to embark a large number of men, horses, guns and stores, transport them by ship, and then disembark them in a neutral port, Beira. They had to pass through the territory of a foreign power, Portugal. They then had to advance by river, rail and road from Beira to Salisbury and extend their line of communications over all of these for a distance of nearly 400 miles. Of this distance, the first part was potentially, and the last 150 miles were in fact, open to attack by the Mashona. Much of the country in which they operated was unknown even to the European settlers living there, and for none of it did they have reliable maps. Their movements throughout were greatly hampered by shortages of food and foodstuff supplies and of transport, and finally had to be hurried in order to conclude operations by a given date. Their enemy was also unusual in having no capital settlement and no main army. Consequently, the Mashonaland Field Force had no definite objective, and taking really decisive action was extremely difficult. The force at Alderson's disposal was very small in comparison with the area of the country covered - about 2000 men operating over 114,000 square miles of territory. His force was made up of disparate elements: regular troops of all arms, except cavalry though most were mounted; irregular troops, both black and white, also of all arms; and friendlies who varied in number and reliability.[152]

From Archer's personal point of view, he had looked forward to active service overseas, and he had got it. A good deal of it was unpleasant and dangerous. He had been seasick on the voyage out; the train on which he was taking his horses from Beira to Fontesvilla had overturned and thrown him out; he had been soaked in getting his horses across the Pungwe river; he had been badly knocked when Mitchell pitched off a horse and landed on his arm, and he had been kicked by a horse the following day; lions had roamed the streets of Chimoio; he had travelled though malarial country; he had marched long distances; towards the end he had been hungry and poorly clothed; he had narrowly escaped injury when rocks had been thrown at him and he was lucky not to have been taken by the enemy when acting as a scout and temporarily got lost. Most serious of all, he had been standing next to Captain Haynes, only inches away from him, when the Captain had been fatally shot in the head: he had had a lucky escape. Then once he was back in South Africa when the campaign was over, he had broken his leg playing football, and, judging by the length of time it took to heal, it had been a serious fracture.

On the other hand, the Mashonaland operation had added greatly to his experience, and many elements of that experience were valuable in displaying him in a promising light from the point of view of progressing his career. In the first place, against a good deal of competition, he had been specially selected by his battalion commanding officer to join the Mounted Infantry. He had played a leading part in the social life of the soldiers during the voyage out, helping to organize concerts and being a judge for the deck sports, in all of which he must have come to the notice of his senior officers. He had been appointed Armourer Sergeant for the whole of the campaign, and Acting Sergeant Major for most of it. When Stephens was down with fever, Archer, as the senior NCO, had taken over command of the Section and was directly responsible to the Company commander. He had been placed in charge of the scouts just before the attack on Makoni's kraal. With Jenner and Haynes, he had led the final bayonet charge on Makoni's kraal. Finally, Alderson had commended him to his Rifle Brigade Commanding Officer as one who was 'very cool under fire, was of great assistance to the officers' and could be trusted with 'the most important duties at any time.'

There can be little doubt that, despite the hardships, dangers and narrow escapes, the Mashonaland campaign - which brought him his first medal - provided valuable experience to Archer as a professional soldier.

CHAPTER FOUR

THE RIFLE BRIGADE - MALTA, EGYPT AND CRETE: 1897-1899

Archer stayed in England, at Aldershot, for only three months before sailing for Malta with the Second Battalion of the Rifle Brigade. They left on the SS *Aroca* from the Royal Albert Docks, London, on Thursday afternoon, 23 September 1897.[1]

In Malta they were stationed initially at the Isola Gate Barracks and later at the Verdala Barracks. He was appointed Caterer, a job he did not like because it kept him indoors more than he wished. For a while, too, he was employed on military topography at Command Headquarters and received an extra duty allowance for this work. At another time he was away at one of the forts learning 'big gun drill' - experience that was to be helpful to him later in South Africa. Thinking that he would have time on his hands, he asked his mother to send him all his letters from Mashonaland so that he could write them into a book: 'they will be all right to read at some future time.' Unfortunately, the book was never written, though he did write notes on his service in Mashonaland. He had gained the Third Class Certificate of Education in December 1889 and the Second Class Certificate in April 1896, and there seems to have been something of an official push to obtain these qualifications. For example, in 1896 three first class certificates were awarded, making a total of ten in the Battalion; 38 second class certificates, making a total of 141; and 39 third class certificates, making a total of 75. He felt he now had time in Malta to take his education further by making a start on studying for the First Class Certificate: 'It won't do me any harm to go to School again for another year, and if I get it, it will qualify me for a Commission.' This was the first time that he mentioned an aspiration to obtain a commission. Although he started his studies, was working hard for the examinations and wished he could get more time to study, he had to postpone them because, contrary to his expectations, he was in fact very busy, with 'so many rumours of wars.' Perhaps this is why he did not write the book on

Mashonaland. That he considered writing about his experiences there indicates how important they had been to him.²

By the end of the year he was feeling the cold of winter, after the warmth of southern Africa, especially since he was living under canvas. He hankered after further active service and, much to his disappointment, he did not think his Battalion would be joining the forthcoming Egypt Expedition, though the Seaforth Highlanders left early in January 1898 and the West Riding Regiment was holding itself in readiness to go. His own Colonel was 'very wild' with the War Office delaying the 1st Battalion of the Rifle Brigade at Singapore: 'If they had come home a month ago we should have been the first regiment for Egypt, as we are getting 500 seasoned men from them.'³

In mid March 1898, now aged 27 and having been in the army for ten years, he re-engaged for 21 years further service with the regiment, and was pleased to be able to tell his mother, 'The Doctor said I was one of the healthiest men he had ever seen for some time.'⁴ She would have been relieved that the dangers and exertions of Mashonaland had not damaged his health.

In April he went on manoeuvres for two weeks, about 13 miles from the Verdala Barracks. They had 'a very rough time' but he enjoyed it, particularly since the Quarter Master Sergeant's wife was ill and he asked Archer to take over his duties, which he confidently and proudly did: 'So, of course, I was a big man on the manoeuvres and got through everything satisfactorily.' His career was continuing to show promise, and one of the Colour Sergeants offered him a bet of a pound to a shilling that he, Archer, would get the next vacancy of Colour Sergeant. He hoped very much that he would get it as he felt he had 'waited long enough.'⁵

He had taken up competitive shooting again, and at the Naval rifle meeting he took two first prizes and one second, winning £4.15.0 in prize money with which he intended to buy himself 'a proper shooting kit.' Everyone was talking about the war between Spain and America but, pessimistically from his point of view, he did not think it would last long. The officers were expecting the Battalion to go to Egypt in June but he personally still did not think they would, though it had been his expectation when he arrived in South Africa in May 1896 that once things had settled down in Rhodesia he would be sent to Egypt.⁶

The recent political and military background in Egypt and neighbouring Sudan was that the Khalifa Abdullah, the Mahdi's successor, and his Dervish forces had dominated the Sudanese territory since 1881. Following the death of General Gordon in January 1885, the British and Egyptian governments decided that the Dongola province should be re-conquered. Since then, 'slowly but irresistibly, the work of re-establishing the authority of the Khedive' in the Sudan had progressed.'

> In successive stages the Dervish forces had been driven from Wady Halfa to ... Dongola [in September 1896]; the valley of the Nile, from Dongola to Merowi, had been garrisoned by Egyptian troops; Abu Hamed had been captured and connected with Wady Halfa by the Desert Railway; Berber had been occupied without opposition [in August 1897]; and an advanced post of the Egyptian Army had been established at the junction of the River Atbara with the Nile. [Late in 1897] the Khalifa Abdullah, successor of the Mahdi, determined to despatch an army under a trusted kinsman, his fighting general Mahmoud, to re-capture Berber, and once and for all to clear his dominions of the detested 'Turk' as his Anglo-Egyptian foes were indiscriminately styled. But his plans [were] reported by trustworthy spies to the Egyptian Intelligence Department. Then began a period of considerable military activity. Numbers of officers were hurried out from England to augment the establishment of British officers serving with the Egyptian Army; and a British Brigade was ordered up the Nile.[7]

Several battles and skirmishes followed, leading to the bloody but successful Battle of Atbara on 8 April 1898. In less than an hour almost 600 officers and men of the Egyptian Army had been killed or wounded. 'The enemy's losses had been very heavy ... not less than 2000 dead bodies were counted in the position and in the river bed alone.'

> Three days later, Kitchener and Mahmoud, victor and vanquished, entered Berber together; the former, the recipient of a great popular demonstration from the rejoicing inhabitants; the latter ... with his hands fastened behind his back.[8]

It was these factors that led Archer's officers to expect to be sent to Egypt. The Sirdar, the officer commanding troops in Egypt, Major-General Sir Herbert Kitchener, not content simply with his victory at Atbara, was planning to press forward up the Nile in order finally to conquer the remaining Mahdi forces and so revenge the murder of Gordon fourteen years earlier. Preparations for this advance - against Abdullah's forces at the Dervish capital opposite Khartoum at the junction of the Blue and White Niles - began at the end of July 1898 when

Kitchener was sent reinforcements from Cairo to Wad Hamad. These reinforcements included the 2nd Battalion of the Rifle Brigade.[9]

The move from Malta to Egypt came sooner than most men had expected. Warning orders were received on 10 June[10], and a number of officers and men failed the medical examination held a week later.

> In fact, the 2nd Battalion had arrived in Malta seriously deficient in numbers and over 500 men had already been detached from the 1st Battalion when it passed through Malta on its return from Singapore in the previous February.[11]

Archer was ordered to sail on the SS *Creole Prince* on 22 June. He went as Acting Quarter Master Sergeant, the senior NCO, leading the advance party to take all the stores and equipment ready for the advance on Khartoum. The Battalion was to follow about three weeks later. He had to pack all his personal kit and leave nothing behind, because the Battalion would not be returning to Malta after the expedition.[12]

The full Battalion of eight companies, having been issued with tropical kit, including helmet shades and spine pads to protect their necks and backs from the sun, and having undertaken 'a series of daily practices in advancing and volley firing', and having also worked out a flexible means of organising fire and movement',[13] followed Archer's advance party and reached Alexandria on 15 July. They then went south by train to Cairo and arrived there the following day, camping in tents on the dusty, fly-ridden and uncomfortable Kasr-el-Nil barrack square. Here the men were kitted out with the equipment Archer had brought, ready for the advance up the Nile:

> Blankets for shelters were issued, each shelter consisting of four blankets strung together by eyelet holes with three poles connected by a ridge-rope. The shelter when erected was in the shape of a *tente-d'abri*, and held eight men, one shelter being provided also for the officers of each company ... The men were also equipped with helmet-curtains and spine-pads, and the officers provided themselves with Wolseley helmets, all helmets in the Battalion having a square dark-green patch sewn on each side.[14]

While they were at Cairo the men were kept busy drawing stores and equipment for the expedition - issued by Archer - but on 18 July, the Battalion paraded at 5.30 a.m. and marched off to see the Pyramids, where they also 'paid homage to the Sphinx.'[15]

Archer wrote to his mother from the Kasr-el-Nil Barracks and, impressed by the number of people and the general bustle in Cairo, said the place was rather like London, except that the people were from 'every nation under the sun.' He was surprised to notice that all the transportation was done on the backs of camels, donkeys and mules, and one rarely saw a cart. Although it was very hot, he preferred Cairo to Malta because it was much cleaner and the streets were wide and had trees along each side. As for the expedition:

> This [Cairo] is where we shall leave our Depot when we go to the front, which will be some time between 27th July and 10th August. It will take us about a month before we all get to Atbara, say about the beginning of September, and we expect to be back here again by December, so it will soon be over ... I shall be quite an old warrior after this affair.[16]

The Battalion set off by rail for the Sudan from Cairo in two parties: the first, known as the right half-battalion, comprised A, B, C and D Companies; and the second, known as the left half-battalion, comprised E, F, G and H Companies. Archer was NCO in charge of the advance party of the right half-battalion, which left Cairo on 27 July. They carried a large amount of equipment 'in Christmas tree order.' The other half-battalion followed them a day later. He arrived at Luxor at noon the day after leaving Cairo and, changing trains because the narrow gauge rail track replaced the broad gauge at Luxor, went on to Shellel - 'about the hottest place on the Nile' - where he arrived two days later. In the four hour interval during which the men changed trains, the officers rode off 'on donkeys to find baths at the local hotel.' The next section of their journey, from Shellel to Wadi el Halfa, was by river, and he and his men embarked four hours later on barges tied to the side of Nile boats. The officers were fed by a civilian caterer of indifferent culinary ability, and the men's, probably better, food was cooked on 'stoves formed of wooden cases filled with dried mud and placed at the stern of each barge.'[17]

> For the officers, the steamer *Ibis* offered a 'ripping' deck with plenty of space since it was fitted to accommodate thirty, and the half battalion mustered but fourteen officers ... By contrast, the men were accommodated in two-decker barges towed alongside and [one] felt sorry for the poor devils confined there and loaded down with greatcoats and two haversacks full of kit for the campaign and water bottles.[18]

Curiously, Archer found this section, travelling by river, with, as he said, 'nothing but desert on either side', the best part of the whole journey, despite the heat – 115° by day and 80° at night. For most of the journey there were low rocky hills, fifty to sixty feet high on both sides of the river, and the banks were 'fringed with the ubiquitous date palms and frequent water wheels.' Some of the officers, too, enjoyed the trip, which one of them, Captain John Gough, described as 'a very jolly party'. Adding '[I am] as happy as I ever hope to be in this life.'[19]

They arrived at Wadi el Halfa at 1.30 a.m. on 1 August, disembarked three hours later and transferred their baggage.

> After a frustrating delay, the men were marched off to breakfast and washed down with Nile water while the officers fared rather better in an Egyptian army mess.[20]

They then all entrained for Atbara in cattle trucks, with 43 men and their kit, 'packed like sardines', in each truck. The officers were eight to a truck.[21] 'The train ... consisted of large trucks with a roof of corrugated iron or wood for officers and men, the men lying on their blankets, and the officers having ... native rope beds placed along the sides of the trucks. The native servants sat on top of the baggage, which was piled in open trucks.'[22] They passed Berber and Darmali and arrived at Atbara on 3 August, the day the Sudanese soldiers, who were at the head of the expedition, left. The other units of the Second British Brigade arrived at Atbara during the following two weeks.

Having reached Atbara, Archer and his men left the train, fell in and marched about a mile to pitch their camp at the confluence of the Atbara River and the Nile. This was not an easy or comfortable task, because they were 'greeted by a frightful dust-storm which half smothered them in about five minutes.'[23]

> The Rifles' first morning [in the] Sudan was not endearing. They were shot out onto a little hillock or platform at half-past one in the morning, in the middle of one of the best dust-storms of the season. [They] had neither tents nor angarebs [light bedsteads or camp beds] nor bags: they were dumped down among their baggage and sat down for five hours to contemplate the smiling Sudan. Then they disinterred themselves and their belongings and marched into camp.[24]

The men were still unwashed and unshaven from the train journey and everyone was soon coated with dust.[25]

Once in camp and the sand storm having died down, their time was quickly and fully taken up in 'zareeba-cutting and making ramps for detraining guns',[26] and putting a telegraph line across the Atbara river.[27] Although initially they had expected to move towards Khartoum fairly quickly, they stayed at Atbara a fortnight, until the whole of the Second Brigade was assembled and everything was ready for them to move up-country. Archer - who, clearly, found the Sudan neither 'endearing' nor 'smiling' - told his mother that travelling in the Sudan was 'worse than any country in the world [with] sand over the tops of your shoes, and whenever the wind blows there is a sand storm.' He continued:

> I had a slight touch of fever coming down here but am all right now. The doctor said it was the old Mashonaland fever working out. I am still employed in the Quarter Master's Department so I get plenty to eat and drink: tea, coffee, cocoa, but no beer is allowed among the troops in the Sudan. An issue of rum is made every week: one sixty-fourth of a gallon per man, so there is no chance of anyone getting drunk. We have been very busy in our Department and shall be until the finish of the expedition.
> We get deserters [from the Mahdi forces] nearly every day from about Khartoum. They get sent further down the Nile to move more goods from the trains to the boats.
> We have lost only one man up to the present. We left him at Wadi Halfa on the way up and have since heard that he is dead (Enteric). Troops are in fairly good health here. Stomach out of order is all that is the matter with nearly all that go to the Doctor ...
> There is talk of keeping two regiments in Khartoum for the winter but I expect it will be Egyptians and Soudanese and not English regiments. The [Grenadier] Guards are lying next to us. They cannot stand the heat so well as our fellows [in the Rifle Brigade]. We shall be glad to get on the move as stopping in one place always causes a lot of work.[28]

Captain Gough, too, commented on the Grenadier Guards:

> The Guardees were very funny when they saw the camp; every officer seemed to want a tent to himself ... Really the way they are pampered is disgraceful; they have been given four more tents a company than us, although they are the same strength. Their officers were given a saloon carriage up from Wadi Halfa, all other officers being stuck into cattle trucks.[29]

Archer did not have long to wait to get on the move, though it did not lessen the amount of work to be done in addition to the training that involved field firing, slow advance, firing on the move and strict control.[30] On 20 August they advanced in very crowded and slow moving boats to Wadi Hamid on the west bank of the sixth cataract, where they disembarked.[31] It is unlikely that the British troops were as tightly packed in their river boats as were the Sudanese troops, who preceded them on the journey south from Atbara to Wadi Hamid. Kitchener dismissed the Plimsoll line with the remark that Plimsoll was dead![32] A war correspondent accompanying the expedition remarked:

> You may have seen sardines in tins; but you will never know how roomy and comfortable a tinned sardine must feel until you have seen [Sudanese soldiers] packed in on one of the Sirdar's steamers. Nothing but the Sirdar's audacity would ever have tried it; nothing but his own peculiar blend of luck and judgement would have carried it through without appalling disaster ...
>
> Every man carried his blanket ... but it was difficult to see how he was ever to get into it. On each deck of each steamer they squatted, shoulder to shoulder, toe to back, chin to knee. Fast along each gunboat were a couple of double-decked roofed barges, brought out in sections from England for this very purpose. Both decks were jammed full of black men till you could not have pushed a walking stick between them; the upper deck bellied under their weight like a hammock. At the tail of each gunboat floated a gyassa or two gyassas; in them you could have laid your blanket and slept peacefully on the soldiers' heads. Thus in the land of impossibilities a craft not quite so big as a penny steamer started to take 1100 men, cribbed so that they could not stretch an arm or leg, 100 miles at rather under a mile an hour.[33]

To be fair to Kitchener, it was also the case that he stopped half a company from boarding a steamer because he judged the barges carrying the men to be overloaded.[34]

At Wadi Hamid the entire force, the full Egyptian and British Divisions, concentrated before advancing to Omdurman. By 24 August they had all arrived - 24,000 men, horses, supplies and ammunition. The men were camped in a 'compact but commodious' mile-long zareeba. For once, none of them was crowded and they all had easy access to water. The Sudanese were encamped at the south end in terraces of straw huts, the Egyptians were next to them under shelters made from their blankets, and the British were located at the north end mainly in their blanket tents. Archer and his British colleagues slept in their boots 'for the sake of practice.' The gunboats were tied up along the shore. There was not much shade but fortunately the camp was covered with tufts of coarse yellow grass that helped to reduce the amount of dust flying around, though not nearly as effectively as did 'the best storm of the season' that descended upon them on the night of 24 August:

> It began, as is its way, savagely and without a second's warning. A flicker of silver lightening, a bloated drop of rain, then the wind rushed down snorting and tearing at the tent-ropes like an angry stallion. It tore up the tents, and left them flapping in agony, while the rain came down and completed the conquest by drenching our kit at its leisure. What was worse, the gyassa, laden with stores and spare kits, belonging to an Egyptian battalion which was just about to start forward, was blown clean over, and everything shot into the river ... The lightening flared and the wind bombarded us till the morning, when we reaped one consolation - the dust was all gone, except that which had formed layers on our faces.[35]

The following morning, 25 August, the army moved out and Wadi Hamid became virtually deserted once more. The Second British Brigade, including Archer's battalion, left at daybreak and the First left in the afternoon – 'a most imposing spectacle'.

A force of Arab irregulars, friendly to the British, under the command of British officers, proceeded up river from Wadi Hamid and cleared the east bank up to the Blue Nile of all opposition. In the meantime Kitchener and his British and Egyptian Divisions moved up the west bank, unopposed. The British Division, under Major-General Gatacre, was made up of cavalry, artillery and the 1st and 2nd Brigades. The Egyptian Division, of four Brigades, under Major-General Hunter, comprised the cavalry, artillery, engineers and a flotilla. In all, their strength was 24,000. The Rifle Brigade 2nd Battalion was part of the British 2nd Brigade, commanded by Brigadier-General Lyttelton also of the Rifle Brigade.[36] They marched off, up the west bank, on 25 August in five columns, the Rifle Brigade on the right and the other regiments - Grenadier Guards, Northumberland Fusiliers, Lancashire Fusiliers and a detachment of Royal Engineers - to their left in order of seniority.

> The first part of the march was among rocks, which soon gave way to sand and the going became a little deep, especially the last mile or so.

We marched between six and seven miles and formed a brigade square. The men were then marched a few hundred yards to the river for water and to cut wood for fires; teas were got ready as soon as the transport came up, after which blanket shelters were laid on the ground and everyone got to sleep very soon.[37]

During the following four days they marched over ground 'varying from very deep sand to hard ground covered with large sharp flints', covering ten to twenty miles a day and bivouacking at night in square in the open under their blanket shelters. The daytime heat was extreme but the nights were cool and they were particularly pleased to be cooled by a couple of nocturnal rainstorms during the journey. By now the deserters from the Dervish forces were 'beginning to arrive in swarms' and provided valuable intelligence as to the enemy's intentions: they were determined to stand and fight on ground of their own choosing.[38] 'For the last two days of the approach to Omdurman and the ruins of Khartoum, Kitchener marched his 20,000 men in fighting formation on a front of nearly three miles.'[39] It must have been a formidable sight.

At noon on 1 September Kitchener's army assembled at the ruined village of Egeiga[40] on the west bank of the Nile, some seven miles north of Omdurman. They took up their positions within a defensive zareeba which they built from mimosa bushes. The zareeba was roughly a semi-circle with a north-south diameter of 2000 yards, based on the west bank of the Nile and centred on Egeiga. The 2nd Battalion of the Rifle Brigade was positioned on the left or southern flank, at the edge of the 2nd British Brigade. Gunships of the flotilla, located in the river on the northern and southern flanks of the zareeba, shelled the forts on both sides of the Nile and breached the wall of Omdurman. About 2200 yards to the north-west of the zareeba, running down to the river, were the Kerreri Heights; and a roughly similar distance to the south-west, between Kitchener and Omdurman, was Jebel Surgham hill, 328 feet high.[41] The officers and senior NCOs were issued with a map on a small card, showing the junction of the White and Blue Niles and the layout of Khartoum and Omdurman.[42]

Members of the Egyptian Camel Corps reported that the Khalifa and his army were advancing from Omdurman - they had in fact bivouaked overnight behind Jebel Surgham hill - and that from the hill they could see 'the whole of the Khalifa's forces, of between 40,000 and 50,000, marshalled in a line stretching for two or three miles, in some places as deep as a quarter-column, and distant about two miles'.[43] This, too, must have been a formidable sight.

After a watchful, wet and blustery night, throughout which the gun-boat searchlights swept the land to detect any enemy movement, the sentries were doubled and the men slept with their rifles, Kitchener's army stood to arms at 3.30 a.m., and at dawn on 2 September the Cavalry moved out - the British on the left and the Egyptian with Camel Corps and horse-battery on the right. The remainder of the army stayed silently in the zareeba.[44] Then, at half past six in the morning,

> a mass of Dervishes with white banners appeared round the north-west corner of Jebel Surgham ... and the first gun proclaimed that the battle had begun ... The guns were doing terrible havoc among the enemy on the north side of Jebel Surgham, when another crowd appeared on the south-east side of the hill [close to the Rifle Brigade position], and the fire was directed on them also, at 2300 yards. This lot, on coming under fire, at first seemed as if they would move round to our left [and outflank us], but apparently thought better of it ... and turned back again to join the main attack which was advancing on us [across the whole of our front] between Jebel Surgham and Kerreri Heights.[45]

The battle was extremely bloody, the Dervishes could never get near [the Anglo-Egyptian forces] and they refused to hold back. They were consequently killed in large numbers. The British and Egyptian rifles grew red-hot; the soldiers seized them by the slings and dragged them back to the reserve to change for cool ones. It was not a battle but an execution.[46]

From their position on the extreme left flank, the 2nd Brigade were unable to take a full part in repelling the Dervishes, and since the main direction of the attack seemed clearly to be on the right flank, they were quickly ordered to move there to support the 1st Brigade. They doubled to the right and took up positions forty yards behind the 1st Brigade, which was under heavy fire, was finding it difficult to fire over the mimosa fence of the zareeba - and had to stand up to do so - and was finding also that the fence offered them little protection. Here they were in support but still could do little firing themselves. Gough and Cockburn recorded the Rifle Brigade's experience, of which Archer was a part:

> A man in my company was hit at once just to my left, and the men had a very poor time doing nothing, just watching the bullets hitting the sand and seeing the Camerons getting hit just in front of us. Altogether as nasty a kind of work as ever I want to do – no

excitement by firing ourselves, simply standing still. Nine of our men got hit, one killed by a bullet through the head. We were really very lucky to get off so light; some of the bullets went uncommon close.[47]

We remained in this position [from 6.45 a.m.] till about 8.20 ... It was not particularly pleasant sitting down to be fired at, with no means of retaliation, but from our position we could see the whole field of battle ... At about 8.20, the enemy's attack having more or less ceased, simply because those Dervishes who had made it had been practically annihilated by our fire, the Sirdar ordered the whole force out of the zareeba. We therefore returned to our place on the left of the line, and the Brigades were formed up; the order was eschelon of Brigades from the left, so we led [at about 9.0 a.m.], moving in a south-west direction towards Omdurman ... We had advanced [about a mile] when we were ordered to wheel to the right, and broke into double time. Soon after we started, a furious fusillade was heard on our right, and we swung round still more; it was a long run all round the left of the Army ... to get between the Dervishes and Omdurman, and we were driving them before us, away from the river and from their town, right into the desert. The firing on the right [which came from a fierce and bloody onslaught on the slow moving Camel Corps by the Dervishes] became hotter and hotter and then ceased [as the attacking Dervishes were wiped out].[48]

They continued driving the Dervishes into the desert - over difficult sand and rocks under a burning sun - to prevent their retreating into Omdurman where they would be more difficult to defeat, until about 11.0 a.m., when they halted. They were then told to march on the Mahdi's tomb at Omdurman. They went about two miles and turned left to find water. None of the men had much to eat that morning, their water bottles were empty and a few fainted. They eventually got to water at about 1.0 p.m. and although it was 'of a rich chrome yellow' colour, they none the less drank thirstily. When the baggage camels arrived, they put up their blanket shelters, ate a meal and had a short rest. Steevens, war correspondent of the *Daily Mail*, observed: 'The Second British Brigade was watering at the Khor – men and horses lapping up the half solid stuff till they must have been as thick with mud inside as they were out.'[49]

At 4.30 we advanced again, and marched into Omdurman, being greeted on the way by the natives with every sign of rejoicing at our victory and the prospects of freedom for themselves. We marched up to the wall of the town, and then turned to the right to get to a camping ground just outside. The way lay through filthy lanes, with a most unpleasant odour, but this last was nothing to the terrible stench that we found at the place where we had to bivouac. It was dark before we got there and there was little water, and no food ... The men lay down just where they were - they were tired out - and in spite of the smells slept soundly. In the morning we found the ground was covered with dead donkeys, which the Khalifa had caused to be killed to prevent the inhabitants from taking away their women or goods and chattels.[50]

No one who took part in it, will ever forget that ride back and its awful sights and smells: the whole road being one mass of dead Dervishes, women, children and donkeys.[51]

The stench of the place was in your nostrils, in your throat, in your stomach. You could not eat; you dared not drink.[52]

The streets were a huge latrine, and dead men, women and donkeys at every few yards the result of the bombardment. The smell was beyond words. The Grenadier's chaplain, Reginald Mosely, vomited.[53]

Archer long remembered the terrible stench. Five years later, when he marched a party of men through part of Old Cairo, the smell was the worst he had ever experienced, and he remarked that it was 'quite like Omdurman two days after the battle.'[54]

The 2nd Brigade fell in, and marched towards the Nile, passing Kitchener on the way, and 'right lustily' cheered him as they passed. They reached the river north of Omdurman at 7.0 a.m., and set about making themselves as comfortable as they could. The whole army was camped here, under their blanket shelters.[55]

The next day, Sunday 4 September, a memorial service was held at Khartoum for Gordon, whose death they now felt they had avenged. Archer was one of those present. The scene and the occasion were described by Steevens:

The steamers ... plug-plugged their steady way up the full Nile ... It was Sunday morning, and that furious Friday seemed already half a lifetime behind us ... On the steamers was a detachment of every corps ... that had taken part in the vengeance. Every white officer that could be spared from duty was there, fifty men picked from each British battalion, one or two from each unit of the Egyptian army ... We were going to perform a necessary duty, which had been put off far, far too long ... The boats stopped plugging and there was silence. We were tied up opposite a grove of tall palms [near] a large building rising from a crumbling quay. You could see that it had once been a handsome edifice ... At that most ordinary sight everybody grew very solemn ... The troops formed up before the palace in three sides of a rectangle - Egyptians to our left as we looked from the river, British to the right. The Sidar, the generals of division and brigade, and the staff stood in the open space facing the palace. Then on the roof – almost on the very spot where Gordon fell ... we were aware of two flag staves ... The Sidar raised his hand. A pull on the halliards: up and out flew the Union Jack, tugging eagerly at his reins, dazzling gloriously in the sun, rejoicing in his strength and freedom ... The Egyptian flag had gone up at the same instant ... Three cheers for the Queen!' cried the Sidar, helmets leaped in the air ... Then the same for the Khedive ... the twenty-one guns banged forth the strength of war. [Then] the Guards were playing the Dead March in 'Saul'. Then the black band was playing the march from Handel's 'Scipio'... Four Chaplains – Catholic, Anglican, Presbyterian, and Methodist – came slowly forward and ranged themselves, with their backs to the palace, just before the Sidar. The Presbyterian read the Fifteenth Psalm. The Anglican led the rustling whisper of the Lord's Prayer. Snow-haired Father Brindle ... read a memorial prayer bare-headed in the sun. Then came forward the pipers and wailed a dirge, and the Sudanese played 'Abide With Me' [which had been] Gordon's favourite hymn ... And there were those who said that the cold Sidar himself could hardly speak or see, as General Hunter and the rest stepped out according to their rank and shook his hand ... Thus with Maxim-Nordenfeldt and Bible we buried Gordon after the manner of his race. The parade was over, the troops were dismissed ... The long-delayed duty was done ... We left Gordon alone again – but alone in majesty under the conquering ensign of his own people.[56]

The day following the memorial service, Monday 5 September, the British Division were taken for a triumphal route march through Omdurman. They marched past the Mahdi's tomb and through the mosque where all the Dervish prisoners were collected and were huddled under a shed. That afternoon the Sirdar distributed loot to the different battalions, the 2nd Battalion of the Rifle Brigade's share being 'a brass gun, a suit of chain-mail and helmet, two banners and a padded 'jibbeh' or dervish patched coat.'[57] Members of the British Division individually collected a great deal of loot, and most 'got together a fine collection of swords, spears, chain-mail and daggers'. A sale of some of this loot was held at the Arsenal and Archer acted as chief auctioneer.[58] He personally collected a number of souvenirs, which he sent home to his mother: a Dervish sword from the battle field of Omdurman, 'some spears, Dervish money and a Koran bible'.[59] This Koran turned out to be a seventeenth century manuscript Koran which eventually his eldest daughter inherited and later deposited in the rare books section of the University of Cape Town Library.[60]

At Omdurman there had been 40,000-50,000 Dervishes and 24,000 Anglo-Egyptian soldiers. These were large armies and the losses were heavy. In round figures, the Dervishes lost 11,000 killed, 16,000 wounded and 4,000 prisoners. The British lost two officers killed and seven wounded, together with 23 NCOs and men killed and 99 wounded. The Egyptian Army lost five British officers and one NCO wounded, one native officer killed and eight wounded, together with 30 NCOs and men killed and 279 wounded.[61]

For his services in Egypt and the Sudan Archer was awarded the Queen's Sudan Medal and the Khedive's Medal with the Khartoum clasp. These he proudly added to the Mashonaland Medal he had already won.

When, at this time, a rebellion broke out in Crete, arrangements were made for the Rifle Brigade to be despatched hurriedly there from Omdurman to quell it and occupy the island. Crete had fallen under Turkish rule in 1669, and subsequently there had been periodic rebellions by the 270,000 Orthodox Greek inhabitants to oust the 70,000 Moslem Turks. A number of these occurred throughout the 1800s and finally, in 1898, the British Vice Consul, his wife and daughter, and 600 Greek Cretan Christians were murdered, by Turkish Cretans,[62] and the great powers - Britain, France, Italy and Russia - decided that the time had come to compel the Turks to withdraw from the island.

On 7 September Archer wrote to his mother from Omdurman, saying that they expected to leave for Cairo and then Crete in a few days' time. There were so many rumours flying around that he did not know what to believe. His Colour Sergeant was trying to get posted to the Depot at Winchester and Archer hoped he would succeed him, 'but he has not gone yet': he was not counting any chickens before they were hatched. The health of his 24 men was good and only one of them was attending hospital. He was indeed promoted to be Colour Sergeant, of G Company - with responsibilities also as Company Accountant - and was placed in charge of the advance party from Omdurman to Atbara. He then took over the Battalion's transport to take them to Crete. He remained Transport Sergeant in Crete until he was appointed Acting Regimental

Quarter Master Sergeant. The main body of the 2nd Battalion followed a few days later.[63]

> On the 10th [September, we] got a telegram ordering the Battalion to Crete immediately in consequence of an outbreak among the Moslems there. The next day, Sunday, we got all our baggages and stores on two barges and two 'gyassas', and started on the 12th, towed by the *Akasheh* ... We picked up a lot of our kit both at Nasri Island and at Atbara, which latter place we reached early on September 14th ... We started on the desert railway on two trains, as before, and reached Halfa at 4.0 a.m. on the 16th; embarked on three steamers with their respective barges, and got to Shellal at 5.0 a.m. the next day ... We did not detrain at Cairo, but were taken right through to Alexandria, which we reached on the 19th and encamped on an open space outside Ras-ed-teen Barracks, embarking on HMS *Tyne* and the SS *Augustine* on the 19th and 20th.[64]

They left their tents behind at Atbara, but took their blanket shelters with them. Thereafter these 'were always struck at retreat, spread out flat, and used for sleeping on at night.'[65]

A few days later Archer was in Crete, after a very rapid and tiring journey, 'with little or no sleep for about 12 days and no chance of much to eat'. He was tired, having moved

> baggage about every two days from boat to train and vice versa, then on arrival here [having] to pitch a camp and move all our baggage to it since when the men have been digging all day making entrenchments, breastworks, latrines and everything required for a standing camp.[66]

He hoped the trouble - 'this row' as he called it - in Crete would soon finish as they were under canvas and the wet season would start in a month's time. He threw all his underclothing away when he arrived because it 'had too many lodgers to be comfortable.' He would be 'glad to sleep in a proper bed again with nice clean sheets.'

There was a great deal of sickness, mainly typhoid - then known as enteric fever - after their arrival in Crete. Archer was 'badly knocked up' and did not feel up to much for about a week, but he took medicine and was soon feeling better, glad not to have had to go to hospital. He was surprised that there were not more deaths after the exertions of Omdurman and the return journey from the battle. The 2nd Battalion suffered 37 deaths from typhoid in 1898, most of them in Crete and a few in Malta.[67]

When about 60 soldiers were sent to Malta for a sea voyage - to recuperate after their exertions on the Nile expedition - including the Quarter Master Sergeant, Archer took over his duties while he was away. He was what the Regiment were beginning to call 'a handy man for any billet'. He was aware that if he could become a Quarter Master Sergeant it could be an important step towards his securing a commission. For example, he pointedly marked the entry in his copy of the *London Gazette* of 4 May 1897, 'the Rifle Brigade (The Prince Consort's Own): Quartermaster Sergeant Arthur White to be Quartermaster, with the honorary rank of Lieutenant.'[68] Also, he kept a photograph of a colleague, labelled 'Sergeant Curtis, promoted Captain' and another, of ten of his former colleagues in India, marked 'A Christmas card from my old pals at Chaubattia', with eight of them marked as being Quartermasters and Lieutenants, Captains or Major.[69]

As Brigade Transport Sergeant he was in charge of the Garrison transport, and had 93 mules under his care. He was responsible for allocating the work to them, mainly convoys to the outposts in the hills, carrying rations to the several regiments and bringing baggage from the quay. It kept him very busy. On one occasion he went out with a convoy, expecting to return at about teatime but in fact did not get back until ten o'clock the following morning, having spent the night in the open in the hills. It then took him two to three days to get his work straight again, and he was rebuked for being absent from his duties. 'The usual thing. As I was away everybody wanted me. If I had been in, none would have wanted me.' He suffered for several years from being constantly in demand: 'It does not matter what time of the day or night ... but what someone wants me, or one of the young sergeants get stuck with their accounts. Of course I have to try and put them right.'[70] Despite being very busy, he found time to play football, including at least one fancy dress football match.[71]

He was still on active service but did not think he would get any fighting, though 'one can never tell.' He thought it would be very foolish for the people on the island to start fighting, as he did not think they would stand a chance of success.

> We have got three Regiments (about 2400 men). [In addition] 200 men Dorset Regiment, 200 men Border Regiment, [and] the Northumberland Fusiliers [are] coming from Egypt tomorrow and the Lancashire Fusiliers and the 22nd Battery, Royal Artillery in a few

days; each Regiment has got two maxim guns and in addition we have got five Battleships in the harbour.

Given this strong build up of forces, Britain and her allies had little difficulty in forcing the Turks to submit to their demands that they leave the island. Archer stayed in Crete for a year and witnessed this end of an era on the island. Though Crete remained under Turkish sovereignty thereafter, it was given independent status under a High Commissioner, Prince George of Greece. Archer was Right Guard, leading his Company, when the 2nd Battalion of the Rifle Brigade ceremonially marched past Prince George and Major-General Chernside on 12 May 1899.[72]

As with the Mashonaland campaign so also did the Omdurman expedition, followed by a period in Crete, provide experience, which, though frequently hard, dangerous and uncomfortable, none the less marked further progress in Archer's career as a professional soldier. In travelling to Omdurman, he had the exhausting changes from sea to rail to boat, back again to rail - often in cramped conditions - and finally several days' marching over rough ground. He encountered stifling sand storms that 'half smothered them in about five minutes' and torrential rain that drenched their kit. He slept in his boots. When he got to Omdurman, the dangers clearly increased as Kitchener's army tackled the Dervishes. Though the Second British Division was not in the very forefront of the fighting, they none the less had an exhausting and dangerous time, having to double long distances to swing round to support the First Division which was being seriously attacked and which was only 40 yards in front of them. Even when the battle was over they had a long and gruelling march to Omdurman town, tired, nauseated by the stench of the place, hungry and very thirsty. They were able to quench their thirst only by drinking filthy water. The journey downstream to the coast and then to Crete had to be made at great speed and they found it very tiring, having had no respite after the ardour of the battle at Omdurman. They had repeatedly to move the baggage from one means of transport to another and had little sleep for twelve days. Archer longed to sleep in a proper bed and he had to throw away his underclothes because they were lice-ridden. In Crete they became further exhausted by having to set up a permanent camp from scratch. Many men were sick with typhoid, and a worrying number died.

Yet, despite the difficulties and dangers, Omdurman, like Mashonaland, provided Archer with experience that was professionally advantageous. For much of the time he was Acting Quartermaster Sergeant, and he became widely seen as a man who was 'handy for any billet' that might become available. He was placed in charge of the advance parties both going to and coming from Omdurman. As Acting Quartermaster Sergeant, he lived well and was not short of food or drink - save during the actual battle. The work kept him very busy and he was constantly in demand, but this was to his advantage because others came to rely on him and he became recognised as a very dependable NCO. In due course he was promoted to be Colour Sergeant, and was made Brigade Transport Sergeant. There were, too, other matters in which he was able to take pride. He attended the memorial service for Gordon and the triumphal march through Omdurman, sharing in the pride and satisfaction of a patriotic vengeance. He was pleased with the trophies that he acquired, and, as a much respected NCO, was the chief auctioneer when some of the loot was auctioned. Several years later, one of his officers wrote to him about a photograph 'of the burning of Wada': 'It was one of the best photographs I ever took. You are marching at the head of the victorious troops, the smoke of the burning city to be seen in the background.'[73] Archer's pride must have been considerable, and he was fast becoming 'quite an old warrior'.

CHAPTER FIVE

THE RIFLE BRIGADE SOUTH AFRICA: 1899-1902

There had been rumours that the 2nd Battalion of the Rifle Brigade would go to Bermuda when they left Crete, but in a very brief note written to his mother on 14 September 1899, Archer said they had just received orders to proceed to the Transvaal, and he expected to leave early in October.[1] He had been in Crete almost exactly a year, the latter part being devoted by the battalion to supervising the civil administration of the island. Then on 2 October he wrote again to say they were off to South Africa that morning on the P&O SS *Jelunga*.[2] The Battalion numbered 26 officers and 864 men. All the boys and invalids in the battalion were left behind.[3] Having been very busy, he would be glad to get on the boat and have a rest. He secured a second-class passage by paying the difference between the contract price and the second-class fare. Only he and five of his NCO colleagues were granted permission to do this. It meant that he would be able to enjoy a more comfortable voyage than on his earlier journey to South Africa, when the conditions were very cramped and he had to sleep in a hammock. Whereas on that voyage he had sailed down the west coast, this time, starting in the Mediterranean, he sailed down the east coast.

He had not been on board many days before he learned that war had been declared in South Africa, and he hoped this was indeed the case 'as we shall then be able to wipe out the old affair of 81.'[4] This was a reference to the First Boer War –the First War of Independence - in 1880-1881 when the British refused the Boer Governments' suits for independence. The Boers won that war and the embittered British regiments were 'prevented from avenging themselves, because the Liberal Government in Britain was eager to seek peace.'[5] Just as the Nile expedition had been seen as a means of avenging the death of Gordon, so the South Africa war was seen, at least by Archer and no doubt many of his colleagues, as a means of avenging the defeat of 1881.

The *Jelunga* arrived for a few hours at Zanzibar on 19 October, having broken down four times on the way, through faulty feed pumps to its boiler,[6] and reached Durban a week later, on 26 October. Here they learned some details of the fighting, and especially the recent British victories of Talana Hill and Elandslaagte.[7] Though this news cheered them, they were surprised at the heavy losses, as they had not expected any fighting for another month.

Two hours after arriving at Durban they were told by a naval officer to 'Land at once!' because they would be going straight to the front instead of, as they had been told at Zanzibar, going first to Cape Town. They were to go to protect Pietermaritzburg as the Boers were expected to make for that town. Archer remarked that there was 'plenty of excitement on board' and, with a stoicism befitting a Colour Sergeant with ten years' soldiering behind him, he added 'especially among the younger officers and men.'[8]

The *Jelunga* drew too much water to risk crossing the bar safely straightaway, so A, B and C Companies left for the shore by surf boats towed by tugs the afternoon they arrived and 'had a bad time of it as there was a regular gale blowing'. 'So rough was it, however, and so slow the progress made, that after five hours' work three companies only had been slung into the lighters, and it was considered too dangerous to continue the practice'.[9] Archer expected, and hoped, that he and his men of G Company would remain on board the *Jelunga*, and go into the harbour the next day, as he was sure he would be very sick if they went on the surf boats.[10]

Much to his relief the sea was a little calmer the next day. 'As the telegrams kept coming in saying we were urgently required, it was decided to try and take the ship in over the bar, on top of the tide next morning.'[11] The *Jelunga* entered the harbour at high tide at about 9.30 a.m. The soldiers discharged all their stores during the morning and then entrained for Pietermaritzburg in the afternoon, in teeming rain, in open and very uncomfortable trucks, only twenty-four hours after they had arrived at Durban. *En route*, the local people seemed very loyal to Britain, gave them a good reception and told them not to forget to 'pull old Kruger's whiskers.' Paul Kruger was President of the South Africa Republic, the Transvaal.

They arrived at Pietermaritzburg, still in pouring rain, at about eight in the evening and were given a much needed meal of tea, bread and butter - 'just the thing they wanted.' Archer met several people he knew from his stay there two years earlier, and he proudly acted as guide when the soldiers were marched to their camp. They were distinctly uncomfortable and their blankets were soaking, but, after their wet and tiring train journey, they all slept well in their tents that night.

They spent a day at Pietermaritzburg, sorting their kit and stores and establishing a depot. Archer then detailed seven of his weakest men to stay behind and look after the depot. He was keen that only the fittest should go forward to the fighting.

On Sunday 29 October, late in the afternoon, they set off by rail for Ladysmith, the British Army's principal station in Natal. It took three trains to carry them, despite their taking very little baggage - two days' rations, two blankets, a waterproof and 200 rounds of ammunition per man[12] - and 'the accommodation was not exactly luxurious, being mostly open trucks.'[13] At Colenso they were warned by the railway authorities to be alert, and by their officers to charge the magazines of their rifles and be ready to jump off the train if they were attacked. For the past week some of the passing trains had been fired on by the Boers.[14] In the event, they arrived safely at four o'clock the following morning, 30 October. They left their baggage on the platform and marched to the camp from where, almost immediately, they were flung into the battle of Lombard's Kop. Martin Evans has outlined the nature and significance of this battle:[15]

> As 14,000 Boers approached Ladysmith, the British realised that, with some 3000 fewer troops, the best chance lay in breaking the developing encirclement. By 28 October a 155 mm Creusot gun [Long Tom], a seriously heavy weapon, had been installed on Pepworth Hill by [the Boers], and therefore Pepworth Hill was the objective of the British attack. The real battle, however, took place to the east of Ladysmith near Lombard's Kop where the British were surprised by Boer forces. Here, and at Nicholson's Nek, the British were defeated and the survivors forced back into the town, facing the certainty of a siege. The day was named Mournful Monday.

As he looked at it from Ladysmith, Archer would have seen Pepworth Hill about four miles away to the north-east. Nicholson's Nek was to its left and Long Hill to its right beyond the railway. Then came the Modder Spruit in a shallow valley running left to right in front of the low kopjes, Limit Hill and Flag Hill. Due east of the town and also four miles distant, was the 'abrupt hump' of Lombard's Kop, with a lesser hump, Gun Hill, in front of it.

> As the country was well overlooked by Boer positions, Lieutenant-General Sir George White decided that his forces should move into positions for attack during Sunday night. Colonel G G Grimwood was to secure Long Hill with the 8th [Infantry] Brigade ... so that

> Colonel Ian Hamilton could use the 7th [Infantry] Brigade ... first in reserve and then to take Pepworth Hill. Six field batteries were left in support, and the left flank would be protected by a force moving towards Nicholson's Nek, while the right was the responsibility of Major-General Sir John French's Cavalry Brigade.
>
> In the course of their deployment in the early hours of Monday 30 October two of Grimwood's battalions by mistake followed the artillery, leaving him with only half his men. At dawn the artillery came under heavy fire from the Boer guns on Pepworth Hill, and had to be repositioned northwards so as to bring the enemy within their range. Grimwood was then surprised by fire from his rear from the Boers on the other side of Modder Spruit.
>
> French moved his men on to Lombard's Kop to support the infantry and they, in turn, had to endure heavy fire. Hamilton was forced to act in support as soon it became clear that the original objective of taking Pepworth and Long Hills could not be achieved. To persist here would be to throw men away needlessly, and so the order to withdraw was given ... The withdrawal was orderly but depressing ... The action at Nicholson's Nek had been yet more disastrous. It was, indeed, Mournful Monday for the British, and the last chance to forestall a siege at Ladysmith had gone.

The 2nd Battalion of the Rifle Brigade arrived from Pietermaritzburg during the early stages of the battle and marched out to join Hamilton just after the artillery had been repositioned to bring the enemy on Pepworth Hill within range. As soon as they got clear of the hills round the town they were 'greeted by shells from a Boer "Long Tom" gun on Pepworth Hill', which made them deploy at the double. In extended formation they eventually reached the rest of the 7th Brigade, under Limit Hill, at about half past six in the morning. Three and a half hours later they deployed and lined the crest of Limit Hill, and stayed there, covering the retirement of the rest of the forces into Ladysmith. The Gloucesters and Irish Fusiliers were forced to surrender 'after a gallant resistance against overwhelming odds in an untenable position.'[16] Gough thought the surrenders 'a disgraceful affair' and that White's abandoning of his men verged on being criminal.[17]

Archer gave an account of his personal experience of what happened when they arrived in camp at Ladysmith on Mournful Monday, 30 October 1899. 'On arrival we had a hurried breakfast [prepared for the whole battalion by the Gloucesters]. Before we could drink the hot tea or eat anything we received the order to fall in as we were to take part in a battle just going to start.'

> After marching about half an hour in Column of Route, i.e. each Company in fours and one behind the other like a big snake moving along, we received a 94 pound shell just over our heads which made us alter our formation very quick[ly] to Column of Companies in extended order. We kept in this order until we arrived in our place in the Centre Brigade, which was to make the frontal attack on the Boer position. We got plenty of shells over us, but none very close as we were under shelter of a big kopje. Heavy firing on the right and left where two Brigades were making flank attacks. The Gordon Highlanders and 5th Dragoons were sent to reinforce the right Brigade, the Imperial Light Horse, [Natal] Carbineers [and] two Colonial Corps of the 1st Brigade.

He had a good view of the first part of the attack of their right brigade from the top of Limit Hill, under which he and his colleagues were taking cover. The Boers had 'a splendid position' on a series of large kopjes 'shaped like small Table Mountains' with guns placed in gun pits on their summits. When he saw their position he anticipated that the British force would suffer heavy casualties in getting them out but he expected they would 'do it all right.' After the Gordon Highlanders had left them to reinforce the right brigade, the Rifle Brigade lined a long kopje, Flag Hill, to their right in extended order, keeping well under cover of the rocks. Archer's Company was on the extreme right. There they remained until about 3.0 p.m., with the enemy occasionally giving them 'a few shells'. Then, when all the other troops had retired, they were ordered to retire on Ladysmith. He thought they were very lucky in having no casualties, though they had several men 'completely knocked up' before they reached the town, the stronger men having to carry their equipment and help them along.

When the 2nd Battalion arrived back at Ladysmith, at nine o'clock at night, worn out, they halted at the east end of the town, near the regular military camp. They piled their arms and lay down. Everyone except the guard was soon asleep, but their day's work had not yet finished, as Archer recalled:

> About 11.0 p.m. we, my Company, received the order to reinforce the King's Royal Rifles that were on outpost duty, as a large party of

Boers had been seen close to their lines. On walking round to find a suitable spot to place a Piquet, my Captain, Captain Paley,[18] was nearly shot by a sentry of the KRR who did not know about being reinforced and mistook him for a Boer in the dark. The bullet hit the ground against his feet.

Archer's Company stayed as escort to the guns on outpost duty, until about eleven the following morning, when they were relieved by another Company. They then occupied huts in Tin Camp, a little north-west of Ladysmith, and spent the following two days sorting themselves out, getting transport wagons and mules and 'generally scraping together the necessities of life.'[19] In their huts they were able to have a 'splendid sleep', the first proper rest for four nights, though they had to stay fully dressed and equipped in case the alarm was sounded. On 2 November, the enemy began shelling, so they moved to nearby King's Post and 'commenced to entrench and putting it into a state of defence.' Archer's Company, G, was accompanied at King's Post by A and E Companies. The other companies dug in at Leicester Post, adjacent to them. These two posts 'were a part of the lines of defence, and now became our permanent residence.'

> Roughly speaking, the position [of the lines of defence] was in the shape of a horseshoe, with the open end to the east, this being rendered secure by the Klip river and a wide stretch of open country. To the south of this horseshoe, a hill [the Platrand] known as Caesar's Camp and Wagon Hill, nearly three miles long and running east and west, stretched out as a long arm, and was joined to the horseshoe at Maiden's Castle.[20]

The day the Rifle Brigade moved to King's and Leicester Posts, 2 November, only four days after Archer's arrival, the Cavalry reported that the Boers had surrounded Ladysmith, and the railway line and the telegraph line had been cut. 'We were isolated!'[21] The siege had begun.

When the siege started there were 1500 troops holding the town with 51 guns; there were some 5400 European and 2400 African and Indian civilians, with two months' supply of food; the troops had plenty of ammunition for their rifles, but their big guns were 'rather short on shells.' As for the Boer forces, 3300 held Pepworth Hill, north-east of the town, 3600 held Lombard's Kop towards the east, 7500 held the south, and 2500 the west, but within a few days reinforcements reached them and the total number of Boer troops besieging the town swelled to 23,000.

The siege began on November 2 with the firing of 'Long Tom' from Pepworth Hill. Soon three more 'Long Toms' were brought into action; one began firing from Lombard's Kop, one from Umbulwana just south of Lombard's Kop and the third from the low hills west of the town. Their 94 pound shells were 'much respected', because when they struck they did great damage inside the town.[22]

A week later, on 9 November, Archer wrote that the enemy attacked Observation Hill, north-west of Ladysmith, where the Rifle Brigade had a small party on look-out:

> They had a sharp fight for a few hours, driving the enemy back. We have since held the hill by a strong party. [During this time 20,000 to 25,000 shots were calculated to have been fired at us.[23]] We lost two killed - 2nd Lieutenant Lethbridge[24] and Private Keech - and six wounded, including the Colour Sergeant, Hodder, of B Company shot through the right shoulder. He is on duty again now. [Hodder was the person with whom Archer had boxed in Ireland on Christmas Day 1894.][25]

Holding King's Post was a dangerous task until it was protected by earthworks, because there was very little natural cover available. Since the Boers directed heavy fire at it by day, the work of constructing defensive works had to be done at night.[26] The weather was 'appallingly wet' and officers and men went for many days on end without removing their boots and without washing or shaving.[27] Archer wrote in his diary about the daily routine they were following, which was 'making our hill a regular fortress'. They started work in parties at four in the morning, working in exposed positions only in the dark, and kept on till it was dark again. They lived underground, and some of the men 'had got holes in the ground like rabbit warrens.'[28] They were proud of the 'fortress' they had built: 'The result of our labour was that when we left these posts, we handed over ... not the bare hills that we had taken over, but, in the case of King's Post, one surrounded by a wall of earth and stones ten feet thick, and liberally supplied with palatial burrows, drained and provided with weather-proof head-cover.'[29] The work involved in making the 'fortress' - supervised by Archer and the other NCOs - was onerous in the extreme:

> To start with, there were invariably from one to two feet of ground to be first got through which consisted mainly of huge boulders, and each of these latter had to be picked round and then levered out with crowbars ... In addition, the lack of suitable tools was disheartening

to a degree ... By hook or by crook, however, the work was done, thanks to the splendid spirit and energy shown by the men, and it did take some spirit to keep on at an eternal round of digging day after day, and outpost work night after night.[30]

One of the King's Post companies was permanently deployed during daylight hours as escort to a battery, held in readiness under King's Post to 'sally forth and keep the Boer guns on Thornhill's Kopje and Telegraph Ridge, north-west of Ladysmith, quiet, when they became too offensive.'[31]

The remaining companies by day exchanged the rifle for the spade ... Defensive works were the first consideration. [Then] at night there was a change; the spade was discarded and the rifle took its place, and practically the whole battalion was out lining the defences. No matter what the weather (and on an average, on four nights of the week the rain fell in torrents) the men had to be at their posts. With our extended and weakly held lines, every possible precaution had to be taken which might help to lessen the chance of a sudden rush by night on the enemy's part being successful.[32]

Their routine changed somewhat when their fortress was completed. At night they moved up into the trenches and slept there, so that they were ready in case of attack. An hour before daybreak they stood to arms, remaining until they got their new advanced posts out for the day. Then they moved back to their shelters.[33]

Today we received orders to hold ourselves in readiness for a column to go and assist our relief column if required, only men in good condition to be taken. The enemy have got guns, some of them very large ones, six inches and 4.7 inches, on all the hills around, completely surrounding us. We get bombarded nearly every day, sometimes more than others. We very rarely get bombarded on a Sunday so we have to work in the more exposed positions. Up to date I have only had two men of my company hit, both slightly, both again on duty.[34]

At half past seven in the morning on 2 December they received orders to parade at once and proceed against the enemy. They marched eastwards in the direction of Lombard's Kop and halted just outside the town. Everyone was expecting a major battle but they were then ordered to 'proceed back several positions' - a somewhat strange expression. It is likely that the strength of the Boer forces there induced a change of mind about attacking them.

Three days later, Archer was involved in another operation, which, though carried through, yielded few helpful results. He was in a party that made a raid on Thornhill's farm. This farm was very frequently used at night by the Boers as a shelter, particularly in bad weather, and was protected by a 'great deal of Boer wire entanglements.'[35] Captain Gough worked out a plan to raid the place 'some stormy night.' This came off on 5 December. Two companies, A under Gough and G under Paley - six officers and 177 men - formed the party, 'but except for a small though comforting haul of fresh vegetables they drew a blank, not a single Boer being found on the premises.'[36] Archer wrote of this abortive exercise:

> At 1.14 a.m. this morning (raining) we, my Company and A Company, received an order to go to a farm called Thornhill's Farm, as the enemy had been seen going there at dusk every evening, and to capture anyone sleeping there. We had Thorn and another man to act as guides. Arrived there at about 3.0 a.m. but did not find anyone. I got some beetroot out of the garden. Got back just at daylight, wet through to the skin. It was a very well carried out night march, the best I have ever seen, nobody lost, which nearly always happens even at Aldershot where you can make plenty of noise after the attack and call out to anyone going wrong.[37]

The gun that was causing them most annoyance at King's Post, more than any other, was that on Thornhill's Kopje, just above Thornhill's Farm. They discovered, however, that by long range rifle fire they could both spoil the Boers' rifle shooting and to a great extent stop them firing their big gun.

> To assist in this good work we also used to send out a few selected marksmen to a small ridge [probably Escort Ridge] about 800 yards in front of King's ridge. A specially enrolled body of Rifle Brigade sharpshooters ... first really discovered that it was possible to frighten the Boer gunners at this extreme range ... The sharpshooters used also to [keep] away the Boers who came down to loot Thornhill's farm which was 2,100 yards away.[38]

Archer, a highly skilled and much experienced marksman, was almost certainly a member of this specially enrolled body of sharpshooters. No doubt he and his colleagues enjoyed this method of keeping the Boers away from Thornhill's farm after their nocturnal attempt to capture them had failed.

Other Boer guns were also being troublesome. On the night of 7 December the Cavalry, the Imperial Light Horse and the Natal Carbineers, left camp at three in the morning to blow up some of them on Gun Hill, the forward slope of Lombard's Kop. Archer and his colleagues heard a number of explosions followed by heavy firing that finished at 9.0 a.m. The Cavalry were also successful in destroying three guns on another hill and seizing a Maseim-Nordenfeldt, but suffered thirty wounded casualties.

Then on the night of Sunday 10 December - following a successful reconnaissance the previous night by Colonel Metcalfe, Gough, Hugh Dawnay, the intelligence officer, a Sergeant and two men, with Major Wing of the Royal Artillery - the 2nd Battalion of the Rifle Brigade, led by Metcalfe, their commanding officer, made an attack on Surprise Hill, where the Boers had a 4.5 inch, 120 mm, Krupp howitzer and a searchlight. As Archer recorded soon after the attack:

> We paraded about 9.0 p.m., A, B, E, G [Archer's Company] and H Companies and half of C Company, a small party of Engineers and Royal Artillery, about 460 all told, to attack up a hill called 'Surprise Hill' on which the enemy had got a big gun, 4.7 inches [and 'throwing a 40 lb shell',[39]] in a gun pit. This gun had been doing a lot of damage and our Artillery could not put it out of action. We had the same guides that took us to Thornhill's Farm. We left camp in Company Column of Sections (each Company has four sections), A Company and half of C Company leading, followed by H Company, B Company, Artillery, Engineers, and G Company, with E Company last, and, except when the moon broke through the clouds, we kept on the march, of course going very slowly.[40]

A Company, with a section of C Company, was commanded by John Gough; B Company by Reginald Stephens - who had been Archer's section commander in Mashonaland; E Company by G B Byrne; G Company by George Paley; and H Company, also with a section of C Company, by George Thesiger[41] - with whom he had served on the Nile Expedition. They were accompanied by six men of the Royal Engineers under Lieutenant Digby Jones and seven of the Royal Artillery for the work of actually demolishing the gun. Though they paraded at 9.0 p.m., they did not start out until an hour later, because the moon was full and bright. For the same reason they had to halt for over an hour under Observation Hill. The Boers had set up a searchlight on Telegraph Hill, west of Thornhill's Kopje and Surprise Hill, and although its powerful beam swept the hillsides, they did not pick up the raiding party.[42]

At last the moon disappeared over the horizon, and on we went to the railway, where another inevitable delay was caused, as a barbed-wire fence on each side had to be cut [by the officers. 'The process of cutting the wires was tedious, and wire fences when cut make a deal of noise. So only small cuts were made, through which the men defiled'[43]], and a five-foot cutting [was eventually] negotiated. After what seemed a very long time, everybody was safely over this obstacle, and now nothing intervened between us and Surprise Hill, which lay across a mile and a quarter of open and fairly level country.[44]

They left Lieutenant Byrne and half of E Company to hold the railway line to cover a retreat should this become necessary. They reached the bottom of Surprise Hill without being seen or giving the alarm - a remarkable feat by so large a body of over 400 armed and equipped men with 'hob-nailed boots, rifle straps and steel-tipped bayonets' in pitch black darkness - though they learned later that they shortly walked 'nearly over the top of a piquet of Boers who gave the alarm to the Hills on our right and left.' A Company, under Gough, formed line, single rank, leaving an opening in the centre - to avoid them all being hit should the enemy fire the big gun - and scrambled up the hill. H Company, under Thesiger, with the engineers to blow up the gun, followed them 30 yards behind but with no opening in the centre. Metcalfe, who led them, ordered them to 'go straight for the hill, [and] the last portion of the ascent was little short of precipitous'.[45] B Company, under Stephens, and G Company, under Paley, halted, formed single rank, B to the right and G to the left, to stop the enemy from coming from Bell's Kopje on the right and Thornhill's Kopje on the left, outflanking the assault companies and cutting off their retreat. They left a gap between B and G Companies - 'between their inner flanks' - through which the assault parties, A and H, could retire. The other half of E Company advanced about 500 yards and halted in a *donga*, a watercourse with steep sides, at the foot of the hill to protect their rear.[46]

A Company had nearly reached the top of the hill ['only a few yards short of the summit',[47] 'scarcely ten yards',[48] 'just fifteen yards,[49] 'within 20 yards'[50]] when the Boer sentry challenged them and fired, which was his last shot as he was shot by Captain Gough immediately. [This gave the alert 'and soon a field gun began firing at them from a nearby hill.'[51]] The firing then became general, half of A Company taking the right top of the Hill, half of A Company to the left top and H Company taking the centre and holding it.[52]

The separation of A Company into a left and a right half, with a gap in the centre not simply ensured against the whole Company being struck should the big gun be fired at them. It also, and more importantly, made it easier for the two halves to take the left and right top of the hill, leaving the centre to H Company. As soon as they reached the top of the hill:

> The Colonel, as had been pre-arranged, shouted out 'Fix bayonets' (the word 'bayonet' was introduced into our drill for the occasion, as we were not quite sure the Boers would fully grasp the meaning of the word 'sword'), and, giving vent to our pent-up feelings, with a wild cheer, over the crest we went ['the men having received instructions to make as much noise as possible'[53]]. [Gough described the action when they reached the summit: 'The Colonel shouted out "Fix bayonets and charge" and in we went.'[54]] The Boers did not offer any opposition, but fled precipitately. Gough and Thesiger quickly formed their companies in a semi-circle about one hundred yards past the gun emplacement, and fired volleys steadily in the direction of the Boers, who, finding they were not further pursued, had halted and started firing. ['The Riflemen swarmed over the top of the hill and ran past the gun emplacement, then formed a firing line and protected the hilltop from Boer attack while the demolition crew worked.'[55]][56]

For an awful moment, when Gough and Thesiger searched for the big gun, they could not find it. It was not in the emplacement and they wondered if it had been taken away - a 'hideous thought'. Then a 'triumphant shout' announced that it had been discovered outside, under a tarpaulin[57] 'about twenty yards away behind some bushes ... It was guarded by four highly-uniformed State Artillerists, who died.'[58] The demolition party placed their charges, and attached the fuses, but these failed, and a fresh fuse was laid and lit. Half an hour later, 'with a tremendous crash, off went the charge, and the chase of the gun likewise.'[59] Archer could hear their colleagues' cheers coming from their camp.[60]

Gough and Thesiger's companies thought nearly everything was over and were taking their wounded down the hill when devastating fire opened on them from right and left and shortly afterwards from the rear, that is from the summit of the hill. 'By the time the gun was blown up almost 2000 Boers were swarming around the hill. The Boers were also dropping shells on to the hill top.'[61] They recorded:

> Down the hill we started, but when we had got about a third of the way down, we were met by a withering fire. For a moment we thought that, by some terrible mistake, our supporting companies had got faced the wrong way and were firing into us, taking us for Boers, [In fact, G and B companies were lying down, not firing] but we were very soon undeceived on that point, and found that owing to our long delay on top of the hill, thanks to the defective fuse [and to the warning given by the Boer piquet as the British moved to the foot of the hill on their way up], the Boers had had time to get round us and cut us off from our supports. ['The enemy had got right up all round us, I never was in such a hot place in my life.'[62]] Orders were given not to fire, and only to use the bayonet, and gallantly the men obeyed; never a shot did they fire. ['The companies had to cut their way back with the bayonet,' Gough] had to prevent some of his men from charging back up the hill at the Boers and ordered them only to fire if they could see the enemy distinctly and rely on the bayonet to fight through any who had slipped around the flanks of the hill.'[63]] On down the hill we went at close quarters with the Boers, now charging out to a flank, now straight down the hill, till at last we were through and on level ground again.[64]

B and G Companies, with the Free State Boers from Thornhill's Kopje and the Transvaal Boers from Bell's Kopje only fifty yards away from them,[65] held their position on the slopes of the hill while the assault companies retired between them, without firing, so that the enemy, joined by others who had advanced from Surprise Hill, generally fired at each other over their heads, though they suffered some casualties. Now that A and H Companies were safely through, B Company, under Stevens, retired, though G Company, under Paley, did not know it at the time. G Company then also began to retire, and had not gone far when they again came under very heavy fire from the enemy. The Boers - 2500 had been detailed to guard the gun[66] - had moved in large numbers into a *donga* between them and their camp and had surrounded them. Paley gave G Company the order to charge and they drove the enemy out of the *donga* with bayonets. Archer, who led the charge with Paley 'did not see the Captain again after that' - he had been shot and badly wounded.[67] 'What added throughout to the confusion was the fact that the Boers picked up all our cries ... and kept shouting them out; this in the pitch darkness made it still more impossible to distinguish friend from foe.'[68] The account in the Regimental Chronicle said that 'Captain Paley was [later] found just at the foot of the hill, very severely hurt. He had been collecting wounded and stragglers on the hill, and was detached from the main body. The Colonel had called for him, and the Boers had taken up the call, crying, "Captain Paley, your Company's here", luring him towards a *donga* in which some of their sharp-shooters were concealed.'[69] Archer's private account recorded:

> On leaving the *donga* there were still some of the enemy between us and the camp, and all the men, some of RA, Engineers and other Companies all mixed up together in a big group, not knowing what to do. I got them into sections with the assistance of three Sergeants of my own Company, who kept very cool, and made for camp. I kept in command until we nearly arrived there when I handed over command to the senior 2nd Lieutenant. My Sergeants told me that I had got plenty of cheek to take command when there were three officers present, but say that if I had not done so we should have lost nearly all the Company. This is well known throughout the Battalion. All the officers were youngsters, the senior not being dismissed drill although he was up the Nile with us.[70]

Archer supplemented this account very soon after the attack, still in December 1899, by making an annotated sketch map of the area between King's Hill and Surprise Hill, three and a half miles apart. In it he deployed to good advantage his training and skill in military topography, first learned in Ireland and later developed at Command Headquarters in Malta. The drawing and annotation add a number of points of information, both on the topography and on the events, which help to clarify and give the setting for the other accounts of the attack.[71] Leaving at 10.0 p.m. and travelling northwards from King's Post at the eastern edge of King's Hill, the column first crossed Escort Ridge, 1000 yards away. Beyond the Ridge, they encountered the railway, which lay at the foot of another hill that gave it cover. Here they left half of E Company and, just before midnight, began crossing a very rocky valley. At a deep *donga* they left the other half of E Company. It was in this *donga* that the Boers later tried to cut off the Rifle Brigade from their return to their camp. Beyond the *donga* and at the foot of Surprise Hill was another deep *donga*. To their right was Bell's Kopje, 1200 yards distant from Observation Hill and from which the Boers attacked the retiring Companies on the east as they left Surprise Hill to return to their camp. Surprise Hill rose to 700 feet above the deep *donga*. To the left of Surprise Hill was a ridge, which the Boers occupied from Thornhill's kopje when the alarm was given, and from which they attacked the Rifle Brigade Companies on the west as they retired from Surprise Hill. Above the ridge was Thornhill's kopje itself, with very rocky slopes strewn with large boulders, and on its top were a 15 pound gun to the left and a 155 quick firing gun to the right. Between Thornhill's kopje and Surprise Hill there was a steep valley with thick scrub. Archer's drawing of Surprise Hill shows, on its summit, H Company and the 4.7 gun in the centre, flanked to left and right by the two halves of A Company. On the slopes were, to the left or west, G Company and, to the right or east, B Company, each below the two half A companies. Outside G and B companies on the slopes were the Boers from the Thornhill ridge to the west, and from Bell's Kopje to the east. On his sketch map Archer wrote a brief account of the attack:

> Attacking party: five companies 2nd Battalion Rifle Brigade with small detachment of Royal Artillery and Royal Engineers. About 460. Column moved off from King's Hill at 9.30 p.m. in Column of Sections. Halted at about midnight in line with Observation Hill on account of the moon. On arrival at the bottom of Surprise Hill A and H Companies formed line, single rank facing the gun. A company then scaled the hill leaving a gap between each half Company. H Company followed about 30 yards in rear, same order, but no gap in centre of Company. B Company formed to the right, G Company to the left to protect the flanks. Half of E Company was left on railway to protect our retirement. The other half Company was left at the *donga* to form our rear. No alarm was given by the Boer sentries until A Company reached within 20 yards of the top of the hill. It seemed a long time before the gun was blown up but [eventually] it was blown up. A and H Company commenced to retire. About this time the Boers' reinforcements had arrived and began firing from both sides. We lay still so they shot over our heads at each other, which was a good thing for us. After A and H Companies had retired we, G Company, retired but only to find that the Boers had cut us off from camp by getting into the *donga* in our rear. Captain Paley gave the order to charge. The Boers ran but Captain Paley and several

others were shot. The Company reformed after crossing the *donga* and marched back to camp, bringing in with us about 25 wounded men. We got back at daylight on 11th December. Total casualties 61 killed, wounded and prisoners. My Company, three killed, four wounded, including Captain Paley, five prisoners and one missing.

Some three months later a war correspondent gave a somewhat different account of what happened when Paley was lured towards the *donga*:

> Ultimately the retirement was duly effected, but Captain Paley and twenty-four men were missing ... From the fire he judged he was in a tight corner, and had just given his men the order to charge with the bayonet when, to use his own words, he was 'bowled over like a rabbit' with a wound through his chest and another that splintered his thigh-bone. This, I think, is one of the bravest actions we have seen in a war that has shown many. Under a heavy cross-fire Captain Paley remained, collecting stragglers, and bringing with him all the men who were able to move, assisting them in the darkness over boulders, and, after incalculable difficulties, getting them into some sort of order, knowing that at the first glimmer of daylight he and his men would be ruthlessly shot down.[72]

Paley, who was, and continued to be, much admired by Archer and who undoubtedly showed great bravery, was more likely to have been wounded in the early stages of the bayonet charge than in the course of collecting wounded and stragglers. Archer did not see Paley after the charge was ordered, and in the morning the Captain was found at the foot of the hill, very severely hurt, and almost certainly incapable of effective further command. It is much more likely that it was Archer, rather than the very seriously wounded Paley, who collected the wounded and stragglers, and - even more likely - got the soldiers 'into some sort of order.'

What seems to have happened during the retirement from Surprise Hill, in summary, was that having destroyed the gun, A and H companies with the Artillery and Engineers, retired down the slopes with their wounded. They were about a third of the way down when they came under very heavy fire from their flanks. The Boers fired at them over the heads of B and G companies, who were lying down between the Boers - only fifty yards away from them - and their retiring colleagues, and not firing. They crossed the *donga* and reached camp. B Company followed them. Not all the personnel of A, H and B companies got through, and, with elements of the E company piquets, a number from each company, 'all mixed up together in a big group, not knowing what to do', with several of them wounded, they were gathered on the camp side of the *donga*, now under heavy fire from their flanks, and effectively leaderless. Their officers had either been incapacitated or had led the rest of their men safely back to camp. Meanwhile, as G company retired from the slopes of the hill, they found, first, that they were being fired on from their flanks, though the firing passed largely over their heads; and then that they were cut off by the Boers who had now moved from a flanking position and had taken up positions in the *donga*. At this time Metcalfe was still in the immediate area because he called out to Paley, who was collecting wounded and stragglers. Paley ordered a charge to remove the enemy from the *donga*. The Boers were driven out, but Paley fell, incapacitated by wounds, before he could cross the *donga*, and stayed there, at the foot of the hill, until morning. G company, with three young and inexperienced subalterns, Archer and three sergeants, but not Captain Paley, having driven the Boers out of the *donga*, crossed it and found themselves with the 'big group' of stragglers and wounded. So Archer got them into sections with the assistance of the three Sergeants of his own Company, who kept very cool, and made for camp. He stayed in command until they almost reached the camp when he handed over command to the senior, but relatively inexperienced, Second Lieutenant.

The Rifle Brigade's casualties were heavy: Lieutenant Fergusson had been killed,[73] Captain Paley had been shot through the chest and hip, Second Lieutenant Bond – aged 20 and commissioned only four months earlier[74] - had been shot through the hip, Second Lieutenant Davenport - 23 and commissioned two years earlier[75] - had been shot through the arm, 12 rank and file had been killed - including Colour Sergeant Saunders of H company, who enlisted the day after Archer, and Sergeant Patterson, 'an old shooting chum' - and three had subsequently died of their wounds. Thirty-six NCOs and Riflemen had been wounded and ten were missing. The total number of British casualties was much larger, possibly 300.[76] When a war correspondent told Paley that he was sorry to hear about the casualties, the Captain whispered in reply 'But we got the gun.'[77]

The British sent out a flag of truce in the morning, and all the wounded, who were left on the ground overnight, including Paley, were brought in and the dead were buried at the foot of the hill. 'The Boers for once in a way, admitted that they, too, had sustained heavy losses.'[78]

Fergusson's death particularly saddened his colleagues. He had been lured towards the Boer guns, as had been Paley, but with fatal consequences.

The Boers caught up the British pass-words and the names of our officers, and it would appear that some of them called out, 'Bring your men this way, Mr Fergusson,' and upon his doing so, under the belief that the order came from someone in the Regiment, he was instantly shot down by a volley at close quarters. He received four bullets, one through the lungs, another inflicting a very severe wound somewhat lower down on the right side, and two more in the legs. Captain Riley, RAMC, states that he found him in great pain, but he only said, 'Never mind me, I'm done for; see to the others.' He lived for a few hours and his body was carried into Ladysmith and buried in the cemetery the same evening, December 11th 1899.[79]

A graphic account of the attack on Surprise Hill was given by a Boer soldier, Deneys Reitz,[80] who was with the Boer Pretoria Commando unit that moved into the deep *donga* vacated by half of E Company when they withdrew to Ladysmith.

> Two other corporalships went on duty at the same time. One under Corporal Tossel, a former police detective, was posted at the foot of Surprise Hill and the other a long way to our left. My brother and myself and Samuel van Zijl were the only members of our tent who were present, the other four being absent with the carrying party. As we walked along in the dark behind Isaac Malherbe we discussed the previous night's attack on the Lombaards-kop gun, and I remember poor Samuel saying he hoped our turn would not come next. But our turn did come next. When we reached the usual halting-place two men were sent forward according to custom, and the rest of us turned in. My time to go on duty was 1.0 a.m. At about half past twelve I awoke, and not thinking it worthwhile to fall asleep again I lay on my blanket watching the stars.
> After a while I distinctly heard the muffled sound of many footsteps in the direction of Surprise Hill, so I [went] to the two sentries to consult them. I found that they had also heard the noise, and the three of us listened for a few seconds to what was certainly men climbing the hill. We thought Corporal Tossel's men had taken fright at something, and were withdrawing up the slope towards the howitzer emplacement. This belief was rudely dispelled, for suddenly there broke from the summit of Surprise Hill a crash of musketry followed by wild bursts of cheering, and we realised that English troops were at the gun. As we stood undecidedly watching the hundreds of rifle flashes lighting up the hill-top, a vivid sheet of

flame stabbed the darkness, followed by a tremendous roar, and we knew that our howitzer had been blown into the air. The two sentries and I rushed back to where our party were already on their feet. Isaac Malherbe now showed the stuff he was made of. Without a moment's hesitation he went straight for the danger-point, the continued cheering of the English soldiery and the volley-firing serving as a guide. His intention was to join hands with Tossel's corporalship if he could find them and then to prevent or delay the troops from returning to Ladysmith, until the whole of the Pretoria Commando could come from camp, and so destroy or capture the intruders.

As it turned out, Tossel's corporalship had bolted when they heard the English coming. They had not only given them a clear field but had fired no warning shot to alarm the unfortunate gunners up above, who were taken unawares and all bayoneted. And as for the remainder of our commando in camp, they stood to arms all night, but Field-Cornet Zeederberg refused to risk the confusion, that he perhaps justly thought would ensue, if he tried to march his men in the dark to an unknown situation. So the twelve of us were left to our own devices.

As we approached we could hear by the firing and shouting that the main body of the attackers were still on the hill, but they had posted a string of pickets at the foot to secure their line of withdraw back to the town, and before we had gone very far we ran into one of these. Isaac and I were a few yards in advance when a 'Halt! Who goes there?' was shouted at us from a few paces away. We simultaneously fired a shot apiece and ran forward. We came on a dead soldier, a Sergeant, as I saw next morning from his badge, but the rest of the picket had run off into the night.

We went forward cautiously and soon we collided once more with another and stronger rearguard party. We were again challenged from close quarters, and, a heavy fire being aimed at us, we took shelter in a dry spruit bed that runs along the base of Surprise Hill. From here we returned the fire, until this outpost too gave us right of way, and we now began to file along the bed in order to seek out a convenient point from which to make a stand against the troops on the hill when they descended.

As we were going, a soldier, lying concealed in the grass on the bank above us, thrust over the muzzle of his rifle, and fired point-blank into us. My tent-mate, Samuel van Zijl was walking immediately in front of me and I had my hand on his shoulder to steady myself on the uneven path. The bullet struck him full in the throat, and so near was the range that the discharge scorched his face and set fire to his beard, which flared up for a moment like a fuse. He staggered, and then dropped. He was still alive, but I could hear from his laboured breathing that he was badly wounded, so I made him as comfortable as I could by placing his blanket under his head, before hurrying up the spruit to rejoin the others.

By now the troops were descending Surprise Hill, and you could hear them clattering down the slope towards us. Their officers were blowing whistles, and calling out 'A Company here!' 'This way B Company!' and so on, to collect their men. They seemed unaware that the road was to be disputed, for they made no attempt to conceal their progress, and there was laughter and repeated cries of 'Good old Rifle Brigade', and here and there we caught the gleam of matches been struck and the glow of cigarettes, to show how little they expected opposition.

In the meantime Isaac had selected a suitable spot on the bank, our faces towards Surprise Hill, our backs towards Ladysmith, and here we crouched, silently waiting for the oncoming troops.

From the sounds that reached us we judged them to be about three hundred strong, and with no sign of Tossel's men or of help from the [rest of the] commando, it dawned on us that we were in a pretty tight corner.

While the soldiers were still some distance away I ran down to see how Samuel van Zijl was faring. He was only just alive, and he asked me in a faint voice to turn him on his side to ease the pain, but as I did so I felt his body stiffen, and then go limp in my arms, and when I laid him down he was dead. I hurried back, for the laughter and talking were drawing very near. As I made up the course, a huge soldier, or it looked so in the dark, loomed up suddenly on the bank above. He lunged at me with the bayonet, but his insecure footing deflected the thrust and brought him tumbling against me. The man was at my mercy now, for I had my carbine against his side, but there came over me an aversion to shooting him down like a dog, so I ordered him to put up his hands instead, which he did at once, dropping his bayoneted rifle at my feet. I told him to sit down until I called him, a command which he so implicitly obeyed that I found him patiently waiting there next morning with a bullet through his leg from the cross-firing during the subsequent proceedings. This soldier must have come on ahead, for when I reached my companions the main force was just reaching the foot of the hill and approaching us in a body.

Isaac whispered to us to hold our fire and each man peered into the darkness until, about 15 yards away we saw a black mass dimly-outlined and then, at his word of command we poured volley after volley into the closely-packed ranks, shooting as fast as we could work the bolts of our rifles. When the blast struck them they thought they were being fired at by their own rearguard pickets, for there were cries of 'Rifle Brigade! Rifle Brigade, don't fire!' But, discovering their error, a commanding voice called out, 'Bayonets, Bayonets,' and they came at us like a wall. In spite of our small number we delivered such a volume of fire that the head of the column swerved to the left and slanted across our front to make the spruit lower down, and, although we continued our volleys, we could not prevent their going by.

Several times, however, parties of soldiers who had lost their way in the dark walked in among us, and of these we shot some and took others prisoners.

A Captain named George Paley came up to where my brother and I knelt, firing over the edge of the bank, and as he failed to halt when called upon we both loosed a round and brought him toppling between us. [One officer, Captain Paley, advanced though he had two bullet wounds already. Joubert gave him another shot and he fell on top of us.[81]] Another time one of our men, Jan Luttig, was seized by some soldiers within a few yards of us, and there was a hand to hand scuffle in which he was stabbed with a bayonet and clubbed on the head with a rifle-butt. [Four Englishmen got hold of Jan Luttig and struck him on the head with their rifles and stabbed him in the stomach with a bayonet. He seized two of them by the throat and shouted 'Help, boys!' His two nearest comrades shot two of them, and the other two bolted.[82]] [Then the English came up in numbers, about eight hundred, along the footpath, and we lay as quiet as mice along the bank. Further on the English killed three of our men with bayonets and wounded two.[83]] In the dark we could not make out what was happening, but when we heard his cry for help and ran up, his assailants were gone. A moment later I made out three soldiers in the spruit behind me and slipped down towards them. One nearly spitted me with a vicious jab of his bayonet, which passed between my arm and body, but before he could repeat the thrust I had him covered and they surrendered. One was an army doctor with a bullet-wound in his foot and the other two said they were helping him along. I ordered them to remain in the bed of the spruit, where I found them in the morning.

About this time we heard four or five shots in rapid succession, followed by groans, from the direction where the troops were still crossing the spruit twenty or thirty yards off. We did not know the meaning of this, and only at daybreak did we find that we had listened to the death-cry of some of our men who had come from the camp to our assistance.

It was now towards three in the morning, and we had nearly exhausted our ammunition so we sat quietly watching the tail of the column vanish into the darkness beyond, on its way to Ladysmith.

When daylight came at last, a grim scene met our eyes. Before us, within a radius of less than twenty-five yards, lay over sixty dead and wounded English soldiers, and as we walked forward among them we came on the bodies of three of our men who had not been with us originally. Two were dead and dreadfully hacked with bayonets and the third was at his last gasp.[In the morning we found Captain Paley and twenty-two of them killed and wounded.[84]]

These had been away to the railway depot with the fatigue party, and [were] on their return [journey], and gallantly attempted to make their way to us when they heard the firing. They nearly reached us but ran into the withdrawing soldiers, and were bayoneted before they could fire more than a few shots. Behind us in the spruit-bed lay poor Samuel van Zijl and close by sat our prisoners, some twenty in number.

Dead, wounded, and prisoners, eleven of us had accounted for more than eighty opponents, an average of seven apiece.

Total casualties 61 killed, wounded and prisoners. My Company 3 killed, 4 wounded, including Captain Paley, 5 prisoners, one missing.

Our work was now done, and shortly after sunrise Mr Zeederberg and a large escort of men came scouting through the bush to see what was left of us and they were surprised to find so many of us still alive.

We stood among the dead and the wounded soldiers, the centre of an admiring crowd, and from now onwards Isaac Malherbe's Corporalship was spoken of as the best in the commando.

A number of interesting points emerge from Reitz's account of the attack on Surprise Hill. First, the Boers defended the gun on the hill by placing units at the foot of the hill and 'a long way to the left'. These were regular placements because Reitz referred to 'the usual stopping place' and the sending of two men forward 'according to custom'. It is unlikely that Metcalfe's reconnaissance had discovered these placements, since had they done so, presumably they would have taken serious steps to locate and neutralize them so that the alarm could not be sounded. It is unlikely, too, that the Boers knew of Metcalfe's reconnaissance, otherwise they would have been better prepared for the attack, especially following the successful attacks on Gun Hill and Sugarloaf Hill a few nights previously. In any event, the unit at the foot of Surprise Hill was not effective in defending the gun: Corporal of the Guard Tossel and his men ran away. It was they over whom the attacking party nearly walked, and although they did not give warning to their colleagues on Surprise Hill, they did give the alarm to those on the hills to their right and left.

Second, the advance of the Rifle Brigade up the Hill slope did not go unnoticed because Reitz and the two forward sentries heard the 'muffled sound of many footsteps' that were 'certainly men climbing the hill.' However, they misinterpreted the sounds and believed that Tossel's men had 'taken fright at something, and were withdrawing up the slope'. In fact, Tossel and his men had heard the English coming and had bolted and given no warning shot. This explains why the Rifle Brigade was able to have a clear field across a mile and a quarter of open and fairly level ground to reach the gun emplacement and why the Boers there were taken by surprise. In accounting for their defeat at Surprise Hill, the Boer generals placed the blame on Tossel and his men for running away.[85]

Third, the attacking party began their cheering as soon as they reached the hill rather than waiting until the gun was destroyed, for Reitz heard the 'crash of musketry followed by wild bursts of cheering' before he saw the 'vivid sheet of flame stab[bing] the darkness, followed by a tremendous roar' indicating their 'howitzer had been blown into the air.'

Fourth, Zeederberg's commando did not come to the aid of Isaac Malherbe's corporalship of twelve men, who were left to their own devices, and it was these twelve who stood in the direct path of the Brigade as they withdrew downhill, and prevented them reaching their Ladysmith camp unscathed by frontal fire. Malherbe's dozen men vigorously engaged the pickets at the foot of the hill, before the attacking parties descended. One of these pickets had their sergeant shot, and the rest 'ran off into the night.' This sergeant was more likely to have been Sergeant Patterson, Archer's 'old shooting chum', than Colour Sergeant Saunders. Saunders was in H Company which was one of the assault companies and not E Company which formed the pickets. The other picket, a much stronger rearguard party, engaged in heavy firing before they, too, 'gave right of way' to Malherbe's unit.

Fifth, as the Brigade 'clattered down' the slope, the officers were trying to collect their men together, by blowing whistles and calling out to direct their companies. The men were laughing, talking, cheering, smoking cigarettes and shouting 'Good old Rifle Brigade', unaware that their passage back to Ladysmith was to be challenged.

Sixth, when they ran into the Boer unit, they thought that the rapid fire into their closely packed ranks, came from one of their own rearguard pickets. When they discovered that this was not so they were ordered - probably by Paley - to charge with their bayonets and they descended upon the Boers 'like a wall'. Though most of the men got through, there was a great deal of confusion in which, on several occasions, 'parties of soldiers who had lost their way in the dark, walked among' Malherbe's men, who shot some and took others prisoner.

Seventh, Paley's injuries were inflicted by the brothers Reitz, who were kneeling in a dry spruit bed that ran along the base of Surprise Hill, and firing over the edge of the bank. When Paley did not answer their call to halt, the brothers 'both loosed a round and brought him toppling' between them. Both rounds struck their target and Paley was wounded in the chest and thigh. Then he was fired on again, by Joubert, though it is unclear whether this inflicted a further injury. Presumably, they thought he was dead or at least fatally wounded, for they neither shot him again to kill him, nor did they take him prisoner.

Eighth, although there was a certain amount of brutality – for example, stabbing with a bayonet and clubbing on the head with a rifle butt during a hand to hand scuffle – there was also some more humane and restrained actions – for example, Reitz's accepting the surrender of a man he had at his mercy. And the war correspondent was wrong when he said that 'at the first glimmer of daylight' Paley and his men 'would be ruthlessly shot down', for, under Archer's leadership, most were able to return to their camp, and the wounded - who had been left unmolested on the ground - including Paley, were recovered under a flag of truce in the morning.

Ninth, Malherbe's corporalship of only eleven men - one, Samuel van Zijl, had been fatally wounded early in the engagement - wreaked substantial damage on the English forces. Accepting that Reitz may have been overstating the numbers he and his colleagues had killed, wounded and captured - more than eighty - and accepting that Archer may have been understating the Rifle Brigade's losses - over sixty dead or wounded and twenty prisoners or 61 killed, wounded and prisoners[86] – it would none the less seem that most of the damage suffered was inflicted by Malherbe's unit directly in the line of the withdrawal, and relatively little by the other Boer forces attacking the withdrawing column from right and left flanks.

Finally, Private J Gibbons of the 2nd Battalion of the Rifle Brigade gave an account of the operation in verse: 'The Night Attack on Surprise Hill':

Yer've erd about the night attack an ow we took the ill
An ow we rushed their sentries to capture or to kill.
Yer've erd about the scramble, an the slashin left an right,
The volleys an the chargin when we took the ill that night.

There wasn't many of us, but wot there was were good.
We couldn't all be eros but we all did what we could.
We left the camp at dead o night adodjin of the moon
An gettin kinder anxious for their searchlight comin soon.

We crept up quiet an gentle when the moon was out o sight
For yer can't afford to make a noise when marchin out at night.
An up we went a scramblin an tumblin all about,
Up,up, an up an near the top when - Bang - the shots rang out.

Fix Baynits. Charge, hooray, hooray, we rushed towards the gun,
Volley firin. Ready. An now the scrap begun.
An now the Sappers av the gun, an now they've lit the fuse,
An now up goes the bloomin gun - Retire -no time to lose.

Our dooty now was finished cos we'd blowed the gun to ell.
But now the job was gettin back, an ow no-one could tell.
For the Boers was waitin down below, an meant to make it ot,
Surrounded us, a sweatin like to capture all the lot.

They thought as we'd surrender an wouldn't make a fight.
They didn't know the sort o men wot took their gun that night.
An bullets fell like drops o rain an lots o men was it
But they couldn't stop our chargin, no damn it not a bit.

We charged em ere, we charged em there, they scattered left an right.
We slashed an stabbed an cursed an swore, good Gawd that was a night.
But no-one shook nor faltered, went at it with a will,
A tumblin, jumpin, pushin an now we've cleared the ill.

An now the firin slackens, the Boers ad ad enuff.
They never did like baynits an our chaps ad used em rough.
An now we've cleared the railway an now the firin's still,
An now we're makin camp again, there's Observation ill.

An then wiv anxious faces we ask wiv arts wots still
Ow many av we wounded an wot's the total killed.
Ay chaps that puts the damper on, just for a time or so,
When yer ears who's give their life's blood, some comrade that yer knew.

Our losses too was eavy, both orficers an men.
Killed an wounded sixty an some won't charge agen.
But wot we done was noble an as brave as ere was seen,
Cos we tried to do our dooty for our country an our Queen.

In Battalion Orders of 13 December, Lieutenant-General Sir George White[87] wrote of the attack on Surprise Hill:

> This was a very bold enterprise, and I have the very highest admiration for the spirit with which it was carried out. Colonel Metcalfe's plan was good, and was founded on personal reconnaissance; his leading on the emplacement was accurate and determined. I am sorry that the Battalion under his command has so many casualties, but success crowned their efforts, and their extrication from a resolute attempt to surround them was due to the good Company system that obtains in the Battalion, to the able way Company Commanders exercised their commands, and to the bravery with which all Riflemen closed with the enemy.[88]

Though it was not said, it also was due to the action taken by Archer in assuming command, albeit with 'plenty of cheek', when his Company Commander, Paley, was so critically wounded, and, with his sergeants, getting the men, from various Companies - not just his own - who were 'all mixed up together in a big group, not knowing what to do', into sections and back to the camp.

Archer had been unable to write home for almost two months because with all communications to the outside world cut, there was no chance of the letters getting through. By Christmas Eve, however, he could hear the guns of General Buller's Force, so expected to be able to get a letter through in a week or so. The Boer howitzers were improving their aim but the staff officers refused to allow any more of the tin huts to be dismantled to provide more material for the bomb shelters.[89]

On Christmas Day he heard that his name had been sent to General Buller, to be mentioned in despatches for his actions on Surprise Hill. He also heard, though he did not then know if it was true, that he had been recommended for the award of the Distinguished Conduct Medal: 'I shall believe it when I see my name in the London Gazette.' He was still not a man to count his chickens before they were hatched.

He enjoyed a very good Christmas 'considering the conditions', with a plum pudding for dinner and a tot of rum in the evening.[90] The pudding was made of currants and raisins, blended with clarified dubbin, issued to grease wagon wheels and often used to waterproof boots.[91] On the other hand, Conan Doyle painted a much blacker picture:

A record of the siege onwards [from the attack on Surprise Hill] until the break of the New Year centres upon the sordid details of the sick returns and the price of food. Fifty on one day, seventy on the next, passed under the hands of the overworked and devoted doctors. Fifteen hundred, and later two thousand, of the garrison were down. The air was poisoned by foul sewage and dark with obscene flies. They speckled the scanty food. Eggs were already a shilling each, cigarettes sixpence, whisky five pounds a bottle: a city more free from gluttony and drunkenness has never been seen.[92]

Although Archer could hear the guns of Buller's relief column from the Rifle Brigade's camp, and although he had a relatively good Christmas, the siege, still less the war, was far from over. Early in the New Year the Boers made a determined attempt to break the British defence of Ladysmith by taking control of the Platrand. This was a high hill, nearly three miles long, running east and west, covering the southern approaches to the town, that so far had been in British hands continuously throughout the siege. If the Boers could take it, the British ability to continue to defend Ladysmith would be severely compromised and probably made impossible. We have already seen how the British defensive lines were secured on the east by the Klip river and a wide stretch of open country, and on the south by the Platrand, with Caesar's Camp and Wagon Hill - two long flat-topped hills - at is ends. Maintaining control of the Platrand was vital to the British if they were to continue to defend Ladysmith. 'Caesar's Camp, a fortified hill just to the South of Ladysmith, [is] the key to its defence.'[93] 'Wagon Hill and Caesar's Camp are the main part of the defences facing south.'[94]

> In the early hours of 6 January the Boers attacked Wagon Hill on the west and Caesar's camp on the east of the Platrand. In a battle that lasted all day both British and Boers hung on grimly, but the Boers failed to hold any ground on the top of the hill as British counter-attacks confined them to the slopes. British reinforcements [including the Rifle Brigade] were summoned by telephone ...
>
> The Platrand was not very strongly manned by the British, but Caesar's Camp had been fortified with the construction of walls about 7 ft. (2 m.) high and emplacements for artillery on the northern edge with a good field of fire across the hilltop, and there was a low wall along the southern side of Wagon Hill. There was also work in progress on Wagon Hill to make emplacements for a naval 12 pounder and one of the Navy's 4.7 inch guns.

The Boer plan was to attack Caesar's Camp with about 1000 Transvaal men under the command of Shalk Burger, while 400 Orange Free State men under Commandant C J de Villiers would take the extreme west, Wagon Point. In the centre 600 men of the Vryheid and Winburg commandos and the German Corps would complete the assault ... In the first rush the British were pushed back, and confused fighting took place in the darkness. The British commander, Colonel Ian Hamilton, was woken by the noise at his headquarters close to the Manchester Regiment positions at Caesar's Camp and used the telephone to contact Lieutenant-General Sir George White and call for reinforcements. Hamilton himself then set off for Wagon Hill with Major Miller-Walnutt and two companies of Gordon Highlanders, cutting himself off from his headquarters and his telephone in the process. He met the expected reinforcements, sent the Gordons back to the Manchesters and took the Imperial Light Horse west to Wagon Hill. As it grew light the artillery came into action, shelling the southern and eastern edges of the Platrand.

Hamilton was at the new, vacant 4.7 inch gun pit [on Wagon Hill] when the Orange Free Staters attacked again. In the confusion two British and two Boers exchanged fire at close quarters around Hamilton; all four were killed, but the colonel survived unscathed. As the afternoon drew on, in a fierce thunderstorm, the men of the Devonshire Regiment clambered up the hill. Hamilton showed their commander, Lieutenant-Colonel C W Park, the place where, in a little nek at the west of Wagon Hill, the Boers were holding out. The Devonshires charged forward into almost certain death. Many fell, but the Boers fled. As night fell the remaining Boers could be heard making their way down the hillside. Holding the Platrand had cost the British 424 casualties, 175 of which were fatal. Boer losses are not known exactly but are said to have been similar. [The cost to both sides was high and no further hand-to-hand attacks were made by the Boers until the end of the siege in February. Had a significant number from the Boer force not elected to absent themselves from an attack considered too dangerous, the outcome might have been different.] [It was the German Corps that stayed away.][95]

The Regimental Chronicle[96] recorded of this attack on Caesar's Camp on January 6th that members of the Rifle Brigade woke early in the morning to the sound of a 'furious rattle of musketry going on at the east end of Caesar's camp and on Wagon Hill'. At about half past five they were ordered to send four companies, and then two more, to reinforce the

Manchester Regiment on Caesar's Hill, leaving only E Company on King's post. The Chronicle continued:

> It was about 7.0 a.m. when we reached Caesar's camp, and found ... that the Boers had got behind the Manchesters' piquets and had made good their footing on the extreme east end of the hill. [Five of the companies went into action, A under Gough, B under Stephens, D under Biddulph, F under Mills and H under Thesiger], G Company, under [John] Harington [who had taken command when Paley was wounded], being kept in reserve ... For nearly the whole day the fighting raged fiercely, first one side and then the other gaining a slight advantage; but we could not succeed in dislodging the Boers. It was fighting at close quarters too, as short a distance of sixty or seventy yards only separating us at times from the enemy. Bulwana 'Long Tom' was rendering them every assistance by trying to throw his huge projectiles amongst us, until Major Abdy brought his battery in the most gallant manner and, to the admiration of everybody, out into the open country at the foot of Caesar's Camp, and drew the attention of the big gun on to himself, to our no small relief. Finally, about 4.0 p.m., a terrific hailstorm came on, followed by a deluge of rain, under cover of which the Boers advanced a short distance; then, finding that the spruit behind them was rising rapidly and that they were in danger of being cut off, they retired. Meanwhile, an equally critical fight was taking place on Wagon Hill; here, also, the Boers established themselves early in the morning in our position, and it was not till late in the evening that they were finally expelled.[97]

During the attack, Lieutenant Hall and seventeen men were killed; Mills - who died in hospital four weeks later[98] - Biddulph, Thesiger, Stephens and Harington and thirty-two men were wounded. There followed a miserable night. All the companies stayed where they were after sorting themselves and connecting up round the crest of the hill. They were all drenched to the skin, and bitterly cold. The next day, 'after a series of contradictory orders', the Rifle Brigade took over Wagon Hill in the afternoon, 'being hurried *en route* by "Long Tom" of Bulwana'.

> On arriving at Wagon Hill we were not best pleased at our change of quarters; we found none of those snug burrows or palatial residences that we had built with so much care in our old habitation [at King's Post], and the defensive works were few and far between. All the weary digging had to be started afresh, only under more

trying conditions, as it all had to be done by night, it being quite impossible to attempt anything of the sort during the day, since we were continually exposed to shrapnel at the convenient range of 3200 yards. Quite two miles of front had to be fortified, but in a very short time a complete set of works made their appearance, continuous *sangars* [defensive breastworks] occupied a large portion of our front, wire entanglements were laid all round the front of our position, and abbatis made in places.

We got some tarpaulins up, with which we made shelters, but suffering a good deal of inconvenience from them owing to their want of stability, when under the influence of [bad weather].

The Battalion was now disposed as follows: Headquarters and four companies, B, D, F and H on Wagon Hill; two companies, A and G under Gough, on Wagon Point, a continuation of Wagon Hill ... One company, E, was left on King's Post.[99]

With two company commanders of G Company wounded – Paley in the Surprise Hill attack, and his successor, Harington, in the Caesar's Hill operation – Archer, under Gough, commanded two sections of A Company and two sections of G Company, while Harington, later to become Inspector-General of the King's African Rifles, commanded the other Company of the defence post - presumably the other two sections of A and of G Company.[100] Gough recorded :

When we got there we could not find anyone in command and no one knew in the least what was going on ... Sydney Mills was first shoved forward to re-inforce No.5 Piquet. He did not know where it was and no one could tell us whether the Boers were on the ridge or not ... Sydney was knocked over and a good many men ... D Company came upon the left and all three officers were knocked over at once ... B Company then came up on their left and worked round the flank, Stephens getting knocked over, George Thesiger in trying to get up to this Coy got shot through the neck .. After Thesiger was hit [and in 'the unexplained absence of Metcalfe who failed to materialise in the firing line at all'[101]] I found myself the senior RB officer under fire, and I could get no orders as to what the authorities were doing on our right; a very nasty position.[102]

It had been unbearably hot all morning, but at about 4.0 p.m. there was a violent thunderstorm. [I] noticed that the Boers were trying to push reinforcements of their own up on to the hill and sensed that it was the moment for [us to take] decisive action. We shoved in all our supports and the Boers went; we then opened a most tremendous fire at them as they went down the slope, but the bush was very thick so that one had to fire at random except at the Klip river which they had to cross 900 yards away. We knocked over a good few at this place, and the ones that got away will remember that place to their dying day.[103]

Archer gave a detailed account of his personal experiences during the defence of the Platrand, - a name he did not use, but rather Caesar's Camp and Wagon Hill - in a letter to his mother on 24 January, telling her about events since Christmas:

6 January. King's Hill. About 1.30 a.m. firing was reported on Wagon Hill (a range of hills south about three miles from us) but it ceased in about half an hour. At about 3.0 a.m. the firing again commenced but more of it and extended along the range of hills to Caesar's Camp. About 4.15 a.m. we got the order to reinforce Caesar's Camp (Manchester Regiment). It is about three miles from King's Post as the crow flies but the way we went made it about five miles. On arrival at the top of the hill we halted just under the crest on our side, the enemy's shells just going over our heads. After waiting about a quarter of an hour, F Company received the order to reinforce the Manchesters on the left. They extended as skirmishers and advanced. (The top of the hill is a plateau about one mile wide.) But instead of finding the Manchesters in possession they found the Boers holding the place they were to reinforce. Several men got killed and wounded before they saw anything. Everyone got behind rocks or the best cover he could and had to remain there until about 4.0 p.m. without anything to eat or drink.

At about quarter of an hour intervals after F Company, companies were moved to different parts of the hill, my company moving round the crest ... where we remained in support. By 3.0 p.m. every company commander was shot except one (Captain Gough, A Company) and things were looking very serious. About 4.0 p.m. all the enemy had been driven off the top of Caesar's camp. The enemy got reinforced ... but were unable to regain the hill. A heavy rain with thunder started about 3.30 p.m. Everybody got drenched to the skin. The firing was kept up till dark on the retiring enemy.

We lost 18 killed including Lieutenant Hall (the Officer who sent the dervish sword home for me)[104] and 38 wounded. The total loss of our force was about 300 killed and wounded. The Boers' casualties must have been very heavy [they were probably in excess of 250 killed[105]] as in addition to the killed and wounded a lot of them must have been drowned when retiring across a *donga* which had become flooded through the heavy rain.

Everybody stopped where the fighting was until the morning. No great coats or anything to keep us warm. It was a terrible night, wet through and very cold. The wounded were all collected during the night but the killed had to stop until the next day. On the 7th we buried the dead, both ours and the Boers', but in separate graves.

About 1.30 p.m. we received an order to proceed to Wagon Hill to hold it at all costs. Here we have remained ever since, putting it in a state of defence. Our rations are getting very short and it is impossible to buy anything.

Putting Wagon Hill in a state of defence was not a simple task, for there were no defences at all when they started. For three days and nights Gough, now in command of both A and G companies, his NCOs, including Archer, and his men worked extremely hard until the position was reckoned to be impregnable.

Unfortunately, it rained solidly and the exposed position laid it open to Boer artillery fire from three sides, so the work could only be carried out safely between 7.0 p.m and midnight. Even then there was no rest as the men had to stand to at dawn in case of any renewed attack. [Gough] and his Colour Sergeant [who may have been Archer since there was only one of this rank in each of the two companies] were also 'horribly frightened' when a huge 100 pound shell landed between them.[106]

Archer completed his letter giving an account of events since Christmas on 2 February, from Wagon Hill. They were in communication with the relieving column by signal and had been for some time. He did not know when they would be relieved but thought it was about time something was done. 'We are getting shorter of rations every day and our daily food at present is one sixth of an ounce of coffee, a quarter of a pound of trek ox or horse and half a pound of biscuits. Sometimes we get bread. We expect to be left on the line of communication to recruit our health etc.'[107]

Then on 1 March at five o'clock in the morning he wrote to tell his mother that the relief force had arrived during the night, 'so our hard work is over for the present.' They had suffered a very bad night in the rain and once again had become soaked to the skin. He was still enjoying good health considering the way he had been living recently, but he must none the less have been feeling weak, because he thought he would not be able to take a long walk. When the 1st Battalion of the Rifle Brigade, who were part of the relief forces, reached Ladysmith they reported of the 2nd Battalion that they 'were clean, but their appearance told of the hard work and privations of the siege.'[108] He expected to be at Ladysmith for another three weeks and then go, with the other regiments, to the lines of communication somewhere in the Colony until they could get fit again. He did not think this would take long once they were given plenty of good food. His daily rations were now a quarter of a pound of biscuit, three ounces of maize meal, one sixth of an ounce of tea or coffee, three quarters of a pound of horse meat and 'Chevril, a kind of Bovril made from horse flesh, which is nearly always bad'. As he remarked, this was 'not much to keep any one in good condition.' He was now using his last piece of paper and envelope so he did not know when he would be able to write another letter.[109] Others commented on the chevril and the way in which horses that were 'on the point of falling down dead from starvation', were shot in order to make chevril from their carcasses. Some found it 'was most sickly, and often by the time it reached [them] it was fermenting. It was dyed mauve, as an encouragement I suppose.'[110] Many found it preferable to the 'cow-heel jelly', made from horse hoof, and quite palatable. For example, Dr May recorded: 'They have killed a lot of horses. As a result we had chevril (horse soup)'; 'Had some choice chevril. It was delicious and very strong.' 'This chevril (they make it very strong) cannot be beaten for nutriment. Sometimes the messes get prime horse meat at the butchers and mince it fine, season it well and call it sausage meat. It is awfully good on bread but you can never get enough of it.'[111] Dr May's stomach had no doubt been strengthened by his experiences. He had spent a decade hunting whales in the Antarctic, had served with the RAMC during the Zulu War and with the British forces during the first occupation of the Transvaal and, suspected by the Boers of spying, had escaped dressed as a woman.

Dawnay, too, wrote of supplies during the siege, throughout the whole of which 'the question of food was one of the most important.'

> As regards meat, we were plentifully supplied, a full ration being issued throughout. [Archer, above, seems to contradict this, his meat ration varying from a quarter to three-quarters of a pound during February.] The last month or so horseflesh became a part of our daily fare. Chevril i.e. Bovril, with horseflesh substituted as an ingredient for beef, was also issued for the last four weeks to supplement our

daily ration. This concoction, if consumed when quite fresh, was fairly good, but went bad very quickly, and was then unapproachable. Another delicacy, which was made on the premises and supplied to the hospitals, was mule's-foot jelly.

The scanty stock of vegetables only lasted for the first two or three weeks, and after that we had to do without. Vinegar was issued towards the end of the siege, and in some way made up for the deficiency; it was known as the 'anti-scorbutic' ration ...

The bread supply lasted in an extraordinary way, but gradually disappeared, giving way to biscuit [which] also slowly dwindled away, till it assumed the almost imperceptible proportions of quarter rations, i.e. one biscuit and a quarter. Mealies were our only other staple food, in fact most of the time mealie porridge was the sole means we had of a comfortable sensation of repletion. Luckily for us it was only shortly before we were relieved that this supply failed.

Clothes and boots constituted another of our difficulties. We were able to procure a certain amount of khaki drill, with which for a time we managed to patch up our uniforms, but this supply failed eventually, and then we bought up any fancy trouserings we could find in the town, and this produced some comic results, as may readily be imagined if one conjures up to oneself the sight of a rifleman on duty in lavender green continuations.[112]

Gough reported that his men were 'painfully weak' and looked 'pinched and worn.' They had been on constant duty for twelve weeks since arriving at Wagon Hill and had got soaked three nights out of every four. Vegetables were hardly ever seen, there was no water for washing and dysentery was rife. Gough found the horse meat steaks 'capital', while Dawnay found mule meat a 'luxury' and biscuit fried in wagon grease a 'welcome change.'[113]

Although Archer had heard Buller's approaching guns on Christmas Eve, it took over two months for the column to succeed in relieving Ladysmith. It was a long drawn-out, disappointing time. One of the nurses at Intombi recalled that there had been so many rumours of Buller's advance and so many acute disappointments, that the men in her ward made a rule that Buller's name was not to be mentioned. There was a penalty for anyone breaking the rule. Then, she continued:

Late one afternoon I saw a man shading his eyes against the sun and looking intently in the direction of Caesar's Camp, where a British regiment was encamped. I asked him what he was staring at. 'Look,' he said. He was seeing men on horseback riding over the ridge towards Caesar's Camp ... Excitement spread among us. All eyes that could stared at the moving body of men. As the column reached Caesar's camp we heard a sudden shout, and then burst upon burst of shouting from the soldiers stationed there ... then we knew! this was really the much-longed-for Relief Force.[114]

On the first day of March the general advance on Ladysmith began. The 1st Battalion of the Rifle Brigade and the 60th Rifles led the infantry. During the afternoon General Lyttelton rode into Ladysmith, and the 1st Battalion 'had the great satisfaction and delight' of meeting their comrades of the 2nd Battalion. On 3 March the relieving army advanced and marched through the town of Ladysmith, 'the Light Brigade bivouacking at the foot of Surprise Hill, the scene of the exploit of the 2nd Battalion on December 11th 1899.'[115]

After they were relieved at Ladysmith, the Rifle Brigade moved to 'a place euphoniously named Arcadia, some seven miles south of Ladysmith', on 16 March, to recuperate from the siege. They camped at Vaalkranz for a couple of nights, and then returned to Arcadia before moving back to Ladysmith on 12 April. During the next five months they were kept very much on the move, marching to Modder Spruit, Tinanyoni, Sunday River, Quaggerkirk Farm, Calabas, Ingagane, Rooipynt and Newcastle, where they stayed two months from 4 June to 4 August. At Newcastle they were engaged in 'three days of turning operations' and manned fourteen posts around the town. They then went by train to Sandspruit and marched on to Meerzicht, Amersfoort, Vaal River, Rietspruit, Ermelo, the source of the Vaal, Witbank, Twyfelaar - resting there for two weeks - Van Wycks Vlei and Geluck Farm, where they arrived on 23 August. In the course of these travels, they shelled, burnt or pulled down a number of Boer farms, and gathered the Boer women ready to be taken in wagons to concentration camps.[116] The burning and pulling down followed incidents in which a Boer had taken up arms again after he had surrendered, and after a patrol had been fired on from a farm flying the white flag. The justification, in Gough's view, for sending Boer women and children to concentration camps was that it solved the problem of feeding the civilians when it was difficult to feed the British soldiers, and prevented the food that was distributed by the British being given to the Boer commandos in the field.[117]

Four days after arriving at Geluck farm, the Battalion was engaged in the Battle of Bergendal.[118] The immediate setting for this battle has been outlined by Christopher Martin:

In the eastern Transvaal, the British effort now was to close the road that led to Komati Poort, which was the point of entry into this country from Portuguese East Africa, and the place where the Boers received their slender supplies that still came in from outside. Sir Redvers Buller had been ordered north and he met with Lord Roberts at the town of Belfast, a few miles west of Machadodorp on the railroad. The object was to move east, rolling up the Boers in front of the British line. For these operations Lord Roberts had some 8700 men and 82 field pieces, while in defence General Louis Botha had 7000 men and 20 guns. One last battle was fought at Bergendal, and although the Boers fought valiantly they could not hope to win. They fell back, giving up Machadodorp, and then the Boer army collapsed as a fighting force.[119]

This battle, that took place east of Belfast on the railway route from Pretoria to Delagoa Bay was the last set-piece fight of the war. Commandant-General Louis Botha's Boer forces had established a 'complex of positions on a line of hills, north of the railway, many protected by marshland.'

> The ridge carrying the railway was held by the ZARP, the [Johannesburg] police, based on a kopje at Bergendal Farm. General Sir Redvers Buller took their position after heavy shelling, and the ZARP were wiped out. With their left flank undefended, the Boers could no longer hold the line and Botha ordered a withdrawal, which was followed by guerrilla warfare.[120]

The enemy occupied a surprisingly strong position, extending from Bergendal along the railway to Dalmanutha four miles to the east. The position was a 'series of carefully-prepared entrenchments, commanding kopjes strewn with huge rocks.' The first kopje was the key of the position and it was to be very difficult for the Rifle Brigade, 'with not even an antheap as cover', to take it. 'But the General said it had to be done, and the Rifles, with the Inniskilling Fusiliers in support, did it magnificently.'[121] On 27 August the British force moved 'upon a high ridge which runs from Belfast on the south side of the railway towards Dalmanutha ... and directed the fire of all our guns upon Bergendal Farm, the kopjes of which apparently formed the left of the Boer position.'[122]

> The final action began at 10.0 a.m. After an hour or more of rifle fire on the right of our advance, the guns opened up at that moment

on the kopje and its neighbourhood. [This bombardment was made by 38 heavy guns firing at a range of 4000 yards and supported by 24 Artillery guns at 2500 yards.] The enemy's guns and 'pom-poms', despite the attention paid to them, kept shelling during these two hours, while the Boers within rifle range on the right maintained a steady fire ... About noon, seeing that the kopje had to be carried at all costs, General Buller directed Colonel Metcalfe to extend his Rifle Brigade in front, and take it by assault, the Inniskilling Fusiliers acting in support.

The Rifles deployed, company after company, like a machine. They found themselves at once under a hot fire from the kopje ... The crucial moment came when the leading line got to within four hundred yards of the kopje. The way was then over ground as flat as a billiard table, and at the other end ... rose the hill, more commanding than ever. The firing became deafening as the devoted band nerved themselves for the last rush ... Then came the final rush of the Rifles ... At the moment the rush began the Artillery nerved themselves for a grand effort. Shells rained on the kopje, and a salvo from the howitzers dropped, with sickening precision, six lyddite charges in a line amongst the rocks. It was more than flesh and blood could stand, and the Boers broke. Not all of them went then, however. Sixty or seventy remained some minutes after the Rifles' final charge began, their bullets finding billets in many a brave fellow ... They too, when the stormers, leaving dead and wounded dotting the veldt, appeared over the crest, realised that the bayonet was already at their breasts, and bolted through the rocks to the back of the kopje, where they took shelter in a cattle kraal immediately in the rear. They were found with their 'pom-pom'.

The Rifles had done magnificently. Bounding up the kopje, bayonet at the 'ready', they found they were too late, and that the set-off to this incomparable charge and a loss of over one hundred killed and wounded was a dozen dead Boers and as many prisoners. [A newspaper correspondent] rode over the field to the kopje as the firing ceased, and saw the dead and wounded as they had been stricken down ... the sight of the field, and the dead bodies of the enemy on the kopje - among them some shredded remains of what had been a man, until a lyddite shell had burst close to him - were eloquent of what war meant.[123]

The Rifle Brigade's losses were heavy. An officer and thirteen men were killed, and ten others died later from their wounds. Metcalfe, six other officers and 57 NCOs and men were wounded, many of them severely.[124] Total British losses were three killed and 107 wounded. Private E Durrant was awarded the Victoria Cross for rescuing a wounded soldier under fire. The Johannesburg Police lost 67 killed and seven wounded and captured.[125] 'As a force, the Zarps had been annihilated.'[126]

Deneys Reitz was also at Bergendal and gave an account of the events there, from the Boer side:

> The British advance started early one morning on a broad front. We of the Pretoria Commando took up a position in the nearest kopjes, but before long we were so heavily shelled that we withdrew, the other commandos also falling back. The direction in which the English were moving was east along both sides of the Delagoa Bay railway line. Up to now this way to the Portuguese port had been open and the Transvaal Government had been importing supplies on a large scale, but apparently Lord Roberts intended to close this final loophole and cut us off completely from the outer world.
>
> Accordingly great numbers of troops, apparently more than 30,000, moved to right and left of the railway, sweeping us easily before them. They were spread fanwise over a distance of 15 miles, and as the usual curtain of scouts approached, followed by shellfire from the guns moving up behind, we pursued the same methods that we had employed in the Free State, falling back from hill to hill and rise to rise, firing when opportunity offered, but not really fighting. In this manner we retreated for four or five days, by which time the English had pushed us along the railway line through the town of Middleburg, and right up to Belfast village 40 miles beyond. On the night we reached this place there was such a press on the road that in the dark I lost the Pretoria men. By next morning they were nowhere to be seen, but, as I was getting accustomed to quick changes of commando, I joined a body of Boksburgers who happened to be passing ...
>
> I trekked from Belfast to Dalmanutha, another 40 miles up the line. After being marched about for some days over mountainous country, we were allotted a position on the edge of the escarpment near Machadodorp, where General Botha intended making a stand athwart the Delagoa railway.
>
> Along this crest he was going to fight a last pitched battle before taking to guerrilla war. All through the retreat we knew that sooner or later it was planned to break away before the English advance and scatter in smaller bands, and this knowledge had kept the men in

good heart ... The position General Botha had selected was a natural fortress. Between us and the enemy there stretched a level plain that could be swept by rifle fire, and immediately behind us the ground fell steeply into a valley, giving excellent cover for men and horses. We were practically on the furthest rim of the high veldt, for a few miles back the country drops into the malarial lowlands that lie towards the Portuguese border. The British had come to a temporary halt at Belfast, and for a week there was no sign of them. Towards the end of that time, while I was working on the defences, I saw the Pretoria Commando come riding up ... and I at once took leave of the Boksburgers in order to join them.

The Pretoria men were given a portion of the line close by [to defend], and at sunrise on the next day heavy dust clouds arose in the distance, and before long masses of British infantry appeared on the skyline.

They were calculated to be 36,000 strong (but it is difficult to count infantry on the march), and within an hour their skirmishers were firing, and their batteries were unlimbering almost within rifle-range of us.

By ten a heavy bombardment was in full swing, although no actual advance was attempted, as they evidently intended first to batter down our works.

This lasted until sunset, but our cover was so good that the casualties were nowhere heavy, and the Pretoria Commando went scot-free. By dark it had all died down, and we passed a quiet night lying around our fires. Next day the programme was repeated. We were shelled to such an extent that one dare scarcely look over the edge of the breastworks for the whirring of metal and the whizzing of bullets. Several of our men were wounded ...

In the afternoon a detachment of infantry came down a defile on our left. We saw them in time to drive them back, killing and wounding about fifteen, but owing to the crossfire we could not reach the fallen men until some time after dark, when we groped our way to get their rifles and equipment. The night was so cold that we found only three soldiers alive, some wounded who might otherwise have survived, having died of exposure. We carried the three men back, and laid them by a fire, where one more died before morning.

As soon as it grew light on the third day, the bombardment recommenced more furiously than ever, but, instead of being spread all over our front, it was concentrated on that section held by the Johannesburg Police, a mile to our right. Tremendous gunfire was pouring on them, and from the massing of the infantry columns we knew that a crisis was at hand. The police behaved splendidly. Twice they threw back the attacks, and hung on doggedly under some of the fiercest pounding of the war ... By sunset the [Johannesburg] police were all but annihilated, and in the dusk we saw the English infantry break into their positions. Here and there a hunted man went running down the slope behind, but the majority of the defenders were killed. Our line being broken, we had to give way too, and after dark General Botha ordered a withdrawal. We fetched our horses from the valley below, and fell back for two or three miles before halting for the night.[127]

Archer described Bergendal as 'the last real stand and battle of the South African War, the break up of the ZARPs and the last time the sword (bayonet) was used.'[128]
The day after the Bergendal battle, Archer marched with the Rifle Brigade east to Machadodorp, then north to Helvetia, the Krocodil River at Badfontein - where they were shelled by Boer 'Long Toms' – and Witklip, and arrived at Lydenburg on 7 September. Here they were made one of the garrison battalions, encamped south of the town and were shelled from the east. Large numbers of Boers surrendered to them. After Bergendal there were no further major battles, and the final phase of the Anglo-Boer armed conflict was a guerrilla war. 'There was interminable movement, with raids and guerrilla action by the Boers, and attempts to capture and contain commandos by the British.'[129]
On 30 October Archer's Company, with four other Companies 'took part in a night attack against Schoeman's Laager, which was captured.' This raid was accomplished without the Rifle Brigade losing any men. They then went to Middleburg where they were stationed for six months, during which Archer, Acting 'RSM of a mixed Force including Boer National Scouts' took part in all night operations with mounted troops under Colonel Bell-Irvine.[130]
The London Gazette of 19 April 1901 announced that Archer had been awarded the Medal for Distinguished Conduct in the Field in recognition of his gallant conduct during the operations in South Africa.[131] In particular, the award would have been for his conduct on Surprise Hill. The DCM was one of Britain's highest military honours, second only to the Victoria Cross. It was awarded to Non-Commissioned Officers and Warrant Officers for distinguished conduct in battle. Captain George Paley, now recovering from the wounds in his chest and hip and about to undergo the last of several operations, had already written to him from

London to say 'You have been mentioned [in despatches] I hear on every possible occasion, which is only what I expected, but I hope it will mean some substantial reward.'[132] Paley now wrote to Archer's mother to say how pleased he was with the award: 'I must write to you a few lines to congratulate you on your son being awarded the Distinguished Conduct Medal ... It is only what he deserved and also what was expected for him, but it is none the less satisfactory now that it has been gazetted so that all can see how well he has done.' The Rifle Brigade had earned more awards than any other Regiment.[133] Archer had also been mentioned in despatches three times: twice in the field - at Ladysmith and at Bergendal. He had spent the whole of the South African War on active service and was awarded the Queen's Medal with the Ladysmith, Laings Nek and Belfast clasps, and the King's Medal with two clasps.[134] He had been offered a sergeant majorship in Thorneycroft's Mounted Infantry by the Deputy Assistant Adjutant General, Captain St Aubyn - with whom he had served in Mashonaland - and agreed to accept it if his own regiment would release him. In the event he was 'shut up in Ladysmith so lost [the] appointment, i.e. if Battalion would have allowed [him] to accept.'[135] At some stage during 1900, too, General Hutton, commanding the 1st Mounted Brigade, applied for him to be appointed RSM of the Mounted Infantry, but again the application was not successful. During 1901 Alderson, now a General, who succeeded Hutton, also applied for Archer to be appointed RSM of the Mounted Infantry but received the reply that he could not be spared.[136]

On 1 June 1902 Archer learned that peace had been signed at Pretoria the previous evening. 'The Anglo-Boer War was over after two years and eight months of hard fighting by two armies ... The number of Boer casualties is not known with any accuracy ... British casualties of all ranks and from all causes, killed, wounded and died of disease amounted to 52,156 of which many more died of disease, particularly typhoid, than in battle.'[137] In the calendar year 1900 alone the 2nd Battalion of the Rifle Brigade lost 68 NCOs and men dying from dysentery and typhoid - 32 of them in February and March - 65 killed in action or dying from wounds, and 143 were wounded and were invalided or recovered. The war had taken a very heavy toll of them.[138]

Two days after the peace was signed, Lieutenant Davies,[139] three NCOs and seven Riflemen left for England to represent the Battalion at King Edward VII's Coronation. A month later, 100 Reservists left for England under Captain Paley. During July and August others, mainly time expired men, also left for England. Archer did not think he would be returning to Britain for some time, and on 17 July he wrote to his mother:

We are still uncertain to what part of the world we are to be sent, all sorts of yarns going about, but at present we are to remain at Middleburg. Several of our officers have gone to England on leave. I don't see much chance of my getting any leave for some time. Have had a cold lately, the first for several years. I think I caught it undressing to go to bed, not being used to it for several years. I saw an account in the paper of Captain Paley's wedding. Shall send him a wedding present as soon as I can get one made. Shall get a part of one of the shells fired at Ladysmith made up into something. Have you seen Major Lowndes or heard if he has left for here again? ... Of course I can do very well without him or in fact any officer, have been so long without one except in name. At present I have three on the strength of my Company. All of them are in England so don't trouble me much. Should very much like to get a Captain like Captain Paley. Makes everything so easy ... It would be good to be at home now the fruit is just getting ripe. We never see any here.[140]

Lowndes had taken over as Company Commander of G Company when Paley was wounded at Surprise Hill and Harington was wounded at Caesar's Hill. In the interim, Archer had been given charge of two sections of G Company - and probably thought he made a better job of doing so than did Lowndes of the whole Company. If Archer did not particularly like Lowndes, the feeling seems not to have been mutual. In replying to Archer's letter of condolence when Mrs Lowndes died in 1909, Lowndes referred to him as 'My dear Sergeant Major Archer' and 'a very dear old Comrade' and spoke of 'dear old G Company in the 2nd Battalion and all the happy years I spent in the Regiment'[141].

On 5 September 1902 Archer left for Pietermaritzburg with his battalion. They arrived there three days later and were accommodated in huts. Three weeks later still they left for Durban. The following day, 25 September, they embarked on the RMS *Malta* and departed the next day at noon for Suez.[142]

Just as the Mashonaland campaign in 1896 and the Omdurman expedition 1898 had provided conditions that had been hard, dangerous and uncomfortable, but had none the less marked significant progress in Archer's career as a professional soldier, so now, the South Africa War in 1899-1902 had added further equally physically hazardous but professionally rewarding experience.

The *Jeluga,* which had carried him down the east coast of Africa, broke down four times on its way, he was sea sick, and the 2nd Battalion's landing at Durban was in rough seas. Without a break, they were rushed to Ladysmith in the pouring rain and immediately were thrown into the battle of Lombard's Kop. They had been able to have very little rest for days on end. As the siege took hold there were grave shortages of food, and, as in Mashonaland, their clothing fast wore out. They were often cold, soaking wet and hungry. They were constantly under threat of bombardment from the Boers' heavy artillery. But they did not allow being under siege to become a passive affair, for they embarked upon a number of active military engagements: Observation Hill, Thornhill's farm, the Platrand, and - particularly important and dangerous - Surprise Hill. Once the siege was lifted, they moved on to march long distances, often under fire, and to fight further battles, including those at Bergendal Farm and Schoeman's Laager. Archer was fortunate to escape the death, wounding, capture and sickness suffered by so many of his colleagues.

Yet the Boer War also provided experience that furthered his career as a professional soldier. As the wounding of a worrying number of commissioned officers depleted the leadership levels, Archer was made Acting RSM and given command of two sections of two companies: he was, in effect, Company Commander. Three separate applications were made by senior officers for him to be appointed substantive RSM of Mounted Infantry regiments. But it was his extraordinary leadership during the withdrawal from Surprise Hill, in pitch darkness, that was the most outstanding of all his service in South Africa. With Paley, he led the bayonet charge at the foot of the hill. When the captain was very badly wounded, and despite the presence of at least three uninjured commissioned officers, he unhesitatingly, almost automatically, though some of his colleagues thought cheekily, took over command, brought order from chaos, instilled discipline into a developing rabble, gathered the straggling men from several units together, and led them back to safety in the camp. He undoubtedly saved their lives, and this was recognized not only by his fellow sergeants but also by Captain Paley and, it appears, by Colonel Metcalfe. Few Distinguished Conduct Medals can have been more deservingly awarded.

CHAPTER SIX

THE RIFLE BRIGADE - EGYPT, THE SUDAN AND INDIA: 1902-1908

By mid October 1902 Archer had arrived in Cairo, having left a number of men with scarlet fever at Aden on the way. He learned later that one of the young men left there had died: 'He was quite a youngster, only just joined us before we left South Africa. Some of the youngsters we have got now should never be abroad.' Since they had no more cases they were allowed to go into the Citadel Barracks, on arrival. He was very busy and had not had a moment to spare since he got there.[1]

> Very old Barracks, plenty of bugs etc. Expect to move into better Barracks (Kasr-el-Nil) in January.[2] I have got very good quarters for this place, with boarded floor, next to the Quarter Master's office and above the store, all the others are stone.

The weather was splendid and 'the Season' had just started, but he did not expect many visitors. 'The cholera will frighten them off', though the number of cases was declining and only two areas of Cairo were out of bounds to soldiers. He was not surprised that there were outbreaks of cholera. When he had to march a party of men through part of Old Cairo the smell was the worst he had ever experienced, 'quite like Omdurman two days after the battle.'[3]

He wrote of the reverse in Somaliland but did not see much chance of his being sent 'as only black troops are being employed.' He did volunteer for service there and was told that application would be made for him to go at the first opportunity. But it was not to be: 'Unfortunately Expedition came to a close.'[4]

> We are very busy at present trying to learn to be peace soldiers, and to forget all the lessons that we have learned during the last few

years. At present we are equipped and clothed for active service, but I expect in about a month's time we shall be model soldiers again, with polished straps, clothing etc.

He was, it seems, becoming nostalgic for the more active life: 'Everyone in the Battalion, except the married men, would be glad to get back on active service again.'[5] 'No shooting now except practice, which a few of us get on Saturday mornings.[6] Indeed, he had written to Gough - now commanding the King's African Rifles - in Somaliland, asking if he could approach General William Manning, Inspector-General of the KAR, to help get him posted to Somaliland. Gough replied on 24 January 1903:

> If I can ever do anything for you I shall be delighted if only in remembrance of old times on Wagon Point and King's Post. But I am separated from General Manning and it takes letters three weeks to reach him and by that time we will be in the desert so that I can't do anything at present. When I meet him I will see if I can do anything about getting you out, as for all we can tell this business may go on for months, as the Mullah is a slippery gentleman and he can bolt south to friendly tribes. If he does this we may or may not follow him up but if we do it will be a very long job. I don't think the Somali is a great fighter, anyway the ones we have on our side are damned funks and probably the others are much the same.[7]

A year later when Archer wrote, as president of the sergeants' mess, to congratulate him on his promotion to Colonel, Gough replied:

> It is nice to know that one is remembered by ones old Battalion. Personally I am not likely to forget the times we had together in Ladysmith and elsewhere. I dare say you remember our night on Surprise Hill as vividly as I do.[8]

He had a new company commander whose knowledge of practical soldiering did not impress him. He was just out from Britain, had recently finished a course at the School of Musketry, 'and of course he knows plenty of theory':

> He told me the other day that I was wrong. I knew I was wrong according to the Book but right practically, and I explained how the method laid down could not be done on service. He then asked me why they should teach one thing and do just the opposite when on

service. The only answer that I gave him was that the people who wrote the books do not as a rule go on service but only see their idea carried out with blank ammunition and it looks well.

Perhaps realising that there was little point in being bitter, and preferring to turn his mind to more immediately important matters, he cut short this line of reasoning and ended his letter by telling his mother, 'the Tea bugle has just gone', and signed off.[9]

Mildly despairing of the quality not only of some of the officers but also of some of the soldiers, and of the role of ill-informed politicians and the denizens of the War Office, he showed other signs that he was feeling things were not what they used to be:

> I should like to see officers commanding companies have more power in recommending a man for discharge as useless. The Battalion Commanding Officer at present has the power to do this but very rarely recommends a man for discharge and then only when he is a thorough criminal. Men who cannot shoot, march or do anything that a soldier should be able to do, very rarely get discharged as long as they do not commit any serious offence. I often wonder if any MP who takes an interest in the service has ever gone to the non-commissioned ranks and found out their views on Army Reform ... I do not mean the advice of an NCO who has spent all his service at home, but of one that has seen them under all sorts of conditions.[10]
>
> I wonder when the War Office will do anything for the army. It seems at present as if all they want is to get a big army on paper; 90% of them being useless for an arduous campaign, and yet they get the same pay as a thoroughly efficient soldier. Nearly all the men that joined us just before we left South Africa and since we arrived here are either in hospital or in prison.'[11]

His mother sympathised and, taking an even more extreme view of declining quality, could 'understand how he felt about the disheartentingly poor quality of private soldiers, judging from the specimens who joined the army from this place ... At present Parndon has too many imbeciles and cripples for a place its size, they want clearing out.'[12]

He even found the Rifle Brigade annual *Chronicle* - started in 1890 and to which he had contributed from time to time - deteriorating, and that of 1902 the worst he had ever seen.[13]

Part, possibly the major part, of this unsettled feeling that he was experiencing was the relative inactivity after the past fifteen years during which he had led a very active life - in Ireland in athletics and thereafter on active service overseas. In May 1904 he ran in a veterans' 200 yards race at the local sports which he won by 20 yards - a margin he may well have felt reflected the declining quality among younger athletes. It was the first time he had run in a race or put on running shoes since he left Ireland - and in the meantime, at the age of thirty three, he had become a 'veteran'![14] Another part was the lethargy of living in an enervating climate:

> We have been having some very hot weather lately, it has not been under 100 degrees in the shade for over a month. My bunk, which is about the coolest in the Barracks, has a temperature of 90 to 96 in the daytime and 86 to 92 at night, so you can tell it is not the sort of weather to give one much energy. We expect it to get a bit cooler next month, as the sun will be a long way north of us. At present it is directly overhead. Of course one cannot do much now.
>
> We generally have a parade at 6.0 a.m which lasts about an hour or a little longer, by which time everybody looks as if he has had a bucket of water thrown over him, change, have breakfast, at which one gets nearly wet through again. After breakfast, lectures, signalling, or various other things that keep one employed until about 11.0 a.m when you return to your bunk, properly washed out, get into flannels, spread out a blanket on the floor and try to keep cool until luncheon at 1.0 p.m. After luncheon same thing, try to find a cool spot and perspire and doze until about 4.30 p.m. when one gets a cup of tea and another wet through. Then parade, office work, school or a walk until about 9.0 p.m. Supper, billiards, cards etc. and dozens of minerals until 11.0 p.m. then bed and sleep, if the sand flies and dust storms will only let you, with only a sheet over you until daylight again. I weigh just the same as I did when in Ireland and in strict training. There are no fat men here.[15]

He could not play cricket in the warmer weather because the asphalt pitch became so hot in the sun that it melted. Nearly everyone was covered in prickly heat. There were several cases of sunstroke, two of them fatal. Some time between 4 May 1904 and 24 May 1905, probably in October 1904, he and his colleagues moved to Khartoum,[16] where he seems to have found life generally depressing. In referring to a person at home, he said, 'I expect he has got the same disease as some soldiers get especially in places like this - melancholia.'[17] His old Colonel, Metcalfe, now a Major-General, wrote to express his sympathy: 'It is pitiful to think of you all being tucked away at Khartoum when you ought to be in London or at some very large station in India.'[18]

None the less, he found diversion and enjoyment in his rifle shooting. In 1903 he came third in the Championship Army Rifle Meeting and the following year came first, receiving distance medals for 200 and 600 yards, the Championship medal and Lord Cromer's special prize. He enjoyed, too, the sports meetings and the picnic river trips on the Blue Nile that the sergeants arranged.[19]

Formal education was important to Archer. We have noted how he felt he had not learned much when he was at school at Harlow, how he attended school at the Castle at Fort Burgoyne within a year of joining the army and had been awarded the Third Class Certificate of Education, and how he had been awarded the Second Class Certificate in April 1892. He had started to study for the First Class Certificate in 1897 but the burden of work forced him to discontinue. Since then there had been gaps in his education due to active service overseas, but, now things had settled down and he had little else to challenge him, he began to study hard again for the First Class Certificate. He recognized that it would not be an easy task: 'The examination for a 1st class certificate is very difficult for anyone who has not had a fairly good education, or has neglected to keep up what one learnt at school.'

There were two parts. The examination to be taken towards the end of October 1903 consisted of arithmetic, military manuscript and dictation, while those to be taken in March 1904 consisted of the history of England and geography. He privately repeated the importance that he attached to the certificates: 'If I can manage these two examinations I shall be eligible for any promotion in the service and may yet finish my career as Captain Archer.' His mother hoped he would not find the examination very difficult, and she was thinking about him a good deal: 'As you have been so successful through life, and got through so far, I believe you will master this if God gives you health and strength.' He in fact passed one part of the examination 'fairly well', though it seems he did not take the second part.[20]

In October 1905 the Battalion returned to Cairo.[21] A few months before this, in June 1905, Archer learned that they were to be moved to India and would be stationed at Chirata in the Himalayas, about 90 miles from Simla. He very much enjoyed the return to Cairo, where the weather was 'splendid':

> Had a very good journey except between Khartoum and Wady Halfa, and Shellel and Luxor where it was too dusty to be pleasant. Visited

the temples of Abu Simbel which are hewn out of solid rock on the bank of the Nile. Also Philae which, as the dam was open, was not covered with water. [Paid] a visit to the Assouan dam, it is a wonderful piece of engineering.[22]

When they arrived at Cairo they were kept very busy in preparing for a Board of Survey of all their clothing and equipment, ready for their transfer to India at which time the Indian Government would take over everything from the home government.[23]

He was getting a little concerned about his future prospects in the Rifle Brigade, and this, too, may have been a partial cause of his feeling unsettled. The years were passing. On 25 June he wrote optimistically to his mother to say: 'I think it almost certain that I shall be promoted QMS when the vacancy occurs, as our present QMS told me a few days ago that if he got promoted Quartermaster he would ask the Commanding Officer for me as his Quartermaster Sergeant.'[24] But four months later his optimism disappeared and he was despondent:

> At present I do not see much chance of any vacancy for promotion occurring in the Battalion (at least not in time for it to do me much good) so that if things do not alter I shall probably come home after about twelve months in India, and try and get a Sergeant Majorship of a Militia Battalion or even a Volunteer Battalion. Our present Sergeant Major has just extended his services for another five years and there does not appear much chance of anything else.[25]

At the end of 1905 the 2nd Battalion went to India, sailing from Suez on the SS *Assaye*,[26] and were stationed in the United Provinces. Early in March 1906 Archer wrote to his mother to tell her:

> We move to Chaubattia on the 20th. At present there is about eighteen inches of snow there, but it will all be gone before we reach there ... Soldiering in India is much different from what it used to be, according to what I am told by men who have been out here several years. Lord Kitchener is making everyone buck up ... and from what little I can see it was about time someone was appointed in command who does not see the reason why some silly thing should be done now just because it was necessary fifty years ago. I expect you have got over the General Election by now ... About the only thing that affects me is: Are the Liberal Government going to increase the pensions? Our Orderly Room Sergeant who left us just before we left Egypt, to

go on pension has been appointed Messenger to the House of Commons at £100 a year rising to £150. Just the billet that would suit me.[27]

He had been in the army for 17 years and was committed to a further 13 years' service. The prospect of a job such as his colleague had secured as Messenger to the House of Commons, would have to await his retirement. In the meantime, he was irritated by what he saw as declining standards at the top, and the ineffectiveness or irrelevance of politicians. These were not new feelings but they did seem to make promotion increasingly important to him. He was in touch with Captain White, with whom he had fought in South Africa and who had been wounded, placed on half pay and stationed at the Rifle Brigade Depot, Winchester.[28] During June and July White urged him to apply for promotion posts outside the Rifle Brigade, where internal competition was fierce:

> Captain Cooke tells me there will be a vacancy in the London Rifle Brigade in August and he thinks you would probably get it. Don't forget that you are not registered here yet and if you are not on the list the job will go to the senior 60th NCO. Of course, I can't say that you will get the job but you would have a very good chance.[29]
> I hope you have sent your name in for the Volunteers as Lord Bingham tells me he is applying for you by name to fill the vacancy which occurs about the middle of August. This ought to be a good job as the London Rifle Brigade is one of the best Corps in London.[30]

Despite this urging and the support of a number of very senior officers, Archer, ever proud of his regiment, preferred to persist in hoping for promotion within the Rifle Brigade. He did not apply for the London Rifle Brigade appointment, and, as White had warned, it went to another by virtue of seniority. It could so very easily have been his, had he applied:

> The LRB appointment has now been given to the senior Colour Sergeant of the 60th. I am not at all sure that you are doing a wise thing in relying on the recommendation for Sergeant Major. Your name is on the list which I am told has over 100 names on it already, and in addition to this you must recollect that there will be 10 Sergeant Majors from the disbanded battalions to be absorbed. You *might* get an appointment, but what I want to impress on you is - don't rely too much on this.[31]

Archer shortly explained this reference to the disbanded regiments and the significance for his promotion prospects:

> Breaking up the regiments by Mr Haldane has I expect put my promotion back for some time as it puts 10 Sergeant Majors without regiments, and of course these will have to be found employment before there is any chance for me. At present the only chance of promotion is if Mr Haldane brings in the Under-Officer system.[32]

None the less, he persisted and asked to be posted back to the Depot where, presumably, he felt he would be more in the eye of those responsible for promotions and would stand a better chance of advancement than he would in India: 'It is, I know, very difficult to hear of things in India. Most of the good jobs go to men serving at home.'[33] White, at the Depot, though still keen to help, was far from convinced, and advised him to think about it carefully:

> As regards your future, I would strongly advise you not to come here; there is no prospect of anything in the way of promotion. The Sergeant Major has just extended for another 5 years and although he may be going shortly to one of the big schools the next Sergeant Major will come from the 60th. The Rifle Brigade QMSgt has no intention of leaving for many years. Re Militia, I don't see much chance ... If you do leave the Battalion, I fancy the Volunteers give the best chance, but a good Corps is essential ... If you decide on registering for the Volunteers, let me know and I will of course do anything I can.[34]

We have seen how Archer had toyed with the idea of writing up his Mashonaland experiences in to a book, but did not do so. In India in 1906 he did write a book, *The Colour Sergeants' Guide*, though, again, it did not see the public light of day: 'Not published. Messrs Gale and Polden wanted £2.2.0 to print each copy. I saw later that they had taken some of my tips.'[35] In view of the fee the publishers demanded to print the book, it must have been of sizeable proportions.

One of the highlights of his service in India was the visit of the Rifle Brigade, with other Battalions, to Agra to welcome the Amir of Afghanistan to that city. They had just finished hill manoeuvres at Chaubattia: 'very hard work but everyone was very fit and [they] had good weather so everything went off very satisfactorily.' It was getting very cold in Chaubattia and they had some hail that cleared the air and afforded splendid views: 'The view of the mountains is now better than I have seen them before. They only look about 6 miles away.' As he told his mother: 'We leave here for Shahjahanpur about 12th November and then go to Agra about 2nd December for the durbar and manoeuvres ... We shall be back in Shahjahanpur before Christmas.' In the event, these arrangements were altered. They left Chaubattia on 13 November and stayed at Shahjahanpur over Christmas and the New Year. Early in January they went to Agra to welcome the Amir and after that they were to return, conducting manoeuvres on the way: 'We are going to march and fight every garrison we come across. This will take us about a month.' He was looking forward to visiting Agra and to the manoeuvres.[36]

At Shahjahanpur he 'had a day's duck shooting with the officers [and] got the biggest bag vis. 24.' He was looking forward to some tiger hunting. The health of the men on the whole was good and they had very little sickness. At the moment only one of his men was in hospital out of 107 - with something wrong with his ears. One of his married Riflemen and his little daughter had died: 'His wife has been well looked after and sent home. Besides other monies, everyone in the Battalion subscribed a day's pay for her, which amount should be a great help to her.'[37]

He recorded, in his diary notes, his experiences at the durbar that welcomed the Amir to Agra:

> 6 January. Paraded at 9.15 and marched to Shahjahanpur station en route for Agra. 7 January. Arrived Agra. Country not up to much. Camped on rifle range. 8 January. Lining streets for Viceroy. Native princes very smart especially the cadet corps. Bikanirs carriage drawn by six camels. 9 January. Guard of Honour to Amir. Battalion lined streets. Amir does himself well. Escort mounted on small hill ponies. Got wet through. Generals in galore. 12 January. Review 33,000 troops. Fine reception by crowd. 13 January. Church Parade. Could not hear a thing. Visited Taj. 18 members of mess had photo taken; bags of medals. Taj wonderful. 14 January. Played hockey for Battalion ... Amir looked on for a short time. Troops in MO [Mounted Order] etc. etc. Went to Bioscope [cinema]. 15 January. Parade under OC Companies, more trouble. Football match PIP v KRR. Three fights. Gurkhas very keen on our medals, had admiring crowds around us vis. S M Townsend and self. 16 January. Secundra. 17 January. Fort wonderful.[38]

After the manoeuvres during their return from Agra to Shahjahanpur they arrived back late in February. A month later the Battalion moved back to Chaubattia, but Archer stayed at Shahjahanpur as Sergeant Major of two companies, so he was preparing himself for a 'hot time' from the point of view of both work and weather. He did not mind the hard work, especially since he was in good company: the other Colour Sergeant left with him had been his 'chum' ever since they enlisted together so he was sure they would 'get on all right together, which means a lot.' Shahjahanpur would not, he expected, be as hot and uncomfortable as Khartoum had been, but he would rather have gone to Chaubattia. At the Battalion Sports he ran in the veterans' 220 yards race but was penalised 20 yards 'so as to give the others a chance.'[39] He was still recognised as a formidable athlete; he captained the Battalion teams from 1905 to 1908 and coached the young soldiers' teams.[40]

For a while he was indeed bothered by the heat: 'I have got a fine lot of prickly heat, look as if I have been partly boiled.'[41] This was the hottest summer for about 30 years, according to an old civilian, and the newspapers said it was ten degrees hotter than the average. 'Everyone here is suffering from prickly heat or boils. I have got the former but not very badly.'[42] Once the monsoon broke, however, life became more comfortable and he felt more energetic:

> We had some Aquatic Sports last week. I swam in the 100 yards and won. This is the first swimming race I have swum in since Belfast when I won the marble clock [16 years earlier]. I also swam in the Relay Race for my Company and we won ... I am going to Chaubattia in September for shooting in the Battalion team for various cups and competitions. Expect to stop there a fortnight or three weeks.[43]

He felt even better after three weeks' holiday in the hills during September. He took a few days rest because he had been hit on the right shin with a hockey ball. The holiday was a relaxing and enjoyable break: 'My Company entertained G Company 43rd Light Infantry here for three days, which made quite a nice change. We beat them at shooting (I made top score of both teams), swimming (of which I won my events) and tug of war ... We also had a very successful concert.'[44] He was free of the prickly heat: 'The holiday to the hills quite freshened me up ... I weigh 10 stone 12 pounds without clothes, plenty heavy enough in tropical countries.'[45]

Christmas 1907, however, was a rather mixed affair, part disappointing and part fulfilling: 'I had rather a hard Christmas. Took 70 men to Lucknow for three days to play a series of games with the Oxford Light Infantry. Saw nothing of the sights as my time was all taken up either by playing games or looking after the men.' On the brighter side, he was presented with the Long Service and Good Conduct Medal on General's Inspection early in January by General Spens, who made 'quite a long speech on [his] splendid record.'[46]

In a way, though proud of the award, the Long Service and Good Conduct Medal served to increase his ongoing frustration about promotion, which grew during his time in India:

> No change in the Battalion. The only Colour Sergeant senior to me leaves on pension in October but this makes no difference to me, as he is not in possession of the necessary certificates for promotion. The next senior to me is going home about the same time. He has been appointed Instructor to the London Irish Volunteers.'[47]

He was still strenuously exploring opportunities for promotion. The Colonel told him that if he heard of any vacancy for a Sergeant Major he would use his influence to try and get it for him, but would be very sorry to lose him from the Battalion.[48] On behalf of his fellow Senior NCOs he wrote to General Wilson to offer their congratulations on his recent promotion, and mentioned his own prospects, including enquiries about a Staff appointment. In thanking Archer for the letter, the General said, 'I will certainly do all I can to help you, if I hear of anything that would suit you.'[49] He wrote, too, to his old battalion commanding officer, Metcalfe, who replied:

> I will of course be glad to do anything I can to help you to promotion, but I cannot do very much, except strongly recommend you, which I have just done to Sir Neville Lyttelton [of the Rifle Brigade, who had commanded the British 2nd Brigade at Omdurman, and who had led the ride into Ladysmith the day it was relieved], who of course knows you well, and I so much hope that something may come of it. I have also written to Captain George Paley who is in the department of the Chief of General Staff at the War Office.[50]

In reply to a similar approach from Archer, Dawson, who had commanded G Company in 1902[51] and was now second in command of the Leicester Militia Battalion, wrote:

> I am so sorry your prospects in the Battalion are not very bright at present, and if I hear of anything I shall be very glad to do what I can, but I am so out of things now I am afraid I cannot do much. I am writing to Mrs Dawson's brother-in-law who is Brigade Major at

Bordon, asking him if he knows of anything, and strongly recommending you. It is, I know, very difficult to hear of things in India. Most of the good jobs go to men serving at home. Major Butler is coming here soon to stay with us, and I will ask him what he thinks. He is much more in touch with everything now than I am.[52]

Then he wrote to congratulate Colonel Gough on his recent appointment as Inspector-General of the KAR in succession to Manning, and took the opportunity to mention the question of promotion. This approach was to turn out to be an important one, and significantly more fruitful than the other approaches he had made. Gough replied:

I was very glad to hear from you and you may be sure that I will remember you if an opportunity turns up. At the present moment there is nothing going but things move quick in Africa as you know. The job that might turn up is Sergeant Major to one of the Native Battalions. The men are good and there is always an off chance of some fighting. The pay comes to about £230 a year (and you pay for your own rations). I do not know if you would care for a job of this sort, but in the event of a vacancy occurring I will let you know and you can decide then. You would have to take on for three years! ... I see you have anticipated my promotion; being no doubt a better judge of my value than the War Office, you promoted me to be a Brigadier-General.'[53]

Whether his mistake as to Gough's rank was diplomatic or inadvertent we do not know, but Archer was much taken by the possibility that had been put to him: a Sergeant Majorship in one of the African Battalions. He did not tell his mother that he was seriously considering it: 'About coming home, if no promotion turns up to enable me to get home before, I shall put in for the Home establishment. This will get me home anytime between November 1908 and March 1909.'[54] In writing to his brother, Harry, however, and explaining that while the immediate prospects were poor, he was optimistic about the outcome of the numerous approaches he had made to senior officers, and he went further in the case of the Africa possibility:

Nothing very stirring here at present, but we hope to have a small war up on the NW frontier about next November, and as we have such a good Battalion there is every prospect of our going there. I received my Good Conduct Medal on the 7th, this makes my 7th medal. At present there does not seem much chance of promotion especially as the Government are to disband so many regiments. If we don't go on service at the end of the year, and nothing fresh turns up, I shall probably come home about next January. I have great hopes of getting something by then as several Generals are trying to get me something. I may get an appointment under the Colonial Office in Central Africa. The pay is fairly good (about £230 a year) but of course the country is not very good (but there is always a chance of getting some fighting). Would not do for a youngster straight out from home. I have not yet told mother about this last billet.[55]

As events turned out, he accepted the offer of appointment to Central Africa as Regimental Sergeant Major of the 1st Battalion of the King's African Rifles, and by the end of July 1908 he had told his mother. He later explained that from 1890 to 1911 there had been only two Regimental Sergeant Majors in the Rifle Brigade and the junior of these had been promoted in 1901. 'I left the 2nd Battalion in 1908 as there appeared no prospect of the Regimental Sergeant Major ever retiring.' Early in August he wrote, 'No news yet of when I start for Africa', and a week later: 'Still no more news of my going to Africa. Of course I know it will take some time, as there is so much red tape and so many offices for it to go through before it reaches me.' He had already told his mother he would have 'two boxes of trophies' to send her to look after while he was in Africa.[56]

There was indeed a good deal of red tape and there were indeed numerous offices to be negotiated, but in fact the processing of Archer's transfer did not take very long. In the middle of August Gough wrote to him to say:

> Official instructions re your appointment as Sergeant Major of the 1st Battalion KAR are being sent to you through the War Office ... About your kit and equipment ... these things are usually supplied direct by us at home, but as you are in India we cannot do this, so we are arranging to advance £16.10.0 (or £17, I forget which) to you for the purpose of bringing your own kit etc. This is the sum that the kit costs at home and I expect that the price will be, if anything, slightly less in India. I would recommend you to invest in a pair of gum boots, as they often come in most useful. I hope you will like your time with the KAR and I am sure that the credit of the Rifle Brigade

will be well maintained. As far as I can see there is no immediate chance of service, but one never knows in Africa. As for the men, I like them very much and think they would compare favourably with any native regiments I know. I expect to be out in Nyasaland in April and I hope I will find you looking fit and well.'[57]

When he received this letter, he wrote to his mother and gave fuller details of his new appointment, which up to this point had been rather vague:

I have been posted to the 1st Battalion King's African Rifles, they are stationed at Nairobi, East Africa ... From what I can hear Nairobi is quite a large town and has a white population of about 500. There are also about 400 European farmers scattered around that district, so for a start I am not going far into the wilds.'[58]

What did not strike him, it seems, was that 1 KAR had moved from Nairobi in British East Africa - Kenya - to Zomba in Nyasaland in July,[59] when they exchanged stations with 2 KAR, even though Gough spoke of seeing him in Nyasaland, when he wrote to him in mid August. Zomba was a much smaller station, and there were not many more than 400 Europeans in the whole of Nyasaland at the time and fewer than 100 - virtually all civil servants - in Zomba District.[60]

On the first day of October the Battalion in India left on manoeuvres, but Archer stayed behind, for he was getting ready to sail for Africa. Before he left he had 'quite a unique send off from the Battalion. The CO had as strong as possible parade and told everyone to take a pattern from me etc. etc.'[61] He left Chaubattia on 7 October, Lucknow on 20 October and sailed from Bombay three days later. It was very hot in Bombay and he was glad to get away. By this time he was clear that he was sailing for Chinde and was going to Zomba in Nyasaland.[62] He was formally transferred to the 1st Battalion of the King's African Rifles, in Nyasaland, and promoted to be Regimental Sergeant Major on 23 October. His annual salary on appointment was £156 plus £36 a year duty allowance and three shillings and sixpence a day ration allowance. He sailed on the SS *Kanzler*, a German boat belonging to the German East Africa Line. Two days after sailing they called at Goa but did not land. It had been 'a very pleasant voyage up to the present, not so hot as on land.' He had a first class cabin as there were very few passengers, and he dined in the second class saloon. The living was 'exceptionally good.'[63]

Having crossed the line on 1 November they arrived at Mombasa two days later. He went ashore and found the area 'very pretty', taking a walk to the other side of the island with 'a Mr Forbes of Klerksdorp, a Scotchman, who was the only other decent second class passenger.' The journey so far had been good but the ship was a very slow one. He had occupied his time on board principally in reading. They left Mombasa the same evening and the ship 'pitched a lot' on its way to Zanzibar, where they arrived the next day. Here again he went ashore with Forbes as soon as it got cool enough, and drove to the Sultan's palace. He dined at the Tippoo Tip Hotel with Mr Tata, headmaster of the Government schools, had another walk and spent the rest of the evening at the Africa Hotel. The following day they sailed at 7.30 a.m. and arrived at Dar es Salaam at noon. He took several walks around the town that afternoon and the following day, and then boarded the RPD *Burgenmeister* at 9.0 a.m. the next morning. They left Dar es Salaam at 2.0 p.m. and arrived back at Zanzibar at 5.30 p.m. On 10 November they left Zanzibar in the late morning and arrived at Chinde on 13 November 1908, almost exactly a year after he had first heard from Gough about the possibility of his becoming a Sergeant-Major in the KAR.[64]

CHAPTER SEVEN

THE KING'S AFRICAN RIFLES NYASALAND AND SOMALILAND: 1908 - 1914

Chinde, on the Indian Ocean coast in Portuguese East Africa, was the port of entry for Nyasaland. It was situated on a shifting sand spit on one of the mouths of the Zambezi river.[1] The journey inland was by shallow draught stern-wheel steamer to the confluence of the Zambezi and Shire rivers, and up the Shire for three to six days to Port Herald, or four to seven days to Chiromo, or five to ten days to Katunga's, depending on how much water there was in the river.

From Katunga's to the settlements in the Shire Highlands the journey was by road but, after 1907, from Port Herald and Chiromo it could also be by rail.[2] In the 1890s and very early 1900s three factors combined to persuade the Government to build a railway from the Lower Shire to the Shire Highlands. First was the fluctuating level of the Shire River that made navigation difficult, and beyond certain points impossible. Second were the persistent pressures from expatriate planters whose agricultural labour costs were high when there was also heavy demand for labour to carry goods and produce between the highlands and the head of navigation on the Lower Shire. Third were the determined representations made by the Scottish missionaries that head porterage, especially by children and women, and particularly on the very steep slopes of the escarpment between the highlands and the river, was inhumane. From 1901 to 1903, the British Government contracted with the Shire Highlands Railway Company to build a railway from Chiromo, at the confluence of the Ruo and Shire rivers, to Blantyre. A further fall in the level of the Shire, however, caused the contract to be extended from Chiromo to Port Herald further downstream. The Port Herald to Blantyre line was opened on New Year's Day, 1908, less than a year before Archer's arrival.

Having reached Chinde in November 1908, Archer recorded the events of the next fortnight in his diary:

> 13 November. Arrived off Chinde - British Concession, gets washed away at the rate of 30 feet a year – 4.0 p.m. Transferred at 6.30 to a small tug by basket. [Because the sea was nearly always rough, passengers were transferred in a large basket by crane from the deck of one boat to the deck of another.] Very rough. Arrived at Chinde about 8.30 p.m. Record not sea sick during voyage or crossing bar. Very rough crossing bar. Went on shore at own risk about 9.30 p.m. Too rough for boats. Took no kit. Stayed at Murray's Hotel. Proprietor a very nice fellow.[3]

The basket mentioned by Archer - and in which he probably very much enjoyed being 'transferred' - was well described by Elsa Green who travelled, as he had, to Beira at the time of the Mashonaland rebellion in 1896:

> A crane lowers the large, bell-shaped arrangement. It has a door in the side, to admit passengers two at a time. As soon as the door is shut and a signal given, the strange conveyance rises from the tug and swings over the ship's decks. The caged occupants are [just] as rapidly lowered and landed, occasionally with a considerable bump, on deck. When once safely landed, it is some amusement to look over the taffrail and watch the other passengers passing through the ordeal. Some of them shrink from it until the very last.[4]

On 14 November Archer reported to the British Consul, Stanley Fletcher,[5] who gave him an advance of £5. He left by the stern wheel steamer, *Centipede*[6] at 5.30 p.m. The Captain was Mr Tennant[7] and the passengers included Commander Edmond Rhoades,[8] Mr Henderson, Dr and Mrs Cahill and Mr A M Ryley.[9] They anchored for the night at 10.0 p.m.

The following day, as they proceeded upstream, they ran aground several times, once for an hour, because the river was very low at this time, the end of the dry season.[10] The country was very flat, there was not a single hill in sight, and there were very few large trees, though 'plenty of reeds etc.' Henderson, who had been in Mozambique nearly 20 years and had 'travelled over nearly all this part for the Portuguese Government', told him that only small portions of the country were fit for cultivation, mainly sugar, even when irrigated. As they moved slowly further upstream the country became covered with scrub and the river banks higher, standing some 20 to 30 feet above the water. He was told that the river overflowed its banks during the wet season. There was 'hardly any population.' On 16 November he saw some hills for the first time, and passed sugar plantations and mission stations. The soil began to look more fertile. He saw several hippopotamuses and many crocodiles, the largest of them being about 12 feet long. The Captain fired a few shots at the crocodiles but did not hit any of them. On 18 November the passengers transferred to the SWS *Scorpion*,[11] and shortly they entered the River Shire. Two days later they transferred again, this time to small houseboats, 'steel flat bottomed boats drawing about six inches of water, with a small shelter built aft to accommodate two passengers, light baggage stowed in bottom of boat.' The boat was punted along by eight men, four on each side, who 'got along when there was sufficient water at a fairly good rate.' There was now 'plenty of cultivation, all native' and it was very hot. The river banks were about 15 to 20 feet high and the river was about 430 yards wide. His military topography training enabled him to estimate the width of the river with such apparent accuracy. He continued his diary:

21 November. Arrived at Port Herald about 3.0 p.m. Very hot. [I am leaving here by train early tomorrow morning for Blantyre and expect to arrive there the same night. I have only got two days' marching to do then to reach my destination.[12]]
22 November. Thunderstorm in afternoon made it much cooler.
23 November. Entrained at 6.0 a.m. Arrived Blantyre 4.30 p.m. Put up with Mr K Metcalfe.[13] Country fairly flat; afterwards commences to rise until Limbe is reached and then slightly downhill to Blantyre. Line [from Limbe to Blantyre] not properly completed. Distance about 130 miles. District around Chiromo thick bush, very little cultivation, but on nearing Limbe one passes a lot of coffee, tobacco and cotton farms. There is also a lot of native cultivation.

On 24 November he left Blantyre at half past eight in the morning and arrived in Zomba nine hours later, covering a distance of about 42 miles. He had expected a two day march, but he was in fact carried in a machila, a hammock hung between two or four poles, by twelve men all the way. The machila men normally trotted or ran as they carried their passengers. On this occasion, sharing the work in three teams of four, they carried Archer at a speed of five and a quarter miles an hour: 'Not bad travelling as I stopped an hour for lunch.[14] When he arrived in Zomba, Major

Stevens, the KAR Adjutant, invited him to mess with him until they moved, 'orders having been received to proceed to Somaliland.' He thought this 'very good of him, as it saved 'a lot of trouble and expense.'

The King's African Rifles was an imperial force maintained in the Protectorates of Uganda, British East Africa, Somaliland and Nyasaland. The 1st and 2nd Battalions were raised in Nyasaland. It was officered entirely by secondments from British regiments for a period of years. Two of these officers were from Archer's regiment, the Rifle Brigade: Captain J Rosborough and Lieutenant H T C Jones-Vaughan. The KAR in Nyasaland had attached to it an Indian Contingent lent by the Indian Government for three years, under officers of the Indian Army.[15]

In a letter written to his mother the day after he arrived in Zomba he told her of his arrival and said he expected to be in Nyasaland for a very short time and to leave for Somaliland, on an expedition against the Mullah, quite soon, indeed before Christmas. He did not know if they would get any fighting there, but he hoped they would 'as it will mean my getting a Warrant Officer-ship.' He thought Zomba was 'a very nice place'. He was already finding it a great disadvantage not knowing the local language, Chinyanja, because few of the soldiers could speak any English, but he expected he would soon pick it up. There were no other European NCOs with him, but the officers were making him very comfortable - as had the Adjutant when he arrived - and he added 'I think I shall like this appointment.' He said he would want his mother to do some shopping for him as he would have to pay for his own keep after his return from Somaliland. Later he wrote to her from Somaliland to follow up this request.[16] He had sent an order to the Army and Navy Stores in London to forward enough food for about 18 months. By doing this he saved about £20 on a year's food as everything was 'so expensive in British Central Africa.' He was arranging for the goods to be forwarded to Berbera, in Somaliland, and from there it would not cost him anything to get them taken to Zomba. He wanted his mother to get him some curtains for his bedroom and sitting room, and some material to make up into small curtains for the glass doors and other windows.

> My house in Zomba is like a small villa: bedroom, dining room, sitting room and bathroom with kitchen built about 20 yards away. I have got crockery, knives, forks etc. but expect I shall find I have forgotten something.[17]

Although he was now thirty seven years old, this was the first time since leaving home almost twenty years earlier, that he had lived in a proper house and needed to equip and furnish it. It was a new experience but one that he seemed to take in his stride and indeed relish.

On his first full day in Zomba he had to go on parade in civilian clothes because his kit had not arrived. He drilled the recruits and reservists and found them much better than he had expected: 'Marking time exceptionally good. Dressing not good - too close together.' At the musketry drill with the reservists the following day he found some very good shots. He was impressed by the condition of the soldiers' rifles, which were 'very old but very clean, hardly any corrosion and no groved chambers or muzzles.'[18]

There seemed to be a degree of uncertainty about the move from Zomba to Somaliland, because for a while there was a rumour that it was cancelled. The rumour soon died down and the advance party was sent off on 24 November.[19] Theirs was not the first expedition to Somaliland, for there had been earlier campaigns in 1901, 1902, 1903 and 1904. The cost to Britain of these last two expeditions was great. In monetary terms the cost was five million pounds, and in human terms 'the lives of many valuable British officers whom our small professional army could ill afford.' Gough had been awarded the Victoria Cross for his bravery in rescuing a badly wounded fellow officer during the third expedition. On the credit side 'the tide of rapine and murder' had been stemmed and they had driven from British territory 'the megalomaniac who had been rapidly ruining his fellow-countrymen in his efforts to further his insensate personal ambitions.'[20]

> [The] Mullah accepted Italian protection in March 1905 and was allotted an area on the Mijertein coast not far from Illig. This agreement was afterwards recognised by the British Government. Although outwardly peaceable during the three years he spent in Italian Somaliland, the Mullah soon opened intrigues with the Dulbahante and Warsanglu tribes. Reports reached Berbera that his agents were constantly at work, seeking to undermine the loyalty of the tribes in British territory and to convince them that one day the Mullah would return and wreak vengeance on all traitors to his cause. In 1908 the exhausted state of the grazing in the Mullah's sanctuary near Illig gave colour to the rumour that he was contemplating a return to British Somaliland ... The prospect of another expedition was viewed by the Government with great distaste. Control of the Protectorate had been transferred from the Foreign Office to the Colonial Office in 1905.[21] Since that date the constant battery of complaints against the authorities at Berbera

Eliza Archer

Thomas Archer

Jack Archer, c 1885

Jack with athletics trophies, Ireland, 1895

Lieutenant-Colonel
John Gough 1904

Major Harold Biddulph
1904

Jack, Acting Regimental Quartermaster Sergeant, Malta, 1897

Jack, India, 1907

Merseburg Prisoner of War Camp, Germany, 1914-1918.
Jack, front row second from left

Muriel Pike, 1917

Jack, at Bisley, 1929

Jack, with shooting trophies, Zomba, 1938

Jack, in Masonic regalia, 1939

Muriel, 1939

Jack, in Prison Superintendent' uniform, Zomba, 1934

Jack, in King's African Rifles uniform, Naiwale, 1944

showed clearly enough that his intentions to be regarded as the ruler of all tribes in the interior were still alive.[22]

In September 1908 it became clear that the Mullah was fast becoming very short of food, and it was understood that he planned to kill and eat all his remaining stock before the beginning of Ramadan at the end of the month. The British thought that as a consequence he would be forced to leave Illig and go on the offensive by attacking the garrisons in British territory. The Government, though deeply reluctant to become involved in fresh operations, decided to reinforce the 6th Battalion of the KAR, the Somaliland Battalion, with 1500 troops from Aden, the East Africa Protectorate, Uganda and Nyasaland, 'to ensure the safety of Burao and the line of communication with Berbera.' The 6th Battalion was only 700 strong and was deployed - very thinly spread - to hold Hargeisa in the west and Sheik, Burao and Ber on the main caravan route.[23]

> 1 KAR was called upon to contribute headquarters and three companies. As it was the home service battalion at the time, Nyasaland was left with a garrison of 100 sepoys of the Indian Contingent and a single African company. The rest of the battalion, numbering six officers and 300 men (of whom 113 were reservists) under Lieutenant-Colonel H A Walker (Royal Fusilliers.) [who, as a Captain, had been with 1 KAR during the third expedition against the Mullah in 1902-3[24]] disembarked at Berbera on 6th January 1909.[25]

Some four years or so earlier, Archer had volunteered for service in Somaliland with the fourth expedition and had been told that he would be sent at the earliest opportunity. He had also asked Gough to approach Manning to get him posted there. In the event, the expedition was withdrawn and he did not go. Now he was looking forward to redressing these past disappointments and going to Somaliland at last.

Archer's first visit to Nyasaland was indeed short. Only two weeks after arriving in Nyasaland, he left with his battalion, most of its officers and 328 askari, for Somaliland. On 9 December they left Zomba and marched south to Namadzi, a distance of about 17 miles – 'splendid soil, covered with trees'. The next day they marched to Limbe, a further 23 miles, in under eight hours, including halts – 'plenty of cultivation and plenty of small streams.' They spent 11 December at Limbe, and the following morning they boarded the train at seven o'clock, arriving at Port Herald nine hours later. Here they embarked on the SWS *Centipede*.

Four weeks earlier, before the rains broke, the river was much shallower and this section had to be covered in small flat-bottomed, punted, houseboats. Now it could be covered by a stern wheeler. The troops were carried in four barges pulled by the *Centipede*. On their way down the Shire, despite the higher water, they ran aground several times but the troops soon pulled them off the sand banks. On 15 December, they passed Shupanga, where Mrs. David Livingstone was buried. Archer saw several hippos, and he and the officers went ashore to shoot buck - unsuccessfully. They arrived at Chinde, 'ankle deep in sand', on 16 December. He stayed at Dishington's Hotel, paying twelve shillings and six pence a day for his board, excluding the cost of drinks. He told his mother:

> This is a very expensive place to live at all decent under twelve and six per diem which means that I am ten shillings out of pocket every day we stop here, but I must not grumble as I still get allowed two shillings and six pence per day whilst on board ship in lieu of rations, and of course it costs me nothing.[26]

On 23 December, early in the afternoon, they embarked on the 6200 ton *Prinzessen*, the largest of the German East Africa Line vessels, pitching a little as they crossed the bar. The officers travelled first class and Archer second class.[27] Presumably the troops travelled either on deck or in the hold. On Christmas Eve they arrived at Mozambique, and he commented: 'The old fort is used as a prison. One white German man in it doing about 20 years for murdering British Vice Consul at Beira.' The murderer is described elsewhere as a Hungarian-American mule-seller, and his victim was J E McMaster, the British Vice-Consul at Quelimane, who refused to lend him money. McMaster had been Postmaster-General of British Central Africa from 1894 to 1897.[28]

On Christmas Day Archer left Mozambique at noon and was pleased when 'Colonel Colville CB, late Rifle Brigade, and Captain Sladen sent [him] a bottle of champagne.'[29] Archer did not think much of the way the Germans decorated the ship for Christmas: 'Christmas tree in second saloon but only bom boms, candles and flags on it.' Over the following six days they travelled north, calling at Zanzibar - where he went ashore in the evening and had a walk round the town with Mr Tata, the headmaster whom he had met there on his way from India - and then Dar es Salaam, Tanga - where he 'went ashore and walked over nearly all the town' - and Kilindi Harbour, where he 'walked to Mombasa and back' to the ship. On New Year's Eve they had 'a bit of a concert in the saloon, and the bar had an extension to see old year out and new year in.' On New Year's Day they crossed the equator and Archer commented on the fact that the 'Germans do not keep up the custom of Neptune coming aboard.' On 4 January they passed Cape Guardafui: 'Very desolate looking country'. Early in the morning of 6 January they arrived at Berbera - 'quite a small place' with very few trees and lots of sand. They disembarked and bivouacked nearby. He commented on the number of camels and the camel tanks from which they were watered. He received ten days' rations and orders to equip himself with two months' supplies. It was a very busy day.[30]

Those whom he accompanied from Chinde to Berbera were: Lieutenant-Colonel H A Walker, Major H W Stevens of the Reserve of Officers, Captains H A Case and G C Sladen, Lieutenants G G S Brander, R Hoffmeister and R H Pipon and 328 Askaris.[31]

With the eye of a soldier trained in military topography and well experienced in the field, Archer described in his diary his first week in Somaliland and the country through which he travelled, its terrain, ease of marching, water resources and game as a source of both food and sport:

> 7 January. After a busy morning loaded camels (102), march about 3.0 p.m. Very hot. In charge 1 Section C Company. Country flat sand, shingle and covered with a low scrub ... Did only 10 miles but then only arrived after dark: loads coming off.
> 8 January. Marched to Byendula ... nearly all the day through ravines with rocks 100 feet to 200 feet high on both sides. A very little scrub on hills. Only animals seen were monkeys. The latter part of journey along bed of stream. Should not like to march through this place in the summer. Good springs, water a little salt.
> 9 January. Marched to Lower Sheikh. Very good day for marching. Missed Colonel Gough as we took a short cut. Rained in the afternoon and nearly all night. Water very bad. It even made me sick. Country sand, stones and covered with thorn trees. Plenty of sheep, goats and some camels. Also saw some gazelle. Looks a good place for shooting.
> 10 January. Marched to Upper Sheikh, about 7 miles with a rise of 2000 feet. Sheikh is about 6000 feet above sea level. A very healthy place. HQ of 6th Battalion KAR. Sergeant-Major Bloomburgh put me up during my stay. Servant Luba from Fort Johnston.
> 11 January. Marched to ? . Slightly down hill. Sand, scrub and rock.
> 12 January. Marched to Burao about 20 miles. Longest halt 20 minutes. Saw several dik dik [small antelope] and plenty of spore of larger antelopes.[32]

The day after Archer reached Burao, he wrote to his mother and told her that he had arrived there, having marched from Berbera in 6 days. The country was 'something like the Sudan round Omdurman but more scrub and bushes.' He expected to leave Burao on 19 January but not to get any fighting until after the arrival of 3 KAR from East Africa on 26 February[33] and 4 KAR from Uganda. He was in charge of the two - later, during the remainder of the campaign, all four - Maxim guns.[34] His comments included some on his changed personal circumstances as the Regimental Sergeant Major:

> I had a very pleasant voyage and a fairly good time here although some of the marches were long and hot. I dined with the officers of the 6th Battalion KAR last night, and the night before with my Commanding Officer [Walker] and Adjutant [Stevens]. I find it a great change from previous expeditions especially in the amount of kit I can get carried. We, that is, the officers and myself, have to provide our own food. I have got about 300 lbs of tinned stuff, enough I hope to last me three months. There is a rumour [we are] leaving here tomorrow.[35]

On Monday 25 January 6 KAR, the Somaliland Battalion, left for Ainabo about 11 miles east of Wadamago, and on 22 February - after six weeks in Burao - 1 KAR followed them. On the way Archer saw 'plenty of game especially dik dik.' At Ainabo, the water was good and the men 'had a good wash and washed their clothes.'

He told his mother that he did not know how long they would stay at Ainbo but expected it would be a week or so. This was 'a desolate, god forsaken country' and so far as he could see no one appeared to know why the Government spent so much money on it. The only reason he could see was to prevent Berbera, just opposite Aden, being made a naval port by some other power. 'As I have been told that eventually we shall have a fight with Abyssinia, holding Somaliland means that our lines of communication for several hundred miles would be through our own country.' He continued, again commenting on his changed circumstances:

> This is different from all other active service I have been on before. In the old days I had to carry a heavy kit, got bad food, had very long marches on foot and was very badly paid for it. Now I only carry very little kit, at present I supply myself with food, but shall soon have it supplied to me (same as the officers receive). Have got a horse to ride and a camel to carry my food and kit, and I hope to be

able to save at least £100 a year. Of course one does not have an easy time of it as we are so very few white men and that means plenty of work. I walked as far as Burao but as I had so much work to do Major Stevens gave me his horse. He has also got a trotting camel and the horse did not suit him: it suits me. I have to employ a syce (groom) to whom I pay 5 rupees per month. I also have to pay for a servant to cook etc. for me (10 rupees). I have also to pay for their food, which I don't expect will come to very much. It is worth the expense, as I am always certain of my food, and the horse is very nice to ride especially if one has been on the go all night and marching all the next day.[36]

A week later he was still at Wadamago and did not expect to leave for another week or so, when he and his men anticipated going into the Ain Valley. 'The Mullah is quiet at present but one never knows when he may make another raid.' And the following week he was still there, uncertain of the future and of the British Government's intentions. Colonel Gough had gone to Burao to meet the Commissioner. Archer thought 'they will hang on like this until the present Government gets thrown out. They will then be able to say that the Conservatives are always getting into trouble.' He did, however, add that there was 'one satisfaction about this place, that one can save money, although anything that one has to get from Berbera is very expensive.'[37]

This was the first of a number of visits Gough made to the Commissioner at Burao.[38] The British Government had ruled out solutions that involved a full expedition to remove the Mullah or indefinite military occupation of Somaliland. The Commissioner, Sir Harry Cordeaux, was shortly joined by Sir Reginald Wingate, Governor-General of the Sudan, on a special mission to advise on which of the remaining alternatives should be adopted: complete evacuation or withdrawal to the coast. Wingate arrived in Somaliland towards the end of April.[39]

The army was slowly getting accustomed to the probability that they would be remaining at Wadamago for a long time: 'There does not seem much chance of this business being finished for some time. We have all made up our minds to stay in this country for at least a year.' 'This looks like being a long job. One thing is that I am saving money.' Uncertainty and impatience about the part that they would play in Somaliland persisted: 'No news here of what we are going to do, but everyone looking forward to a move either against the Mullah or back to our various [home] stations.' 'Still no news of our moving either way. Expect we shall hear something when the present Government either gets thrown out or settles down for another year.' Consequently, at an early stage they built a 'proper camp', which became 'quite a little town' over the course of time. This kept Archer busy, and he found the time passing quickly. The weather was changing and it was starting to warm up: 'It is beginning to get fairly warm now. The officers and NCOs just out from England feel it a good bit. They will soon get used to it.' The Mullah was still very quiet, but Archer expected he would start raiding again as soon as the troops left the country.[40]

> Nothing fresh here. I expect you have seen that a defensive policy is to be carried out. Same old thing, letting the Mullah do practically what he likes. This also means he will have more time to prepare and will be joined by several tribes who would not join him if we were allowed to advance. I expect we shall sit down here until the present Government is defeated. The only way to settle this trouble is to send plenty of troops and keep at it until the Mullah is captured or killed. It would cost a good bit of money but would be a saving in the long run.[41]

Clearly, Archer favoured the option of a full scale expedition to remove the Mullah. The waiting continued as Wingate's negotiations with the Mullah were long drawn out and fruitless. Archer felt that 'something will have to be done shortly as over 100 men of my Battalion have finished their term of service.[42]

During this somewhat frustrating period of waiting, they occupied their time in regular route marches, drills, parades, machine gun and rifle practice, sorting the ammunition and other stores and keeping their equipment and arms in good order. Archer also kept himself busy and fit by playing games - hockey and football - and by taking part in the Brigade Sports - 'Won officers' 120 yards race; prize one dozen bottles of beer presented by Colonel Gough'; taking part in rifle meetings - 'Won 400 yards, second at 200 yards, tied 150 fixed target, tied running man, won volley rapid at 500 yards, second volley at 200 yards ... won Maxim gun competition'; and in hunting - mainly dik dik and jackal. His health was good, save that when it first rained he had a bad cough that lasted several days, and a little later he was 'laid up' and 'bad with lumbago'.[43]

The British forces used a large and varying number of 'friendlies'. These were Somali groups, some of them very large, and individuals opposed to the Mullah and willing to fight against him, either on their own account or for the British, but in either case for the loot they hoped would fall to them. They were required to hand over some of the loot, especially bullocks, which Archer slaughtered to supply his men with food. They joined the British forces on military exercises and manoeuvres - 'We are having plenty of parades with friendly Somalis acting as an enemy, so everyone is up to all their little dodges' - and much of the actual fighting was in fact left to them.[44]

Using friendlies so extensively had many disadvantages. Their loyalties were fluid. They were difficult to control. Exercising even minimal supervision over them was a troublesome matter and engendered internecine rivalries - sometimes encouraged by the British - with uncertain outcomes.

Early in October the friendlies at Bohotle made a successful raid south to Gerlogubi, capturing a large number of camels and rifles and killing several more dervishes. This so pleased them that they thought they might capture some more, but their further forward movement was unsuccessful. At the end of a day's march they had just watered their camels when the headman received news that a strong party of dervishes was quite close. He made a zareeba for his stock at a well, and leaving a small party to take care of them, went out, attacked the dervishes, defeated them and seized their rifles. During his absence another party of dervishes attacked his zareeba and captured his stock. They then formed an ambush 'which of course the joyful raiders walked into' on their way back to the well, losing about 60 men, all their stock and several rifles. They scattered, and for several days parties of them sought the security of Bohotle. Archer did not expect they would ever know the true number of casualties.[45]

> In my last letter I told you we were making a forward movement. We only went as far as Badwein, to which place we had to go by forced marches owing to our friendlies striking. It appears that the Political Officer (Captain Dawnay) had collected about 1500 friendlies at Badwein with the idea, with our assistance, of making a raid into the Nogal Valley. They were promised all loot i.e. camels, ponies etc. that they captured, but this [it] appears did not suit them. They also wanted to be paid which of course could not be thought of. Consequently, the same afternoon, they proceeded to fire off their rifles, a lot of the bullets falling into the 6th Battalion camp. We received a message at about 3.30 p.m. to proceed at once, reaching Badwein about 10.30 p.m. having marched all the way in square. Everything quiet there when we arrived. It appears that after firing

off their rifles they split up into two parties, those who wanted payment going off, the others staying. It appears to have been an unpleasant place for an hour or so as the 6th Battalion had two Companies away on patrol, consequently were only about 300 strong. The party that remained wanted permission to go after the others and loot them, but of course this was not allowed. On the 3rd November the 6th Battalion and Camel Company 3rd Battalion left in support of about 400 friendlies for a raid into the Nogal Valley. News has just come in, 11th, that they have been fairly successful. They have captured about 100 camels, 70 ponies and three rifles. Also killed six dervishes ... The friendlies who kicked up the row have been disarmed.[46]

9 November. Friendlies who kicked up the row [over demanding to be paid] disarmed, except a proportion who were willing to proceed with the column. Raid near Shimber Berris.

11 November. The party 6th Battalion, Camel Company 3rd Battalion and about 4000 friendlies made a fairly successful raid. They captured about 100 camels, 37 ponies, four rifles and killed six dervishes. No casualties on our side ... The friendlies in this raid captured the ponies etc. east of Gaulo. They report about 200 dervishes in the Halin Haisimo Gaulo districts but scattered ... Several (17?) headmen killed in trying to leave Mullah. Three only escaped.[47]

The British were often unclear as to the Mullah's whereabouts and movements, and what he was up to. He and his followers continued their sporadic attacks and kept up the pin-pricks with raids on communities opposed to them, as Archer's letters and diary entries indicate:[48]

The Mullah is reported to have a force at Horsasamma about 70 miles east of here.

About 13th March the Mullah raided, 200 camel, killed 5 friendlies, 2 others since dead, about 45 miles east of here.

The Mullah has made another raid and as he could not get away with the camels he killed about 100.

Mullah reported to have detached a force of about 700 to the Nogal valley about 75 miles from here to watch our movements. Reported capture of four ponies from Mullah friendlies; also fight; firing heard from Eil Dab.

8 August. Some 40 of the Mullah's men raided about 30 miles east of Eil Dab yesterday. 6th Battalion left here early this morning.

> 9 August. Mullah's men killed 40 Somalis, captured about 200 camels as well as sheep and took away women of eight different families.
> 26 September. Have just heard that some of the Mullah's men have made a raid near Bohotle last night. Camel Company, 3rd Battalion left this morning.
> Mullah raided about 200 camels and killed five friendlies and hamstrung two others about 25 miles east of Eil Dab two days ago.
> About 40 spearmen reported between Burao and here. Convoys will have to keep their eyes open.
> Mullah's men made attack on friendlies and killed 13. Supposed to be 200 strong of whom 100 have rifles.

Archer's letters and diary entries also indicate that the British were none the less encouraged by splits in the Mullah's ranks, by defections from him and by indications that he might wish to retreat or seek peace:[49]

> The Sheikh's followers are now reported to be fighting with a part of the Mullah's force.
> The Mullah wants peace but nothing is known what is going to be done ... I hear the Mullah has sued for peace. His followers appear to be discontented. If they give him peace now he will only raid again in a couple of years' time as the only way in which he keeps his followers together is by raiding stock etc.
> Everything is quiet here now, the Mullah being at present in Italian Somaliland about 14 days journey from here.
> It appears that the British Government wrote to the ... representatives of the Somali Mohamadans at Mecca and stated that the Mullah had broken his word passed as a true Mohamadan etc. The [representatives] wrote a letter to the Mullah telling him to keep his word and act in accordance with the Koran. The letter was handed over to the Italians to deliver to the Mullah at Illig by gunboat and floated it ashore in a tin, (the Mullah occupies Illig) asking the people to forward it to the Mullah. On receipt, the Mullah read it out to his Sheikhs and, afterwards, turning towards the principal Sheikh, asked him his opinion on it. The Sheikh answered that they had also talked among themselves about the same thing in that the Mullah was not keeping to the Koran. The Mullah had him promptly executed. The Sheikh's tribe and some others, consisting of about 80 riflemen under the command of an old Sheikh, left the Mullah, taking with them their stock etc. The Mullah sent a party after them

to wash them out. The Sheikh, putting his riflemen to act as a rearguard, defeated the Mullah, the old Sheikh being wounded in the shoulder. The Mullah has sent out a much stronger party to try and wash out the Sheikh's party. Messenger from Sheikh asking for assistance reached Eil Dab 17th April. After sending to us, the Mullah appears to have sent a much stronger force. The old Sheikh, hearing of this, scattered his force in the bush and lots of them have joined us near here. Our friendlies are hunting for the others in the Haud, where it is thick bush.

During the last week about 400 men women and children have joined us here [Wadamago] having deserted the Mullah. The Mullah captured nearly all their camels, goats etc. also several of the headmen whom he is keeping as prisoners.

Rumour that one of the Mullah's Sheikhs has had a row with him and that he (the Mullah) promptly had him shot.

Archer was saddened to learn that Colonel Gough was having to leave Somaliland. On 2 June 1909 the Colonel issued a Special Order from Sheikh. In it he said that he greatly regretted that he had been placed on the sick list and was having to hand over his command. Before leaving he expressed his sincere thanks to all ranks for the loyal co-operation they had consistently given him in Somaliland. He added a passage that highlights the difficult conditions under which Archer and his colleagues were serving and the way in which they were coping with them:

> The conditions under which we have been serving have been trying. An enforced inactivity is about the most severe test that Troops can be put to; it tries the loyalty and discipline of all ranks. I wish to place on record my appreciation of the cheerful and soldierlike tone that has been shown throughout the whole Force. To the constant fatigues and other extra work incidental to active service have been added unpleasant climatic conditions and exceptional difficulties about the water supply, yet I cannot remember having heard any complaints, nor have I ever noticed a fatigue party not working hard and cheerfully. In fact the whole Force has acted up to the soldierlike maxim, 'The dirtier the work the more necessary it is to put one's whole heart into it'. I only regret that I am obliged to leave the country without an opportunity of seeing the Troops in a fight.[50]

He was pleased, however, with Gough's successor as Inspector-General: 'The new Inspector-General King's African Rifles is Colonel Thesiger,

Rifle Brigade. He was in the 2nd Battalion from 1889 (Dover) until 1901 (South Africa) so of course I know him well. He is a very keen soldier but has not previously served with Native troops. I hear he is not coming out at present so it does not look like any movement forward out here.'[51]

In his letters he made a number of interesting comments on the environment in which he was living in Somaliland, particularly rain and water supplies and his diet:[52]

> We have had several heavy showers of rain so the country looks much better, the camel thorn trees being quite green. We get our water from *balis* now, i.e. ponds formed in hollows from rain water, as the water in the wells now is filthy, the heavy rain having washed all the camel, sheep etc. etc. dung into the wells.
>
> Had a surprise for this country last week i.e. had our camp flooded out. Had two heavy thunderstorms in one day with very heavy rain. Our camp had about two feet of water in it. We have since moved camp, so have been fairly busy.
>
> Burao, situated about 80 miles south south east of Berbera on the Tug Dur, a river that has water in it when it rains. Several wells which appear to be fed from an underground river. Plain covered in camel thorn bushes during the dry season. No grass anywhere.
>
> Water is the great drawback of this country. From Burao to this place there is no water, so every drop had to be carried. The allowance was one gallon, officers and men; horses and mules two gallons; camels nil for every 24 hours. One gallon appears a lot but when one has to cook, wash etc. with it, it does not go far. A bath is a thing to be talked about for some time after. It is not a very great hardship to myself as I have very often had to manage on less, but anyone just out from home must feel it very much. The water at this place is very brackish and looks as if a coal heaver had been washing in it, but still it does not taste very bad when one is thirsty and the colour saves putting in so much tea into the kettle so it saves on tea ... If one had good water this place is ideal as regards weather just at present; very hot in the sun but beautifully cool in the shade. In the evening one has to put on a jersey to keep warm. I hope we get to a better place before the summer, as this place will be about the worst one could select.
>
> The weather here is fairly hot during the day, but splendid at night. Everyone in splendid health except the 6th Battalion (who are about 20 miles from here) who have had about 10% of their men down with fever. [Sergeant-Major] Townsend [who had been Colour Sergeant

of H Company in South Africa when Archer was Colour Sergeant of G Company] sends me enough mustard and cress seeds [from India] so don't trouble to send me any. I grow it in boxes under a grass shelter I have had made. If the sun gets at it, it dries up as if it had been put in front of a big fire.

Yes, I get a fair amount of fresh meat, principally goat, sometimes camel, also deer. Vegetables are our greatest need, (except good water), we get an issue of onions and Townsend sends me a regular supply of mustard and cress seeds so I don't do badly.

I have had a little shooting here [Eil Dab] and have got several good heads and skins, but am afraid I shall not be able to get them down country. Am looking forward to getting back to Central Africa where one can get plenty of fresh vegetables all the year round. I wonder how much mustard and cress I have eaten since I came to this country.

October and November 1909 was in many ways an irritating period in which 1 KAR seemed repeatedly to be on the verge of being involved in operations either directly against the Mullah's men or in support of others - militia posts, the Indian Camel Company, 6 KAR - and in disputes among Somali groups friendly to the British forces. It involved a good deal of lengthy standing by and standing down, marching from Wadamago via Ainbo and Eil Dab to Badwein, and preparing for an advance into the Nogul Valley:[53]

1 October 1909. We had quite a scare about noon. We received orders to move at 4.0 p.m. for Eil Dab as the Mullah was reported to be raiding. About 2.0 p.m. when everything was packed up the order was cancelled. It was afterwards reported that some dervishes had attacked one of our Militia posts (Yaguri), killing three men. Enemy's casualties not known. The 6th Battalion are now patrolling as far as Adad.

11 October. Reported fight between about 200 Mullah's men and Indian Camel Company under Captain Carter VC Indian Army. It appears that Captain Carter's Company had just relieved Captain Lawrence's Company 6th KAR on detachment, when returning they were fired on by the Mullah's men estimated at 200. Captain Lawrence, who heard the firing, immediately zaribered up his animals and rode to the assistance of Captain Carter. Major Ward with the remainder of the 6th Battalion hearing some firing at once collected all their ponies etc. and had just gone to find out what had

happened. They had just started when a messenger (Somali) came in to say Captain Carter was engaged and that both sides had had casualties. Standing by ready to move to their assistance.

12 October. Still standing by.

27 October. Marched to Ainabo, 2.30 p.m. Very hot.

28 October. Marched to Eil Dab early morning. About 3.0 p.m. received instructions to march to Badwein, owing to friendlies (1500) having a row. It appears they struck for pay and as they could not get it fired their rifles off. Several of the bullets dropped in the 6th Battalion camp but did no damage. We arrived at Badwein about 10.30 p.m. having marched from Eil Dab in Square. Good job it was moonlight. One lot of friendlies offered to wash out the others if they could keep their stock, women etc.

There were many blank days in Archer's diary in November; a few were marked 'Parades' and recorded a little shooting but on the whole it was a period of uncertainty and relative inactivity. Enforced inactivity, however, was, as Gough had pointed out, 'about the most severe test' that soldiers could be put to; for it 'tries the loyalty and discipline of all ranks', and must have placed a considerable burden of supervision and discipline on the officers, Archer and the other senior NCOs.

On 12 November instructions reached the headquarters staff of the KAR in Berbera 'to abandon altogether the interior of the Protectorate and retain control only of the coast. It was hoped that the Mullah would be kept in check by the tribes themselves, who were to be issued with arms for their protection.'[54] It appears that this decision was not immediately conveyed to the other ranks, though by early December it was clear to them that there was to be no further advance, and indeed that the British forces in the interior of Somaliland were shortly to be withdrawn completely:

I am still at Eil Dab. Any further advance is off at present principally owing to the row the friendlies kicked up. An Indian Battalion (Natives) lands at Berbera on the 10th. Everyone seems to think that this means our leaving this country during the next few months. There is nothing official yet but I should not be surprised if we leave this part of the country and retire on Burao, and on the arrival of the Indian Battalion there for us to march to the coast and proceed to our various stations. It is thought that the Indian Battalion will occupy various posts, forts, as far as Burao, leaving the 6th Battalion to try and prevent raids. Everyone very tired of this country especially as we have had no fighting. Expect it will mean another expedition to this place in about two years time or even less.[55]

We march to Burao on the 17th, and we arrive on the 20th [December]. Expect we shall stop there for Christmas. No definite news yet of our leaving this country, but we have sent a lot of our stores to Berbera.[56]

9 December. Marched to Ainabo. 10 December: Wadamago. 17 December: Marched from Wada 2.0 p.m., camped at Kirrett, first eight miles flat, remainder hilly. 18 December: Marched 22 miles, two marches, rocky ground, plenty of scrub and bush, also grass. 19 December: Marched 21 miles, two marches, sandy soil, remainder same as yesterday. 20 December: Marched to Burao 13 miles, country flat, sandy with camel thorn, very little grass.[57]

Early in January 1 KAR left Burao, following 4 KAR who had left just before Christmas, and began their withdrawal down to the coast at Berbera ready to leave Somaliland. Archer, as so very often, keenly observed and recorded details of the terrain on the way:[58]

7 January 1910. Left Burao. Country flat for about 10 miles, thick camel thorn, open plains with camel thorn bushes ... last part of journey uphill, rocky high hills to right, east.

9 January. Marched through Sheikh. Stopped with Sam Bloomburgh for breakfast. Camped at Wagon Rest. Bad going for camels. About 3000 feet drop from Sheikh.

10 January. Marched to Byendula, very stony, bad for camels marching. Country all rock and small bushes and trees, little grass, dak bungalow and [?] rooms. Plenty of water, underground river, comes up as a spring here, with steam on it.

11 January. Had a swim ... Water splendid. Cold after getting out. Marched about six miles through narrow gorge with stream.

12 January. Marched about 12 miles across plain with hills all round. Plenty of Dura [sorghum].

13 January. Marched to Berbera and camped near fort (3rd and 4th Battalions on sea shore.)

On 21 January 4 KAR embarked while 1 KAR loaded their baggage on lighters - a 'very slow job.' Two days later 1 and 3 KAR embarked on the SS *Pundua*, a British India Steam Navigation Company ship of about 3500 tons. Archer was pleased to have a bunk to himself. There was 'very little accommodation on deck as camels and ponies took up both well decks.' A painful tooth had been troubling him for some time and he had it drawn during the voyage: 'very hard to get it out.'

On 6 February they arrived at Chinde, where he found it very hot. Disembarking was something of a minor catastrophe, for the *Adjutant* tug of the German East Africa Line on which he did so broke her mast and got it fouled in the anchor chain of the *Pundua*. He dined at Dishington's hotel. The following day he embarked on the SWS *Centipede* and left Chinde in the afternoon. He visited Mrs Livingstone's grave on 10 February and during the next two days he had some duck shooting: 'I was very successful with Captain Hart's gun, a 35 inch barrel.' On 13 February he arrived at Port Herald and there met 'Jeffries, Scout with my column during Mashonaland Expedition. He is hunting at Chimbwe, Portuguese East Africa.' The next day he left Port Herald by rail at 7.0 a.m. The train made very slow progress because of the heavy rain and the large number of passengers. They stopped overnight at Luchenza, carried on next morning and arrived in Limbe at 11 0 a.m. Here he had lunch, and dinner at the Imperial Tobacco Company, where, he commented, 'Mr Howard and Mr Rowe did me very well.' On 16 February, he marched with his men to Namadzi, about 20 miles. On the way six men fell out, and Archer sympathetically attributed this to their 'Long march after being on board ship so long.' Unusually, he confessed to feeling 'very weary' before they finished the march. The following day they marched to Zomba, very hot and extremely stiff from the previous day's march. The Governor inspected the Battalion when they arrived in Zomba.

Moyse-Bartlett, the KAR historian, wrote of this withdrawal from Somaliland:

> On 17 December 1 KAR left Wadamago for Burao, and on 6th January 1910, for Berbera on relief by an Indian battalion. A fortnight later the men embarked for home, after a year and sixteen days in Somaliland without firing a shot or seeing a dervish. On arrival at Zomba the reserves were demobilised and the rest of the troops were sent on two months' leave ... The dispersal of the KAR from British Somaliland at the beginning of 1910 was the result of a decision taken a few months previously to abandon the interior of the Protectorate and retain only Berbera, Zeila, Bulhar and a strip of the coast. This represented a complete reversal of the policy of the previous ten years.[59]

The Somali coastal towns of Berbera, Zeila and Bulhar were now garrisoned by Indian infantry who had arrived from Aden. A few Somalis were retained as mounted police and their movements were restricted to a three-mile radius of their stations. Arms, ammunition, ponies and mules were given to the Somali tribesmen, 'who at once turned savagely upon one another to pay off old scores.'[60] For his service in Somaliland Archer was awarded the Africa General Service Medal with 1908-1910 clasp, his eighth medal.[61]

Although he had been Regimental Sergeant-Major of 1 KAR for over a year, Archer had not experienced 'normal' regimental life in Nyasaland, because, save for a fortnight, all his time had been spent on the Somaliland expedition, and even that fortnight had been taken up by preparations for the expedition. His was an unusual position, for he was the only European NCO in the Battalion. All the commissioned officers were British and all the other NCOs and men were African. His style of living - accommodation, food and leisure activities - was very much closer to that of the officers than it was to that of the other NCOs and men, in fact in most respects it was identical to the officers' style of living. It is unlikely that he was a member of the sergeants' mess, if indeed there was one, and he was not a member of the officers' mess. Yet he 'belonged' to neither group. Nothing in his diaries or letters deals with this situation, he did not comment on it and there is no indication that he was in any way troubled by it, but it must have had a considerable effect on his way of life. The African NCOs and men would have looked upon him very much as being a 'bwana' and the officers would inevitably have seen him as being not quite 'one of themselves', though they invariably treated him with great respect, kindness, courtesy and as closely as they could as if he were.

Not being on active service, and with no prospect of such service, he and the rest of 1 KAR settled themselves into a routine with route marches, parades, drills, musketry practice, manoeuvres, field days bivouacking on Zomba Mountain and other military exercises. He also trained the recruits, the band and 'casuals' at musketry, and fitted them out with uniforms. In all of this Archer played an important role as the pivotal point between officers and men. He was 'specially mentioned in the Commanding Officer's reports on the musketry training of the KAR.'[62] Of one of the field days, he said:

> Left camp with 65 men at 7.0 a.m. and ran to Mkanda, about 7 miles, arrived 8.30 a.m. cross-country, grass up to one's head. Chimanga [maize] about eight feet tall kept hitting me in the face. Arrived back at 10.0 a.m. Hockey in evening. Completely done up. No more hockey after a hard field day.

Reveille was at 6.0 a.m. the main parade was from 7 to 8.0 a.m. and the recruits' parade was from 11.0 a.m. to noon. In winter they were three quarters of an hour later.[63]

Ensuring the desired standard of discipline of the soldiers in the battalion - and, it seems, of private servants and of discipline generally in Zomba - also played an important part in his life at this time, as his diary reveals:

> 6 May. Heard a lot of shouting about 6.30 p.m. but thought it was a lot of *Tenga Tenga* [carriers] who had been paid off, until the Acting Adjutant came and told me it was our men and asked me to bike to the troop lines and find out who they were. I got 29 names. It appears that a man, Kambenzi, of my Company, C, has lately been making love to another man's wife in Zomba, visiting her during her husband's absence. Her husband heard of this and returned suddenly, catching Kambenzi and his wife on the charpoy [bed]. The husband commenced to hit Kambenzi but got the worst of it so called on other natives to assist. A small boy belonging to the camp ran back to the camp and told the Askaris who immediately armed themselves with sticks and ran into town. When they arrived the native police had arrested Kambenzi. The Askaris rescued Kambenzi and returned to camp in triumph. Result: 29 Askaris 10 days confined to barracks.
>
> 7 May. The Governor confined the [whole] Battalion to camp.
>
> 11 May. Confinement to Barracks cancelled. Three men who were the ringleaders in the rescue are to be tried by civil power but I expect they will let the CO settle the case. Their [argument] is that they are Askaris; therefore if they have got to be punished, the punishment should be given by their own Bwanas.[64]

Then on 19 June at about half past ten in the morning, the Sergeant Prison Warder reported to Archer that one of the prisoners had escaped. Archer immediately sounded the alarm and fell in all the Askari and sent them off 'in various directions' to search for the prisoner. He offered a prize of two shillings to the man who caught him. At about noon the soldiers came back, with the prisoner, and about a dozen claimed the two shillings. Eventually Archer gave 'one man two shillings, two men one shilling and a Sergeant who saved him being brought back in pieces one shilling.' The soldiers had placed a necklace of *chintechi* bean vine and grass round the prisoner's neck: 'The *chintechi* bean causes the most awful itching and lasts for such a long time, enough to drive one mad.'[65]

A few days later, Archer was annoyed when his personal servant, Dini, having used his bicycle, returned it with the pedal, brake and oil case broken, the front wheel buckled and its tyre in tatters. He took Dini before the Commanding Officer, who ordered twenty lashes, which he received the following day. It seems that Dini did not learn his lesson, because a little later he was sentenced again by the Commanding Officer for stealing four shillings from Archer, and this time he got 42 days imprisonment with hard labour and 24 lashes.[66]

There were other matters involving Archer personally that also resulted in court cases. For example, late in September he gave evidence against an African who, by using 'chits' made out in western script, and purporting to bear Archer's signature, had obtained 36 yards of white drill cloth and two packets of Sunlight Soap from Storey's store, and another 24 yards of white drill from Kabula Stores. He had also obtained goods from the African Lakes Corporation in Lieutenant Collins's name. Archer was puzzled as to how this could have happened because the African could not write except in Swahili script. 'I cannot make out how they came to serve the man on the chits presented especially Storey's as they see my writing nearly every day and their order was spelt Stores for Storey, Whit for White Drill.' No one had been able to find out who wrote the orders and he thought they probably never would. It was unlikely that the accused had written them.[67]

Nor was this the only case of theft in which Archer was involved, for he had to take action - unorthodox and pragmatic but successful - in one which only narrowly missed being fatal:

> 7 January. Just as I was having my lunch Mr Collins came and reported that the Capitao of the machila men had poisoned nine machila men. We took a tin of mustard and a bottle of salad oil with us and went to their lines. I got the men out of their huts and they all complained of pains in their tummy. We mixed the mustard with some water in a big tin and made them all have a good drink. Result a general scatter and vomiting. The Doctor arrived shortly after with a tin of mustard but we did not require him. Ordered men to hospital. It appears that one of the Adjutant's (Mr Baxter's) boys had got hold of a bottle of tabloids for making up stuff for photographic purposes and gave it to the Capitao of the machila men, saying it was good stuff, what the Bwanas took. Nine of them tried it. Juma, the Adjutant's boy put on guard. I wonder how many lashes the CO will give him tomorrow. 8th. Juma got 16 lashes, good ones laid on his back by Grant.[68]

There was, however, one amusing case when he was mistaken in thinking that larceny was afoot. He was awakened at about half past four one morning by noises of something moving about his room:

> I listened and again heard something move. I thought it was someone trying to steal something so slipped quietly out of bed and lit a match. Saw nothing, but going on to the verandah I saw Hooker's tame female bushbuck which had evidently been taking a stroll round my bedroom.[69]

Despite all the routine military work and discipline, Archer was left with ample leisure time, and - as always - he filled it with athletics and sports, to which he now added field shooting and game hunting. The dry season from April to October was very fully occupied with games and to a lesser extent athletics and shooting. After three in the afternoon, except when there was musketry or reservist training, he had generally finished work for the day. He played tennis except during the heavy rains. Hockey and football matches were played for about six months during the year, generally one football and two hockey matches a week. He played cricket on Saturdays for about two months before the annual sports week against Blantyre in August.

Although he was getting older and was now a 'veteran', he continued to play games a great deal, though he played wicket keeper at cricket and goal keeper at football, and he seems to have been more vulnerable to injury in the course of his still very energetic playing. Even when injured and unable to play he often acted as umpire, for example when he hurt his thumb at hockey. His diary from late May to mid August illustrates the volume of sports played and the injuries incurred:[70]

> 26 May. Cricket match. Took one wicket and made 12 runs. [On another occasion he made 34.] Got hit on the shin bone with the ball. 31 May. Hockey. Got hit in the left eye with the ball, fine black eye. 7 June. Hockey, strained back muscle of left leg. 20 July. Cut my eyebrow playing cricket; had to get it stitched. 21 July. Football with one eye bandaged over. 26 July. Hockey, bad hit with ball and then another hit with a stick on the same place right leg on old football wound. The biggest lump I have ever seen. 28 July. Doctor says it burst a vein that made it swell so much. 29 July. Ran a quarter mile with Ryley. Beat him easily. 30 July. Cricket, got caught, second ball. 2 August. Ran 220 with Ryley, he beat me. Played in hockey match. 3 August. Had a long run and then played cricket in the nets.

4 August. Played goal in football match. 8 August. practice shoot 200, 500 and 600, made 91. Ran 100 yards with Northern and Ryley. First Northern, Second dead heat Ryley and self. 9 August. Hockey match. 10 August. shot in camp team against the Volunteers. Got second top score. 11 August. played football. 12 August. played hockey. 15-20 August. Rode bicycle to Namadzi and slept at rest house. Rode to Blantyre, put up with Cox.[71] Sports, won 440 yds, second in 220. Played in hockey and football teams. Returned to Zomba, stayed at Jay Williams plantation for lunch.[72]

This visit to Blantyre was to participate in the Annual Sports meeting at the Blantyre Club on 18 and 19 August 1910. He was a member of the Zomba shooting, hockey, football and athletics teams.[73] As one of Zomba's hockey half backs - he usually played at centre half - he 'played magificently at times', and in the football match he 'made a brilliant save in goal.'[74] Two years later he again cycled from Zomba to Blantyre for the annual sports meeting, and Norman of Kabula Stores put him up. He played in the cricket match, won the 220 yards race, came second in the 100 yards race and there was a 'Dead Heat in the quarter mile in which [he] threw [him]self at the tape, cutting [his] knee rather badly.' Then in hockey he 'got a whack' on his sore knee that stopped him playing. He returned to Zomba on 17 August and was lucky to get a ride on 'the motor trolley' for the last 29 miles.[75]

Apart from his sports injuries, he maintained good health, though there were occasional bouts of fever:

> Had a sharp touch of fever, felt very sore and stiff in the morning, high temperature in the afternoon, rotten all night. Three spoonfuls of soup for lunch and dinner. Quinine 15 grams midday, 10 in evening. [Next day] Went on parade but still not very fit. Laid down in afternoon. Better in evening. Head a bit thick.[76]

He frequently climbed Zomba Mountain to shoot quail, enjoying the wild 'raspberries', taking a puppy with him for early training[77] - presumably to recover the quail - and contemptuously bemoaning the shortage of birds 'because civilians have been shooting them.' He also shot duck on Lake Shirwa:

> Started for Lake Shirwa about 6.0 a.m. by bicycle. Took wrong path and went a good bit out of my way which made me trek cross-country to regain pathway, bad for bicycle. Arrived Shirwa about 9.30 a.m,

the path being overgrown with grass about six feet high. Went straight out onto the lake and shot eight teal. Saw no other duck. This was the best bag for that day. Had a good lunch and started back. Arrived at Zomba about 5.0 p.m. completely done up and with a splendid thirst.[78]

On other occasions he went duck shooting at Shirwa with Lieutenant Jones-Vaughan and Captain Morland, and did well. For example, on one such occasion he got 44 out of a total bag of 69, and a fortnight later he recorded, 'My bag of 91 is the biggest that has been got at Shirwa.'[79]

A little later in the year, at the end of the dry season and beginning of the wet season he went on a number of game hunting trips. In mid September 1912, in the course of a three day shoot, he saw gwapi, sable, eland, water buck, gnu, hartebeest, wild dogs and buffalo.[80] There were times when getting to the area where there were game animals could be fraught with difficulty. For example, in the middle of November 1912, he recorded:

> 16 November. Left Zomba and rode bicycle to Likwenu. Stopped with Robinson.
> 17 November. Left Likwenu about 6.0 a.m., soon punctured. Put on new inner tube. After passing Liwonde, valve tubes went wrong. Had five spare ones but they broke as soon as I put them on. Eventually fixed one up. Very hot. Completely knocked. Arrived at Mvera about 12.30 p.m. with a thirst. Went out in the evening but hit nothing.

Mvera was a wooding station for the river boats on the Shire at the outlet of Lake Malombe, and Charlotte Mansfield who stayed at Mvera at about the same time as Archer said the rest house there 'gave one the creeps after being in it for only a few minutes.' The window of the 'best bedroom' was broken and she found the two Africans in charge of the rest house 'not of very fascinating appearance.' However, she quickly forgave their appearance when they brought her a meal of chicken and, to her surprise and delight, some fresh fish.[81] Archer gave a few more details of his hunting trip in a letter to his mother, telling her that from Mvera he walked to Fort Mangoche where he stayed with Captain H A W Bockett Pugh.[82] On arrival he had a light lunch of four hard boiled eggs and a piece of bread.[83]

Over the Christmas break, 1913, he again went on a ten day shooting trip. He was not very successful but was comforted by the fact that he did better than any of the others who also went on shooting trips at the same time. He was somewhat irritated by finding on his return to camp after a day's hunting, that Storrs, the Resident, and McCall, the Director of Agriculture, had camped near his tent: 'I don't know what they are going to do, as it is no good three of us shooting from the same place. One can hear a shot for miles and after that game requires too much stalking as it is on the lookout for danger.'[84]

By the time Archer returned to Nyasaland from Somaliland in February 1910, he was 39 years of age and had been in the army for 21 years, more than half his life. He had done well: he was a substantive Colour Sergeant in the Rifle Brigade and Regimental Sergeant Major of 1 KAR on secondment. Although his ambitions were partially fulfilled by his appointment as RSM, this was but a temporary measure and in a sense an oblique step towards securing the fuller ambition after which he still hankered: substantive Sergeant Major in his own Regiment, the Rifle Brigade, and ultimately a commission. Once again, as in India, he was not on active service and, despite the diversions of sports, athletics, shooting and hunting, his mind turned frequently to his future in the army.

He was still in touch with Captain White at the Winchester depot, who continued to be both realistic and helpful. White was not aware of anything that stood in his way in a recent application he had made for a Quartermaster Sergeantship 'except the lack of the first class certificate' of education.

> I don't think there is much chance of a messengership either in the Lords or Commons. Simpson has been down for (I think) 8 years and I heard the other day that he had not the least chance for years and then he would be too old. I think the Yeoman of the Guard is a good thing: not worth very much in itself but as an aid to other things. However, I think a man with your record would not have much difficulty in getting something suitable when you want it.[85]

His ambition to become a Regimental Sergeant Major - to become the senior of NCOs - in his own regiment was, not unnaturally, one which others of his colleagues shared. It was an ambition accompanied by pride in the regiment and their own progress in it, by envy of those who succeeded - unworthily as they saw it - before they did, and by general disillusion. Soon after arriving in Nyasaland, he received a letter from a close friend and fellow freemason in the battalion in India, Billy Dickinson:

You will have heard that someone from Home has got the 4th Battalion. I don't know who but I believe little Wombwell. [Wombwell, then an Acting Sergeant, had been wounded at Surprise Hill[86]] Captain Harman ... hoped I would allow my name to be registered for anything going after this. I have declined for it's a bit rough after asking a man to take a job, to allow another to jump in front (and little Wombwell at that). I should not care to take service with anyone, knowing that I was only taking second place. It's rather a come down for me, Jack, and the usual rotters have not been nice with their quiet remarks etc. I quite made up my mind I was going and got all sort of kit ready but that cannot be helped now ... About your silver, if you wish it sent home will you please give me the address ... It will be a bare mess when it goes but they cannot expect it to remain forever ... No soldiering here, just musketry and then day after day stupid parades which no one can take any interest in. Soldiering is not expected of the men, just heaps of sentry go and staff jobs ... so you can see that we have fallen sadly from our splendid state up in the hills.[87]

Archer went to Britain on leave, sailing from Chinde, on 17 April 1911 and caught the *Carisbrook Castle* from Delagoa Bay.[88] It was a very full leave. At his own request he spent part of his time at the Vickers armaments factory at Erith for instruction in the operation and repair of maxim guns.[89] With Jones-Vaughan he tried to get an East Africa rifle team together to compete at Bisley, but was disappointed: 'I stayed at Bisley to receive members arriving and to make all arrangements, but was unable to get a team of eight.' While in England, too, he pursued with Colonel Thesiger the question of promotion and suitable alternative employment. The Inspector-General replied in August to say, 'I shall be at the Colonial Office tomorrow. I went to the War Office and they have over 40 names registered for such billets; they tell me many of them are Sergeant Majors who have been down for years.'[90] Thesiger's reference to both the War Office and the Colonial Office suggests that he was making enquiries on Archer's behalf for both a military post in a British regiment and either a civilian or military post in the colonies, probably Nyasaland. Thesiger recommended him for a Quartermastership with a view to his getting the Gosport Discharge Depot, but the War Office said that he was too old to register for the post.[91] He was then 40 years of age. At the end of his leave, early in October, he travelled by rail across France to Marseilles, where he boarded a ship to take him back to Africa. In this way he avoided sailing through the Bay of Biscay and risking being seasick. The train journey was 'bad' but the sea voyage to Naples, where the ship called, was 'splended'. He arrived at Chinde on 10 November 1911.[92]

Some six months after he arrived back from leave, he received letters from Colonel Dawson offering him the Sergeant Majorship of the 6th Battalion of the Rifle Corps.[93] 'Let me know as soon as you can as there are several applicants. Don't think I shall be hurt if you don't think it good enough. Do what you think best.' Four days after receiving the second letter he declined the offer. The reason he did so was that he felt he stood a good chance of being offered the Quartermastership of 1 KAR. Indeed, Thesiger recommended him for a commission on the Quartermaster-General's list at the War Office, and the Commanding Officer of 1 KAR recommended him for appointment as Civilian Pay and Quartermaster of the KAR. In this latter case, the Governor, Sir George Smith, considered the post to be a 'special Treasury plum' and not open to recommendations of military men by the Commanding Officer.[94] Apparently in compensation, the Colonial Office offered him appointment as Chief Constable of the Falkland Islands. He declined the offer on four grounds: he still hoped for a Quartermastership in the regular army, the climate was cold, he did not fancy living on a small island and there was no chance of active service.[95]

He was making good progress in the KAR and he took over command of half of C Company from Lieutenant Giffard and the whole of B Company on other occasions. On the Governor's recommendation, the Secretary of State gave permission for him to draw extra duty pay of £2 a month while acting as Subaltern and Company Commander at various other times between 1911 and 1913. This received the approbation of at least one of his friends: 'Get all you can out of them while you serve. The rotten authorities at home will not give you a penny extra when you leave.'[96] Archer took pride in the fact that Giffard, from whom he took over half of C Company, later became General Sir George Giffard and Inspector-General of the KAR.

Despite this good progress, from early 1913 onwards he was seriously contemplating leaving the army and had in mind trying to get a civilian job in Nyasaland.[97] He was advised by Thesiger not to leave it too late.[98] Gough, too, thought it wise to consider a civilian appointment in Nyasaland, and indeed it appears that he actually applied for such a job:

> I think you are right to think of a civil billet under the Colonial Office, but I know they are not easy to get, as there are any number of applicants for such jobs. I hope you have been successful. You can

always rely on me to say a good word if it would be useful to you. The person to get interested in your case is the Governor, he could probably do more for you than anyone else.[99]

Shortly, one of his former Rifle Brigade officers, who had also been in 1 KAR and served on the Somaliland expedition, and with whom he had tried to set up a Bisley team and had done a good deal of duck shooting, Jones-Vaughan, wrote and offered him a job managing his coffee plantation in Uganda. 'As you must be getting towards the end of your time with the KAR and getting near drawing your pension, I am writing to ask if you would like a job as manager of a coffee estate in Uganda.' He had bought land there, near Jinja, and was looking for someone he could trust to manage it for him, get the land cleared of bush and planted with coffee and cocoa. He wanted a man who was good with Africans, as the principal work for the first two years would be getting the ground cleared.[100] In the event Archer did not receive this letter for several months, by which time he was unable to accept it, even if - as was unlikely - he had felt inclined to do so.

On the first Sunday morning in May 1914, he left Zomba in Jay Williams's motor sidecar and travelled to Limbe, where he arrived late in the afternoon. He stayed at Copeland's Hotel, where Mrs Ryall was the manageress. The next day he left Limbe by train at half past eight in the morning and arrived at Port Herald at five in the afternoon. He slept that night on board the sternwheeler *Empress*, and the next day, Tuesday, left Port Herald at 9.0 a.m. On Thursday he arrived at Chinde and stayed at Dishington's Hotel. It had been a 'good voyage down the Zambesi: nice and cool.' He sailed from Chinde on 10 May[101] at 1.0 p.m. It was a smooth passage over the bar and 'Jimmie' gave him some of his home made pickles, which were sufficiently outstanding for him to record the fact in his diary. He also 'made the acquaintance of Miss Taylor':

12 May. Arrived at Mozambique at 6.0 p.m. Went on shore and walked all over the island with Miss Taylor. She got very tired. Hot but not so bad as the last time I was here [five years earlier]. Left at 2.0 p.m.

13 May. Arrived at Port Amelia about 6.0 a.m. Fine harbour. All houses blown down by cyclone. All boats in harbour driven up on to the beach. Unable to land. Left about 10.0 a.m., heavy rain.

14 May. Hot night last night. Arrived at Zanzibar about 1.0 a.m.

15 May. Went on shore about 9.0 a.m. Returned about 11.30 a.m. Left Zanzibar about 5.0 p.m.

16 May. Arrived Mombasa (Kilindini) about 6.0 a.m. Went on shore at 4.30. Dinner at Hotel Metropole with Miss Taylor. Returned at 9.0 p.m.

17 May. Went on shore at 3.30 p m. Walked round the Pepper Pot. Tea at Metropole. On board at 6.0 p.m.

18 May. Left Mombasa at 4.0 p.m.

23 May. Arrived at Aden about 4.30 p.m. Went to the Wells with Miss Taylor. Dined at Grand Hotel. On board about 9.30. Very hot.

24 May. Left Aden about 1.0 a.m. this morning.

26 May. Arrived Port Sudan about 8.0 a.m. Left about 10.0 p.m. Went on shore with Miss Taylor.

5 June. Arrived at Marseilles about 10.30 a.m. Left by 8.25 train.[102]

He was expecting to return to Nyasaland after his leave,[103] but this was not to be, at least not for some time. We do not know whether he had sufficiently 'made the acquaintance of Miss Taylor' as to wish to take their relationship further by meeting her again while on leave, but in the event this also was not to be.

CHAPTER EIGHT

THE FIRST WORLD WAR: 1914-1919

Almost exactly five years earlier Archer had forecast that there would be a 'war with Germany who [were] preparing for it'. He had continued to hold this belief, and about a year before he left to go on leave in May 1914, his mother had written to him, 'As you say - rumours of war; let us hope it will stop there.' Her hope was not to be fulfilled.[1]

He had been on leave in Britain less than two months when the First World War broke out. When mobilization was ordered he was on a visit to Aldershot and he immediately returned to London, to the Colonial Office, where he volunteered for the front. Shortly he was told by Captain Ffrench of the Hampshire Regiment, 'Your services have been placed at the disposal of the War Office for the duration of the war.'[2] This ended his secondment to the KAR as Regimental Sergeant Major, a Colonial Office responsibility. On 8 August he received a cable from Winchester ordering him to report to the Adjutant, 1st Battalion Rifle Brigade at Colchester. He did so the same day. Initially, for a very short period, he found the place in some confusion: 'They know nothing about me and don't know what to do with me - the only soldier in khaki drill.' This was not surprising so soon after the outbreak of hostilities. It very soon changed.[3]

Men of Archer's experience were rare - rarer, no doubt he thought, than they would have been had Haldane not disbanded so many regiments - and consequently were much needed. With the prospect of early fighting and an immediate vast expansion of the army, his regiment was very pleased to have him back and was determined to put him to full use. He was soon working from six in the morning to eight at night every day, building defence works against the possibility of invasion. He was in great demand because there were 'very few with [his] practical experience of defences', gained mainly in South Africa.

On 12 August, only four days after he arrived at Colchester he saw Colonel Biddulph,[4] who knew him well. They had served together in the Sudan, South Africa - including the attack on Caesar's Hill, when

Biddulph, then a Captain, commanding D Company, had been wounded - and India. Biddulph asked him if he would accept a commission. Delighted, he accepted without hesitation. Although he had in mind accepting the commission only 'for the duration of the War, as afterwards the pay is not good enough to keep one going', he was elated with this fulfilment of a long held ambition. No longer need he concern himself with becoming a Sergeant Major, whether in the Rifle Brigade - as he preferred - or, as it had increasingly become more likely, in a Volunteer or Militia regiment, for he was now offered a commission in the regiment of which he had proudly been a member and in which he had served with distinction for twenty-five years. He was keen to get on with the job and go out with the battalion to France as soon as he could. Given to understand that he would be granted a kit allowance of £100 with his commission, he immediately bought, at Colchester and at his own expense, officers' equipment including field glasses and a compass.[5]

In his diary he recorded details of his activities during the remainder of his first week at Colchester, building defences, mainly of barbed wire, until relieved by territorial soldiers, in conditions that were often uncomfortable:

> Wednesday 12th August. Left Colchester with Colonel Biddulph in his car.[6] Joined A Company under Captain de Moleynes,[7] at Rowhedge. Worked up to 7.30 p.m. putting *sangars* right that had not been made properly. Left with 19 NCOs and men for Wivenhoe [on the River Colne to take charge of a party of men making defence works and] to release a party of A Company.
> Thursday 13th. Building *sangars*, making trenches, putting up barbed wire etc. ... block houses to be built.
> Friday 14th. Same as yesterday.
> Saturday 15th. Hands cut a good deal with putting up barbed wire defences. Rained in the early afternoon, my blankets got wet as the roof of half a small boat that I sleep in let the rain in. Worked up to 12 noon. Afternoon men washed clothing and bathed, inspection of rifles, field dressings, emergency rations etc. etc. at 6.30 p.m.[8]

He was formally restored to his regiment, the Rifle Brigade, on 17 August,[9] and a few days later he left with the 1st Battalion for France as part of the British Expeditionary Force. He went as A Company Sergeant Major and a platoon commander - a position normally held by a 2nd Lieutenant. Having been offered and accepted a commission, he was 'in every way treated as an officer' by his colleagues, both officers and men.

As soon as he arrived in France, he was attached to the Headquarters Staff and was immediately involved in active fighting. The men were tired after an exhausting journey from England to the front in scorching heat relieved only by sudden downpours of rain. The British Expeditionary Force was defeated at Mons on Sunday 23 August and fell back to the south, towards Le Cateau, in a fighting retreat, pursued by the Germans. It was a disastrous beginning to the war:

> Just after dawn three confused days later, on the anniversary of the Battle of Crecy, [the German] army caught [the British] tired II Corps at Le Cateau from where, after a morning's battle, the retreat continued. British casualties were about 8000 men and 38 guns. German casualties are estimated at 9000 ... Shortly after dawn on 26 August, the German troops ... entered Le Cateau and came up against elements of 5th Division ... near the railway bridge, when after a short fight conducted from the windows of the houses the British withdrew to the high ground behind the town ... Inexorably [the German] forces built up against the open right flank and by 1300 hours the British on the exposed spur were under artillery fire from three German divisions and under frontal and flank attacks by a dozen infantry battalions. It was time to get out. [The British] decided to withdraw by divisions from right to left. [The] order was issued at 1340 hours but much of the line of communication had been destroyed by the artillery bombardments and the message had to be delivered by runner. 5th Division HQ received the order at 1400 hours, forward units got it at 1500 hours. [Some regiments] never got it at all and by 1600 hours they were surrounded and wiped out.[10]

The official history of the Rifle Brigade in the War deals specifically with the part played by the Brigade and Archer's platoon:

> Shortly after 4.0 a.m. on August 26th the fighting troops ... stood to arms in the first light of a glorious morning and, discovering that the enemy was at hand, engaged him hotly in the best tradition of the British Army. Dawn had broken upon the First Battalion [Rifle Brigade] standing to arms in cultivated fields on a forward slope covering the village of Fontaine-au-Pire, and had revealed to the outpost company a body of hostile cavalry and artillery advancing upon Cattenieres. [The] Battalion, taking advantage of natural cover ... fell back in succession of companies at a steady walk - almost, despite the hostile rifle and shell fire, as though on Salisbury Plain.

During this manoeuvre one platoon [of 68 men] of 'A' Company which was covering the movement of the remainder of the company came to close quarters with the enemy on the right of the Battalion, and C.S.M. Archer, who was in command, was severely wounded and taken prisoner; there were also a number of other casualties - the first to be suffered by the Regiment.[11]

Archer gave a great deal more specific information in his own account of the events of those fateful few days, starting two days after the defeat at Mons.[12]

On [Tuesday] the 25th August we entrenched but did not come under fire until just before dark. Just as we were ready to retire, a Staff Officer rode up and said that some Regiment was in difficulties and getting cut up. I was ordered to take back my platoon to investigate. Sent off two men to my left flank to let the Herts (who had occupied our old trenches) know they should not shoot us. The two men rejoined during the night. After going about a quarter of a mile Captain de Moleynes caught me up and told me to return as quickly as possible as the enemy were on another road and would cut us off. Sent word to my point (Corporal and two men) and by running and walking eventually caught up the Battalion. My platoon was rear guard to the Battalion with orders to fire on anyone coming up from the rear ... We retired and marched nearly all night with the enemy close on our heels. Got a little sleep but at daybreak 26th we advanced about a quarter of a mile and soon came under shell and rifle fire, retired gradually for about a mile where we (three Companies) took up a position in a sunken road. We soon began to get shelled and as we had not a very good field of fire, our Brigadier, General Hunter-Weston, ordered C Company to advance a short distance and dig themselves in. My Company, A, was ordered to retire a short distance. I lay down in reserve. The enemy soon began to pepper our advance Company and shots that just skimmed the ridge caught us, killing and wounding several men. I pointed out to the Officer in Command (Major Rickman)[13] that it was too exposed where we were. He ordered the Company to advance. Again to the sunken road. No sooner had we arrived there than a battery of six guns turned on the sunken road. The shooting was splendid but fortunately for us a little too high. The willow trees were very much cut about and practically all the shrapnel hit the ground just where my Company had lain extended. Occasionally of course a shell would burst a couple of yards short causing casualties. Our Artillery fired a few rounds, which caught our advance company, (our Artillery could not see them) causing the ones still left to retire on us. The OC C Company said it was impossible to stick there any longer now our own Artillery was on them too. Some of the enemy's infantry had now crept up to within 100 yards of us. They also made an attempt to get round our left flank. Several officers unnecessarily exposed themselves. I spoke to Major Rickman. He told officers not to expose themselves unnecessarily. Sometime afterwards Major Rickman said he thought the enemy were concentrating to charge us, and got up on the bank to look. He was mortally wounded before he could get down.[14] Major Salmon now took command.[15]

Archer was told that the remainder of the Brigade and a French Division would come to their assistance and that they would then advance. The Brigade started its advance but only a few of the Somerset Light Infantry joined them. He continued his account:

The Brigade disappeared. They got a tremendous shelling, and whilst they were such a good target the enemy left us alone, but when the target disappeared they again devoted themselves to us. We now began to get a larger number of casualties. Shells were coming from all directions ... The last one who passed near me was Captain Hon. Prittie[16] who I think in order to get away had discarded his equipment. In fact at first I thought he was a doctor looking after wounded. Later I saw someone looking for wounded and waved my handkerchief, which only drew fire. None of the bullets hit within six yards of me. The enemy were searching among the corn and the two small woods which were on the opposite slope to where I was lying, and just before dark they eventually dropped on the hiding place of two of our men. As I saw them get up and run, the Germans fired at them. They dropped but soon after I again saw them running and would run until shot at when they dropped. This they repeated several times before I lost sight of them. Sincerely trust they got away. There were several wounded men near but none seemed able to move.[17]

The officers had a quick conference and then - aware of, and valuing, Archer's long experience of active service - asked him his opinion as to what should be done. Conscious of the dire position in which they found themselves, he immediately replied, 'Stick it out till dark or let anyone get away who likes.' They also asked a Company Quarter Master Sergeant who took a different, more belligerent but less prudent, view and replied, 'Fight it out to a finish.' The officers then had another talk between themselves and soon Major Salmon came and told Archer to take his platoon and try to get away. They would watch the result and then decide what further they should do, presumably to follow Archer's advice, if he were successful, or the Company Quarter Master Sergeant's, if he were not. Archer got permission for his men to take off their packs, so as to make escape easier. He then led the retirement, reformed under cover of the nearby railway line, was joined by other men and officers, including Captain Prittie, and in extended line they continued the retirement. Archer continued to lead the retirement, despite the presence of commissioned officers, just as he had done at Surprise Hill in South Africa in 1899. This time he was not so fortunate in escaping injury:

> The enemy turned and fired on us and I was unfortunate enough to get bowled over, just like a rabbit [almost precisely the wording Paley had used when he was wounded at Surprise Hill], by one of their last shells. Corporal Bentley, an NCO in my platoon, stayed and bandaged me up and made me as comfortable as possible. Nearly all the unwounded officers and men got away.

He thought the Germans were very slow in not charging them, because had they done so they, the Germans, would have saved themselves a lot of casualties. Archer's men had been firing badly in the early morning when they were first shelled, but later in the day 'they shot as well as on the range; as soon as one of the enemy showed his head it went down like a falling plate!' Indeed, so rapid and accurate was the fire of the Brigade riflemen - 15 rounds per minute - that the Germans believed they were using machine guns. In fact the British had only two machine guns for each battalion.[18] He was convinced that the enemy did not realise they were such a small party and although aeroplanes went over them he thought they were too small for the pilots to report their presence, 'which was fortunate although we should have given a good account of ourselves in a hand to hand fight.' A little later he discovered that his injury was considerably worse than he had initially thought:

> Later I learned that I was still bleeding from a wound not bandaged but managed to get a shirt out of my haversack and stick it between my legs where it stuck onto the wound and stopped the bleeding. I spent a very miserable night. It rained and what with the loss of

blood and the cold brought on an attack of fever and ague. I got picked up by French civilians and put in a wagon about 9.0 a.m. 27th. Only one other man was alive anywhere near me. Others wounded had either got away or died during the night. Taken to Legney-en-Cambresis (a small village about 12 kilometres from Cambrai) and put into a small gymnasium.[19] Wounds dressed by Captain Stevenson RAMC. About 300 wounded in the village. A couple of days later, on being carried out in order to clean out and put down fresh straw, an artery in my leg that had been damaged burst and I lost a lot of blood. Five or six days later I was sent into Cambrai with other special cases. By this time I had got a fine attack of fever. A few days later the artery burst again, soaking the bed. The same day I was sent to the operating hospital where I had three operations [and 'nearly bled to death'[20]] before they managed to finally stop the haemorrhage.

He thought the French doctor who operated on him at Cambrai was 'a very clever surgeon.' He was able to watch him operate on a number of German soldiers with half a dozen or so German doctors looking on, and when the operation was completed there was 'a great salaaming' of admiration and congratulations. The French and English soldiers called him 'the Butcher' because of the large number of arms and legs that he amputated.

It was to be several years before he learned of the gratifying number of his Rifle Brigade comrades who escaped at Cambrai[21] and of the sad irony that the day after he was wounded and captured, the German offensive was halted for ten days.[22] Indeed, the shell that wounded him was one of the last they fired before halting the offensive.

When, a little later, he was medically examined, the doctors attested that he had been wounded at Ligny en Cambresis on 26 August 1914, *Scrapnell, sitay musculaire aussi droite sortie pli inguino scrotal.*[23]

His mother was officially notified of his wounding on 13 October,[24] though it is likely that at about the same time she received his first letter, dated 9 October, from the *Institution Notre Dame de Grace*, Cambrai, saying, 'I am in hospital ... Wound (bullet through thigh) doing well.'[25] Two weeks later he wrote again, this time from *Gefangenen Lager Cruppen*, Uebungsplatz, Darmstadt, Hessen:

> You will see by the above address that I am a prisoner. I was wounded (bullet through the right thigh) on 26 August near Ligny. My wounds are now quite healed up and I left hospital last week. At

present I am lame and very stiff but hope to be walking about again as usual in less than another week. We are in huts and get sufficient food ... we are allowed to receive letters. Please do not worry about me.[26]

Despite his attempts to reassure her in this letter, his mother must have been desperately worried about him, and, sadly, she died ten weeks later, on 1 January 1915, his birthday, at the age of 68, and a day before the anniversary of her husband's death 32 years earlier.[27] She had been looking forward for some months to the time when Jack would return permanently: 'Of *course* I shall be glad when you can come home.'[28] She, and he, would have been pleased that he had been on leave and able to be together only six months earlier.

His wound, during the first few months, may well have taken his mind somewhat off the fact that he was now a prisoner of war. 'Most of the men in the front line expected to be either killed or wounded. Most hoped for a wound heavy enough to get them home, but light enough not to ruin their lives. Very few ever thought they would become prisoners, and didn't prepare for the eventuality.'[29] Though this may have been true of the many non-professional soldiers, it is very unlikely that Archer, a regular soldier, expected to be either killed or wounded and he certainly would not have wanted to be taken home and away from the fighting. Nor does he seem to have experienced the 'feelings of humiliation and shame [that] were almost too much to bear', felt by others when they were taken prisoner,[30] though he did later make the passing remark that the First World War was the only campaign that he had not 'seen out to the finish.'[31]

He had no more haemorrhaging, so was moved to another hospital where he began to get a little stronger, though it was not until the middle of October that he was passed fit to be moved again. As for the doctors and nurses, he recalled:[32]

> At Ligny [the gymnasium to which he was first taken when wounded] only English doctors and French women who volunteered to be nurses. At Cambrai, first hospital, French doctors all did their very best; in fact they killed some of the men with mistaken kindness. French doctors very good except one old French Colonel, who in the opinion of the patients, French and English, knew nothing about his work. Eventually the French refused to be dressed by him. Our men, finding this out, asked to be dressed by someone else. The complaint did some good as we were handed over to a French Lieutenant who

was a splendid surgeon. German and French nurses. In the first room I was in, the German nurse was not at all good; she did her work but did not like the English. Second hospital (Hospital Militaire), where I was sent to be operated on, there were two German professional nurses in my ward. Both were very good and although they gave the German troops anything special that came up they gave us every attention. Third hospital, French doctors, nurses and orderlies under German supervision did everything possible for us but were not regular nurses and knew nothing of their work, but most willing to learn.

He left Cambrai - birthplace of the painter Matisse - by rail in mid October. At the railway station the Germans tried to take away the prisoners' greatcoats - which were essential if they were to keep warm. While at Ligny, Captain Stevenson - the doctor who had first dressed his wound - had made sure that every man had a greatcoat taken from packs left on the battlefield by retreating or dead colleagues. A German under-officer ordered Archer to take off his greatcoat, but he refused, saying he was cold and badly wounded. He refused, too, to accept two marks and a blanket in exchange for his greatcoat. When the under-officer then brought a more senior officer who ordered that the coat should be taken forcefully, Archer 'shouted and groaned, in fact rather put it on but it stopped the under-officer taking [his] coat.' He had been a soldier long enough to know when to dig his toes in. He and his close colleagues were the only ones to keep their greatcoats. He was convinced they would have lost them had they not been 'laying down cases and on stretchers'.

Three days rotten journey and then we arrived at Darmstadt where I was taken to the camp lazarettes [hospital wards for diseased patients]. Plenty of 'swine Englander' but no striking. A *feldwebel* who told me he had a business in London, which was still being run, upon my asking him for a separate bed on account of the other men hurting my leg, said, 'The first time there are any natives [by which he meant eastern Europeans and Russians] arrive here I shall put you between two of them and only give you two beds.' Fortunately I was ordered to move to another camp. Arrived at Mersburg in November and taken to the town hospital after not a bad journey for Germany. The under-officer in charge of our truck would not allow civilians to hardly look in the carriage, sent them away to other carriages saying that we were all wounded. Part of a Company of Gordons [in kilts] were on the train and a certain number of them had to get out on the platform at each stopping place for the civilians to see the English soldiers dressed like women.

He recalled that in the hospital at Mersburg 'everything and everybody [was] German. Good food, very clean, not a speck of dust. In fact I was very foolish, as soon as my wound had healed, in continually asking to be sent to a laager, as I could have stayed there until I was able to walk a bit better.' He was fortunate in having a French professional masseur in the camp with him. Indeed, he later attributed his ability to walk after being so badly wounded, to the skills of this man, who had been captured at the same time as he had. The Germans also held the masseur in high regard and made full use of his skills: 'A car would arrive to escort him to the hospital where he was expected to work on patients, and the car would return him to the camp in the evening and he would then work on his fellow prisoners of war.'[33]

His long rail journey to a prisoner of war camp was similar to that experienced by most prisoners, though Archer was fortunate to be taken prisoner near a railhead and thus was not forced to undertake the long march that many other prisoners had to suffer. In any case, he would not have been able to walk far. Whilst many were kept in France 'to work behind the German lines, carrying supplies and mending roads', most were sent on long route marches to railheads. Here they were put in cattle-trucks, with up to sixty in a truck. They then began a two to six day journey, travelling deep inside Germany towards one of the 600 camps that had been hastily built to accommodate them. After every big offensive, these became overcrowded with men, and the conditions could be very primitive.'[34]

He was gradually recovering from his injury and could walk a little but could not go up or down steps without being helped. He was having trouble, too, from one of the under-officers. During an evening in November, not long after he arrived at Mersburg from Darmstadt, he went for a walk from the hospital.

> Everything went all right until we met an under-officer who returned to camp with us. We marched over cobbles covered with mud. I could have managed with this but the under-officer appeared to consider it a great joke to keep the light of a bullseye lantern constantly in my eyes and it appeared to be a great joke when I stumbled and nearly fell down. Luckily I had nothing to carry. On arrival in camp I was put into a filthy dirty hut, no blankets were given me the first night but a Frenchman lent me one of his, so I

wrapped it round me and laid down. The next day I was given a damp dirty bed and two blankets.

Walking over 'cobbles covered with mud', his mind may well have gone back with a degree of nostalgia to January 1893, when he marched to the Ship Stree Barracks in Dublin, despite it having been a 'rotten march over wet muddy cobbles' and he having had difficulty in keeping step when marching to bagpipes.

During the next two months he was 'continually being moved from one barrack to another either as a punishment or because [he] was English.' He was up to his knees in mud in the camp, and 'very little was done in way of sanitation.' 'Every German who saw me thought it was his duty to send me outside with my bed, but I soon got to know how to make my way to another hut and keep out of sight.'

Just before Christmas he was allocated to a room with about a hundred men of all nationalities, only one other of whom was English. At night it was difficult to get up without stepping on someone, as there was only just enough space for all of them to lie down. Again, his mind may well have gone back to his service with Kitchener on the Nile Expedition with its crowding of men in river boats and on trains. Daily, now, he was verbally abused by the senior *feldwebel*, Gunter, who called him 'Swine' and other abusive names and 'who tried to lead [him] a dog's life.' Archer had a book and a copybook in his hand one day when Gunter asked what they were. He handed it to him and when Gunter found that the book was in French - which presumably he could not read - he threw the book in one corner and the copybook in another. Following Gunter's lead, the other under-officers also treated him badly. After a while, eleven other Englishmen joined him, all from hospital. On one occasion Gunter struck a man called Carr for not standing to attention quickly enough. Carr had been very badly wounded and could not stand up without first turning round. He complained to the German Captain of the Company, and the treatment of Englishmen began to improve slightly. Archer found the Captain 'quite a good officer, strict but fair.'

When, as was not infrequently the case, prisoners were treated badly, Archer attributed it to having 'a bad Company OC or bad *feldwebels*', whose cruel behaviour was copied by their under-officers. 'The things that make life so miserable in laagers are the pin pricks, i.e. punishments given by the *feldwebels* and under-officers. Beds and bedding put outside when it is raining and kept out until everything is wet. Kept on parade for hours without knowing why, etc. etc.' One of the *feldwebels* at Mersburg was so bad that the men christened him 'Dr Crippen' after the notorious murderer. He was known to prisoners of all nationalities by that name. On one of the visits by the Dutch Attaché to the camp, a man made a complaint and when asked the name of the German against whom he was complaining he said 'Crippen'. He thought that was the real name, 'which caused a great laugh.' *Feldwebel Lieutenant* Gunter was reported to the American Attaché and *Feldwebel Lieutenant* Richter to the American and Dutch Attachés for badly treating prisoners.[35] Archer's experience was not unusual:

> The threat of summary punishment and violence was never far from the prisoners' minds. In camps, and particularly on work commandos, the men were vulnerable to the whims of the guards. Many excesses were committed, particularly where the commandant cared little for the men's welfare.[36]

It may be that Archer was picked on by such men as 'Crippen' because he stood out among his fellows, with his imposing appearance, neat beard, erect bearing, his Sergeant Major badge on his right sleeve, his highly polished boots and his two rows of medal ribbons on his chest, and was clearly looked up to by his fellow prisoners, most of whom were only half his age, or less.[37]

Archer found the living conditions poor. At first the food was not too bad but as time went on it gradually worsened as some of it was sold by the Germans employed in the camp kitchen. Fortunately he had about £4 on him when he was wounded and had, while in France, sewn it into various parts of his clothing, so was able to buy a little extra food. He was also affected by the way the food was served:

> We used to fall in two deep in the rear of the large soup tub. If I was in the first half dozen I was often taken out and put in the last row. This was very unfortunate especially if it was raining or snowing. One day an under-officer ran at me with a soup pole [used for stirring the soup], but stopped when he found that I did not run away from him. I was very lucky he did not knock me down but he used up his temper by calling me names.

As for the general living conditions, he 'got a rotten cough during the winter, caused by continual wet feet, wet bed and blankets and never being able to get thoroughly dry. The rooms were crowded, vermin and filth everywhere. In fact, try as one could it was impossible to keep clean.'

Hunger was described by many prisoners of war as 'the greatest torture'. As the war dragged on food supplies became more and more difficult because of the Allies' blockade of Germany and the country's economic collapse. Most of the available food went first to the German army and then to the civilians.

> The prisoners were at the bottom of the food chain and many died from malnutrition, or from illnesses which they contracted but were too ill to fight. Inside the camps, the men survived on whatever could be scrounged or stolen in order to supplement the meagre food they were given, which usually amounted to half a loaf of bread shared between five and some thin gruel.[38]

More than 10,000 British prisoners died in German prisoner of war camps, and an equal number in occupied France and Belgium. Their weakened physical condition rendered them vulnerable to disease.[39]

The shortage of food, however, bad as it was, would have been very much worse had it not been for food parcels, both generally and for Archer specifically.

> Such was the desperate plight of the prisoners in Germany that many charitable organisations supplied food to the camps in Germany. Individual families, army regiments, the Salvation Army, the YMCA, all sent parcels to the prisoners. By mid 1916, the Red Cross managed to co-ordinate the sending of regular food parcels. After that, most prisoners eventually received two parcels weighing 6 kgs (13 lbs) every fortnight. These included not only food but also badly needed clothes and were a lifeline to prisoners. They undoubtedly saved many thousands of lives ... When we got the Red Cross parcels, things changed for the better. We got bread and biscuits, soup, chocolate, cigarettes, dripping and cake, [a tin of bully beef and cheese]. They were a godsend.[40]

Specifically in Archer's case, too, the food situation improved. In May 1915, when he had already been a prisoner for nine months, parcels began to arrive from England, which bucked him up considerably. Prisoners who received regular parcels did not eat their soup. If they had done so there would not have been sufficient for everyone. He and his fellow prisoners, it seems, received all the food parcels sent to them even when, in the latter part of the war, the civilian population was very short of food.[41]

He experienced other helpful changes, even if they were not permanent. By February 1916, the volume of enquiries made to the camp about missing Englishmen was so great that he was ordered to make a list of all British Prisoners of War in the camp, and to answer all enquiries about missing people. To enable him to do this he was given a pass to visit other Companies in the camp, which gave him much fuller freedom of movement and more contacts than formerly. Just as important was the fact that he was also allowed to live in a small room with only five others - all French. He considered living in this small room 'a great privilege as it enabled [him] to keep fairly clean', but it was short lived: 'When [a] German submarine crew were imprisoned in England, [he] was put on punishment, taken out of the small room and put to sleep between a dirty Russian and a dirty Zouave both selected on account of their filthy state.' During the day he had his bed in its correct place in the room but he never slept there.

Once more, things did change for the better, albeit temporarily again, for in May 1916 a small part of a room partitioned off from the men was given to him and another senior NCO to share. From then onwards they made themselves a little more comfortable. At the beginning of the winter 1916-17 he got permission to buy a stove and get it fixed up in their room, and to close in the room partition up to the ceiling. Electric light was also extended to their room. This was done at their own expense but no charge was made for electricity. 'We were then quite comfortable for a prison camp.'

> Unfortunately, in January 1917 we got another second in command of our camp; he ordered our stove and the top of our partition to be taken away, so we got frozen for the remainder of the winter, ice a good three inches thick on our window and one never got warm except when walking. Each room contained two large stoves and our partition was in one corner near the double doors, but we very rarely got any coal. Consequently, we occasionally made a fire of beds, tables, forms and posts that held up wires for drying clothes. We were given back the stove in January 1918. A charge was made for things burnt and of course the Germans were very angry when they found out what we had burnt.

Prisoners did not have much unused time on their hands, since all the camps relied for their functioning on their labour. 'Men were assigned to jobs, from cooking to growing vegetables, from managing the stores to cleaning the toilets ... The majority of men, however, were sent out on working parties, or commandos, to jobs in agriculture or industry.[42] In Archer's case, he was made President of the British Help Committee in the camp. An important part of his tasks was to keep the Red Cross informed of all British casualties transferred to the camp. In carrying out his work he had a number of serious disputes with Richter - Crippen - who was the German officer in charge of parcels. For example, in October 1917 eight cases, each containing 20 emergency parcels, arrived at Mersburg addressed to the President, British Help Committee. Archer applied to take over these cases and permission was given to bring them to the camp and put them in the Help Committee store. He sent a fatigue party and wagon to collect them, but after they were loaded they were ordered to unload them because no order had been received from the Commandant that they were to be sent to the camp. Archer reported this to the Chief Censor and after several days he was told he could collect the cases but that they were to be censored when they arrived at the camp. Richter was instructed to hand the cases over.

> Again [I] sent down a fatigue party, which returned without them. Made another report. Reply: everything must be censored before leaving the parcel office. About 13th November I was informed I could now receive the cases as they had been censored. Again sent for them and obtained the 160 parcels complete, but the [wooden] cases had been stolen. I was informed that the cases had been taken by ... *Feldwebel Lieutenant* Richter. I sent a written complaint to my Company Officer that they were addressed to the President, British Help Committee and were the only asset available for the Help Committee to carry on its work. I was sent for by the Company Sergeant Major whom I told that I had been informed that the cases had been taken by [Richter]. Some time after that, *Feldwebel Lieutenant* Richter sent an order for me to report to him in town, but as I had received an order from my Company Officer that I was not to go to the Parcel Office unless I obtained special permission, I did not go. The *Feldwebel Lieutenant* then came to my Company. At first he tried to bully me but, finding it no good, again ordered me to attend the parcel office in town. I informed him that I was not allowed to go there. He then offered to pay me for three cases and stated that the other five had been used in the parcel office. I refused to accept payment except for the eight cases. As no further notice was taken of my complaint, upon the arrival of the Dutch Attaché on 4th February I made a complaint in the presence of my Company Officer about the cases ... The *feldwebel* referred to takes all wood of

the Russian parcels and at one time boxes belonging to the French Red Cross. These are taken to his private house in town ... It is very difficult for anyone to accuse him of taking anything as it would only be a person's evidence against unlimited other evidence.[43]

After he left Mersburg, on 6 February, he heard that a small payment had been made to his successor as President of the Help Committee as compensation for the stolen cases and it had been agreed that no other cases would be taken.

Archer, like many others, did not make an escape attempt. Of all the British prisoners of war, 'it is not known how many attempted escape, although the number probably ran into hundreds rather than thousands. Success was limited, many being captured on the heavily protected Dutch border. The punishment was solitary confinement on starvation rations.'[44] He collected everything necessary for escaping, such as a compass, clothing, maps and wire cutters but, as it turned out, he did not use them. During the first eighteen months in camp he could not walk far enough, and later, after his leg was healed, there was 'always something cropping up' to delay his attempt.

> It was a very difficult undertaking from Mersburg, not on account of getting out of the camp which could easily be arranged but the great distance, 500 miles, from both Switzerland and Holland. Only two out of the hundreds who made the attempt succeeded in escaping. They went by rail all the way; it was a clever move. In 1917 I got in touch with a German who said for £50 to be paid to his brother when I arrived in Holland he would give me every assistance [to escape]. His scheme was a good one and I think would have been successful, but I was so fed up with being shut up inside barbed wire [that] when the exchange [plan] was agreed [under which some prisoners would be transferred to Holland on a reciprocal basis] I was not keen to stay longer on the chance of escape. Indeed he advised me not to volunteer to stay in Germany as he could not be certain when, if ever, he would be able to get me to Holland. I only went outside Mersburg Camp about six times during my three years and three months stay there, and from the summer of 1916 never put my foot outside until I left [in 1918].

He occupied his time in Germany by assisting the other prisoners as much as he could - both personally and informally and also officially as President of the British Help Committee - by learning a little French and in the winter by trying to keep warm. He habitually walked several miles every day so as to keep fit: '40 paces and about turn.' And he was always on the lookout for vegetables and other food to supplement the normal prison diet and the parcels he received. He had, of course, earlier successful experience of stealing fresh food - for example, beetroot and peaches - when under siege at Ladysmith.

By the middle of February 1918 he had been moved from Germany to Scheveningen in Holland.[45] Here he felt much freer and physically much better. Relative freedom took some getting used to: 'One did not realise how soft one was until one arrived here', and it took quite a while for him to get over 'the prison feeling.' Except the *Hotel Les Galaries*, which was used as a depot, transferred prisoners were accommodated in private houses, some terraced, others detached, that the Dutch Government had requisitioned and converted into temporary barracks. Archer was billeted at 50 Van Aassen Straat.[46] The bedding, much to his pleasure, with its white sheets, was 'very good' and 'everything was very nice and clean.' After three and a half years in prison, without sheets, having to sleep in wet and usually unhygienic bedding, these were profoundly welcome changes, his earlier experience of poor sleeping conditions when on active service notwithstanding. In Holland, too, he shaved off the beard that he had grown in Germany, but retained his moustache.[47]

At Scheveningen he had 'a small room like a bunk in barracks' - another treat. He told a friend he was quite fit again and could walk well, though his football days were over. Major Day of the Warwickshire Regiment was his Commander in Holland. There were just over 50 members of the Rifle Brigade, though no officers, with him, and they expected shortly to be put together in a group with the King's Royal Rifle Corps. He was pleased to learn that so many of his Rifle Brigade comrades had escaped at Cambrai on 26 August 1914 and that the majority were doing well.[48] In a letter which he drafted at this time he brought a friend up to date:[49]

> The health of the troops is very good. The only drawback in this place [Scheveningen] is the food, which is not sufficient even for an old chap like myself. It would not be so bad but it is so difficult to buy anything and the prices are intended for millionaires, but still we manage to rub along. One gets so very hungry here what with the sea air etc., and after being shut up in a filthy dirty laager one always feels hungry. This is one of the cleanest places I have ever seen. The contrast from what one has been used to since being taken prisoner impresses itself so much on one.

My wound does not trouble me although I have lost a good deal of my thigh muscle of my right leg, but I can still walk well. Did 30 kilometers a few days ago and can still kick a football. Have got rid of the barbed wire feeling and am feeling better than I have done for the last three and a half years. It was rotten luck to get captured so early in the war - my only campaign that I have not seen out to the finish.

You cannot tell what a miserable time I had in Germany and knowing that everybody was getting promoted, and being laid by the heels did not improve one ... I am now getting into condition again. I am walking about twelve miles a day just to get myself in trim. You cannot tell what a relief it is to practically have ones full liberty, but the greatest relief of all is to get into the fresh air again. In the laager one could never get away from the smells. The rooms were always crowded and in the winter windows were very rarely opened, and what with tobacco smoke, small fires in out of the way corners (both strictly forbidden) one could very rarely see from one end of the room to the other, everything covered with smuts, and ones nostrils always filled with blacks. The only place for exercise was between the huts or on the small Barrack square, about 60 by 50 yards.

The matter of others being promoted while he was a prisoner, to which he referred, troubled him a great deal. Now that he was in the relative freedom and comparative comfort of Holland, he pursued the matter. He wrote many letters, both official and personal, in attempts to secure the commission of which he had so narrowly been deprived by being wounded and captured.[50] In his private papers, he kept numerous scraps of paper on which he drafted letters for his application to be commissioned. The replies were deeply disappointing: 'The case of Colour Sergeant Archer has been carefully considered and it is regretted that he cannot be granted a commission whilst he remains a prisoner of war.'[51] He continued to pursue the question and received a good deal of support in doing so. General Howard said: 'We must get Colonel Biddulph's evidence that he recommended you for a commission, that you accepted it, and that you did duty as an officer.'[52] He wrote to a number of influential people for their help, and everyone he approached seemed genuinely to support him and do all they could to assist. He felt it was very unfortunate that Brigadier Gough had been killed - in action at Estiaire on 20 February 1915 - for he would undoubtedly most strongly have pushed his case for a commission. Lady Gough had written to him 'as an envelope was found in his despatch case addressed to' Archer.[53] His case, basically, was:

On about the 10th August Colonel Biddulph asked me if I would accept a commission. I accepted, Colonel Biddulph informing me that he was going to get me out to the front with the battalion but was not certain how it could be managed. I was sent to Wivenhoe in charge of a party of men on defence work and remained there until the 1st Battalion left for Harrow. From then until I was wounded on 26th August I performed officer's duties and was i/c a platoon ... Since 1908 when I was seconded under the Colonial Office I served in the Somaliland Expedition, 1908-10, and had charge of the Maxim guns etc. etc. In 1911 Colonel Thesiger [killed in action in France, on 29 September 1915], who was then Inspector-General KAR, recommended me for a Quartermastership with a view to my getting the Discharge Depot, Gosport, but the War Office said 'Too old for registration for a Quartermastership'! At Harrow again the Colonel drew the attention of General Snow to me but I do not know what the conversation was as the General only told me 'You will have a fine chest of medals after this show, Archer'.[54]

His firm belief was that he had been recommended for a commission in the Rifle Brigade not only by Biddulph but also by Brigadier Hunter Weston, Brigade Commander, and General Snow, Divisional Commander. Indeed Biddulph acknowledged in a letter to General Howard that he had recommended Archer for a commission in 1914, that because of the shortage of officers he performed officers' duties as a platoon commander, and that had he not been severely wounded and taken prisoner at the Battle of Cateau he would in the ordinary course of events have been promoted to be Second Lieutenant.[55]

He was both profoundly disappointed and resentful about not being commissioned, as he revealed to a former colleague: 'I am in a rather rotten position. Officially I am the same rank as when you left the Battalion, i.e. Colour Sergeant, and I am junior in rank to many who were in short frocks when I was promoted Colour Sergeant, and who have never left England until this war.'[56] And to another colleague he wrote: 'Like myself, I expect you are awfully fed up being a prisoner especially when one sees how promotion is flying about for the lucky ones.'[57] His total daily pay in 1898 had been four shillings and three pence, and this had been increased by seven pence in 1902. From 1914 to 1917 it was only three shillings and six pence, which was increased by sixpence in September 1917. It rankled, too, that he had in good faith incurred expenditure on officer's equipment at Colchester before going to France in August 1914.

Eventually it became clear that the War Office would not give in and grant him a commission. A recommendation from Major de Moleynes was rejected because he was over 32 years of age. About 8000 officers had to be absorbed and this had a dampening effect on promotions.[58] The War Office persisted in their principal explanation that it was not possible to promote a person while he was a prisoner of war. Those who so strongly supported his application began to realise it was a lost cause, despite its undoubted merits: 'The commission was an impossibility, I'm sure - after all you only lost it by bad luck in being taken prisoner.'[59]

Archer had eventually to accept the inevitable, all the high level support he was receiving notwithstanding. As he told General Howard somewhat bitterly:

> I don't think there is any point in pressing my case further. I was unfortunate in getting bowled over so early in the war. I expect when my leave expires on the 12th January I shall be discharged with a Colour Sergeant's pension. At present I have not the slightest idea what I am going to do, but shall probably apply to the Colonial Office for an appointment. They may overlook my age as I have served under the Colonial Office before [when in the KAR]. At times it makes one regret having been so foolish as to constantly volunteer for service, especially when one sees shirkers etc. who have stayed at home and getting all the plums etc.[60]

Rumours that the war was nearly over became prevalent in many prison camps several weeks before 11 November 1918 when the Armistice was signed. 'When peace did arrive, many prisoners in western Germany were able to make short train journeys to Holland or France. Prisoners in eastern Germany were not so fortunate.'[61] Archer was already in Holland, and on 15 November he left Scheveningen for Rotterdam and at midday embarked on the small SS *Stockport*. They sailed at five o'clock the next morning and were 'nearly blown up by a floating mine anchored.' On 17 November they arrived at Hull at 1.0 p.m. and received a 'great reception', though the camp there was 'rotten', with bad accommodation and with all ranks mixed. He was then moved to Rippon, and on 21 November he left there on leave. 'The only good organisation at Rippon was the medical and food.' He was awarded the 1914 (Mons) Star, the General Service Medal and the Victory Medal. The ribbons of these now joined the other eight on his chest.

Other prisoners have described their parallel experiences at the end of the war:

[They] took a train from [their] camp in Germany to Rotterdam and then sailed to Hull. 'There were crowds of people on both sides of the Humber, waving and shouting out "Welcome Home!", hundreds waving all kinds of handkerchiefs and Union Jacks.' ... For many of the first prisoners who came home [such as Archer], there was a rousing reception, but, as the weeks passed, many prisoners arrived home and were met by no one. For most, there was a brief return to the regiment - to take advantage of the two months' special leave granted to POWs - before they returned home for good. But after a long time in captivity, some were unable to adjust to civilian life ... All in all, although most of the prisoners of the Kaiser eventually returned home, about 20,000 - almost one in eight - didn't come back. Of those that died, maybe half of them ended up in unmarked graves. And even those that did return were soon forgotten.[62]

Archer's wounds had been so severe and so many of his colleagues had been killed at Cambrai that he was lucky to have escaped death, and his incarceration had been so long - virtually the whole of the war - that he was lucky to have survived the rigours and privations of imprisonment. During the long hours in hospital and especially in the prison camps, and on his eventual return to Britain, he may well have contemplated his escape from death and his survival and have reflected on his mother's reminder, written to him a year before the war: 'There is a Providence who watches over all our ways, rough hew them as we will.'[63]

While in prison, he 'kept a rough diary but it was confiscated when [he] left for Holland.' His mental recall, however, was exceptionally good and the details of his recent experiences were deeply etched into his mind, so that in the months following his release he was able to re-write the diary from memory. He almost certainly started this during his time in Holland, when events were still very fresh in his mind, and completed it within the following year. It was written for his friends because he thought they 'would all like to have a short account of what has been happening since the outbreak of war.'[64]

He spent Christmas at Leighton Buzzard,[65] where his Aunt Finch lived, and New Year's Eve with Harry Green and his family, after which he went on to another party, leaving at 2.30 a.m. 'K and I great chums.'[66] The following day he went for a walk with Dora, from 10 to 11.0 a.m.[67] and with Nellie from 11.15 a.m. to 12.30 p.m. In the evening he went to the Masonic Lodge for dinner and responded to the toast, 'The Visitors.' On 22 January he saw Colonel Lord Henniker about employment possibilities. Henniker knew of none but said he would make some recommendations on his behalf. That same day he applied to be discharged from the Army at the end of his leave. He then packed up his kit at Parndon and bought a suit of clothes for four pounds fifteen shillings and a raincoat for four pounds three shillings and eleven pence.[68] Had it not been for the fact that the final four years of his army service had been discoloured by his being a prisoner of war and unable to secure the commission that was, many would think, rightly his, he may well have found this experience much more sad than, it seems, he did. He was discharged from the army on pension on 20 February 1919, at the age of 48. For the first time in just over thirty years he was no longer a soldier.

CHAPTER NINE

THE PRISON SERVICE - NYASALAND: 1919-1939

The day after he applied to be discharged from the army - and pursuing the idea that he might try to secure a Colonial Office appointment - Archer wrote to the Colonial Office seeking employment. Two days later he wrote to the Governor of Nyasaland, who was on leave in England, and told him that he had applied for the post of Superintendent of the Central Prison in Zomba. Sir George Smith had been appointed Governor before the war, on 17 May 1913, and had known Archer when he was in the King's African Rifles. In his reply Smith said that the post of Superintendent had been offered to another person, Warren, but he had declined it. He did not know if Sir Hector Duff, who was acting Governor, or the Colonial Office, had made any further plans to fill the post, but he sent Archer's letter and its enclosures to the person in charge of Nyasaland at the Colonial Office. It is likely that Warren declined the Prison post knowing that he was about to be promoted to a more remunerative, less troublesome and less onerous post in the customs department.[1]

Smith was a little anxious about whether Archer's wound would harm his application. The Governor need not have worried, because, shortly, he was passed medically fit and received an offer of appointment to the Nyasaland post, which he promptly accepted on 21 February, the day after he was discharged from the army. He expected to leave by the first available boat after 1 April.[2]

Before the war there had been no separate prisons department in Nyasaland, nor any European officer appointed specially to take charge of prisons. A central prison to cater for long-service prisoners existed in the military cantonment at Zomba under the control of the officer commanding troops. Those with sentences less that six months were accommodated in district prisons, with the civil police acting as warders under the control of District Commissioners. As soon as Archer was appointed, the Governor wrote to tell him of the important changes that were intended in Nyasaland and what he expected of him:

> It is the intention to make prison life in Nyasaland very different from what it was when you were in the KAR. The new building has been designed for this purpose and will be, when completed, as fine an institution of the kind as you will find in any of the British Colonies. I am glad you are to have before you leave some experience of prison work and discipline in England. You have as Deputy Superintendent a good man who has been trained in Prison work in England and his detailed knowledge and experience should be of great assistance to you.[3] However, during your attendance at a convict establishment here [in England] you should make yourself acquainted generally and, as far as possible, with all matters of control, discipline and punishments and the books and records kept. The following points should be attended to: 1. Separate or cellular confinement. 2. Close confinement as punishment. 3. The employment of convicts both in 1 and in association. 4. Moral and other instruction of prisoners. 5. Distribution of duties of the Prison staff. Of course there must be a marked difference between what is done in England and what is attempted in Nyasaland, arising partly in the difference in local conditions and in the physical and mental condition of the prisoners concerned, but the more you can learn about prison work in England the better it will be, I am sure, for the discharge of the duties which lie before you. The new house which is being built for you near the Prison will not be ready by the time you arrive but other arrangements will be made temporarily for your accommodation.[4]

Each day from 10 to 21 March Archer went to Wormwood Scrubs prison and worked with Prison Warder Stone. The journey across London was 'quite a rush' to get to the prison by eight o'clock. He left Brockley Station at two minutes to seven in the morning and then had to run or walk fast from London Bridge to Wood Lane to catch another train to arrive in time at the prison.[5]

On Friday 9 May he left England for Nyasaland. He caught a train from St Pancras station late in the morning and arrived at Tilbury an hour later. Unused to the absence of military - and to some extent prison camp - discipline, and keen to be on his way to start his new life, he was exasperated by delays in embarkation but was pleased with his cabin once he was on board: 'Rotten arrangements re inspection of embarkation tickets. After passing Embarkation Officer, had to wait two hours then another wait to give up ticket Embarkation Officer had given us. Good berth. Port side outer cabin.'

The weather was foggy and cold during the first few days of the voyage, and the ship, the *Saxon*, was 'a great roller', pitching a good deal, though he seems not to have been seasick - maybe his years on a prison camp diet had, if only temporarily, hardened rather than weakened his stomach. He enjoyed the visit on 14 May to Madeira and its 'splendid views', the walks and the ride in a bullock cart taxi, but was irritated by the number of people asking for money: 'almost as bad as Egypt'. He commented critically - as one used to military discipline and public decorum - on some South African officers and troops having a row on shore and returning to the ship 'frisky and helpless'. It was soon getting 'rather hot'. His daily routine was: '6.0 a.m. bath in sea water, wash down with fresh water to take off the stickiness - shave etc. 8.0 a.m. breakfast. Walk, bridge etc. 12.30 lunch. Afternoons, sports. Dinner 7.0 p.m. - dress. Evenings, concerts, dances etc. 11.0 p.m. bed.' There was a band on deck in the late evenings and he attended a fancy dress ball, which was a 'very good show'. After two weeks at sea he saw 'lots of flying fish' and 'whales spouting about a mile away.' On the last night of the voyage there was 'a bit of a bust up ... several passengers got frisky and got a telling off the next morning.'

They docked at Cape Town at 9.0 a.m. on 28 May and - like many thousands of other voyagers over the years - Archer enjoyed the 'splendid view coming into the bay'. He spent much of the rest of that day arranging his baggage, and was irritated that one box from the Army and Navy Stores was missing. He stayed at the Grand Hotel and in the course of the next two days visited Camp Bay - 'splendid scenery' - the Cape Town pier and a naval concert, and arranged for his rail ticket to travel north. He left Cape Town by train mid morning on Saturday 31 May and over the next four days travelled via Paarl, the Orange River, the Modder River - where he had marched almost exactly nineteen years earlier after Ladysmith had been relieved - Kimberley and Mafeking to Bulawayo. Here he changed trains and went on to Salisbury, where he took a walk round the town but did not recognise anywhere he had been during the Mashonaland campaign: the settlement had grown a great deal in the meantime from the 'few tin huts' of 1896.[6]

He arrived at Beira - also now much larger than when he was last there - at 7.30 a.m. on 5 June and 'saw Sir Hector Duff and Mr Pratt Barlow'. He put up at the Savoy Hotel, 'Beira's leading hotel, a three storied brick building replete with all modern conveniences, in a central position on the sea front', according to the hotel's advertisements.[7] For its time it was a fine hotel, with 'well ventilated bedrooms opening on to spacious verandahs [with] bathrooms and lavatories on all floors [and] electric light throughout.' The following day he embarked on the SS *Ipu*. The next day, having anchored outside the bar, he transferred to the SWS *Empress*. This was the boat on which he had slept overnight in May 1914 before travelling downstream on his way to England. His journey up river was comfortable and he was pleased with the 'splendid weather' and the absence of mosquitoes.' They stopped at Shupanga, which he had visited on his way both to and from Somaliland ten years earlier, and he was disappointed to see how much the place had deteriorated in the meantime:

> This place is going to ruin. It is now occupied by Portuguese. Mrs Livingstone's grave is broken, cross broken off, top cross still there. The gardens, which when the French priests were there were the best in the country, are now overrun with grass etc.

On 10 June he arrived at Chindio on the north bank of the Zambezi River. A further fall in the level of the Shire River after he had first travelled this route in 1908 had brought about an extension of the railway south of Port Herald to Chindio. This extension, of 60 miles, was constructed between 1913 and 1915 by the Central Africa Railway Company, a subsidiary of the Shire Highlands Railway, and was largely in Portuguese territory.[8] At Chindio he met two old friends, Walker and Eldridge, who were going on leave from Nyasaland.[9] He left Chindio by train at 6.0 a.m. the next day and arrived at Port Herald two hours later. Here he noticed significantly more planting in African villages than when he had left. He travelled on from Port Herald by train. When he arrived at Limbe he stayed at Copeland's Hotel.[10] The next day he went on to Zomba in a lorry - there had been few, if any, in the country when he left in 1914 - and only narrowly escaped disaster on the way.

> Left Limbe about 8.0 a.m. At a store near the old Blantyre Road I was standing off the road when a motor car coming from Zomba passed our lorry. At the same time another motor coming from Blantyre came by on the right side and knocked me over. It did not stop but near Thorburn's[11] it came back and the fellow apologised. Put up at Keyte's.[12]

The next day he called on the Acting Chief Secretary, Ernest Costley-White.[13] He was told that he was not to take over the prison formally until he had seen the Governor. He called on Colonel Baxter[14] and then visited the prison: 'Quite a fine building or will be when completed.' On 18 June he took over the prison from A C Hayter, who had been looking after it while awaiting his arrival.[15] The following day he was given permission by Colonel Baxter temporarily to occupy a house next to the Governor's, and he made arrangements with the Public Works Department to move in. Two days later the Governor - who had arrived back from Britain a few weeks earlier - inspected the prison and selected a site for Archer's new house and for a temporary leper prison.

One of Archer's earliest visits on his return to Nyasaland was to see what had happened to the property he had left behind when he went on leave in 1914:

> I went to KAR Boma to look up my kit. Most things have been taken. Remainder have been destroyed by weevils [more likely white ants]. Visited Prison, Lunatic Asylum, Isolation etc. Lots of prisoners knew me [The prison had been in the KAR cantonment when he left in 1914]. All the old KAR askari knew me.[16]

He was pleased to be back. The African prisoners and soldiers seem to have played a major part in helping him immediately to feel at home after five years' absence. Those prisoners who knew him must have been in gaol for at least five years - or had returned to gaol in the meantime. Since he himself had been in a prison camp for most of that intervening period, and in at least as uncongenial conditions, it would not be surprising if he sensed a fellow feeling with them.

His European colleagues, too, helped him. He was made a member of the committee arranging the 19 July Peace Celebrations and Sports, and was soon playing a full part in Zomba's social and sporting life, taking up, as it were, where he had left off five years earlier, save that he was older and somewhat less robust physically than he had been then.

During his first tour of duty, from 1919 to 1921, he played a great deal of cricket and hockey and did a good deal of competitive shooting.[17] On his first Sunday back in the country, 15 June 1919, he played cricket for Zomba against the Army, made two runs and 'dropped a sitter of a catch whilst fielding on the boundary at leg.' He was, of course, several years out of practice. The next day he was 'very stiff after cricket'. Later in the year he played centre half at hockey and was pleased that he was not as stiff the next day as he thought he would be.

On 4 July he shot on the KAR rifle range and the following day on the Nyasaland Volunteer Reserve range, securing the second best shot on each occasion. It seems that he had lost little of his rifle shooting skill despite having been a prisoner of war for so long. On 26 July he shot for the Edwards Cup and equalled first with Purves. James McLennan Purves, the Chief Forest Officer, had been in the Nyasaland civil service since August 1900, and consequently he and Archer were well known to each other.[18]

By attending the annual sports at Blantyre, as in other ways, he was resuming part of the life he had led before the war. In August 1920, he was captain of the Zomba shooting and athletics teams, and played in the Zomba hockey team, but not cricket or football.[19] He was quickly and comfortably settling back into Nyasaland life. His relationships with the KAR were still close:

> 12 August 1920. Left Zomba by Packard about 8.30. Caught up by Colonel Baxter with his car and taken to Blantyre. Saw finish of cricket match. 13 August. Won Shire Highland Cup. Won 10/- at bridge. 14 August. Returned to Zomba in KAR mess car.

The wound to his thigh does not seem in any way to have hindered his physical activities but, possibly because he was out of practice, or possibly because he was not as young as he had been, his hockey and tennis playing incurred a number of injuries. Early in January 1921, while playing hockey, he and Northern,[20] struck a ball at the same time. The ball shot up into the air and hit Archer hard on the bridge of the nose: he 'saw stars'. Further injury followed in the same match when Callow[21] hit him hard with a ball inside his right thigh, the very place where he had been wounded at Cambrai. The next day his nose was very sore and he had black eyes, but his thigh seems not to have troubled him. Maybe because of these injuries, his recreation for the next few days was sedentary: playing chess. Then a fortnight after he received his black eyes, when playing hockey again, Stewart[22] ran his shoulder into Archer's nose, which bled profusely. His nose was again very sore, especially since it had not recovered from the earlier injury. Later in the year he strained a muscle in his right calf when playing tennis. At first he thought one of the tennis boys had thrown a ball hard and had caught him on the back of his leg. The following day he could barely walk and only with his knee bent, and shortly a bad bruise appeared.

Socially, he enjoyed entertaining fellow officers and being entertained by them.[23] For example, on New Year's Day 1921, he dined at the KAR officers' mess and stayed till 4.0 a.m. His 'medals made a great impression on the company' and he was 'introduced to Miss ... and [they] had a very interesting talk'.[24] The following morning he slept till 11 a. m. Two days later he spent the morning at Likangala river and then played centre half at hockey in the evening. On Sunday 9 January 1921 he had tea and dined with Frederick Lock[25] and Mrs Lock, and the following Thursday he 'dined with Major Francis Trant Stephens, OBE MC [and they] discussed the Prison Ordinance.'[26] The next Saturday William Bithrey, the recently arrived Depot Police Superintendent, moved into his house to join him, Archer clearing out his dining room to make space.[27] At some of the dinner parties he played bridge. He enthusiastically took up his freemasonry activities again.[28]

The Prison Ordinance, enacted in 1920, set up a Prisons Department with headquarters at Zomba. The newly appointed Commissioner of Police, Stephens, was made Chief Inspector of Prisons. Archer was in charge of the only central prison, that in Zomba. In those districts where European police officers were placed in charge, they also became superintendents of the local prison. In other districts the prisons remained in the charge of the District Commissioner. It was to be Archer's responsibility to introduce the more rigorous discipline that was required by the new rules made under the Ordinance.[29]

It fell to him to supervise a good deal of construction work at the Central Prison during his first few years there, and he was determined to make the new, purpose-designed building, in the Governor's words, 'as fine an institution of the kind as you will find in any of the British Colonies.' In 1919 his deputy's house was built, and his own was completed the following year. Work started on the lunatic asylum in 1920 and a boiler house and incinerator were built in 1921. Work on the new prison building was carried out over a number of years and was substantially finished in 1922, though a drying room and kitchen extension were added the following year and other works followed.[30]

Archer took a keen interest in the personal welfare of the African warders working under him, and he was anxious not to lose the services of those he felt were good prison staff:

18 September 1919. During the last week Cpl Sekamoja has had a lot of trouble with his wife. She ran away from him about a fortnight ago and took some cloth. Cpl Sekamoja obtained the Resident's order for his wife to return and restore the cloth. This was done but the next day she ran away again and refused to return. Cpl Sekamoja went and fetched her back but she went off again and complained to the Resident that he had thrashed her. Cpl Sekamoja summoned for assault. Result: Divorce and wife to pay 5/- for cloth taken.

> 19 September. Cpl Sekamoja complained to me that his late wife and Sgt Lubana KAR came through the lines and jeered at him. His wife had told the Resident that there was no other man in the case so Sekamoja has been done out of his marriage fee to above. He is very cut up about it and wants to leave Zomba so as not to see his wife with another man. He says: 'I don't know but she must have put some medicine in my food as I still love her very much. Also that if her present husband comes through the lines (Barracks) I shall fight him.' Have got the Adjutant to order Sgt Lubana and his wife not to come through my [Prison] Barracks. If he does he will get punished. Cpl Sekamoja on my advice is going to keep at work.

This incident no doubt reminded him of the earlier trouble he had experienced with Kambenzi, of C Company, who was caught in *flagrante delicto* 'on the charpoy' before the war.

There was great agitation in Zomba in October 1919 when one of the long term, and presumably dangerous, prisoners, Jali, escaped. At about 4.30 p.m. the warder, Moloni, who was in charge of a group of nine prisoners working in a garden run by the prison, let them wash in the Bwaila stream on their return from work. While the others were washing, Jali went up stream to a place where he had previously hidden a blanket, and then after dark made off in the direction of Namiwawa, leaving his prison jumper behind. Archer sent warders out 'in all directions' to find Jali, but to no avail.

> 16 October 1919. Telegraphed to Residents Mlanje and Blantyre. All available warders still out, returned from about 3 to 7.0 p.m. Lance Corporal Amani and two others saw Jali at Namiwawa about 2.0 p.m. and Amani fired at him. Jali was evidently pushed rather closely as he left his blanket (a prison one), boots and trousers, but still had a hat, khaki jacket and trousers. Wrote to all Residents.
>
> 23 October. Bet with Colonel Baxter that Jali is captured in 6 months, £1.
>
> 13 December. Jali, who escaped on 15th October and captured on 6th November, when being tried by the Resident Zomba (Aplin[31]) for escape and stealing a prison blanket, when being questioned why he escaped, stated that he had been a prisoner for a number of years. All the Bwanas had been good and he had plenty of food. Since the new Bwana had arrived he had had less food and very much more work. He did not intend to leave the country but escaped so as to tell the judge how much harder it was in prison etc. The Resident reported

this to the judge but sentenced Jali to six months and ten lashes for escape and six months for stealing the blanket. Judge confirmed [the sentence]. Minute papers asked me to make comments on Jali's statements. This I did. Governor's answer: '1. No further action in this case but I should like Mr Archer next time I am at the Prison to show me a pair of leg-irons and the process of attachment to the person of the prisoner. 2. I am quite satisfied with Mr Archer's government of the Prison and with the manner in which the more rigorous discipline under the new rules and system is being introduced by him. Signed G S 17.12.19.'

Archer seems to have made a number of wagers - some of them rather strange - with KAR officers. In addition to that with Colonel Baxter about Jali being recaptured - which he won - he also bet Baxter £1 that he, Baxter, would marry before he returned from leave and he 'bet Colonel Stevens £1 that he won't go to England before 31st December 1920.'

He occasionally met with violence from the prisoners. This was not unexpected, though it occurred infrequently, and he was well able to handle it:

> I remember [him] one day saying that he had been attacked when on his rounds in the prison by a couple of men with a crowbar. He said that his boxing prowess came in handy and he escaped to the gatehouse - the administration block - with minor injuries, a couple of cuts and bruises.[32]

By early February 1921, he had been in the Nyasaland Service for almost two years and was comfortably and happily settled into his new career. He was, therefore, disturbed to receive a somewhat bluntly expressed letter from the Chief Secretary, Richard Rankine,[33] who told him that he would neither be confirmed in his appointment nor be considered for promotion until he had passed the Government language examination in Chinyanja. Archer spoke Chinyanja well, though he had sat none of the required examinations, but being an old soldier, he wrote back to enquire whether the 'colloquial examination passed in 1902' was not sufficient for him to be confirmed in his appointment. This was an obscure request because in 1902 he had been in South Africa and Egypt, nowhere near Nyasaland and its languages. It was not accepted, and he was required to sit an oral examination. On 23 March he took a test before the examiners, Costley-White and Cecil Wade.[34] He passed, and promised 'to look up the language further.' To keep him at his word, he shortly received another message from the Chief Secretary that he would have to pass a further oral test in six months' time, which he did.

It was not simply Africans, such as Sergeant Labana carrying on with Mrs Sekamoja, and prisoner Jali escaping from gaol, who caused him a certain amount of bother. In addition to his prison duties, Archer was also Superintendent of the Lunatic Asylum, in which capacity he was caused a good deal of trouble by a European who had become mentally unstable. Bertram Mason had first joined the Nyasaland civil service on 1 April 1905 and ten years later had been appointed Clerk to the Attorney-General - not that it was this which caused the problem![35] By 1920 he was showing significant signs of being deranged, and it was decided to repatriate him. It fell to Archer to ensure that he was taken safely out of the country as the first step in getting him back to Britain.

> 28 October 1920. To Blantyre with Mason.
>
> 29 October. Rotten night. Mason on the go all night. Talks of knocking Dr Old's head off.[36] He went out just after 5.0 a.m. but when he found that I would not run after him he came back to me. Trying to put the 'wind up' me he told me.
>
> 30 October. Luckily I got a couple of Askari to stop in the entrance to the hospital so got a better night's rest. Mason went off again about 5.30 a.m. and hid himself in the sports pavilion WC and then laughed at me. In the morning he threw his boots at a hospital boy and scored two hits, then before we could stop him he threw two lemonade bottles. Luckily he broke nothing except the bottles
>
> 31 October. Very bad last night, crying etc this morning. Dr Old came in just after 8.0 a.m. I met him at the door. He said something about us being in pyjamas. Then came into the room. Mason got excited and told him about murdering natives and doing nurses out of their money. Mason got hold of him and shook him. Just got hold of him in time. Tried to kick Dr Old but I prevented him. Dr Old called for boys to assist but they kept away (luckily). The doctor went off, has applied to Resident for a new coat.
>
> 1 November. Mason much better but still keeps one awake at night.
>
> 3 November. Fixed up everything for Mason's departure tomorrow. Armfield [who was to accompany Mason on the journey from Nyasaland] nearly as mad as Mason.
>
> 4 November. Mason woke up during night screaming, went to Armfield's bed and would have been alright if Armfield had put his arms round him like a child, but Armfield rolled out of bed further side and Mason rolled over on him. Armfield called for help and I

got hold of Mason and helped him back to bed. Armfield says Mason got hold of his throat - I don't think so. Mason now knows he can frighten Armfield. Returned to Zomba with Colonel Baxter.
5 November. Very tired after a week of looking after Mason.

Dr Old, born in 1868, had qualified as a surgeon and physician in 1895 and had been in the Nyasaland service since April 1900. In his earlier years he had been stationed in the remote northern part of Nyasaland. About two months after his encounter with the demented Mason, though probably unconnected with it, he handed in his resignation and retired with effect from 3 July 1921.

Archer's, in retrospect comical, experience with Mason was not to be his last tussle with an unhinged European. He was due for leave towards the end of 1921, but it was to be no ordinary leave. On the last day of April the previous year, Stewart Galton had been appointed Second Class Clerk in the Lands Department of the Nyasaland civil service. By early October, five months later, he seems to have become insane and was admitted to hospital in Blantyre. It fell to Archer to escort him back to England. On Monday 10 October Archer saw Dr Bury[37] and Bertram Lilley, the Lands Officer,[38] and was told that Galton had left the hospital and could not be found. He arranged to stay in Blantyre and for Dr Bury to hand Galton over to him at ten o'clock the following morning. Some time after Archer had left Bury and Lilley, Dr Hearsey, the Principal Medical Officer,[39] found Galton and ordered him to the hospital. The next day Archer was still having trouble in getting Galton back to the hospital, and he arranged to stay there until Friday while awaiting instructions from Dr Bury about Galton disappearing. He searched the town for him but without success. At about noon Mr Partridge[40] brought Galton back to the hospital. Archer recorded in his diary: 'Bad night, Mr Galton wanting to leave hospital. He is a lunatic and wants a proper attendant and valet. Had to give him a cut with cane to bring him back to hospital by force. Two bruises.'

The following two days Galton was 'still bad' but on 15 October he was 'a little better'. The next day he was also 'better' and went for a walk in the morning. That afternoon at 5.0 p.m. he ran away once more. He was back again the following day and Archer was able to get him to look at some pictures though he was unable to read. On Tuesday 18 October it was time to board the train to start taking Galton to the coast and then back to England. Archer had his own and Galton's luggage to look after: he had three uniform cases, a leather bag, a leather hand bag, a dressing case and a helmet case, and Galton had a valise inside a camp bed, a box, a trunk and a leather dressing case. All of these had to be got onto the train, off it and then onto the ship.

At the very outset of their journey, Archer had great difficulty in getting his ward to the Blantyre railway station. He put him in a *garetta*, a rickshaw pulled by a man in the front and pushed by another at the back, but Galton wanted to box him. Unless he was unaware of Archer's record as a boxer, Galton's wish to box him must have been compelling evidence of the man's insanity! Archer eventually got him on to the train. Galton was not well and was suffering from a boil. They were accompanied by Senior Prison Warder Chipande, who took his own servants with him. The next day, on the train, Galton still looked ill but was sleeping better, and the following day he slept nearly the whole of the day and night, though he continued to want to walk off into the bush. They arrived at Chinde early in the afternoon of Friday 21 October and disembarked two hours later. He met Dr Milne-Tough[41] and Ernest Davey,[42] both of whom had recently arrived at Chinde on their way back from overseas leave, and they messed together on board the ship. Chipande was 'very bad' with malaria, the mosquito nets having large holes in them and the bedsheets being old table cloths. Archer took a walk alongside the beach, relieved to get a breath of fresh air and to be away from his charge for a while. He put up at the African Lakes Corporation boarding house. On Saturday he and Galton went for a swim at 6.30 a.m. and in the afternoon Archer swam again. By this time Galton was 'queer'. The following day, Sunday, Archer and Galton embarked on the SS *Ipu* at 7.0 am. This farcical operation, being hoisted by crane in a basket, must have been a nightmare. Galton was very sea sick. Archer himself succumbed to sea sickness at about 6.0 p.m. and missed his dinner. They arrived at Beira the next day and put up at the Savoy Hotel, where Galton was 'a nuisance'. Later that evening Archer went for a walk and - as if things were not bad enough - it rained heavily. The next afternoon, Galton left the hotel at about three o'clock by the back stairs. Archer searched for him all afternoon and then reported his disappearance to the British Consul, who in turn reported it to the police. Galton returned to the hotel by himself at about half past one the next morning, very tired.

On Wednesday they embarked on the RMS *Guildford Castle* and Archer had a cabin to himself. With great relief, he handed Galton over to the ship's doctor. Two days later they arrived at Lourenco Marques early in the morning and spent the day there. He went for a walk to the Polana, a large hotel in the course of construction, and admired the 'splendid beach and fine hotel.' When they left late the next morning the sea was rough. There was trouble when they arrived at Durban the following day because Galton did not have a passport. The local authorities threatened to put a guard on the ship and charge two shillings an hour for his services. Archer was able to enjoy going to the Empire cinema in the evening and spending the next two days watching Natal play Australia at cricket. The ship left Durban on Wednesday 2 November early in the afternoon. The next stops were at East London, where the ship anchored off shore and Archer was able to relax by going ashore for dinner followed by a walk along the beach; and Port Elizabeth, where again he went ashore, and had a swim. He arrived at Cape Town on 11 November and sailed again the following day. The ship arrived at Tilbury Docks on Tuesday 6 December and he disembarked with Galton in the afternoon.

Even now, Archer's troubles were not over, for Galton was still troublesome and refused to leave London. Instead, he wanted to stay with relatives who, he said, lived at 153 St Quentin Road, West Kensington. When Archer took him there, he found that the highest number house was Number 85. Patiently, he tried several nearby houses that Galton thought were the right ones, but to no avail. They slept that night at Waterloo. The next day, with much relief, he saw Galton off from Waterloo station at 9.30 a.m. but only after considerable difficulty in getting him to leave for Bournemouth. He wired Galton's mother, at Lesbourne, 123 Hankinson Road, to tell her he was on his way. He was later allowed £20 for escorting Galton to England. He had earned every penny of it!

The preparations that he had to make before going on leave, though typically those of an expatriate civil servant of the time, were numerous and often tedious. He had to check on such matters as the detention allowance - fifteen shillings a night at Chinde, Beira, Cape Town and on the train, and ten shillings at Marseilles; handing over his government quarters and furniture; obtaining a medical certificate; insuring his personal effects - arranged by the African Lakes Corporation; checking on hotel charges - fifteen shillings a day at Limbe, twelve shillings and sixpence a day on the train, seventeen shillings and sixpence a day at Chinde, twenty-five shillings a day at the Savoy in Beira; securing an advance of salary; getting permission to defer some of his leave; obtaining firearm licences in England; and arranging with the Vice-Consul at Chinde the return of his personal servant after he had accompanied him there. No doubt, the difference between the detention allowances being quoted per night and the hotel charges being quoted per day was a fruitful source of dispute between the government and its expatriate officers.

Archer's ability to hand Galton over to the ship's doctor while at sea, enabled him more fully to enjoy the voyage back to Britain. This turned out to be important for his future, because it was during this trip that he met Emma Muriel Pike, the daughter of Elizabeth and Jack Pike, an architect who worked in London and later in South Africa. She was returning to Britain after visiting her elder brother, Percy, who was a civil engineer and gifted water-colourist, married to an opera singer, living in South Africa. Muriel, as she was invariably called, had been born at Kennington in London on 18 December 1888.[43] Jack and Muriel spent a good deal of the two weeks voyage together, relaxing in deckchairs, playing deck games and taking photographs of each other. From the outset they enjoyed each other's company.

They spent Christmas and Boxing Day 1921 together, with Muriel's parents at 331 Croxted Road, Herne Hill in South East London. On Saturday 21 January 1922 they left Kings Cross railway station mid morning, arrived in York just after noon, and stayed with T C Atkinson, probably a relative of Muriel's. It was a wet day, but they enjoyed visiting York Minister. The weather turned colder and two days later in snowed. This did not stop them going out, and they visited the Willows and Rowntree's cocoa works and walked round the city walls. It was a happy break together. It is likely that during these four days he proposed to her and she accepted, though the possibility had almost certainly been raised, or at least crossed their minds, while they were on the ship. He left by train on Tuesday 24 January and Muriel followed him four days later.

As early as twenty years previously, in May 1902, his mother had pointedly written: 'I have noticed a good many of your Rifle Brigade swells getting married lately.'[44] And, possibly as a result of her having raised the question again, or having renewed the hint, in June 1909 he wrote: 'Expect I shall settle down one of these days when I find the right woman.'[45] Now, at the age of 51, he had found her.

On the first day of February he bought a wedding ring for £3.10.0, and he and Muriel were married at Holy Trinity Church, Tulse Hill on Saturday 4 February, less than three months after they had first met. Their witnesses were Muriel's mother and father.[46] They went to Bournemouth for their honeymoon, staying at the Empress Hotel. Fortunately they did not run into Galton there! They spent most of their mornings on the beach, even in February, and in the afternoons visited the pier, Christchurch Priory, the Winter Gardens, Boscombe and the Cliff and the Homeric White Star liner. On their last day Muriel was not well and they returned to Croxted Road in the evening of Saturday 10 February. Later in their leave they visited Chudleigh, Ivybridge, Harlow, Parndon, Southend-on-Sea, Frinton, Felixstowe, Leighton Buzzard - to visit Jack's Aunt Finch[47] - and Wolverton.

Having made arrangements with the Crown Agents, Archer spent from 6 March to 11 April almost every day at the School of Weaving, Old Cavendish Street, Oxford Street, London, learning all he could about weaving so that he could introduce the craft to the prisoners in Zomba when he returned.

On 7 April he visited Dr Stannus in Russell Square, London, for a medical check: 'He advises me not to have veins or piles cut out, but to get an elastic stocking. Not to wear puttees.'[48] He was regaining his weight after the privations of the war. When he returned to England at the end of 1918 he weighed nine and a half stone with his coat on. By the middle of 1922, three and a half years later, he weighed just over thirteen stone. He combined this visit to Dr Stannus with attending the Rifle Brigade Veterans' dinner at the Imperial Hotel, and was pleased to meet a number of former colleagues, including Swaine, now a General, whose skill on the parade ground he had so much admired when he first joined the army.[49]

On 5 May Jack and Muriel boarded the SS *Modasa* at the Royal Albert Docks, London, and sailed in the late afternoon. The Government allowance for travelling was £138 but he paid the additional sum of £62 so that he and his bride could travel first class from London to Beira. Not surprisingly, since they were about to set up a married home for the first time, they took rather more goods back with them than they had, separately, brought to England. Although the free allowance for baggage was 3 cwt each they still had to pay excess for another 2½ cwt.[50] They had 19 items of baggage between them.

The day after they sailed from London, they passed Portland and Weymouth Harbour, three days later Cape St Vincent and the following day Gibraltar. Muriel had her fortune told when they were at Port Said - we do not know with what results. At Port Sudan they visited the town during the day and went for a row in the harbour in the evening. Shortly they saw a 'shoal of porpoises under the bow of the boat at night and Muriel took a photograph of one leaping out of the water.'[51] At Aden they visited the Tanks, and during the next few days the monsoon was blowing and he was sea sick. He won ten shillings on the sweep and she won third prize in the Derby Sweep. At Mombasa Muriel was very tired and she rested while he was shown round the prison. At Zanzibar they were 'too lazy to do anything' the day they arrived, but the next day he was shown round the local prison. At Dar es Salaam, too, he was shown round the prison, and noted - with a view to doing the same things eventually in Nyasaland - that they did tailoring and a little carpentry and would probably start mat-making in about a year's time. South of Dar es Salaam the sea was very rough and Muriel was sea sick. They arrived at Beira at three o'clock in the afternoon on Sunday 11 June and stayed overnight on the *Gloucester Castle*, which was anchored there in the harbour. They disembarked at half past nine the next morning, and the Consul advised them to book their tickets to Limbe themselves rather than through the consular office. They had so much luggage that it was difficult to get it all on the train. They left at 1 p.m and it was a bad journey. They arrived at Marraca on the southern bank of the Zambezi at half past two in the morning, were kept hanging about and arrived at Chindio on the northern bank at half past ten at night. It was a 'hot crossing' over the Zambezi by ferry and Muriel was not well. Twenty hours in the low lying, hot and humid Zambezi valley, especially with its myriads of mosquitoes after dark, must have been an uncomfortable experience. They completed their journey by arriving at Limbe at three o'clock the following morning and leaving for Zomba six hours later. They arrived in Zomba after a further two hours' journey, had lunch with the Locks, and stayed with them until they moved into their own house five days later, 19 June 1922. Exhausted, they, and certainly Muriel, must have been glad to arrive.

On 29 July 1922, six weeks after they arrived back in Zomba, Muriel had a distressing attack of malaria - the result of their journey through the Zambezi valley. Archer, deeply concerned, recorded that she 'had high temperature last night. M O to see her 1.30 p.m. Ordered 30 grains quinine per diem. Temp 104^{0}'. She was 'very little better' the next day and the day following that she was admitted to hospital and stayed there for six days.

After this anxious and worrying start, the next three years were spent happily, he at work at the prison and she settling into her new home, shortly getting it ready for their first child, a daughter, Elizabeth - named after her maternal grandmother - known as Betty, who was born on 19 May 1923. Their second child, also a girl, Mary Rose, was born the following year.

Archer devoted a good deal of his leisure time to rifle shooting. Very soon after he returned from leave he spent five days in competitions for the preliminary shoot and for the Manning Cup against Blantyre. Ten days later he qualified at shooting for the Nyasaland Volunteer Reserve. A little later, on 9 September, he shot for the Schmarson Cup and lost it to Allen by four points. On 16 and 17 September, however, he won the Binnie Cup and the Gosling Cup competitions, winning £3.18.6 in prize money. The importance he attached to shooting is demonstrated by the fact that these references to shooting are the only entries in his diary at this time.

On Wednesday 4 February 1925 the Archers left Zomba to go on leave. This was Muriel's first leave from Nyasaland. Before they left he made arrangements for their domestic staff to be paid allowances during the family's absence. The allowances were paid on his behalf by George Paveley, his Deputy Superintendent at the prison, the day before they left Zomba.[52] Their head servant, John Machemba, accompanied them from Zomba to Beira and then returned to his home at Msosa village.

Archer, his wife and two small daughters left Zomba and travelled by road to Limbe, where they stayed the night at an hotel before going on by train the next day to Port Herald. Here they boarded the *Empress* to journey down the Shire River to its confluence with the Zambezi. This was his third trip on the *Empress*. A day later they arrived at the small Portuguese town of Fontes Villa, on the southern bank of the Zambezi River. Already with two tiring days behind them, they now faced two further days of discomfort:

> 6 February. Disembarked in main street of Fontes Villa 2.0 p.m. House boat for about one and a half miles. Walked one mile. Trolley two miles to Caia.
> 7 February. Slept in train at Caia last night. Had no nets. Thousands of mosquitoes. Left Caia at 8.0 a.m. Went about six miles. Wash out on [line, so proceeded on a] trolley to [another] train. Arrived Beira midnight.
> 8-14 February. Queen's Hotel Beira - £11, including milk two bottles daily and 5/- baggage.

The trolleys to which he referred were later described by Winifred Tapson:

> These jolly vehicles have vanished now ... But in those days they made movement easier for the shod feet of Europeans across the sandy wastes ... They were small ramshackle affairs propelled by two almost naked savages, along diminutive railway lines, which scampered along in every sandy street, crossing and criss-crossing without apparent design. Whenever we met a trolley coming in the opposite direction, and only a moment before impact, either one or the other vehicle would be lifted bodily off the track, with its human cargo aboard, to give way to the other.[53]

This last part of their journey to Beira was extremely uncomfortable, especially with a two-year-old child and a very small baby; and the danger of malaria from the mosquitoes would have concerned them greatly. They must have been relieved to get on board ship and to settle for a while, after a journey that had started in a motor car, and then was successively by rail, stern wheel steamer, house boat, walking, trolley, rail, trolley, and train, before they reached the coast at midnight. On 14 February they boarded the SS *Guildford Castle* - the ship on which they had met three years earlier - and, having two small daughters, occupied two cabins. They sailed the following day. After the exertions of the journey to Beira, they found the sea trip relaxing. Their voyage took them via Delagoa Bay and South Africa to Tilbury, where they landed early in the afternoon of 20 March. It had been just over six weeks since they left Zomba.

They spent part of their leave - from 24 April to 26 June 1925 - at Church Farm, Bosham, where their accommodation cost them £2 a week for a large bedroom, their own sitting room and 'attendance', which included all cooking. They paid extra for fires and lighting. After this holiday Archer spent a fortnight, from 29 June to 11 July, with the firm of Newton and Cook, learning about mat-making, which he planned to introduce into the Central Prison in Zomba when he returned. He also visited the Crown Agents to arrange the buying of mat-making materials.[54]

On 25 July he attended the unveiling ceremony of the Rifle Brigade war memorial, and met Colonel Harington, with whom he had served in South Africa, and a number of other former colleagues.

He was saddened to learn of the death of Lawrence Smith, recently retired as Treasurer in the Nyasaland Government, who was killed by lightening one evening on Mitcham Common. He had been playing golf and although there was a thunderstorm he refused to stay in the Club, but made his way in the direction of Mitcham station. He made a habit of never staying late at any Club. Archer attended his funeral at Tooting Parish Church on 27 July, and met Keith Tucker, Smith's successor, and George Tuckett, Postmaster General, there. Smith was a fellow freemason, and on an earlier occasion when he went on leave, Archer took over his responsibilities as Secretary of Lodge David Livingstone.[55]

By mid August their leave in England was at an end. On Thursday 13 August they went by taxi to St Pancras station and then by train to Tilbury where they boarded the ship to return to Africa. They passed Dover at about 10.0 p.m. and arrived at Plymouth at 7.0 a.m. the following morning. They sailed again six hours later, in calm weather. 'Betty [was] bitten badly with bugs or mosquitoes.' The calm weather continued through the Bay of Biscay and, it seems, throughout most of the journey to Cape Town. They left Cape Town on 25 September on the SS *Kakoa*, travelled along the south and east coast of South Africa, arrived at Beira on 16 October, and stayed again at the Queen's Hotel. Things were not going well and they were desperately worried about their daughters' health: 'Betty diarrhoea. Baby very ill.' They left Beira early on 19 October and reached Limbe in the evening of the following day. Here, they stayed at the hotel overnight and went on to Zomba the following afternoon. Five days later, on Monday 26 October, in the evening, Mary Rose died, of gastro-enteritis. She was buried late the next morning in the Zomba cemetery, then, and now, a wonderfully quiet and private place, in the shade of tall dark green Cyprus trees, the resting place of more than one beloved baby.[56]

In 1927, on 31 October, the Archers had two more children, twins, Rosemary and John; and on 26 May 1930, their last child, Beryl, was born.[57]

Archer invariably took his long leaves, as did many expatriate civil servants, to coincide with the British summer. Whilst this meant that they left towards the end of one rainy season and returned at the beginning of the next and therefore had to travel to the coast at a time when malaria was prevalent, they did so in order that they would not have to put up with the cold northern winters. In 1929, for example, they were away from Nyasaland from 11 March until 20 November and had the whole of the summer in England.[58] In Archer's case, the timing was only partly for him and his family to enjoy warmer weather, but partly, too, for him to be able to attend the Bisley shooting competitions. On this leave they rented a house at Southend-on-Sea, where they were visited by Muriel's sister-in-law, Elsie. When Muriel told her that she believed one of Elsie's children had whooping cough, this was strongly refuted. None the less, Betty was soon suffering from whooping cough, and was closely followed by the twins and their father. She later recalled:

> Rosemary and John went down with it, as also did Dad, but he still went to Bisley, sporting bloodshot eyes from the coughing. Many years later he told me that while he was on the range at Bisley he overheard someone behind him saying, 'That man has been on the tiles. Have you seen his eyes? He can't possibly shoot straight.' Whereupon Dad proceeded, with glee, to pick up his cash winnings in some minor event. He amassed a fair amount of pocket money in this way.[59]

In the 1930s Muriel bought the Zomba Hotel from 'Pop' Smithyman, a settler of many years standing in the country, who then built himself and his large family a new house further east in Zomba township.[60] She bought it in order to provide extra income for their retirement. On one of their leaves from Nyasaland she attended the Technical School in Durban to study catering and hotel management.[61] She was a remarkable woman, bright, cultured and hard working:

> My mother was a very intelligent and cultured woman with many accomplishments. When young she came second in the whole of England in a civil service examination. When living in Zomba she and Dad would attend musical evenings where my mother played the piano - my Dad used to say he went out to pour the drinks! [We had a piano at home which she played.] When he retired from the civil service they [lived in] the Zomba Hotel and my mother ran that very successfully before selling it and buying Naiwale. It was she who used to organise the picking and selling of the tung nuts as well as buying tobacco from the locals and then air-drying it to sell.[62]
>
> Mum was a highly intelligent and very private person who could turn her hand to anything. She left school at the age of 14 to work in the post office, working her way through the various departments to be a book-keeper in the Savings Bank. She was one of the family's bread winners in London. She played the piano and sang, mezzo-soprano ... At the prison house Mum belonged to a circle that held musical evenings when people sang, accompanied them on the piano, and there were refreshments ... After her marriage she became an excellent dressmaker - she made me two warm suits, jackets and skirts when I went to University - she made bedside rugs, did upholstery and tried her hand at photography, developing and printing.[63]
>
> She could turn her hand to almost anything. She could sew, knit, crochet and embroider. She made our clothes, stitched fitted covers for furniture for which she had done the upholstery in the first place. She made rugs and did some photography ... She kept the books for the Zomba Hotel. It was my impression that she was the financier for the family.[64]

She also taught some of the women prisoners and those in the lunatic asylum to knit, both as a source of income and as a therapy for them. It is likely that she learned some of her photography from James Lennon, one of Archer's two assistant superintendents, whose hobby was photography, mainly pictures of lizards, frogs, snakes and chameleons, and who had a snake pit in his garden.[65]

Until Archer retired, the family lived in the official Prison house, about a quarter of a mile from the prison itself, with 'snakes in the garden, and convicts cutting the grass.'[66]

> The house we lived in was originally standard government issue: sitting room, dining room, one bedroom and a bathroom. The kitchen was an outhouse, likewise the loo. Over the years, with increasing family, it was added to, to have finally four bedrooms and large pantry, bathroom and adjoining bucket loo using sawdust. To start with there was neither running water nor electricity. Later electricity was supplied from Zomba, for lights only, not for appliances. I don't think we ever had running water. The only taps were in the bathroom, supplied from outside tanks. Each bedroom had a wash stand with jug, basin and pottie. I remember water being rolled [by the prisoners] down the hill in 44-gallon drums from the stream near the lunatic asylum.[67]

Later, in 1939 when Archer retired, the family lived in the hotel until about 1943 when they moved to Naiwale.

In the early 1920s, after he was married, Archer bought a cottage on Zomba Mountain. Before the war he had much enjoyed his climbs to the top of the mountain to shoot quail and to enjoy wild raspberries and the company of his puppy. It was here, too, between the wars, that he and his family enjoyed the coolness, peace and relaxation of the plateau. They all loved it.

> During the hot weather the family used to move up to our cottage on Zomba Mountain, with my father going down the mountain every weekday to work [usually in a *garetta*] - up on the hour and down on the half hour as the road was so narrow [that vehicles could not pass]. One day he went up the mountain in a motorbike and side-car. The dog [who accompanied him] started to play up so Dad put a restraining hand on him, when both they and the side-car went over the side of the mountain. They both got up and shook themselves and there were no broken bones. As small children we were taken up the mountain in a machila carried by four Africans. The cottage was a wonderful place for us children, somewhat primitive and surrounded by fruit trees and pine forests. The fruit trees were planted and grafted by my parents and they taught us how to graft. I remember, as a very small child, we had a donkey up at the cottage, which carried my brother and me on walks and picnics. One day this

wretched donkey decided to go over a rock instead of round it and John and I shot out of our basket seats to the ground. I always remembered this as I broke a tooth.[68]

In about 1930, in replacement of, or in addition to, his motor cycle and side car, he bought a Ford Tudor saloon car which he sold almost twenty years later for the same price - much to his delight.[69]

Archer always enjoyed having dogs around him. He fed them himself and they were devoted to him.[70] As a small child he enjoyed coursing with greyhounds, and when he was first in Nyasaland he took a puppy with him quail shooting on Zomba Plateau. There was, too, the dog that caused the toppling of the motorcycle, sidecar and occupants on the precipitous slopes of the same plateau. He also inherited a large mastiff dog from a colleague who had to leave the country because of ill health. It was chained to its kennel outside the children's bedroom at night and spent much of the day accompanying its master on his rounds.

> It followed Dad everywhere, killed visiting jackal, and, discovering that the Africans stepped aside when Dad was on his rounds of the prison estate, required a likewise obeisance for himself! ... It contracted some skin disease and I remember Rosemary and I taking this dog on a leash to visit the vet. over a mile away. Eventually when it was time to put the dog down, Dad wouldn't leave it to the vet. but took it out for a walk and shot it himself.[71]
>
> The first dog I remember was a large mastiff cross which slept, chained to his large packing crate kennel, just outside the bedroom which Rosemary and I shared at the prison house. If the moon was full, or if anything else disturbed him, he would drag his kennel off the verandah and down the steps. We were not allowed to go near it when it was feeding. Dad had acquired this dog from someone who had to leave the country because of ill health. I was told that the first thing the dog did was to chase and kill some of my mother's chickens. Dad said that he thrashed the dog and it never killed another chicken. It would, however, hunt and kill jackal, grabbing the animal by the back of the neck and giving it two shakes.[72]

It is little wonder that African prisoners deferentially stood aside when this dog passed them. Maybe they were glued to the spot, petrified and unable to flee!

Two of the children went to school in Zomba, run by Mrs Daly, wife of the local garage owner. Betty asked to be allowed to go there at the age of four and her parents allowed it.[73] Beryl went to school when she was about six, travelling from and to their home in a *garetta*. There were about seven children at the school, and Mrs Daly was the only teacher. In the hot weather she moved the school up onto Zomba Plateau. The twins were sent to the Catholic boarding school in Limbe at the age of six. Then, when they reached the age of eight, they were sent to school in Southern Rhodesia.

> We went to Rhodesia by train. Limbe to Salisbury via Beira. One day and one night to Beira. One day in Beira. One night and one day to Salisbury. All this three times a year with the corresponding attacks of malaria from the Shire-Lower Zambezi area. A few times we stayed in Rhodesia on a farm for the April-May holiday together with other kids from Nyasaland. All the European children from Nyasaland and the Fort Jameson area [in Northern Rhodesia] did this train journey. Parents were given a free ticket if they would escort the train. I never knew anyone to do it twice! [Later, the Nyasaland Council of Women designated a member to escort the school train. The trains burned coal in Rhodesia and wood in Nyasaland.[74]] When there had been wash-aways on the line - common round the Chiromo, Port Herald areas - we'd do part of the trip by paddle steamer. We also used the Lower Zambezi bridge and it was one of the interests of the senior boys to get off the train at Dona Anna on the northern side of the river and run across the bridge to Sena on the southern side of the river, a distance of some three miles.[75]

Betty, the eldest child, left Mrs Daly's school at the age of six and was then sent to Oakford Priory boarding school outside Durban in South Africa, for three years before returning to Nyasaland and attending the Catholic boarding school in Limbe and then the Girls' High School in Salisbury.[76]

Archer taught his children to swim, to shoot, to drive and generally to be tough and self-reliant in life. His son, John, later 'did all sorts from whaling in Antarctica to crocodile shooting on the Lower Zambezi, tobacco farming at Fort Jameson, farming in Uganda, game ranging in Tanganyika' and farm management in Tobago.[77] Archer's youngest daughter recalled many years later:

> I remember him teaching me to swim. I had a band round my waist which was attached to a fishing line so he could walk alongside the pool and keep dry! But I also remember swimming with him at

Monkey Bay [on Lake Nyasa] when he must have been in his late seventies.

As a 14 or 15 year old I was bored one holiday and requested a lift from Naiwale to Zomba [a distance of ten miles] in order to have a swim at the club. 'Take the bike', said Dad. The bike - John's - a boy's model, was the only one ever owned by the family. Ten miles downhill to Zomba - fine - lovely swim - ten miles back uphill to Naiwale - not such fun.

He taught me to drive. The test at the age of 16 consisted of driving the policeman from his office to the club. 'If Dad thought I was competent to drive, then I was competent to drive!!'

He also taught us all to ride horses but I never mastered this. The old pony - Toby was his name - used to munch grass to his heart's content until headed for home, which was at a gallop.

He taught us to shoot. He also coached the Zomba Ladies Rifle Club. Mum was a good shot with a .22 rifle. When Naiwale was an army camp [during the Second World War] the officers' mess challenged the Archer family to a shooting match. The Archers won comprehensively.[78]

His eldest daughter also recalled that at school at the age of four she learned to recite the alphabet: 'When I proudly recited this to Dad his only comment was "Can you say it backwards?" So I promptly learned that too.'[79] She, also, long remembered her father's tuition of his children in shooting:

We had a .22 rifle range at the prison house and I remember being taught to shoot with a .22 rifle when I was 10 or 11. John was taught at the same time. We started prone on the verandah and we were not allowed to proceed to the range until we could squeeze the trigger without wobbling! Rosemary and Beryl also became competent shots. When we were at Naiwale, the rifles and shotgun were kept on an open rack in a hallway with the ammunition on the top shelf. The only weapon under lock and key was Dad's revolver. Rosemary used to take the gun out after partridge. We would all take turns in grabbing the shotgun to try and shoot the crows which would come onto the verandah after the scraps in the dog's and cat's feeding bowls. We were never successful, the crows had always flown by the time we got through the door with a loaded gun, which, of course had to be unloaded and put back on the rack. When we were at the prison house we would on occasions meet Dad at the KAR rifle range where he had been involved in a local competition ... Frequently we were involved in the intricacies of cleaning a rifle properly. Dad always used an ordinary army type issue of .303 for competitions.[80]

He also taught them to play tennis and they had a clay court at Naiwale. 'Although we were all pretty good tennis players, Dad always managed to place the ball just out of reach - he was a Senior Citizen then.'[81]
Another of his daughters recalled her father's great energy:

In spite of our father being an older Dad he managed to keep up with all our activities - what I should really say is that we managed to keep up with him. We had a rifle range on Naiwale Estate and we were all taught to shoot with my mother's .22 rifle and progress on to the heavy .303. My mother belonged to the Zomba Ladies Rifle Club - coached by my father - and she was an excellent shot. I still have odd bits of silver that she won.[82]

Rifle shooting played an important part in Archer's life, from his earliest times in the Rifle Brigade, his days as RSM of 1 KAR and, with an inevitable break while he was a prisoner of war, all the way through his time as Superintendent of the Central Prison and well into his retirement. His successes in shooting competitions between the two world wars were remarkable. He had a 25 yard miniature rifle range at the prison house and also frequently used the KAR .303 range. He was a member of the Nyasaland team shooting at Bisley in 1929, 1932 and 1936 and was a member of the Nyasaland national team every year from 1920 to 1939 except when he was on leave. The annual inter-territorial competitions between Nyasaland, Kenya, Uganda and Tanganyika were held at first light to avoid the mirage effect resulting from the earth warming up in the sun. They were held on a given date, regardless of the weather, and the scores were compared by telegram.[83] He won the Shire Highlands Vase Championship under Bisley conditions six times: in 1919, 1920, 1931 and 1938, having also won it while in the KAR in 1912 and 1913. He won the Armed Forces Championship, instituted in 1925, four times: 1926, 1933, 1937 and 1938; and the Duncan Cup, instituted in 1927, five times. He won the longer established Edwards Cup eight times: to his successes while in the KAR in 1912 and 1913, he added 1920, 1923, 1934, 1935, 1937 and 1938. He won the Schmarsow Cup outright in winning the competition two years running and the following year tying for first place. He won the Binnie Cup at the Nyasaland Volunteer Reserve meeting seven times: 1922, 1924, 1927, 1933, 1934, 1935, and

1938. He won the Gosling Cup at the NVR meeting seven times: 1921, 1923, 1933, 1934, 1935, 1937 and 1938. He won the Governor's Cup, instituted in 1934, three times: 1935, 1937 and 1938. He also won the Hodgson Cup in 1933, and in that year, at the NVR annual at home, Lock, the President of the Zomba section, said:

> He wished specially to mention Mr Archer who has been such a stalwart figure in the shooting history of Nyasaland both in this country and at Bisley. Time does not diminish the skill which had enabled him to win no less than five of the trophies in one year. These were the Armed Forces Trophy, the Duncan Cup, the Hodgson Trophy, the Binnie Cup and the Gosling Cup. This was a record in the annals of the section.[84]

Then, *The Nyasaland Times* of 13 February 1936, when Archer was 65 years old, carried the report:

> Vol. J Archer MBE DCM has well and truly qualified as a marksman for 1936. Firing on the NVR range in a qualifying shoot this week, the Zomba veteran scored 96 out of a possible 97. He made a four inch group, obtained 20 points for snap shooting, 32 for rapid and dropped only one point at 500 where he scored 19 out of a possible 20. Congratulations!

But it was 1938 that was his most outstanding year for competitive shooting, when he won all the available scratch cups in Nyasaland, a feat never before accomplished.

By the mid 1930s, when Betty, Rosemary and John were at school in South Africa and Southern Rhodesia, the Archers arranged their overseas leaves differently. Instead of spending nearly all their time in England, they - and Beryl, their youngest child, who stayed with them - now spent part of it in South Africa to be near the children. In 1936, for example, the parents and Beryl left Zomba by road at 9.0 a.m. on Sunday 23 February and left Limbe by rail late in the morning. They arrived at Beira after a twenty-one hour journey and stayed at the Savoy Hotel - where he had stayed on his journey to take up his prison superintendent's post, and also when he had taken the demented Galton back to Britain. Two days later, on 26 February, they boarded the *Llandaff Castle* and sailed the following morning. They called at Delagoa Bay and then Durban, where they spent the following two months, staying at the Torquay Hotel. As always, he combined a certain amount of work with his holiday: he visited the Durban and Pont prisons and made a day trip by rail to see the Pietermaritzburg mental hospital.

He left Durban by himself on the SS *Sterling Castle* on 7 May and arrived at Southampton on 1 June, travelling on the same day to London where he stayed at the Lincoln Hall Hotel, Russsell Square. He then moved to 116 Westbourne Terrace in West London on 9 June and shot at Bisley from 10 June. On 15 June he wrote to the Colonial Office and asked if he could spend the last part of his leave, from 14 August, in South Africa and Southern Rhodesia because his children were at school there. Still combining work with pleasure, late in June he visited Broadmoor Asylum. His request to spend the end of his leave in southern Africa was granted and he sailed on the SS *Llanstephen Castle* from Tilbury on Friday 14 August. He arrived at Durban on 12 September and stayed at the Parade Hotel. The next two months were spent partly in South Africa, where Betty was at school, and partly in Southern Rhodesia, where Rosemary and John were at school. While in Salisbury he visited the new gaol, which was not yet finished or occupied, and 'brought away plan of gallows'. He was responsible for supervising, though not carrying out, sentences of judicial execution in Nyasaland, all at the Central Prison. From 1922 to 1938 inclusive, there were 109 executions at the Central Prison in Zomba. These averaged six a year but there were great variations from 17 in 1928, 11 in 1925 and 10 in 1933, to none in 1930, two in 1923 and 1937 and three in 1926.[85]

From Salisbury he flew back to Nyasaland - his first flight - and arrived at Chileka airport on 20 November. He travelled on to Zomba the following day.

By this time, the mid 1930s, Archer had established for himself the public reputation of a progressive prison reformer. He abolished unproductive labour as a punishment for rule infringement, and substituted extra string-making. We have already seen how he spent part of his leaves studying rope and mat-making and how he took many opportunities to visit other prisons to study their methods and particularly the trades that they taught. He ensured that all long term prisoners left the Central Prison with a skill that would help them re-enter society and remain there: bricklaying, carpentry, tailoring, metalwork, weaving.[86] At his instigation, four African trade warders were appointed in 1931, and helped a great deal in this respect.[87] He always insisted on very high standards of cleanliness of both prisoners and premises, and he continued these high standards after he retired from the prison and was placed in charge of army recruits. When the medical officer examining the recruits said they seemed so much better than those he had examined elsewhere regarding general health and cleanliness, Archer told him that he had paraded the recruits first and ensured that they showered and washed their clothes before seeing the doctor.[88] His keenness on making enforced labour productive and his insistence on cleanliness undoubtedly derived from his experience as a prisoner of war. In the case of cleanliness it derived, too, from his long experience, often serving in trying conditions, as a soldier and particularly as a senior NCO in charge of troops.

He also built the prison estate into a flourishing concern, and he was able to boast that, apart from the salaries and wages, the place was virtually self-supporting, and the only supplies that had to be bought were meat and nails.

> The prison vegetable garden [had] a small mountain stream flowing through it ... Maize was grown for the staple grain, also fruit trees - lemons and the ubiquitous mangoes and pawpaws. Sisal was grown for rope- and string-making and the standard punishment for infringement of prison rules was extra string-making. Long staple Egyptian cotton was grown, spun and woven into cloth from which the prison uniforms were made. We [members of his family] had curtains and bath mats made from the same yarn. Beautiful stuff, soft and silky in feel. The prisoners hated it because it was almost indestructible, would not tear and was probably on the heavy side for a garment. Bricks were made on the site and fired. Blue gums were grown for timber, and sisal poles used for scaffolding. The bricks probably supplied the whole of Zomba.[89]

Almost certainly, his interest in growing foodstuffs for the prisoners - and the effect on their health – also owed something to his own experiences in times of confinement, both at Ladysmith and, particularly, as a prisoner of war.

There was inevitably always the danger when prisoners were employed on outside work, that some would escape. Given a total inmate population averaging over three hundred, the number of escapes was relatively low and of those who did escape the majority were recaptured. We have seen how Jali escaped from the gaol in 1919 only to be recaptured three weeks later. In the twenty years from 1919 to 1938 that Archer was Superintendent of the Central Prison, 123 prisoners escaped - an average of six a year - all from outside working gangs, and 93 of them were recaptured: a 76% recapture rate.[90]

From late 1937 to the middle of 1938 Sir Robert Bell headed a commission enquiring into the financial position of Nyasaland. His report on the prisons is a revealing statement of the position they had reached, especially the Central Prison under Archer just before he retired:

> Technical training is possible only at the Central Prison. Instruction is given in the following trades: tailoring, shoemaking, blacksmithy, tinsmithy, string-making, [mat-making] and weaving. Since the appointment of a European gaoler and four African trade warders in 1931, more effect has been given to this training and it has been possible to make all uniforms for the subordinate African staffs of the civil service, including the khaki uniforms of the police and the warders. [The number of civil servants in the subordinate class, the police and prisons increased from 943 in 1919 to 2097 in 1939. The annual value of the uniforms made for all of these must have been considerable.[91]] Apart from Government work, the Central Prison workshops earn about £100 annually. Labour not required for the upkeep of the prison or not employed in the [work] shops is used on public works in Zomba. The value of the output of the workshops and of labour supplied to other departments in 1936 was £2030.[92] [The expenditure on rations for all prisoners, whether in the Central Prison or in District prisons, in 1936 was £1900, so the value of output of the workshops and labour supplied to other departments, more than paid for the rations.[93]]

In that year, 1936, under Archer's management, the annual cost of maintaining a prisoner in Nyasaland was £7.9.7 as compared with £9.3.9 in Kenya, £14.11.10 in Tanganyika, £18.0.2 in Uganda and £24.0.0 in Zanzibar. The cost of the Central Prison was £4758, against which Archer's income of £2030 contributed 43%. Until 1928 the prisoners at the Central Prison had also grown food crops, valued at £540 a year, specifically to reduce expenditure against the prison ration vote. Archer abandoned this practice in 1928 because it restricted the amount of unskilled labour available, more profitably, to other departments, though he kept the garden going with a smaller number of prisoners. Within a few years of the practice being abandoned, the value of labour used by other departments rose to £900, a 66% increase in value.[94]

In his final annual report on the Central Prison, in 1938, Archer commented on the accommodation there. It was a vast improvement on the conditions he had found when he became Superintendent. The position now was the outcome of the intended reforms Governor Smith had indicated to him in 1919 and, particularly, of his own management and development of the prison. Smith had told him it was intended to 'make prison life in Nyasaland very different from what it was' and he had asked him to pay particular attention to whether convicts should be accommodated in 'separate or cellular confinement'; the question of 'close confinement as punishment'; the employment of convicts both in confinement and in association; and the 'moral and other instruction of prisoners.' Archer's 1938 report said:[95]

> Accommodation at the Central Prison for non-European prisoners consists of two blocks. One block contains 28 association wards, twelve to accommodate six prisoners each and the remaining 16 eight each. The second block contains 66 single cells, four association cells with a capacity for eight prisoners each and six association wards each of which will accommodate six persons. [Almost half of the prisoners, 47.8%, were accommodated eight to a cell; nearly a third, 32.3%, six to a cell, and nearly a fifth, 19.7%, were in single cells. By the standards of the time in African prisons this was good accommodation. In 1918 all prisoners had been accommodated 22 to a cell, save that there were two small solitary confinement cells for 'violent or refractory prisoners.'[96]]
> Within the main walls of the Central Prison are the hospital and some of the workshops. The hospital contains two large wards and a smaller one for serious cases.
> A large building contains the shops, in which are employed tailors, leather workers, weavers, mat-makers and tinsmiths. The carpenters' shop is outside the main walls, as are also the wards for lepers, for those suffering from venereal and other dangerous diseases, and for the observation of new arrivals. [In 1918 there had been no separate accommodation for the observation of new arrivals.[97]]
> The female prison is entirely separate and contains one ward and four single cells. This section has a large exercise yard and is surrounded by a wall. Female prisoners are usually employed on garden work [and, as we have seen, some were taught to knit by Mrs Archer].
> Recidivists are kept apart from first offenders while young prisoners are separated from the older ones. [In 1918 there had been no classification of prisoners.[98]] The younger prisoners are housed in association in 'A' block and work apart from the others. Prisoners who have to serve a sentence long enough to make it possible to teach them a trade are put into the workshops. Numbers of prisoners who have been of exemplary character and have proved trustworthy, have, on release, been given letters of recommendation by the

Superintendent. Many of them have thus been able easily to obtain work as artisans, bricklayers, etc.

Management of the prison was not the only matter in which Archer wrought changes. When he was appointed Superintendent of the Central Prison in 1919 he was also appointed Superintendent of the Lunatic Asylum. Before 1910 lunatics were kept in the then central prison at the KAR camp. In that year a small asylum was built at the camp and continued to be in the charge of the officer in command of troops. In 1919 the lunatic asylum passed to Archer's charge. The following year he started work on having a new asylum built. He was very keen to have the asylum managed as a separate institution from the prison but his proposal to transfer it to the Medical Department was not approved. It may well be that senior members of the Medical Department, with their experience of such mentally sick people as Mason and Galton, besides African patients, had no wish to become formally responsible for the asylum. To emphasise the volume and importance of the work involved in managing the asylum - and to bring pressure to bear to have something done about it - he then made representations that he and his Deputy could not be expected to cope with the increasing responsibilities of the Central Prison and the lunatic asylum without devoting a great deal of their spare time to work which was not part of their main employment. In 1927, in lieu of additional staff and until the asylum could be run as a completely separate institution, he was granted an annual allowance of £100 and his Deputy £50 for their work in relation to the asylum. He continued to be Superintendent of the Asylum and to draw this allowance until he left the service. When, in January 1925, three penthouses, simple lean-to buildings, were blown down at the asylum hospital in a gale, he immediately asked for them to be re-built, and made three new cells for female inmates.

By the late 1930s and the time of Archer's retirement, there was 'temporary accommodation for one European and one Asian, and inadequate accommodation for 87 [African] males and 20 African females' at the asylum. There were 21 male attendants and six female attendants, and the inmates averaged 75 - of whom 34 were classified as 'chronic, presumably irrecoverable, turbulent and dangerous.' This was a ratio of one attendant to fewer than three patients. The accommodation, however, was poor and, at Archer's instigation, it was decided gradually to replace the existing wards and thereby, over a period of years, build a new and separate institution, which would then be transferred to the medical department.[99]

Archer always firmly believed that the asylum should be in the charge of medical officers. He observed a form of madness that he believed had a dietary basis: the patients improved while in the asylum but reverted to their disturbed condition when they were released and returned to their home villages. He complained that the medical officers took no notice of what he said about the inmates and showed little interest, though he admired Dr Shelley[100] for his 'skills and his knowledge of African medicines.'[101] Archer was surprised when Dr Shelley asked, 'When were you in the Sudan?' and went on to explain, 'Your malaria is typical of that region.' It had been almost forty years since he was in the Sudan.[102]

Jack Archer had every reason to be proud of the work he had done as Superintendent of the Central Prison and Lunatic Asylum, and when he retired from the Nyasaland civil service at the very end of 1938, aged 67, the *Nyasaland Times* wrote of him:

> Although a strong disciplinarian, he has a pronounced human touch, for which he found ample scope for expression in his reformatory efforts and in the personal interest he took in the welfare of the unfortunate inmates of the Lunatic Asylum who look upon him in the character of father and friend. His iron nerve and strong fearless personality have had a powerful influence on the many natives who have passed through his hands at the Central Prison, and it can be said with truth that there is no man in the country for whom the average native has greater respect.[103]

CHAPTER TEN

THE SECOND WORLD WAR AND RETIREMENT: 1939-1954

By early 1939 it was clear that another war with Germany was inevitable. Archer was about to take his final retirement leave in Britain and, though he did not say so, he did not want to be caught there again when war broke out, as he had been in 1914. This was not because he was fearful of being placed in personal danger - that thought would not have occurred to him - but because Nyasaland had become his home, and his children were at school in southern Africa. Most importantly, he felt that there might be the opportunity to serve in some capacity in Nyasaland, where, unlike Britain, he and his abilities were well known, and his age was less likely to count against him.

Early in the New Year, on 25 January, he joined the Supplementary Reserve of the KAR, Southern Division, for 'special confidential duty.' This was almost certainly concerned with planning the emergency measures - including recruitment and training for the army - that the Government undertook after the forewarning given by the Munich crisis in September the previous year.[1] Shortly, he wrote to the Brigade Major at Dar es Salaam, in accordance with the Reserve Regulations, and told him that he proposed to leave Beira to go on retirement leave in February 1939 and return to Nyasaland in May. His address would be in London.[2] He and Muriel - the children were at school - sailed from Beira on 28 February, and he formally retired on 18 May 1939 on his return from England.[3] War was declared three and a half months later.

> When war came the transition from peace-time conditions was made smoothly and without delay, thanks to [the emergency planning]. From the start Nyasaland [was] a recruiting and training centre ... The military authorities began to function on a war basis on 1 September 1939, with Nyasaland organised as a sub-area of the Lines of Communication Area, the headquarters of which were in Dar es Salaam ... The Nyasaland sub-area [was] used almost exclusively as a

recruiting ground for the infantry battalions of the KAR and also for the formation of units of the East Africa Army Service Corps. The first thousand native ranks were recruited in two and a half months solely in the Southern Province.[4]

On 18 October 1939 Archer was passed medically fit for garrison duty and depot service, and two days later he was commissioned as a Second Lieutenant, at long last fulfilling the ambition he had held during his thirty years in the Rifle Brigade, and of which he had so narrowly and unfortunately - indeed unjustly - been deprived in 1914. Astonishingly, he was now almost 69. He was commissioned in the East African Army Service Corps and attached to the KAR Depot in Zomba. From 6 November 1939 to 1 April 1940 he was appointed Officer Commanding H Company and then G Company at the Depot. It was a time of great activity during which everyone was kept very busy at the Depot, and especially Archer, as the accommodation had to be expanded to cater for the large numbers of new recruits:

> During the early part of 1940 the establishment of the KAR Depot at Zomba was considerably increased. An intensified recruiting campaign was conducted in the Northern Province by the District Commissioners with the aid of African sergeants. Accommodation for the expanded establishment of the Depot proved a source of difficulty and this was met for the time being by sending companies into temporary camps in the vicinity of Zomba.[5]

From April 1940 until June 1941 he was Officer Commanding the Garrison and Headquarters Company at Zomba, and during this time, on 17 April 1941, he was promoted to the War Service rank of Lieutenant. During February and March 1942, on the instructions of the General Officer Commanding East Africa Command, and the Governors' Conference, he was seconded as Acting Superintendent of the Central Prison and Lunatic Asylum, paid for by the Nyasaland Government. This was to cover for the absence of his successor, Paveley, while on leave, and until Lennon, his deputy, could be appointed Acting Superintendent.[6] No doubt he was pleased to return temporarily to his old post, though he would have been keen to return to his military work. For the following six months he was Officer Commanding Details at Zomba.

As the war situation in East Africa developed it became increasingly necessary to speed up recruiting for the KAR and it was decided to raise additional battalions, [and] the accommodation of the Depot at Zomba was greatly enlarged. Special training camps were constructed at Ekwendeni in the Mzimba District, amongst the Angoni-Atumbuka people, at Mandimba in the Namweras area in the Yao country, and at Mpata Milonde between Dedza and Lilongwe ... The authorities in charge of training have been at pains to ensure that the first month of army life should not be exacting, and measures were taken to recondition recruits who through some deficiency or other were not immediately fit for full duty.[7]

Such was the intensity of recruitment that nearly a third of the fit African adult male population of the country was recruited into the army during the war.[8] Enlisting such a large number of men was a huge exercise. 'In order to meet the increasing demands of the Military for recruits, [another] intensive recruiting campaign was opened at the end of September 1942.'[9]

Civil habilitation camps [were] established at Mpata Milonde and Ntondwe where recruits [were] kept for treatment, when necessary, until they [were] fit to be attested and drafted either to the Military Holding Wing at Namweras or to military training camps.[10]

For the first six months of 1943, Archer was Officer Commanding Details and Camp Commandant with the powers of Commanding Officer at Ekwendeni and then Mpata Milonde.[11] The recruiting campaign continued during the early part of 1943 until 'the requirements of the Military were fully met.'[12] Then,

at the end of June the recruiting organisation was closed down and arrangements were made for recruits presenting themselves after that date to be sent forward to the military reception depot at Ntondwe, and the civil habilitation camp at Mpata Milonde in the Northern Province was closed down.[13]

With this closure Archer left Mpata Milonde and was posted to Ntondwe, where he took over the duties of Quartermaster of the habilitation camp that had been established there.

While at Ekwendeni a convoy passed through, one of many coming down from Kenya on the Great North Road. Archer asked the young major in charge to sign the necessary papers. The major was reluctant to do so, asking why he should 'listen to an old man who knows nothing about the army.' Archer, a Lieutenant at the time, working in his shirt-sleeves, simply reached for his jacket and put it on. He made no comment, but when the major saw the rows of medal ribbons on the jacket, he promptly signed the papers and proceeded on his way.[14]

Early in 1943 the Archer family moved from the Zomba Hotel to land, which they had bought from the bank, some ten miles south of the capital: Naiwale Estate near Ntondwe. This became an army camp - and for six months in 1943, was under Archer's command.

> During the war we had officers and men of the KAR stationed on Naiwale, the officers staying in converted tobacco barns. We [Archer's children] only met them during our school holidays.[15]

After six months stationed at Ntondwe he was posted again to Zomba, to the Initial Training Centre. At various other times he was Officer Commanding Recruits and the Discharges and Dispersal Centre. During much of 1946 he was at the Dispersal Centre at Ntondwe and was given the task of trying to 'clear up all African rank releases from Lilongwe and Namadidi', which numbered over 2000.

He was formally released from the Army, with the honorary rank of Captain, on 25 April 1947. Forty four years earlier, in writing of the army certificates of education, he had told his mother, 'I may yet finish my career as Captain Archer.'[16] Neither he nor his mother could have anticipated how long it would take, nor the manner in which it would come about. He had served seven years and 101 days since 1938, bringing his full army service up to 37 years and 241 days, and his total crown service to almost 58 years. He was awarded the 1939-1945 Medal and, in 1951, the Meritorious Service Medal.

Whilst he was immensely proud of the large number of medals he had won, he was generally quiet and modest about them, though from time to time, almost ritualistically, he would take them out and polish them.[17] When his teenage daughter asked why he had been awarded the Distinguished Conduct Medal at Ladysmith he replied, 'For going through the Boer lines at night and coming back with peaches from the farms.' She long remembered, too, that her father would often bring up the conditions during the Siege of Ladysmith when his children did not finish the food on their plates![18] He may well have thought that the nocturnal expeditions, for example to Thornhill's farm, were more important than the bravery - and leadership in a very tight corner - at Surprise Hill for which he was in fact awarded the medal. Indeed one of the officers of the Rifle Brigade said shortly after the siege was broken:

The peaches, unappetising though they looked, proved our salvation, as there was almost an unlimited supply, and when stewed they were really excellent; they would doubtless have been improved by a little sugar, but as there was none we could not afford to despise such an excellent substitute for vegetables, which latter we had not tasted for many a weary week.'[19]

When his daughter asked why he had been awarded the MBE he replied, modestly but playfully, 'For telling the Chief Secretary to go to hell.' It is likely that this was a reference to differences of opinion that he had with senior secretariat officers who did not fully agree with his prison reforms and his enlightened treatment of inmates of the lunatic asylum, for which the award in fact was almost certainly made.[20]

After he left the army in 1947 Archer spent his time running the Naiwale estate, and leasing part of it to a local farmer. His leisure time was taken up mainly in reading - biographies and military histories. He also enjoyed playing billiards on 'a half sized table with very dead cushions', a table on which he had taught his children to play and on which they all 'had an immense amount of fun.'[21] The family also had another piece of land, further south still, at Namadzi where they did some tenant tobacco farming for a while as well as selling timber from Naiwale.[22] They made a number of alterations to the Naiwale house - a large house some 60 feet by 100 feet - replacing the grass thatch with corrugated iron sheets, repairing the windows and doors, and - welcome innovations for the family - adding a flush toilet and a bathroom. The water supply was from rainwater tanks. Later, when the estate - except the house and garden - was leased to the KAR as a recruiting and training camp, the army drilled a deep bore-hole well that gave an excellent supply of water. The house was connected to this supply - another welcome innovation.[23] Archer planted tung trees, tung oil then commanding a high price as the demand for its use in the paint industry was great during the post war period of reconstruction in Europe.

They did not lose all their Zomba contacts in retirement. They entertained a few old friends, and the cottage caretaker from Zomba Mountain continued to walk down the mountain every week during the fruit season, carrying a large basket of fruit for the family, as he had when they lived in Zomba.[24] Also, as Archer's daughters recalled:

> When we lived at Naiwale, an old African man called Jali used to make watering cans out of corrugated iron; Jali was an ex-convict, a house breaker and a very good welder. He would disappear

periodically and we would be told he was back in gaol. He was invaluable when Mum lost her keys, as he could open anything with a piece of wire.[25]

A regular inmate, Jali, who had been a frequent inmate of prisons from Cape Town to Nyasaland and further north – for theft – worked in the metal shop. Later, when Dad had alterations made to the Naiwale house, Jali was employed to make the gutters and do the other metal work. Jali would never have stolen from my father. I remember Jali working at his forge in a lean-to to the garage. He had some wrinkles and some white hair by then.[26]

One wonders if this multi-talented African gentleman was the same Jali who had escaped from prison in 1919, and had learned the skills of welding - and unofficially of locksmithing - which he put to good and generally legitimate use, but somehow or other found it difficult completely to avoid returning – or being returned – to the place where he had spent so much of his life and had learned most of his trade: the Zomba Central Prison.

Early in 1954 Jack Archer complained of cystitis but this was shortly diagnosed as prostate cancer. He was nursed at Naiwale before undergoing surgery in Zomba hospital. The prostatectomy was unsuccessful, as the cancer re-grew. When Muriel enquired about further treatment, such as radiation, which would have involved his being taken to Salisbury in Southern Rhodesia, the doctor believed that this would be a waste of effort, time and money. He returned to Naiwale and though confined to bed was happy to be at home.[27] He died on 30 July 1954 at the age of 83, in the country where he had spent half his full life and the whole of his married life.

CHAPTER ELEVEN

A MAN AMONG MEN

Jack Archer's was a long, immensely rich and wonderfully varied life. Born into a small yeoman farming family on the Essex-Hertfordshire border in 1871, his earliest years were spent in a rural setting, leading a robust open-air life, horse-riding, coursing with greyhounds, climbing, shooting pigeons, and generally enjoying the countryside in the company of his cousin Fred. School seems not to have been an unhappy experience even though he said little about it save to remark that he did not learn much there. His father's death brought about a family move to Lewisham, and his aunt's death caused his mother to return to Essex, but Jack stayed in London, where, although he took little pleasure in his work in the wine and spirit trade - and eventually escaped to the countryside with his uncle in Hampshire - he did enjoy learning to box and becoming skilled in the sport. Indeed, save briefly from time to time to see his mother and, finally, immediately after the First World War, he did not return to his Essex home. Even the short period in Lewisham had its benefits, because it was here that the family came in contact with Captain Lawrence with whose help Jack joined the army, which became his 'home' for the next three decades.

His relationship with his mother was close. He invariably spent his leaves from the army with her, and visited her whenever he was in England on his way to or from athletics meetings. Throughout the remainder of her life he wrote to her regularly and was always generous to her in money matters: 'I am sending you £130, my savings since I joined the KAR. Don't forget to use what you want of it' 'Don't forget that if you do want the money that you have in the bank you are to consider it as your own.' He confided in her and to no others, for example, his hopes of promotion and his aspirations to be commissioned: 'I think it almost certain that I shall be promoted QMS when the vacancy occurs.' 'I may yet finish my career as Captain Archer.' It was a tragedy for both of them that she died while he was a prisoner of war. He was less close to his brother, Harry, and rarely mentioned him in his letters, though he was generous to him, too: 'Yes, I sent Harry some money years ago and also lent him the money I saved whilst in Mashonaland.'[1]

To many modern ears thirty years in the army may sound a boring and uninteresting way to spend a large part of ones lifetime, yet this was far from the case with Jack Archer. In the course of those thirty years he served on three continents, in England, Ireland, Rhodesia, Egypt, the Sudan, Malta, Crete, South Africa, Nyasaland, India, France and – involuntarily – Germany and Holland. On his journeys he called at other countries: Madeira, Kenya, Tanganyika, Zanzibar and Mozambique. He was on active service, in most cases fighting, in Rhodesia, Egypt and the Sudan, Crete, South Africa, Somaliland and France. He became a much travelled man.

Even when not on active service, his life was far from boring. In his early army years in England and Ireland his time was full, with military training, sports, athletics, boxing and shooting. When travelling he carefully observed the countryside, briefly recorded the features of the landscape, took an interest in all that he saw and appreciated the beauty of the areas through which he passed, frequently using the word 'splendid' to describe attractive views. Of a journey from Belfast to Dublin while a young soldier he remarked that 'the country looked lovely, greener than anywhere I have ever seen before'; and he enjoyed the 'splendid view' from the Hill of Allen. On his way to Mashonaland, he found Wynberg 'a pretty place with splendid views'; and he enjoyed the 'splendid views from the top' of Table Mountain. He admired, too, the good view of the coast from the ship, especially Zululand: he could 'see the surf breaking on the cliffs ... It looked grand.' On the journey from Fontesvilla to Chimoio he was impressed by the forest with its 'splendid trees'. In Egypt he was fascinated by the Abu Simbel temples, 'hewn out of solid rock', and the 'wonderful piece of engineering' at the Aswan Dam. He found Mombasa 'very pretty'. When hail cleared the air at Chaubattia, revealing 'splendid views', better than he had seen before, he commented that the mountains 'only look about 6 miles away.' And just after the First World War he wrote of the 'splendid views' at Madeira and the 'splendid scenery' at Camps Bay, on his way back to Nyasaland.

Many prisoners of war in Germany inevitably found some of the time weighing heavily on their hands, but this again was not so with Archer, despite his being incarcerated for virtually the whole of the war, far, far longer than the majority. Being President of the British Help Committee occupied a great deal of his time, and it was work to which he fully committed himself and which he found worthwhile, even, under the circumstances, enjoyable. He kept himself alert, too, by writing a diary and memorising much of it.

Physical activity and keeping fit added to the richness and variety of his life. As a boy he led an active life, learning to ride, shooting and coursing, and a little later boxing. When he joined the army the opportunities to develop the range of physical activity widened enormously and he seized them all. Indeed, one might be forgiven if one gained the impression that in Ireland his life was one long round of running, shooting, swimming and playing football and hockey. Throughout his life he regularly walked long distances as a means of keeping fit. A good deal of this was in the form of marching while on active and other service but much of it was voluntary. In Ireland, for example, when parades were cancelled because of scarlet fever, he walked to the Hill of Allen and then across the Bog of Allen. As he was recovering from a broken leg in Pietermaritzburg hospital, he 'walked about two miles round the grounds with the aid of a stick.' Whenever the ship on which he was travelling called at a port, he was off walking. Having worked all night getting the horses on board at Durban on his way to Mashonaland, rather than going to sleep, he went ashore and had a good walk; at Mombasa he 'walked to the far side of the island'; at Dar es Salaam he 'took several walks around the town'; at Tanga he 'walked over nearly all the town'; and from Kilindi Harbour he 'walked to Mombasa and back.' As a prisoner of war, once he was fit enough, he habitually walked several miles every day: '40 paces and about turn.' And at Scheveningen he wrote, 'I am now getting into condition again. I am walking about twelve miles a day just to get myself in trim' and 'I can still walk well. Did 30 kilometres a few days ago.' There were, of course, a few occasions when he did not have to walk and he gratefully accepted other means of transport. For example, when he first arrived in Nyasaland, he had expected to march two days to take up his post in Zomba, but instead he was carried in a machila all the way. Again, in Somaliland he had a horse to ride and a camel to carry his food and kit. In getting to the places where he wished to hunt game he used a - not invariably trustworthy - bicycle. During the hunting expeditions themselves he thought nothing of walking huge distances. But he did not always, or indeed often, take advantage of other available means of travelling. On their return from Somaliland he marched with his men the twenty miles from Limbe to Namadzi, and the following day the remaining sixteen miles to Zomba. Though 'very weary' himself, he was not going to have his tired soldiers march in the heat without his being - and suffering - with them. The reason given for not allowing him to join the navy as a teenager – that he had flat feet – is scarcely likely to have been genuine!

He did not allow injury to stand in the way of his continued enjoyment of physical activity, though he was pragmatic in guarding himself against additional injury whilst continuing the contest in which he was currently engaged. For example, when his nose had been broken in a boxing match while working in the wine and spirit trade, he carried on but was careful to avoid further injury. Again, in the army in 1893, early in a game of football against the gym staff, he dislocated his shoulder; the medical staff pulled it in and he played on but took good care that no one touched him. In a mile race at Manchester in 1895, despite being bumped and spiked, he ran on to finish third. When he cut his eyebrow playing cricket in Zomba and had to get it stitched he was careful to bandage the eye when playing football the following day. As he got older he more frequently played wicket-keeper in cricket matches and goalkeeper in football matches rather than in positions that required more robust agility. The many serious knocks he received when playing hockey, tennis and football were soon pushed to one side and he doggedly refused to let them curtail his playing. Nor did he allow a severe bout of whooping cough, and the sore eyes that accompanied it, to prevent his competing - successfully - at Bisley. Above all, he overcame the difficulties presented by the very serious wound he sustained in France. Many men, indeed most, with a huge chunk of muscle torn from their thigh, would never again have wanted to play competitive sports, but not so Archer. As soon as he was free from incarceration, he resumed his sporting activities as if nothing had happened, and as if he was not conscious of being out of practice and now several years older than when they were suspended at the outbreak of the First World War.

The pragmatism that accompanied his physical toughness, the belief that in some cases discretion is the better part of valour, extended in tight corners to his professional life. At Mons, conscious of their disastrous position, his advice was that they should 'stick it out till dark or let anyone get away who likes.' This was undoubtedly a wiser view than that of the Company Quarter Master Sergeant who thought they should 'fight it out to a finish.' In the prisoner of war camps he would not let the Germans provoke him. When a *feldwebel lieutenant* tried to bully him he found it 'no good' and stopped. The under-officer who ran at him with a soup pole stopped when he found that Archer did not run away from him. When attacked at the Zomba prison, instead of fighting off his attackers, as he might well have done successfully though at some cost, he retired to the gatehouse and dealt with them later.

His refraining from smoking - he teased his daughters that he was not old enough to smoke - and his modest drinking of alcohol - in the evenings he would 'have a scotch and soda, rarely two' - were deliberate decisions taken to improve his 'wind' and his sporting performance, and no doubt contributed to his longevity. There can be little doubt, too, that given the harsh life that he led during many parts of his army career, for example in Mashonaland - where 'the effects of climate, exposure, and indifferent food' brought about a severe form of malaria and landed most officers and many men in hospital - and in Egypt and South Africa, his lifelong steps to maintain a high level of physical fitness contributed to that longevity. As he approached his eighties he was affected by arthritis in his knee and he walked more carefully, but his general state of health continued to be excellent. When he was in his eighties, 'a young man came to Naiwale and tried to sell him a life insurance policy!'[2]

But luck also played its part in his survival. Unlike many of his army comrades, he escaped being struck down by typhoid, cholera and scarlet fever. He had many other narrow escapes, of varying degrees of seriousness, when wounded. These ranged from the knock on his head when he fell off the barn roof as a boy and the consequent impairment of his vision, mercifully not permanent, to the wounding in France at the beginning of the First World War. But there were many others. Had he stood but a few inches to one side at Makoni's kraal, the shot that immediately killed Captain Haynes would have hit Archer, with similarly fatal consequences. There were other very close calls in Mashonaland, where he narrowly escaped injury when rocks were thrown at him and when, as a scout, he got lost temporarily and was lucky not to be taken by the enemy. There were many more in the battles in which he fought in South Africa, particularly at Surprise Hill and Bergendal. And in Nyasaland after the war he was lucky that the further injuries he sustained while playing hockey and tennis did not exacerbate his war wound to the extent that he might have to give up at least some of his sports playing. A degree of luck was on his side also when he was attacked on his prison rounds by inmates with a crowbar. He was lucky, too, that the periods of serious hunger he experienced in Mashonaland, Ladysmith and Germany did not so weaken his constitution as to render permanent impairment of his general health and physical ability. On the other hand, although when in Somaliland he admitted that in the past he had 'got bad food', he took as great a care of his diet as was possible under the circumstances in which he was living: growing and eating cress and mustard in Egypt; paying for a servant to cook for him in Somaliland - 'It is worth the expense, as I am always certain of my food'; stealing vegetables in

Ladysmith and Germany; and maintaining a fruit and vegetable garden at the Zomba prison, at his cottage on the plateau and at Naiwale. His game hunting was not simply to secure trophies, for he put the game meat to good use. For example, he interrupted his hunting on Christmas Day 1913 to eat a lunch of 'plum duff and a saddle of eland beef weighing 20 pounds.'[3] Perhaps he was subconsciously making amends for the Ladysmith Christmas pudding made of sultanas and wagon wheel grease.

He kept himself mentally active as well. In his early days in the army he studied for the various classes of the education certificate. Until he married, he was a constant letter writer, mainly letters to his mother but also to others, and he kept a diary, or wrote diary notes, sometimes, as with those written in Mashonaland, with a view to putting them together in book form. His record of mail and parcels received at Merseberg, a small leather bound notebook, with hundreds of neat entries made in the tiniest handwriting, must have taken him hours and hours over long periods to compile. As a young sergeant in Ireland, he took advantage of his mess companions' sleepy and befuddled minds, by being mentally alert himself and winning the games of cards that they played. In more than anything else, his mental power of concentration, was displayed at its best in his rifle shooting. In competitive shooting he was superb, and his concentration and skills remained with him until he retired and there is evidence – for example in the Archer Family versus the KAR Officers competitions at Naiwale – that they remained with him for several more years.

Jack Archer's chosen career – after his mother's intervention to keep him out of the navy – was as a soldier, and it is difficult to imagine that any other career, including the navy, would have suited him nearly as well, though undoubtedly there were aspects of his general make up that would have been valuable in other careers. From the very outset he took great pride in his regiment and its traditions, its uniforms and its perceived superiority to other units: in Egypt he remarked that 'the Grenadier Guards cannot stand the heat so well as our fellows.' He took pride, too, in the precision and skills of parade ground foot and rifle drill: 'Colonel Swaine was a splendid drill. He could manoeuvre the Battalion at the double on the South Front Barracks parade ground, which was very small, very easily.' He was proud, also, of the camaraderie in the regiment, as his letters to and from colleagues and the photographs that they collected and exchanged show. This was a camaraderie shared by men, NCOs and officers. Archer was at pains to write and congratulate his officers when they were promoted, and they wrote warmly in return, especially those who had been engaged with him in battles, such as

Gough: 'It is nice to know that one is remembered by ones old Battalion. Personally I am not likely to forget the times we had together in Ladysmith and elsewhere. I dare say you remember our night on Surprise Hill as vividly as I do.'[4] When Archer sent a photograph to Gough, he received the reply, 'Many thanks for your photo. I was very glad to get it indeed. Next expedition I am on I hope you will be there too.'[5] 'If I can ever do anything for you I shall be delighted if only in remembrance of old times on Wagon Point and King's Post'[6]. During his recovery in London Paley wrote to Archer to ask him to let him know the addresses of any colleagues who had died, since he would 'like to visit their people' when he was well enough. He asked to be remembered to 'all section commanders and the Company.'[7] Even though he may not particularly have liked Major Lowndes, Archer wrote to him when his wife died in 1909, and in reply Lowndes addressed him as 'My dear Sergeant Major Archer', called him 'a very dear old Comrade' and spoke of 'dear old G Company in the 2nd Battalion and all the happy years I spent in the Regiment.'[8] When one of his married Riflemen and his daughter died in India, Archer and his colleagues collected money for his widow, and 'everyone in the battalion subscribed a day's pay for her.'[9] In India, too, Archer and his sergeant colleagues invited 'an old Second Battalion Rifle Brigade Sergeant, who had fought in the Indian Mutiny, to come up to Chaubattia for a holiday.'[10] Although, inevitably, he was only intermittently able to be in touch with his former regimental colleagues after he left the army, he did, for example, attend the Rifle Brigade Veterans' dinner when on leave in 1922 and the unveiling ceremony of the Rifle Brigade war memorial when on leave again in 1925, on both occasions being pleased to meet a number of former colleagues, including Swaine.

Archer's promotions up to the level of Colour Sergeant in the 2nd Battalion of the Rifle Brigade were comparatively rapid. He was respected by his colleagues and by his senior officers - some of them very senior officers - including Lyttelton, Metcalfe, Paley, Biddulph, Thesiger and, again, particularly Gough. He saw service in a remarkable number of campaigns and was awarded the medals appropriate to them. But the most outstanding of all his achievements was that for which he was awarded the Distinguished Conduct Medal. Official and media reports may have given Paley much of the credit for the successful withdrawal from Surprise Hill but Archer's crucial part was 'well known throughout the Battalion' and was fulsomely acknowledged by Paley himself - 'it was what was expected for him' - and by Metcalfe in recommending him for the award.

In the withdrawal from Surprise Hill, Archer's leadership qualities came to the fore. It was he who kept his head, gathered together a rabble of lost men and stragglers and led them back to safety. And he did so with a fine balance of pragmatism and propriety. Despite the presence of three commissioned officers, Archer took command. He did not ask permission, nor was he asked, to do so. It seemed to him that under the circumstances, it was the job of an experienced Colour Sergeant to get his men - and other men and officers - out of a tight corner in which they could all so easily have been wiped out, as Steevens expected them to be. The officers did not object - they may well have been mightily relieved - and Archer, having got them all to safety, acted with great propriety and handed back command to the senior second lieutenant present, who then led his men the final few steps back into camp. Again, at Le Cateau, in the general retreat from Mons, he led the retirement of his men, reformed them, was joined by others and then continued to lead the retirement, despite the presence of officers.

From an early date he was seen as a sound, reliable man upon whom one could depend. At a relatively early stage in the army, for short periods, he was given the posts of Chosen Man, Caterer in the sergeants' mess, and Regimental Postman, and he was placed in charge of the regimental transport. The authorities at the School of Musketry wanted him to stay on as an instructor. He was quickly selected to join the Mounted Infantry for the Mashonaland campaign, was made Sergeant Armourer and was given the vital responsibility of seeing that their horses were safely transported to Beira and then quickly from Beira into Mashonaland. At Omdurman it was he who was photographed marching at the head of the victorious troops after burning Wada and it was he who was appointed chief auctioneer when loot was sold. He was much in demand by people seeking his help: 'It does not matter what time of the day or night but what someone wants me.' Frequently he was placed in an acting post prior to substantive promotion, which followed soon afterwards. He was seen as 'a handy man for any billet.' At both Surprise Hill and Le Cateau he was the senior NCO covering his colleagues' withdrawal: they needed a reliable man to cover their backs. Just before the First World War, a former officer, Jones-Vaughan, wrote to offer him a job as manager of his newly acquired coffee estate in Uganda. He was looking for someone he could trust to manage it for him, and Archer quickly came to mind. At Le Cateau the officers consulted him closely over whether they should stand and fight or withdraw. And in the prisoner of war camp, fellow prisoners and the Germans in charge relied on him to deal with enquiries about missing men and to handle the food parcels efficiently. In Nyasaland after the First World War he was entrusted with the task of implementing reforms at the Central Prison, and the Governor expressed confidence in him. He was asked to organise the Victory celebrations very soon after he arrived back in Zomba, and this was not simply a gesture of kindness to a returning soldier. Finally, he was entrusted with the huge and vital task of recruiting soldiers to the KAR during the Second World War.

The greatest disappointment in his life was the failure to be commissioned at the very beginning of the First World War. The commission, that to which he had so long aspired, was virtually his; only formal confirmation stood in the way. Had he not been so keen to get to the front immediately, had he delayed but a day or so - taken a little longer to buy his field glasses and other accoutrements - that confirmation would undoubtedly have been forthcoming. But to have not shown that keenness and to have delayed his departure would have been utterly contrary to his nature. Instead, he went immediately and as a consequence he stayed a substantive colour sergeant though acting sergeant major, was severely wounded, captured and remained a prisoner for the rest of the war. That the commission should not have been granted at the end of the war, from officialdom's viewpoint, is understandable, but that did not lessen the hurt to Archer nor the basic injustice. Once it became clear to him that the War Office was not going to commission him, he accepted the position, and there is nothing in his papers to suggest that he subsequently harboured any elements of resentment, even if, as is likely, his disappointment was profound. Yet, like the best of fairy stories in which all turns out well in the end and other stories in which the good guy finally wins, Jack must have been overjoyed - though no doubt quietly so - when, at the beginning of the Second World War, he was commissioned. A delightful photograph of him, in his seventies, wearing khaki drill tropical uniform, with medals covering the left part of his chest, with pips on his epaulettes and wearing the KAR officer's bush hat with brim turned up at the side and fastened with a black ostrich feather, only just conceals the pride, the joy and the contentment that he so deeply felt.

Thirty years in the army, much of it overseas, starting at the young age of just eighteen and with the final four years spent in a prisoner of war camp, gave him little opportunity to meet many young women, still less to consider marriage seriously. As he began to get older the matter did cross his mother's mind. She observed, pointedly, that a number of his colleagues were getting married, and when she again mentioned it he replied, 'Expect I shall settle down one of these days when I find the right woman.' It was not a matter that seemed particularly to concern him, though he did correspond with a number of women over the years. As early as November 1904 Kathleen Brown wrote to him a chatty letter on three postcards which she sent in an envelope because she had not left enough space for the address. In it she told him some items of local news, and wrote, 'We all think your photo grand and it occupies the place of honour on the drawing room mantelpiece and is gazed upon by all friends and relatives with "awe and wonder and with bated breath."'[11] In the first part of 1909 he wrote almost daily to Cully.[12] In 1912 until the middle of the year he wrote frequently to a lady named Edith and she replied equally frequently.[13] Then he started to write and receive frequent letters from another called Dim or Dimples. Although there was the intriguing entry in his diary of 3 November 1912, 'Two letters from Dim. Chucked', they continued their correspondence well into 1913. Furthermore, they resumed their letter writing after the war, in 1919, 1920 and 1922, Archer usually writing by return of post. One does not know what, if anything, might have transpired from his making the acquaintance of Miss Taylor on the boat returning to England in 1914 had it not been for the war. After he was released from prison at the end of the war he went from a New Year's Eve party to another party, leaving at 2.30 a.m. and commented in his diary, 'K and I great chums.' This was Kathleen, and he mentioned her again in May when he 'went to Luton to see Kathleen.'[14] The day following the New Year's Eve parties he went for a walk with Dora, from 10.0 to 11.0 a.m. and with Nellie from 11.15 a.m. to 12.30 p.m. From 27 January to 2 May there are several entries in his diary referring to 'D', followed by oblique marks in varying numbers. Whether 'D' was Dim or Dora or another lady is unknown as is the significance of the oblique marks. In the twelve months from March 1919 to March 1920 he received twenty-one letters from Kathleen and fourteen from Rose.[15] During the course of dinner at the KAR officers' mess on New Year's Day 1921, when his medals 'made a great impression on the company', he was introduced to an unmarried - and unnamed - lady, they had a 'very interesting talk' and he stayed until four o'clock in the morning. The occasion would be insignificant were it not made the subject of a longer than usual diary entry.

It would appear that he was by no means a misogynist, indifferent to the company of women. It is more likely that, as he indicated to his mother, he was waiting to 'find the right woman' before he settled down.[16] It was on the *Guildford Castle* steaming its way northwards from Cape Town to Tilbury shortly before Christmas 1921, that he met her. She was well worth the long wait.

Jack Archer's life was in two distinct parts, indeed, there were almost two lives. The first was as a professional soldier, a bachelor without a settled home, leading a life that he shared intimately with very few, if any, others save to a limited extent his mother. His companions were overwhelmingly male. His accommodation was in barracks or, when on active service, tents. He seems to have enjoyed and been proud of some of the camps that he helped to build on active service, for example the new fort at Mazoe in Mashonaland; the King's Post 'regular fortress' in South Africa; and the 'proper camp' in Somaliland, which became 'quite a little town' over the course of time. He made himself as comfortable as possible, and was always pleased when he was able to acquire some privacy, but there was nowhere he could call his own home.

The First World War, spent not on active army service but in a prisoner of war camp, marked the dividing line between the two halves of his life, and it was, with one blurring, a clear division. The division was emphasised by the death of his mother and with it, the severing of any remaining elements of a family 'home' that he had in England: his return to Parndon to pack up his kit after the war was a very brief one. The blurring of the line between the two parts of his life was the period of his first tour in the civil service of Nyasaland, the period before he met Muriel. Once they were married the change in his life and lifestyle became distinct. Life now became settled. He had a wife, and soon a family of four daughters and a son. He had a permanent house, made into an attractive home by Muriel, and a cottage on Zomba Plateau in which they spent the hotter weather and their leisure hours. Later there was the Zomba Hotel and later still a new home at Naiwale. Professionally he was the senior officer in charge of an important institution, faced with the challenging task of implementing prison reform. His wandering life was at an end, as were the dangers implicit in a military life, when the calls to active service could be at short notice and to any part of the world.

For some seven years after his retirement from the Nyasaland civil service, he was able to return to his army life and to combine it with his married life, joining, as it were, the two parts in one. To his happily married life, with a wife and family, settled in a comfortable home of their own, he now added his wartime service in the KAR. Once again - though this time never posted far from his family, nor engaged in actual fighting - he was in military uniform, in charge of various bodies of men and responsible for their training, discipline and welfare, able to put to use all the skills and experience of his earlier years.

When he died in 1954, Jack Archer had served under the first nine of Nyasaland's twelve Governors.[17] He was still living in Nyasaland during the term of office of the tenth,[18] and had he lived but a few months longer, he would have lived there during that of the eleventh.[19] He also lived through the reigns of six British sovereigns and through the terms of office of twenty-six governments in Britain. He had been awarded sixteen medals and these occupy a proud place on display in the Royal Green Jackets Museum at Winchester: an abundantly well deserved and truly fine chest of medals.

Jack Archer was buried in the cemetery in Zomba, the country's tiny but beautiful capital, the headquarters of the King's African Rifles and the location of the Central Prison, still referred to by Malawians over sixty years after he retired as Superintendent, as *pa Achala*, Archer's. His children, John and Beryl were at his graveside. There was a 'large military presence' and he was buried with full military honours. The KAR band - which he had trained over forty years earlier soon after it had been formed - the Nyasaland Police band and a contingent from the prison were also there to pay their last respects.[20] A neighbouring farmer, a former KAR officer, sent his lorry to Naiwale Estate to collect the African staff there, so that they too could attend the funeral.[21] The granite headstone on his grave is inscribed with the words, 'A Man Among Men', a fitting epitaph, selected by his widow.[22]

NOTES

Chapter One

[1] Material in this and the following three paragraphs is from *The Hertford Mercury* of Saturday 31 December 1870 and Saturday 7 January 1871.

[2] Until the currency of the United Kingdom was decimalised in 1971, it was based on the pound (£), each pound being divided into 20 shillings (s) and each shilling being divided into 12 pence (d). Thus, ten pounds, ten shilling and ten pence was referred to as £10.10s.10d or £10.10.10. Ten shillings was referred to as 10/-.

[3] Material in this and subsequent paragraphs of this chapter, unless otherwise stated, is from the Archer Papers (hereafter AP) and correspondence with Archer's daughters.

[4] In a note written many years later, Archer said he stayed with his Uncle William Thurlow at Thruston Downs Farm.

[5] See *Rifle Brigade Chronicle* 1896, pp. 294-5.

Chapter Two

[1] Material in this chapter, unless otherwise stated, is from AP Notes, Diaries and unreferenced newspaper cuttings.

[2] Later he said he spent seven days in hospital with catarrh: AP Notes.

[3] Hon. Arthur Charles Edward Somerset, b.11.11.1859, ed. Eton, 2nd Lt. 22.2.1879, 1 Rifle Brigade India 1880-86, 2 Rifle Brigade UK 1886-89, retired as Captain 1901, d. London 24.3.1948: W P S Curtis *The Rifle Brigade Register 1905-1963* (Winchester: 1964). Unless otherwise stated, subsequent personal details of Rifle Brigade officers are from this source.

[4] Sir Leopold Victor Swaine, b. 15.12. 1840, 2nd Lt. 24.7.1859, retired as Major-General 15.12.1902, d. London 13.3.1931.

[5] Sir Harry Hughes Wilson, Bart., b. 5.5.1864, ed. Marlborough, Lt. 26.11.1884, Field Marshall 31.7.1919, assassinated London 22.6.1922.

[6] Annotated photograph in Beryl Groves's photograph album.

[7] Letter to Mother dated 16 June 1893, from Curragh Camp. All letters to and from Archer's Mother are in AP.

[8] Elizabeth Saunder to author 5 July 2002.

[9] Hon. Wenman Coke, 2nd son of Earl of Leicester, b. 20.11.1855, ed. Harrow and Trinity College Dublin, 2nd Lt. 30.1.1878, retired as Lt.-Col. 8.3.1904, d. London 30.5.1931.

[10] See *Rifle Brigade Chronicle* 1905 p.43, and 1896 pp.294-5.

Chapter Three

[1] Letters to Mother dated 4 January and 19 February 1896 from Aldershot.

[2] Foreword, *The '96 Rebellions*, originally published as *The British South Africa Company Reports on the Native Disturbances in Rhodesia, 1896-97*, Rhodesiana Reprint Library - Silver Series, Volume Two (Bulawayo: 1975).

[3] Hugh Marshall Hoole, *The Making of Rhodesia* (London: Macmillan, 1926), pp.362-4.

[4] E A H (Edwin Alfred Hervey) Alderson, *With the Mounted Infantry and the Mashonaland Field Force, 1896* (London: Methuen, 1898).

[5] Alderson op. cit. pp.4-5.

[6] Albert Jenner, 'The Rifle Company in South Africa', *Rifle Brigade Chronicle* 1897, p.162.

[7] *The Regiment: An Illustrated Military Journal for Aldershot*, Vol.1, No.5, 2 May 1896, p.3.

[8] Sir Reginald Byng Stephens, son of General Sir F Stephens, b. 10.10.1869, ed. Winchester and Sandhurst, commissioned 2nd Lt. 9.4.1890, retired as General 1.10.1931, d. Lechlade 5.4.1955.

[9] Captain Albert Victor Jenner, DSO.

[10] The Riflemen were Bellamy, Bottomley, Broad, Collins, Coshill, Davies, Davis, Dunkley, Fitch, Gibbons, Gough, Herrington, Honey, Johnston, Keene, Kemp, Mitchell, Rogers, Rose, Smith, Tracy, Wayman, Wide and Woodward: *Rifle Brigade Chronicle* 1897, p.163.

[11] Captain Hubert Edward Vernon, the Rifle Brigade, awarded DSO for service in Rhodesia 1896. Jenner's staff officer for ten weeks, 'Cool and dashing. An ideal Mounted Infantry officer': *The '96 Rebellions* op.cit. p. 147.

[12] *Rifle Brigade Chronicle* 1896, p.166.

[13] Jenner op. cit. p.162.

[14] Photograph on p.40 of C J Harris and B D Ingpen, *Mailships of the Union-Castle Line* (London: Patrick Stephens, 1994), p.164.

[15] Alderson op. cit. p.7.

[16] Jenner op. cit. p.164.

[17] Ibid.

[18] Ibid. 12 May is the date given here by Jenner.

[19] Alderson op. cit. p.7.

[20] Ibid. Jenner op. cit. p.164 says 'Baden Powell very kindly kept us all in roars of laughter with a couple of excellent musical sketches.'

[21] Jenner op. cit. p.164.
[22] Unless otherwise stated, material in this and the following six paragraphs is from Letter to Mother dated 26 May 1896 from Wynberg.
[23] Alderson op. cit. p.8.
[24] Jenner op. cit. p.164.
[25] Jenner op. cit. p.165.
[26] Alderson op. cit. p.16.
[27] Jenner op. cit. p.172.
[28] Alderson op. cit. pp.9-10.
[29] Letter to Mother dated 26 May 1896 from Wynberg.
[30] E Goodwin Green, *Raiders and Rebels in South Africa* (London: George Newnes, 1898), p.4. Elsa Green arrived in Cape Town in December 1895.
[31] Jenner op. cit. p.165.
[32] Alderson op. cit. p.9, and Letter to Mother 26 May 1896 from Wynberg.
[33] Jenner op. cit. p.165.
[34] Alderson persistently says it was 16 June.
[35] *The '96 Rebellions*, op. cit. pp.112-113.
[36] Letter to Mother 23 June 1896 from Wynberg.
[37] Alderson op. cit. pp.11-12.
[38] Captain Sir Horace Westropp McMahon, Bart., Royal Welsh Fusiliers. Awarded DSO for service in Rhodesia, 1896. 'Worked hard and loyally, did good work in collecting and embarking horses at Durban; continued with his men when wounded at Mashingombis': *The '96 Rebellions*, op. cit. p.147.
[39] Alderson op. cit. p.15.
[40] Alderson op. cit. p.14.
[41] Alderson op. cit. p.16.
[42] Jenner op. cit. p.165. The *Arab*, launched in 1879, weighed 3192 tons and was 106 meters long, with a speed of 12 knots. She could carry 110 first class passengers, 90 second and 50 third. In 1882 she had been used as a troopship for the Sudanese campaign. In 1883 she was placed on an experimental voyage between Liverpool and Baltimore. Two years later she was the headquarters ship for naval transport staff in the Sudanese war. In 1891 she was transferred to the intermediate service and in 1900 was broken up: C J Harris and B D Ingpen op. cit. p.164.
[43] Jenner op. cit. pp. 165-166.
[44] Alderson op. cit. p.16.

[45] Green op. cit. chapters VI and VII.
[46] J. Archer 'The Rebellion in Mashonaland', *Rifle Brigade Chronicle* 1896, p.97.
[47] Jenner op. cit. p.166 says 'Apparently we were not expected by the harbour people, and had to wait till the afternoon tide to get in.'
[48] Ibid.
[49] Jenner op. cit. p.165.
[50] Letter to Mother dated 4 July 1896 from SS *Arab*, Beira.
[51] Jenner op. cit. p.166.
[52] Alderson op. cit. pp.19-22.
[53] Green, op. cit. p.53.
[54] Lieutenant-Commander Hunt RN. He 'afforded much assistance and hearty cooperation in the disembarkation of troops': *The '96 Rebellions* p.148.
[55] Alderson op. cit. p.50.
[56] Green op. cit. pp.66-67.
[57] Archer op. cit. pp.97-98.
[58] Material in this paragraph, except where otherwise stated, is from Alderson op. cit. pp.25-27.
[59] *The '96 Rebellions* op.cit. p.145.
[60] Green, op cit. p.51.
[61] Alderson op. cit. p.44.
[62] Alderson op. cit. p.42 and p.47. Nurse Elsa Green described the tug *Kimberley* more flatteringly as the 'SS *Kimberley*': Green, op. cit. p.55.
[63] Alderson op. cit. p.47.
[64] Green, op. cit. pp.55-56.
[65] AP Notes.
[66] Green, op. cit. p.67.
[67] Alderson op. cit. p.50.
[68] Alderson op. cit. pp.54-55.
[69] Ibid.
[70] AP Notes.
[71] Alderson op. cit. pp.56-57.
[72] Alderson op. cit. p.51. See also Green op. cit. p.63: 'The various stopping-places on the line were as yet unnamed; they were designated only by their distance from Fontesvilla.'
[73] Green op. cit. pp.59-62. Jenner op. cit. pp.166-167 describes Fontesvilla as 'a hot, sleepy place ... not a very nice place.'
[74] Green op. cit. p.52 and p.72.

[75] Archer op. cit. p.101.
[75] Green op. cit. p.59.
[76] Green op. cit. p.59 and p.66.
[77] AP Diary 9 July.
[78] Alderson op. cit. p.58 and p.60, and Archer op. cit. p.98.
[79] Letter to Mother - a small scrap of paper – no date, no place, but text indicates still in Portuguese East Africa and still down country. In most of the contemporary documents *waggon* is a more common spelling than *wagon*.
[80] Alderson op. cit. p.59.
[81] Green op. cit. p.67: 'The remainder of the officers and men of the West Riding regiment came up from Fontesvilla, and marched on to Umtali very early in the morning of the day on which we started in the coach for Umtali. We passed them on the road at their first halt.'
[82] Jenner op. cit. p.167.
[83] Archer op. cit. p.98.
[84] *The '96 Rebellions* op.cit. p.114.
[85] Green op. cit. p.68.
[86] Alderson op. cit. pp.62-63.
[87] Green op. cit. p.69.
[88] Green op. cit. p.73.
[89] *The '96 Rebellions* op.cit. p.114.
[90] Green op. cit. pp.75-76.
[91] Green op. cit. p.78.
[92] Hoole op. cit. pp.376-7.
[93] Green op. cit. p.82.
[94] Jenner op. cit. p.169.
[95] Jenner op. cit. p.168 says 28th. Archer op. cit. p.98 also says 28th.
[96] Alderson op. cit. p. 78.
[97] Archer op. cit. pp.98-99.
[98] Archer op. cit. p.99.
[99] Alderson op. cit. pp.81-82.
[100] Alderson op. cit. p.83 and Jenner op. cit. p.168.
[101] Green op. cit. p.81, from a copy of the wire sent by Alderson for transmission to the High Commissioner at Cape Town. Archer op. cit. p.99 says Irish Company and RA took the north, RE Volunteers the east and Rifle Company and Scouts the south with Mr Ross acting as guide. Jenner op. cit. p.168 says the Irish Company and the guns went to the left, the Rifle Company and the Volunteers to the right.

[102] Jenner op. cit. p.168.
[103] Archer op. cit. pp.99-100.
[104] Green op. cit. p.81 says 60 were killed.
[105] Royal Irish Regiment, wounded in the thigh: Green op. cit. p.81.
[106] Irish Brigade, wounded in the leg: Green op. cit. p.81.
[107] Trooper in the Umtali Volunteers, wounded in the chest: Green op. cit. p.81.
[108] Alderson op. cit. p.95. See also Green op. cit. pp.80-82.
[109] 4 August 1896: *The '96 Rebellions* op.cit. p.137.
[110] Green op. cit. pp.79-80.
[111] Green op. cit. pp.82-83.
[112] Green op. cit. pp.81-82, from a copy of the wire sent by Alderson for transmission to the High Commissioner at Cape Town.
[113] Jenner op. cit. p.168: 'The next day [4 August] some of us went down the Devil's Pass, the telegraph line was repaired and we got into communication with Salisbury.'
[114] *The '96 Rebellions* op. cit. p.112.
[115] *The Rhodesia Herald* Wednesday 19 August 1896. For the subsequent defeat and execution - on 4 September - of Makoni, see Green op. cit. Chapter X. Details of the attack on Makoni are in Chapter V of Alderson op. cit. and Jenner op. cit. pp.162 ff.
[116] Letter - a small scrap of paper - to Mother 1 August 1896, no place. See also Archer op. cit. p.101.
[117] Alderson op. cit. p.83.
[118] Alderson op. cit. pp.99-115. See also Jenner op. cit. p.169. For a brief note on Gatzi's and the death of Major Evans, shot through the heart, see Green op. cit. pp.137-138.
[119] *The '96 Rebellions* op.cit. pp.112-113.
[120] Alderson op. cit. p.116 and pp.140-141.
[121] *The '96 Rebellions* op.cit. p.116.
[122] Jenner op. cit. p.170.
[123] *The '96 Rebellions* op.cit. p.117.
[124] Jenner op. cit. p.172.
[125] Jenner in Alderson op. cit, pp.147-148.
[126] Jenner op. cit. p.171.
[127] *The '96 Rebellions* op.cit. p.73.
[128] Jenner op. cit. p.171.
[129] Jenner in Alderson op. cit. pp.153-155.
[130] Jenner op. cit. p.171.

[131] Archer op. cit. pp.101-102.
[132] *The '96 Rebellions* op.cit. p.132, and Jenner op. cit. p.172.
[133] AP Notes.
[134] Hoole op. cit. pp.376-7.
[135] Pendoola.
[136] Jenner op. cit. p.172.
[137] Alderson op. cit. p.259.
[138] Jenner op. cit. p.173.
[139] Jenner op. cit. p.172.
[140] *The '96 Rebellions* op.cit. p.74.
[141] Alderson op. cit. pp.248-262.
[142] Jenner op. cit. p.173.
[143] Letter to Mother February 1897 from Pietermaritzburg. He spent a total of 115 days in hospital: AP Notes.
[144] Stephens may have been unusually susceptible to fever. Jenner, *Rifle Brigade Chronicle*, 1897, p.164, recorded that even when it was so hot that the thermometer on the ship had to be iced every hour, Stephens 'remained in his bedroom [and] had all the windows shut, put on a great coat, shooting stockings and a sweater, and [said] he was feeling the cold less than he had for years.'
[145] Letter to Mother February 1897 from Pietermaritzburg.
[146] Letter to Mother 5 March 1897 from Pietermaritzburg.
[147] Letter to Mother 10 April 1897 from Pietermaritzburg.
[148] Letter to Mother 15 May 1897 from Pietermaritzburg.
[149] *Rifle Brigade Chronicle* 1897 p.273.
[150] Battalion Orders for Tuesday 28 December 1897, issued by Major G F Leslie, Commanding Verdala Barracks, Malta, quoting from a letter received from Officer Commanding Mounted Infantry South Africa: cited in letter Archer to Mother dated c31 December 1897 from Malta.
[151] Carrington to Lord Rosmead, 6 May 1897: *The '96 Rebellions* op.cit. p.152.
[152] Alderson op. cit. pp.viii-ix.

Chapter Four

[1] Letter to Mother dated 16 September 1897 from Malta.
[2] Letters to Mother dated 30 October and 23 December 1897, 16 January and 20 March 1898 from Malta; AP Notes; and *Rifle Brigade Chronicle* 1896 p.169.

[3] Letters to Mother dated 31 December 1897 and 16 January 1898 from Malta.
[4] Letter to Mother dated 20 March 1898 from Malta.
[5] Letter to Mother dated 30 April 1898 from Malta.
[6] Ibid.
[7] H G Majendie 'The Battle of Atbara, April 8th 1898', *Rifle Brigade Chronicle* 1898 pp.41-42.
[8] Majendie, op. cit. pp.46-47.
[9] *The New Encyclopaedia Britannica*, 15th Edition, 1975, Vol. VII, p.531, Col.1.
[10] Ian Beckett, *Johnnie Gough VC: a Biography of Brigadier-General Sir John Edmond Gough, VC, KCB* (London: Tom Donovan, 1989), p.33.
[11] Beckett op.cit. p.35.
[12] Letter to Mother dated 21 June 1898 and AP Notes.
[13] Beckett op. cit. p.35.
[14] B H Cooke, 'Cairo to Khartoum, August 1898', *Rifle Brigade Chronicle* 1898 p.48.
[15] Beckett op. cit. p.35; and 2nd Battalion Letter to the Editor, *Rifle Brigade Chronicle* 1898 p.108. Archer kept a number of photographs in his album of the places he visited in Egypt.
[16] Letter to Mother dated 4 July 1898 from Cairo.
[17] Beckett op. cit. p.36 and Cooke op. cit. pp.50-51.
[18] Beckett op. cit. p.36.
[19] Ibid.
[20] Beckett op. cit. p.38.
[21] Ibid. Gough says there were 33 men to a truck.
[22] Cooke op. cit. p.52.
[23] Cooke op. cit. p.53.
[24] W Steevens, *With Kitchener to Khartoum* (London: Blackwood and Sons, 1898), p.194.
[25] Beckett op. cit. p.38.
[26] Cooke op. cit. p.53
[27] Beckett op. cit. p.39.
[28] Letter to Mother dated 10 August 1898.
[29] Beckett op. cit. p.39.
[30] Ibid.
[31] AP Notes.
[32] John Pollock, *Kitchener: the Road to Omdurman* (London: Constable, 1998), p.126.

[33] Steevens op. cit. pp.192-3.
[34] Beckett op. cit. p.40.
[35] Steevens op. cit. pp.234-6.
[36] Brigadier-General Lyttelton joined the Rifle Brigade in 1865 and saw active service in India, Egypt and South Africa. He became the first Chief of the Imperial General Staff after WW I: Martin Marix Evans, *Encyclopedia of the Boer War* (Oxford, ABC-CLIO, 2000), p.159.
[37] Cooke op. cit. p.56.
[38] Steevens op. cit. p.245.
[39] John Pollock op. cit. p.127. The true figure was 24,000.
[40] Also spelt Agaiga.
[41] George Cockburn, 'Battle of Khartoum, September 2nd 1898', *Rifle Brigade Chronicle* 1898, pp.62-63 and maps at end of volume. Major Cockburn was 2 Rifle Brigade's second in command.
[42] Archer later kept his card map in one of his photograph albums.
[43] T Green-Wilkinson, 'With the Egyptian Camel Corps, 1898' *Rifle Brigade Chronicle* 1898, p.76. See also Steevens op. cit. pp.249-258.
[44] Steevens op. cit. p.260.
[45] Cockburn op. cit. pp.64-65. See also Steevens op. cit. pp.263ff and Pollock op. cit. pp.130 ff.
[46] Steevens op. cit. p.264.
[47] Beckett op. cit. p.42.
[48] Cockburn op. cit. pp.66-67.
[49] Steevens op. cit. p.298.
[50] Cockburn op. cit.p.69.
[51] Green-Wilkinson op. cit. p.79.
[52] Steevens, op. cit. p.209.
[53] Pollock, op. cit. p.136.
[54] Letter to Mother dated 11 October 1903 from Cairo.
[55] Cockburn op. cit. pp.66-70.
[56] Steevens op. cit. pp.310-316. See also Pollock op. cit. pp.139-142.
[57] Cooke op. cit. p.60.
[58] Ibid.
[59] Letter to Mother dated 5 October 1898 from Crete, and AP Lieutenant L D Hall to Archer dated 2 March 1899.
[60] Elizabeth Saunder to author 5 July 2002.
[61] Steevens op. cit. pp.284-287.
[62] The ringleaders were hanged by volunteers from the Rifle Brigade under the supervision of George Cockburn, and others implicated were

shot. Archer was present at the public execution of the seven ringleaders: photographs in Archer's albums.

[63] Letter to Mother dated 7 September 1898 from Omdurman; AP Notes; *Rifle Brigade Chronicle* 1898, p. 145 (Archer was promoted Colour Sergeant on 21 November 1898).
[64] Cooke op. cit. pp.60-61.
[65] Cooke op. cit. p.48.
[66] Material in this and the following four paragraphs, unless otherwise stated, is from Letter to Mother dated 5 October 1898 from Crete.
[67] *Rifle Brigade Chronicle* 1898, p.145.
[68] AP *London Gazette* of 4 May 1897.
[69] Beryl Groves's photograph album.
[70] Letter to Mother dated 7 January 1903 from Cairo.
[71] Photographs in Archer's album.
[72] Ibid.
[73] AP, HA Case to Archer 18 April 1913.

Chapter Five

[1] Letter to Mother dated 14 September 1899 from Crete.
[2] For departure from Crete for South Africa, see *Rifle Brigade Chronicle*, 1899 p.112.
[3] H Dawnay, 'The Siege of Ladysmith', *Rifle Brigade Chronicle,* 1900, p.68; and Beckett op. cit. p.54.
[4] Letter to Mother dated 2 September 1899, but must be 2 October 1899, probably posted at Aden.
[5] Evans *Encyclopedia op. cit.* p.xi.
[6] Letter to Mother dated 19 October 1899 from Zanzibar; Beckett op. cit. p.49, and Dawnay op. cit. p.68.
[7] Dawnay op. cit. p.68; Evans *Encyclopedia* op. cit. pp.246-8 and 86.
[8] Letter to Mother dated 26 October 1899.
[9] Dawnay op. cit. p.68.
[10] Letter to Mother dated 26 October 1899 from Durban and Letter to Mother dated 24 December 1899 from Ladysmith but not posted until after the siege was lifted. What follows, except where otherwise stated, is from this Letter to Mother dated 24 December 1899 from Ladysmith.
[11] Dawnay op. cit. p.68.
[12] Beckett op. cit. p.55.
[13] Dawnay op. cit. p.69.

[14] Kate Driver, *Experience of a Siege* (Ladysmith Historical Society, 1978, Mimeo), p.4.
[15] Evans *Encyclopedia*, op. cit. pp.155-6. For a good account of the battle of Lombard's Kop, see Christopher Martin, *The Boer War* (London: Abelard-Schuman, 1969), pp.66-81.
[16] Dawnay op. cit. p.71.
[17] Beckett op. cit. p.55.
[18] George Paley, ed. Eton and Sandhurst, b. 21.7.1872, wounded at Ladysmith, Major 8.7.1908, killed in action at Chateau Hooge, Ypres, 31.10.1914.
[19] Dawnay op. cit. pp.71-72.
[20] Dawnay op. cit. p.72.
[21] Dawnay op. cit. p.73.
[22] Martin op. cit. p.128.
[23] H M Biddulph and R B Stephens, 'The Attack on Observation Hill, November 9th, 1890' in *Rifle Brigade Chronicle* 1900 p.96.
[24] For obituary of B E Lethbridge see *Rifle Brigade Chronicle* 1900 pp.389-390.
[25] Archer's diary enclosed with Letter to Mother dated 24 December 1899. For a detailed account of the attack on Observation Hill, see Biddulph and Stephens op. cit. pp.94-96.
[26] Dawnay op. cit. p.76.
[27] Beckett op. cit. p.58.
[28] Archer's diary for 29 November 1899 enclosed with letter to Mother dated 24 December 1899.
[29] Dawnay op. cit. p.74.
[30] Ibid.
[31] Dawnay op. cit. p.73.
[32] Dawnay op. cit. pp.73-76.
[33] Archer's diary enclosed with Letter to Mother dated 24 December 1899.
[34] Ibid.
[35] Beckett op. cit. p.59.
[36] Dawnay op. cit. pp.77-78. See also Beckett op. cit. p.59. Sir John Edmund Gough, son of Brigadier-General Sir Charles Gough VC, and nephew of General Sir Hugh Gough VC; b. 25.10.1871, ed. Eton and Sandhurst, 2nd Lt. in the Westmeath Militia 12 April 1890, 2nd Lt. in Rifle Brigade 12.3.1892, seconded for service in BCA Protectorate 3.9.1896, m. Dorothea d. of General Sir C Keyes 1907; awarded VC 1904, Brigadier-General 19.10.1913, killed in action at Estiaire

20.2.1915, knighted posthumously [R Doherty and D Truesdale, *Irish Winners of the Victoria Cross* (Dublin: Four Corners Press, 2000), passim., and Beckett op. cit.

[37] Archer's diary enclosed with Letter to Mother dated 24 December 1899.

[38] Dawnay op. cit. pp.77-78.

[39] *Rifle Brigade Chronicle* 1900, p.166, quoting *The Morning Post*, March 1900, 'Surprise Hill, December 10th-11th, 1899' by a War Correspondent.

[40] Archer's diary enclosed with Letter to Mother dated 24 December 1899.

[41] George Hancock Thesiger, b. 6.10.1868, ed. Eton and Sandhurst, 2nd Lt. 19.3.1890, 2 Rifle Brigade, Nile Expedition 1898, South Africa 1899-1900, Inspector-General KAR 1909-1913, Acting Major General 27.8.1915, killed in action in France 29.9.1915.

[42] Ruari Chisholme, *Ladysmith*, (London: Osprey 1979), p.132; Dawnay op. cit. p.81; Thomas Packenham, *The Boer War* (London: Weidenfeld and Nicolson, 1979), p.271, quoting from Gough's diary.

[43] *Rifle Brigade Chronicle* 1900, p.167, quoting *The Morning Post*, op. cit.

[44] Dawnay op. cit. p.81.

[45] *Rifle Brigade Chronicle* 1900, p.167, quoting *The Morning Post*, op. cit.

[46] Archer's diary enclosed with Letter to Mother dated 24 December 1899.

[47] *Rifle Brigade Chronicle* 1900, p.167, quoting *The Morning Post*, op. cit.

[48] Chisholme op. cit. p.132

[49] Beckett op. cit. p.60.

[50] AP sketchmap.

[51] Martin op. cit. p.131

[52] Archer's diary enclosed with Letter to Mother dated 24 December 1899. Beckett op. cit. p.60 makes no specific reference to Gough shooting the sentry but says he loosed off a shot in the gun emplacement as he rushed past.

[53] *Rifle Brigade Chronicle* 1900, p.167, quoting *The Morning Post*, op. cit.

[54] Pakenham op. cit. p.271, quoting from Gough's diaries.

[55] Martin op. cit. and Beckett op. cit. p.60.

[56] Dawnay op. cit. p.82.

[57] Martin op. cit. p.131.

[58] *Rifle Brigade Chronicle* 1900, p.168, quoting *Morning Post*, op. cit.

[59] Dawnay op. cit. p.83.
[60] Archer's diary enclosed with Letter to Mother dated 24 December 1899. The howitzer was replaced by another ten days later. Surprise Hill was formerly known as Vaalkop: H M Jones and M G M Jones, *A Gazetteer of the Second Anglo-Boer War* (London: The Military Press, 1999), p.213.
[61] Beckett op. cit. p.60.
[62] Pakenham op. cit. p.271, quoting from Gough's diaries.
[63] Beckett op. cit. p.60.
[64] Dawnay op. cit. p.83.
[65] *Rifle Brigade Chronicle* 1900, p.168, quoting *The Morning Post*, op. cit.
[66] Ibid.
[67] Archer's diary enclosed with Letter to Mother dated 24 December 1899.
[68] Dawnay op. cit. p.84.
[69] *Rifle Brigade Chronicle* 1900, pp. 169-170, quoting *The Morning Post*, op. cit.
[70] Archer's diary enclosed with Letter to Mother dated 24 December 1899. One of the young officers may have been Second Lieutenant Maurice Bazley White, who was commissioned on 20.11.1899.
[71] AP. A photograph in Archer's album, with the monument, erected to the memory of those who were killed, in the foreground, shows Surprise Hill in the background.
[72] *Rifle Brigade Chronicle* 1900, pp. 166-170, quoting *The Morning Post*, op. cit.
[73] For obituary of G C D Fergusson see *Rifle Brigade Chronicle* 1900, pp.390-391 and photograph.
[74] Algernon Arthur Garneys Bond, b. 21.1.1879, ed. Eton and Sandhurst, 2nd Lt. 9.8.1899, wounded in attack on Surprise Hill, Ladysmith, d. India 13.6.1911.
[75] Samuel Davenport, b. 10.8.1876, ed. Winchester, 2nd Lt. 22.9.1897, retired 19.4.1902, re-employed 1914, d. 2.10.1954.
[76] *Rifle Brigade Chronicle* 1900, p.84 and p.355.
[77] A Conan Doyle, *The Great Boer War* (London: Smith, Elder and Co., 1901), p.221.
[78] Dawnay op. cit. p.84.
[79] *Rifle Brigade Chronicle* 1900, pp.390-391.
[80] Deneys Reitz, *Commando: a Boer Journal of the Boer War* (London: Faber and Faber, 1929), pp.54-59, and a letter that he wrote at the time and reproduced in Conan Doyle, op. cit. pp.220-221. Deitz was the son of

Francis William Reitz, Chief Justice of the Orange Free State, 1874; President 1888; State Secretary 1898; first president of the Senate of the Union, 1910.

[81] Conan Doyle op. cit. pp.220-221.
[82] Ibid.
[83] Ibid.
[84] Ibid.
[85] Chisholme op. cit. p.133.
[86] Martin op. cit. gives a total of 64: 'one officer and 16 men were killed and three died later of wounds, four officers and 34 men were wounded, and six men were missing and presumed to be captured.'
[87] George Stewart White, born in 1835, was commissioned in the Gordon Highlanders in 1853. He served in the Indian Mutiny at Charasiah and won the Victoria Cross in 1879. He fought in the Afghan War of 1878 to 1880 and commanded a brigade in Burma in 1885 to 1886. He succeeded Lord Roberts as commander in India. He was appointed to command the Natal Field Force in 1899 and, contrary to the pleas of Sir Redvers Buller, moved well north of the Tugela River and became besieged in Ladysmith. Under his leadership the garrison held out, but White was ill and exhausted at the end of it. He was invalided home and, on recovery, became Governor of Gibraltar: Evans *Encyclopedia* op. cit. p.272.
[88] *Rifle Brigade Chronicle* 1900, pp.355-6.
[89] Beckett op. cit. p.61.
[90] Archer's diary enclosed with Letter to Mother dated 24 December 1899.
[91] Dawnay op. cit. p.85.
[92] Conan Doyle op. cit. p.222.
[93] Driver op. cit. p.44.
[94] Biddulph and Stephens op. cit. p.97. For detailed accounts of the attack on Caesar's Camp, see also W E Davies, 'Captain Sydney Mills' Company (F) at Caesar's Camp, January 6th 1900', in *Rifle Brigade Chronicle* 1900, pp.101-106; Evans *Encyclopedia*, op. cit. pp.207-8; Conan Doyle op. cit. pp.223-231.
[95] Evans *Encyclopedia* op. cit. pp.207-208. For a good account of the Platrand operations, see Martin op. cit. pp.133-138.
[96] W E Davies op. cit. pp.101-106.
[97] Ibid.
[98] For obituary of Sydney Mills, see *Rifle Brigade Chronicle* 1900, pp.391-392.
[99] Dawnay op. cit. pp.85-88.

[100] AP Notes.
[101] Beckett op. cit. p.63.
[102] Pakenham, op. cit. p.274, quoting from Gough's diaries. See also Beckett op. cit. pp.62-64.
[103] Beckett op. cit. p.63.
[104] For obituary of Louis Duval Hall, see *Rifle Brigade Chronicle* 1900, p. 391. Born 18 3 1875, ed. Eton, gazetted from the Militia on 24 August 1897, posted to 2nd Battalion Rifle Brigade, served in Malta, Sudan, Omdurman, Crete and South Africa.
[105] Biddulph and Stephens, op. cit. p.100. See also Henry John May, *Music of the Guns: Based on Two Journals of the Boer War* (London: Jarrolds, 1970), p.185: British losses 400, Boer losses 200.
[106] Beckett, op. cit. p.64.
[107] Letter to Mother, completed 2 February 1900 from Wagon Hill.
[108] J D Heriot-Maitland, 'The Composite Battalion, 1900' in *Rifle Brigade Chronicle* 1900, p.128.
[109] Letter to Mother dated 1 March 1900 from Ladysmith.
[110] Driver op. cit. pp.48-49.
[111] May op. cit. pp.2-3, p.35, pp.56-57 and pp.60-61.
[112] Dawnay op. cit. pp.92-93.
[113] Beckett op. cit. p.65.
[114] Driver op. cit. p.49. Dawnay op. cit. pp.89-91 also deals with the long drawn-out approach of Buller's forces.
[115] C Lamb 'The Relief of Ladysmith', in *Rifle Brigade Chronicle* 1900, pp.122-123.
[116] Photographs in Archer's album.
[117] Dawnay op. cit. p.93; Beckett op. cit. p.69 and p.74; *Rifle Brigade Chronicle* 1900, pp.356-357.
[118] See George Cockburn 'The Fight at Bergendal, 27 August, 1900' in *Rifle Brigade Chronicle* 1900, pp.143-146.
[119] Martin op. cit. p.170.
[120] Evans *Encyclopedia* op. cit. pp.19 to 20.
[121] *Rifle Brigade Chronicle* 1900, p.179 quoting *The Standard*, September 1900, 'Storming of Bergendal. Gallantry of the Rifles. A Brilliant Charge', from our Special Correspondent. Near Helvetia, August 31.1900
[122] *Rifle Brigade Chronicle* 1900, p.175. 'Bergendal, August 27th 1900' quoting from *The Times*, August 30th, 1900, 'Lord Roberts's Advance. The Fighting at Bergendal. The following telegrams from Lord Roberts have been received at the War Office'.

[123] *Rifle Brigade Chronicle* 1900, pp.177-183, quoting from *The Standard* September 1900, 'Storming of Bergendal. Gallantry of the Rifles. A Brilliant Charge', from our Special Corespondent, Near Helvetia, August 31.
[124] *Rifle Brigade Chronicle* 1900, p.176. 'Bergendal, August 27th 1900' quoting from *The Times*, August 30th, 1900. 'Lord Roberts's Advance. The Fighting at Bergendal. The following telegrams from Lord Roberts have been received at the War Office'.
[125] Jones and Jones, op. cit. p.17.
[126] Pakenham op. cit. p.456.
[127] Reitz op. cit. pp.117-121.
[128] Archer's photograph album, annotation.
[129] Anthony Baker, *The Battles and Battlefields of the Anglo-Boer War, 1899-1902* (Milton Keynes: The Military Press, 1999), p.231.
[130] *Rifle Brigade Chronicle* 1900, pp.356-358; AP Notes.
[131] *The London Gazette* 19 April 1901 p.17.
[132] AP Paley to Archer dated 5 December 1901 from 29 Wimpole Street, London.
[133] AP Paley to Mrs Archer dated 22 April 1901.
[134] *The London Gazette* 8 February and 19 April 1901.
[135] AP Notes.
[136] Ibid.
[137] Anthony Baker op. cit. p.235.
[138] *Rifle Brigade Chronicle* 1900, pp.360-366.
[139] Warburton Edward Davies, b. 14.7.1879, ed. Eton and Sandhurst, 2nd Lt. 4.2.1899, retired as Colonel 1928, d. Camberley 1956.
[140] Letter to Mother dated 17 July 1902.
[141] AP Lowndes to Archer dated 6 December 1910.
[142] AP Notes.

Chapter Six

[1] Material in this and the following two paragraphs, unless otherwise stated, is from Letter to Mother dated 18 October 1902 from Cairo.
[2] They did not move into the Kasr-el-Nil barracks until October 1903: Letter to Mother dated 11 October 1903 from Cairo.
[3] The following year, however, things had improved and he was expecting Cairo to be crowded with tourists during the winter as there had been no cholera that summer: Letter to Mother dated 11 October 1903 from Cairo.

NOTES

[4] AP Notes.
[5] Letter to Mother dated 7 January 1903 from Cairo.
[6] Letter to Mother dated 6 September 1903 from Cairo.
[7] AP, Gough to Archer 24 January 1903.
[8] AP, Gough to Archer 8 February 1904.
[9] Letter to Mother dated 18 October 1902 from Cairo.
[10] Letter to Mother dated 6 September 1903 from Cairo.
[11] Letter to Mother dated 11 October 1903 from Cairo.
[12] Letter Mrs Archer to Archer dated 1 November 1903.
[13] Letter to Mother dated 3 September 1903 from Cairo.
[14] Letter to Mother dated 4 May 1904 from Cairo.
[15] Letter to Mother dated 24 May 1905 from Khartoum.
[16] Ibid.
[17] Letter to Mother dated 18 June 1905 from Khartoum.
[18] AP, Metcalfe to Archer 17 June 1904.
[19] Archer's photograph album.
[20] Letters to Mother dated 20 August and 6 September 1903 from Cairo and 25 June 1905 from Khartoum; AP, Captain White to Archer 15 May 1909: 'Re Quarter Master Sergeant - No there was nothing except the lack of the first class certificate that I know of.'
[21] Letter to Mother dated 25 October 1905 from Khartoum.
[22] Ibid.
[23] Ibid.
[24] Letter to Mother dated 25 June 1905 from Khartoum.
[25] Letter to Mother dated 25 October 1905 from Khartoum.
[26] Photograph in Archer's album.
[27] Letter to Mother dated 7 March 1906 from Shahjahanpur.
[28] Maurice Bazley White, b. 5.7.1879, 2nd Lt. 20.11.1899, half pay on account of wounds received at Vlakfontein 26.12.1900, d. Alresford 8.5.1925. He may have been one of the subalterns at Surprise Hill.
[29] AP, Card from Captain White to Archer dated 19 June 1906.
[30] AP, Card from Captain White to Archer dated 2 July 1906.
[31] AP, White to Archer dated 1 August 1906.
[32] Letter to Mother dated 2 October 1906 from Chaubattia. Richard Burden Haldane, first Viscount Haldane of Cloan, b.1856, d.1928 was Secretary of State for War, 1905-1912, when he remodelled the Army and founded the Territorials.
[33] AP, Dawson, 7th Militia Battalion, to Archer dated 6 November 1907 from Leicester.

[34] AP, White to Archer dated 20 November 1906 from Winchester.
[35] AP Notes.
[36] Letters to Mother dated 2 and 30 October 1906 from Chaubattia.
[37] Letter to Mother dated 1 December 1906 from Shahjahanpur.
[38] AP Diary Notes 1907. Archer's photograph album contains several pictures of the Amir's visit to Agra.
[39] Letter to Mother dated 6 March 1907 from Shahjahanpur.
[40] AP Notes.
[41] Letter to Mother dated 11 July 1907 from Shahjahanpur.
[42] Letter to Mother dated 24 July 1907 from Shahjahanpur.
[43] Ibid.
[44] Letter to Mother dated 22 August 1907 from Shahjahanpur. In Archer's photograph album are photographs of the 'G Company Minstrel Troupe 1906, winners of the Battalion competition', and of the 'G Company Dramatic Group 1907, winners of the Battalion competition', in both of which Archer is seated on the front row.
[45] Letter to Mother dated 2 September 1907 from Shahjahanpur.
[46] Letter to Mother dated 10 January 1908 from Shahjahanpur.
[47] Letter to Mother dated 11 July 1907 from Shahjahanpur.
[48] Letter to Mother dated 2 September 1907 from Shahjahanpur.
[49] AP, General H F M Wilson to Archer dated 14 October 1907 from Poona. Archer marked this 'Ref Staff job.'
[50] AP, Major General Charles Metcalfe to Archer dated 3 November 1907 from Piccadilly, London.
[51] Annotation on photograph in Beryl Groves's photograph album.
[52] AP, Dawson, 7th Militia Battalion, to Archer dated 6 November 1907 from Leicester.
[53] AP, Gough to Archer dated 10 November 1907 from London.
[54] Letter to Mother dated 10 January 1908 from Shahjahanpur.
[55] Letter Archer to his brother Harry dated 16 January 1908 from Shahjahanpur.
[56] Letters to Mother dated 15 July, 4 and 10 August 1908 from Chaubattia; and AP Notes.
[57] AP, Gough to Archer from Colonial Office dated 14 August 1908.
[58] Letter to Mother dated 15 September 1908 from Chaubattia.
[59] *Nyasaland Protectorate, Report for 1908-9* (London: HMSO, 1909), p.15.
[60] Nyasaland Government Blue Book 1908, passim.
[61] Letter to Mother dated 23 October 1908 from Bombay.

[62] Letters to Mother dated 30 September 1908 from Chaubattia and 23 October 1908 from Bombay.
[63] Letter to Mother dated 25 October 1908 from the ship, SS *Kanzler*, off Goa.
[64] Letter to Mother dated 14 November 1908 from Chinde.

Chapter Seven

[1] For fuller details of Chinde see Colin Baker, 'The Chinde Concession, 1891-1923', *The Society of Malawi Journal*, Vol. 33, No. 1, January 1980, pp.6-18.
[2] Colin Baker, *Development Governor, a Biography of Sir Geoffrey Colby* (London: I B Tauris, 1994), Chapter 9.
[3] D Dishington was the owner of Murray's Hotel at Chinde. Archer later referred to this as Dishington's Hotel.
[4] Green, op. cit. p.49.
[5] Stanley Hewitt Fletcher, Member of the Chartered Institute of Accountants, 1892; 2nd Accountant, British Central Africa Protectorate, June 1893; Manager, *British Central Africa Gazette*, October 1894; Acting Chief Accountant, 1895; Central Africa Medal and Clasp, 1896; Collector, Zomba, April 1900; British Vice-Consul and Agent, Chinde, January 1901. Unless otherwise stated, details of Nyasaland civil servants are from the Nyasaland Blue Books.
[6] The *Centipede* was one of the stern wheel paddle steamers of E C Sharrer's Zambezi Steam Navigation Company, 85 feet long and 17 feet broad: S G Williams, 'Some Old Steamships of Nyasaland', *Nyasaland Journal*, Vol. XI, No.1, January 1958, pp.42-56.
[7] This was probably John Tennett, who went to Nyasaland in 1907 as captain of one of the river steamers and later settled at Mangunda near Luchenza: 'Obituary, Basil Tennett', *Society of Malawi Journal*, Vol. 55, No.2, 2002.
[8] Edmond Lushington Rhoades was educated at Rugby School; appointed to BCA Naval Service to command H M S *Pioneer* March 1895; promoted from Second Officer to First Officer, Marine Transport Department 1904. See also excellent description in *Nyasaland Journal*, Vol. X, No. 2, p.26.
[9] Arthur Mylius Ryley, appointed 3rd Grade Clerk in the Secretariat, Zomba, April 1903; promoted Clerk in Deputy Governor's Office, May 1913; resigned April 1914.

[10] Letter to Mother dated 21 November 1908 from Port Herald.
[11] Also of Sharrer's Company, 70 Feet long and 14 feet broad: S G Williams op. cit.
[12] Letter to Mother dated 21 November 1908 from Port Herald.
[13] For a brief biography of Kenneth Metcalfe and his elder brother, Claude, both of the British Central Africa Company, see Colin Baker, 'Claude Metcalfe, 1866-1941 and Kenneth Metcalfe, 1869-1959' *Society of Malawi Journal* Vol. 43, No.2, July 1990, pp.20 ff.
[14] For a fuller description of machilas and machila men, see F Winspear, *Some Reminiscences of Nyasaland*, 1957.
[15] See H Moyse-Bartlett, *The King's African Rifles, a Study in the Military History of East and Central Africa, 1890-1945* (Aldershot: Gale and Polden, 1956), p.3. The Commanding Officer of 1 KAR was Lieutenant-Colonel H A Walker, the Adjutant and Quartermaster was Major H W Stevens. There were four Company Commanders: Captains J Rosborough, H A Case, G C Sladen and R H Pipon. There were also six Lieutenants: D Mills, H A R Hoffmeister, G Wynne Finch, G G S Brander, B Edwards and H T C Jones-Vaughan: Nyasaland Blue Book 1910, pp.N 13-14.
[16] 'The stores I ordered from London have arrived at Berbera so I shall be all right for food when we move back to Central Africa.': Letter to Mother dated 4 July 1909 from Wadamago.
[17] Letter to Mother dated 6 June 1909 from Wadamago.
[18] AP Diary 25 and 26 November 1908.
[19] Letter to Mother dated 25 November 1908 from Zomba.
[20] Douglas Jardine, *The Mad Mullah of Somaliland* (London: Jenkins, 1923).
[21] It had been transferred to the Foreign Office from the India Office in 1898.
[22] Moyse-Bartlett op. cit. p.190. See also Jardine op. cit. Chapter VI.
[23] Jardine op. cit. pp.172-4.
[24] Moyse-Bartlett op. cit. p.179.
[25] Moyse-Bartlett op. cit. p.148.
[26] Letter to Mother dated 21 December 1908 from Chinde.
[27] AP, Passagier-Liste des R-P-D "Prinzessin", Kapitan A Stahl.
[28] *British Central Africa Gazette*, 31 July 1900. See also Colin Baker, *Johnston's Administration, 1891-1897* (Zomba: The Government Press, 1970), pp.39-40; and Fred J Melville, *British Central Africa and the Nyasaland Protectorate* (London: Melville Stamp Books, 1909), p.17n.

[29] For Colville, see Colin Baker, 'The 1905-1910 Journeys of Olivia Colville, Mary Hall and Charlotte Mansfield', *The Society of Malawi Journal*, Vol. 35, No. 1, January 1982, pp.11-29. Olivia was travelling with her husband, Colonel Colville, on a hunting expedition in Central Africa. Arthur Edward Colville b. 20.11 1857, 2nd Lt. 13.9.1875, to half pay as Lt. Colonel 15.12.1903, m. 1883 Olivia d. of Lord Alfred Spencer Churchill, d. 26.2.1943.

[30] AP Diary 23 December 1908-6 January 1909.

[31] The staff and departments serving in Somaliland were: OC Troops, Colonel J E Gough; CSO, Captain Hon H Dawnay - both of the Rifle Brigade and with both of whom Archer had been at the attack on Surprise Hill; SO, AG and QMG, Major L R H Pope Hennessey; Orderly Officer, Captain E R Hayes-Sadler; Senior Intelligence Officer, Captain C E Dansey; Assistant Intelligence Officer, Mr R C Corfield; Lieutenant R A Boger; Major G E Piggott; Captain N G Anderson; PMO Captain M J Quirke; Finance, Treasurer Somaliland Protectorate: Somaliland Order No. 110 of 15.2.1909.

[32] AP Diary 7-12 January 1909.

[33] Letter to Mother dated 27 February 1909 from Wadamoga.

[34] AP Notes.

[35] Letter to Mother dated 13 January 1909 from Burao. Archer's diary entry for 26 September 1908 shows that he 'Ordered from Cowasgee: 1 lb curry; ½ doz whisky, ½ doz lime juice, ½ doz gin, ½ doz tins peas, ½ doz tins carrots, 3 bottles pickles, 3 bottles vinegar, ½ doz tins butter, ½ doz tins cornflour, ½ doz tins Quaker oats, 1 tin mustard.'

[36] Letter to Mother dated 28 January 1909 from Wadamago.

[37] Letters to Mother dated 6 and 14 February 1909 from Wadamago.

[38] See, for example, Letter to Mother dated 20 March 1909 from Wadamago.

[39] Jardine op. cit. pp.189-190.

[40] Letters to Mother dated 18 February, 13 March, 20 June and 4 July 1909 from Wadamago and 17 April 1909 from Eil Dab.

[41] Letter to Mother dated 4 April 1909 from Wadamago.

[42] Letter to Mother dated 5 September 1909 from Somaliland, and Jardine op. cit. p.192.

[43] AP Diary 3 March-6 August 1909.

[44] Letter to Mother dated 14 February 1909 from Wadamago.

[45] AP Diary Notes 1909

[46] Letter to Mother dated 11 November 1909 from Somaliland.

[47] AP Diary 9 to 11 November 1909.
[48] Letters to Mother dated 6 and 20 March 1909 from Wadamago, and 17 April 1909 from Eil Dab. AP Diary 3 March to 26 September 1909 passim.
[49] Letters to Mother dated 17 April 1909 from Eil Dab and 25 April, 1 and 23 May and 4 July 1909 from Wadamago; AP Diary 3 March to 17 August 1909 passim.
[50] Archer hand copied this in Letter to Mother dated 6 June 1909.
[51] Letter to Mother dated 2 December 1909 from Somaliland.
[52] Letters to Mother dated 17 April and 2 December 1909 from Eil Dab; 23 May, 20 June and 18 July 1909 from Wadamago; another Letter to Mother, no address but had moved from Burao, no date but before the summer; marked 29th but no month or year; AP Diary 23 December 1909; *Rifle Brigade Chronicle* 1900 p.359. There is a photograph of Townsend in Archer's photograph album.
[53] AP Diary 1 to 28 October 1909.
[54] Moyse-Bartlett op. cit. p.191. See also Jardine op. cit., p.193.
[55] Letter to Mother dated 2 December 1909 from Somaliland.
[56] Letter to Mother dated 12 December 1909 from Somaliland.
[57] AP Diary 9 to 20 December 1909.
[58] AP Diary 7 to 13 January 1910.
[59] Moyse-Bartlett op. cit. p.149.
[60] Moyse-Bartlett op. cit. p.191.
[61] AP Notes.
[62] Ibid.
[63] Ibid.
[64] AP Diary Notes 6-11 May 1910.
[65] AP Diary Notes 19 June 1910.
[66] AP Diary Notes 18-21 August 1910 and 25 February 1913.
[67] AP Diary Notes September 1910.
[68] AP Diary Notes 7-8 January 1911. Grant may have been Colin Grant, 2nd Grade Resident, but more likely an African soldier or prison warder.
[69] AP Diary 26 May.
[70] AP Diary 26 May-20 August 1910.
[71] This was probably V J N Cox of Nyamateti Estate, Cholo.
[72] A Jay Williams, Chief Assistant Secretary, Secretariat 1908. Owned and managed the British Central Africa Company Shops in Limbe 1922. He specialized in engineering works and was agent for all Ford motor products: Handbooks of Nyasaland, 1908 and 1922.

73 AP, Programme, Blantyre Sports Club, 18-19 August 1910.
74 *Nyasaland Times* 25 August 1910.
75 AP Diary 11-17 August 1912.
76 AP Diary 2-3 April 1912.
77 AP Diary 31 July 1910.
78 AP Diary 8 May 1912.
79 AP Diary 3 and 17 July 1912.
80 AP Diary 12-15 September 1912.
81 Charlotte Mansfield, *Via Rhodesia* (London: Stanley Paul, nd but c 1909), p.354.
82 Nyasaland Blue Books 1912 and 1913: Lieutenant Bockett Pugh, of the Gloucester Regiment, was seconded to the KAR, arrived 11 August 1909, promoted Captain 22 June 1912.
83 AP Diary 16-17 November 1912.
84 AP Diary Notes, 21 December 1913.
85 AP, Captain White to Archer dated 15 May 1909 from Winchester.
86 *Rifle Brigade Chronicle* 1900 p.360.
87 AP, Dickenson to Archer, dated 5 May 1910 from Calcutta. Dickenson shortly became RSM of 2 KAR: Dickenson to Archer, 10 August 1910.
88 AP, List of Passengers on Union Castle *Carisbrook Castle*. The Carisbrook Castle, weighing 7594 tons, was launched in 1898. It sailed from London until 1900 and thereafter from Southampton. It was transferred to the East Africa route in 1912, and became a hospital ship in 1914. It was scrapped 1922. Photograph in CJ Harris and B D Ingpen op. cit. p.166.
89 AP Notes.
90 AP, Thesiger to Archer dated 25 August 1911.
91 AP, draft letter Archer to General Sir Francis Howard, nd but probably 1918.
92 Postcard to Mother dated 15 October 1911 from Naples. While Archer was on leave, 2 KAR returned to Zomba from East Africa, with RSM W Dickenson, to be broken up. In Zomba they formed two new Yao companies and took them back to East Africa for service with 3 KAR, leaving Zomba on 28 August 1911: W Dickenson 'With the KAR', *Rifle Brigade Chronicle*, 1912 pp. 96-106.
93 AP, Dawson to Archer 12 May and 4 April 1912.
94 Francis Staunton Silas Wright was appointed Paymaster on 1 April 1914: Nyasaland Blue Book 1915 p.N 17.
95 AP Notes.

[96] AP, Slattery to Archer 20 July 1913. Slattery had been a Sergeant Major in the KAR and was living at Mtonia, a place three days journey from Fort Johnston and not far from Fort Maguire, in Portuguese East Africa.
[97] AP, H A Case to Archer 18 April 1913.
[98] AP, Thesiger to Archer 29 April 1914.
[99] AP, Gough to Archer 10 February 1914. The words 'I hope you have been successful' suggest that Archer had applied for a civilian job.
[100] AP, H Jones-Vaughan to Archer 6 May 1914.
[101] AP Diary 10 May 1914.
[102] AP Diary 9 May-5 June 1914 and Nyasaland Government Gazette 30 May 1914.
[103] AP, Dickenson to Archer 21 July 1914.

Chapter Eight

[1] Letter to Mother from Wadamago dated 1 May 1909 and Letter Mother to Archer 29 May 1913.
[2] Elsewhere – AP Notes – Archer says that his rejoining his Regiment was granted 'for three months.' Perhaps this was the length of time the War Office expected the war to last.
[3] Letter to Mother dated 8 August 1914.
[4] Harold Mavromichall Biddulph, b. 26.9.1869, 2nd Lt. 6.2.1889, 2nd Battalion Rifle Brigade, Sudan 1896-99, South Africa 1900-02, India, 1906-11, pppromoted Lt. Colonel 16.12.1911, retired 1919, d. France 12.1 1961.
[5] AP Diary 12 August and AP Notes.
[6] This was the day Biddulph recommended him for a commission.
[7] Richard Philip Arenberg de Moleynes, b. 13.12.1881, 2nd Lt.. 8.5.1901, d. London 4.1.1939.
[8] AP Diary Notes 12-15 August 1914.
[9] Nyasaland Government Gazette, 31 October 1914.
[10] Tonie and Valmai Holt, *Battlefields of the First World War* (London: Pavillion Books, 1995) pp.15ff.
[11] Reginald Berkely, *The History of the Rifle Brigade in the War of 1914-18, Vol I, August 1914 - December 1916* (Frome and London: Butler and Tanner), pp.11-12.
[12] AP Diary Notes.

[13] Stuart Hamilton Rickman, b. 11.5.1872, ed. Eton, 2nd Lt. 29.11.1893, killed in action near Cambrai 26.8.1914. 2nd in command to Biddulph.
[14] See also AP, three letters from Rickman's mother to Archer.
[15] Geoffrey Nowell Salmon, b. 26.11.1871, ed. Sherborne, 2nd Lt. 2.6.1894, Major in command of C Company 1st Battalion Rifle Brigade, France 1914, retired as Colonel 1926, d. Winchester 7.12.1954.
[16] Hon Francis Reginald Denis Prittie, b. 15.10.1880, second son of Lord Dunally, 2nd Lt. 2.6.1900, killed in action on the Marne 19.12.1914.
[17] AP Notes.
[18] Elizabeth Saunder to author 5 July 2002. See A J P Taylor, *The First World War: an Illustrated History* (London: Penguin Books, 1966), p.29.
[19] There is a post card of Ligny in Archer's photograph album.
[20] AP, draft letter Archer to Lane, nd but probably early 1918 in Holland.
[21] Ibid.
[22] Taylor op. cit. pp.29-30.
[23] AP Notes.
[24] AP Casualty Form letter E of 13 October 1914.
[25] Letter to Mother dated 9 October 1914 from Cambrai.
[26] Letter to Mother dated 23 October 1914 from Hessen.
[27] Beryl Groves to author 14 February 1999.
[28] Letter Mother to Archer 29 May 1913.
[29] Richard Van Emden, *Prisoners of the Kaiser* (London: BBC Publications, 2000), p.5.
[30] Van Emden, op. cit. p.6.
[31] AP, Archer to 'Arthur', draft, nd.
[32] AP Diary Notes - headed 'Zomba Gymkhana Club, Zomba, Nyasaland.' What follows in this chapter about Archer's time as a prisoner of war, except where otherwise stated, is from this source.
[33] Elizabeth Saunder to author 5 July 2002.
[34] Van Emden op. cit. p.9.
[35] AP Notes.
[36] Van Emden op. cit. p.14.
[37] Photograph in Elizabeth Saunder's album.
[38] Van Emden op. cit. p.16.
[39] Van Emden op. cit. p.18.
[40] Van Emden op. cit. pp.18-19.
[41] Elizabeth Saunder to author 5 July 2002.
[42] Van Emden, op. cit. p. 13.
[43] AP rough notes. nd.

[44] Van Emden op. cit. p.19.
[45] AP, Archer to Adjutant, Rifle Depot, Winchester, dated 16 February 1918 from Scheveningen, and J Todhunter to Archer 26 May 1918.
[46] AP, Prisoners' Identification Card issued by War Department, Heerengracht 13, Hague.
[47] Photographs in Archer's album.
[48] AP, draft letter Archer to Lane, nd but probably early 1918 in Holland.
[49] AP, Archer to 'Arthur', draft, nd.
[50] E. g., AP, Archer to Adjutant, Rifle Depot, Winchester, dated 16 February 1918 from Scheveningen.
[51] AP, J N Gardey to Archer 15 April 1918.
[52] AP, General Sir Francis Howard to Archer 25 May 1918.
[53] AP, draft letter, Archer to Lane, nd but 1918 in Holland. We do not know what that envelope contained.
[54] AP, draft letter Archer to General Sir Francis Howard, nd but 1918.
[55] Ibid.
[56] AP, fragment of draft letter, nd but 1918. The reference to short frocks relates to the short frock coats worn by other ranks.
[57] AP, draft letter, Archer to Lane, nd but 1918 in Holland.
[58] AP, draft letter, Archer to General Sir Francis Howard, nd but before 19 January 1919.
[59] AP, Lord Henniken to Archer 5 March 1919.
[60] AP, draft letter, Archer to General Sir Francis Howard, nd but before 19 January 1919.
[61] Van Emden op. cit. p.21.
[62] Van Emden op. cit. pp.22-23.
[63] Letter Mother to Archer 29 May 1913.
[64] AP Diary Notes - headed 'Zomba Gymkhana Club, Zomba, Nyasaland.
[65] Introductory pages to 1919 Diary.
[66] Other references to K include 7 May 'Went to Luton to see Kathleen.' Letters received 13.2 19 to 29.3.20, 21 letters from Kathleen.
[67] From 27 January to 2 May 1919 there are several entries in diary 'D' followed by '//' in varying numbers. D may be Dora or, less likely, Dims.
[68] AP Diary 27 January and 10 February 1919.

Chapter Nine

[1] AP, Archer to Colonial Office 23 January 1919; AP, Smith to Archer 27 January 1919 and 16 February 1919. Edgar Herbert Warren was born on

29 July 1880 and served in the Transvaal civil service from 1903 to 1908 when he joined the Nyasaland service as a clerk in the Customs department. He had been promoted to be Principal Immigration Officer just before the war. Not long after he declined the post of Superintendent of the Central Prison, he was again promoted, to be Assistant Comptroller of Customs on a salary scale of £450-£550 as compared with that of the Superintendent of the Central Prison, £400-£500, the same as Superintendents of Police: Nyasaland Civil List 1923 and Nyasaland Blue Book 1919.

[2] AP, Archer to Smith, date removed by termites but probably late February 1919.

[3] William Henry Crosby, appointed 23 July 1918.

[4] AP, Smith to Archer 5 March 1919.

[5] Material in this and the following six paragraphs, unless otherwise stated, is from AP Diary 10 March-22 June 1919.

[6] *Nyasaland Times* 29 December 1938.

[7] For photograph of the Savoy Hotel and a description of its services, see Nyasaland Handbook 1922, p.xxxii

[8] See Colin Baker, *Development Governor: a Biography of Sir Geoffrey Colby*, Chapter Nine.

[9] There were two Walkers in the Nyasaland civil service: Charles Henry, born in 1873, and Arthur Henry, born in 1878. Both were Assistant Treasurers and both had been appointed on 1 April 1910. Charles's office was abolished in 1922, when he retired from the service, and Arthur went on to become Controller of Police and Prisons until he retired in 1931. Dr Arthur George Eldred had joined the Nyasaland service as Medical Officer in 1911.

[10] J C Copeland also ran the Chiromo Club.

[11] T Thorburn of Makamba Estate Blantyre or J O Thorburn of Magomero Estate Namadzi: Nyasaland Handbook 1910, p. 86.

[12] Vincent John Keyte joined the Nyasaland service on 14 October 1897 and was made Chief Transport Officer on 21 December 1911.

[13] Ernest Costley-White was a Second Grade Resident who had been in the service since 16 June 1900.

[14] G L Baxter of the Cameron Highlanders had been a Major and Second in Command of 1 KAR in 1918: Nyasaland Blue Book 1918.

[15] Arthur Clement Hayter was a member of the Nyasaland Volunteer Reserve. He was temporarily commissioned in the Nyasaland Field Force during the First World War. His commission was terminated in December

1918, when he took temporary charge of the Central Prison awaiting Archer's arrival.

[16] AP Diary 14 June 1919. Later he was allowed £10 for the loss of this kit: 19 August 1919; but received a cheque for £20 for it: 27 Aug 1919.

[17] Material in the remainder of this chapter, unless otherwise stated, is from AP Diary and Notes.

[18] Nyasaland Blue Book, 1920. Archer joined the Nyasaland Volunteer Reserve on 12 July 1920.

[19] AP, Annual Sports at Blantyre, August 1920, programme of events.

[20] Albert William Beves Northern, 1st Class Clerk in the Treasury.

[21] John Albert Callow, Clerk in the Department of Agriculture.

[22] Archibald Colin Stewart, 1st Class Clerk in the Department of Agriculture.

[23] His domestic staff in 1919 comprised Poly the Cook who was paid 10/- a month; Nyayala the House Boy who received 6/-; and Mataya, the *Sukambale,* dish washer, who was paid 3/- a month.

[24] In his diary Archer does not identify the lady concerned. Whether this was a matter of discretion or whether he did not catch, or soon forgot, her name, is unclear.

[25] Frederick John Lock, appointed to Nyasaland service 14.7.1915; promoted 1st Class Clerk in the Treasury 23.7.1918.

[26] Francis Trant Stephens, OBE MC, Chief Commissioner of Police.

[27] On 7 February he received a cheque from Bithrey for £10.15.4, presumably for accommodating him.

[28] AP Diary passim. Archer had become a Freemason, a member of the Raghet Lodge, soon after he arrived in Egypt in 1902. On 26 April 1906 he became a member of Lodge Affinity, Moradabad in India, and a little later a member of Lodge Fidelity. He joined Lodge David Livingstone in Nyasaland soon after he returned to the country in 1919 and was an active member until he finally retire in 1947.

[29] R D Bell, *Report of the Commission Appointed to Enquire into the Financial Position and Further Development of Nyasaland* (London: HMSO, 1938, Colonial No. 152), pp.180-181.

[30] Nyasaland Blue Books: 1919 p.J3; 1920 p.H3; 1921 p.H3; 1922 p.H7; 1923 p.H7.

[31] Charles Edward D'Auvergne Aplin, appointed to Nyasaland service 8.8.1903, promoted 1st Grade Administrative Officer 1.4.1919.

[32] Elizabeth Saunder to author 24 May 1999 and 5 July 2002.

[33] Richard Sims Donkin Rankine, appointed Chief Secretary 31.10.1920.

[34] Cecil Henry Wade, appointed to Nyasaland service 5.8.1911 and promoted First Assistant Secretary 1.6.1921.
[35] Nyasaland Blue Book 1919.
[36] John Edgar Sidney Old, Medical Officer, first appointed to Nyasaland service 25.6.1900, retired 3.7.1921: Nyasaland Blue Book 1920 and Nyasaland Government Gazette 1921 p.246.
[37] Raymond Bury, Medical Officer who had been in the country since 1911.
[38] Bertram Edward Lilley, Lands Officer who had been in the country since 1919.
[39] Herbert Hyde Young Hearsey, appointed to Nyasaland service 6.6.1896 and promoted Principal Medical Officer 29.4.1902.
[40] Partridge was an expatriate resident in Nyasaland.
[41] William Milne-Tough, Medical Officer, appointed to Nyasaland service 19.5.1919.
[42] Ernest William Davey, appointed to Nyasaland service 18.1.1906, promoted Assistant Director of Agriculture 13.11.1920.
[43] Beryl Groves to author 14 February 1999 and Elizabeth Saunder to author 24 May 1999.
[44] Letter Mrs Archer to Archer 20 May 1902.
[45] Letter to Mother dated 20 June 1909 from Wadamago.
[46] Holy Trinity Church Tulse Hill Marriage Register and Rev Dr Bill Musk, Vicar, to author 7 February 2001.
[47] Elizabeth Saunder to author 5 July 2002.
[48] Hugh Stannus Stannus had retired from the Nyasaland Medical Service in December 1919 and had gone into private practice, having served in the country since May 1905.
[49] Photograph in Beryl Groves's photograph album.
[50] A 'hundredweight', cwt, was 112 pounds.
[51] AP Diary 23 May 1922. This diary entry is not in Archer's handwriting but possibly Muriel's.
[52] George Sanders Paveley was the Deputy Superintendent of the Central Prison, and had been appointed to this post in April 1921.
[53] Winifred Tapson, *Old Timer* (Cape Town: Howard Timmins, nd c 1957), p.2.
[54] AP Diary 5 June 1925 gives details of the equipment he purchased for mat-making, costing £12.12.0.
[55] Lawrence Smith, formerly Treasurer, joined the Nyasaland service in 1899. Keith Ravenscroft Tucker, appointed in 1916, had succeeded him as

Treasurer in 1924. George Henry Tuckett, appointed to the Nyasaland service 31.8.1897, promoted Postmaster-General 1.8.1912.

[56] AP Diary: 'Monday 26 October 1925, Baby died 8.0 p.m. Tuesday 27 October 1925, Baby buried 11.0 a.m.'
[57] Beryl Groves to author 14 February 1999.
[58] Nyasaland Government Gazette 1929.
[59] Elizabeth Saunder to author 24 May 1999 and 5 July 2002.
[60] F and D Bompas interview with author 13 June 2000.
[61] Elizabeth Saunder to author 24 May 1999 and 5 July 2002.
[62] Rosemary Page to author 27 September 1999.
[63] Elizabeth Saunder to author 24 May 1999.
[64] Elizabeth Saunder to author 5 July 2002.
[65] Elizabeth Saunder to author 24 May 1999.
[66] Beryl Groves to author 14 February 1999.
[67] Elizabeth Saunder to author 24 May 1999.
[68] Rosemary Page to author 27 September 1999.
[69] Elizabeth Saunder to author 24 May 1999.
[70] Beryl Groves to author 8 July 2002, and Rosemary Page to author 22 July 2002.
[71] Elizabeth Saunder to author 24 May 1999.
[72] Elizabeth Saunder to author 5 July 2002.
[73] Elizabeth Saunder to author 24 May 1999.
[74] Ibid.
[75] Beryl Groves to author 14 February 1999.
[76] Elizabeth Saunder to author 24 May 1999.
[77] Beryl Groves to author 14 February 1999 and 10 November 2002.
[78] Beryl Groves to author 14 February 1999.
[79] Elizabeth Saunder to author 24 May 1999.
[80] Elizabeth Saunder to author 5 July 2002.
[81] Rosemary Page to author 27 September 1999.
[82] Ibid.
[83] Elizabeth Saunder to author 24 May 1999 and 5 July 2002.
[84] *Nyasaland Times* 15 September 1933.
[85] Nyasaland Blue Books. No data are available for 1919 and 1920.
[86] Elizabeth Saunder to author 24 May 1999.
[87] R D Bell op. cit. p.181.
[88] Elizabeth Saunder to author 24 May 1999.
[89] Ibid.
[90] Nyasaland Blue Books 1919-1938.

[91] Nyasaland Government Annual Estimates of Expenditure, 1919 to 1939.
[92] R D Bell op. cit. pp.180-185.
[93] Nyasaland Blue Book 1936 p.B7.
[94] R D Bell op. cit. and Nyasaland Blue Book, 1936 p.X3.
[95] *Annual Report on the Social and Economic Progress of the People of Nyasaland, 1938,* Colonial Office No. 1902, (London: HMSO, 1939), pp.56-57.
[96] Nyasaland Blue Book 1918, p.Ba2.
[97] Ibid.
[98] Ibid.
[99] R.D.Bell op. cit. p.186.
[100] Horace Minton Shelley, a Pathologist, was appointed to Nyasaland in 1924.
[101] Elizabeth Saunder to author 24 May 1999.
[102] Elizabeth Saunder to author 5 July 2002.
[103] *Nyasaland Times* December 1938.

Chapter Ten

[1] *Nyasaland and the War, September 1939-April 1941, Sessional Paper No.1 of 1941* (Zomba: The Government Printer, 1941), pp.1-2.
[2] AP Notes and copy of letter to Brigade Major KAR Dar es Salaam.
[3] Nyasaland Government Gazette 1939, p.72 and p.108.
[4] *Nyasaland and the War, September 1939-April 1941, Sessional Paper No.1 of 1941* (Zomba: The Government Printer, 1941), pp.1-2.
[5] Ibid.
[6] Nyasaland Government Gazette, 1942, p.36, p.86 and p.128.
[7] *Nyasaland and the War, September 1939-April 1941, Sessional Paper No.1 of 1941* (Zomba: The Government Printer, 1941), pp.1-2.
[8] *Colonial Office Annual Reports, Nyasaland, 1946* (London: HMSO, 1948), p.1.
[9] *Nyasaland and the War, November 1941-December 1942, Sessional paper No.3* (Zomba: The Government Printer, 1943), p.1.
[10] Ibid.
[11] AP Notes. Unless otherwise stated, material in the remainder of this chapter is from this source.
[12] *Nyasaland and the War, January 1st - December 31st, 1943* (Zomba: The Government Printer, 1944), p.1.

[13] Ibid.
[14] Elizabeth Saunder to author 24 May 1999.
[15] Rosemary Page to author 27 September 1999.
[16] Letter to Mother dated 6 September 1903.
[17] Rosemary Page to author 22 July 2002.
[18] Ibid.
[19] Dawnay op. cit. p.89.
[20] Elizabeth Saunder to author 24 May 1999 and 5 July 2002.
[21] Beryl Groves to author 10 November 2002.
[22] Beryl Groves to author 14 February 1999.
[23] Elizabeth Saunder to author 24 May 1999.
[24] Rosemary Page to author 27 September 1999.
[25] Beryl Groves to author 14 February 1999.
[26] Elizabeth Saunder to author 5 July 2002.
[27] Beryl Groves to author 8 July 2002.

Chapter Eleven

[1] Letters to Mother dated 21 January 1910 from Berbera, 6 September 1903, 25 June 1905 from Khartoum and 1 December 1906 from Shajahanpur.
[2] Rosemary Page to author 22 July 2002.
[3] AP Diary 25 December 1913.
[4] AP, Gough to Archer dated 8 February 1904.
[5] AP, Gough to Archer, nd but when Archer was in Egypt: Beryl Groves's photograph album.
[6] AP, Gough to Archer 24 January 1903.
[7] AP, Paley to Archer dated 5 December 1901.
[8] AP, Lowndes to Archer dated 6 December 1910.
[9] Letter to Mother dated 1 December 1906 from Shahjahanpur.
[10] Photograph and annotation in Beryl Groves's photograph album.
[11] Enclosed in Beryl Groves's photograph album.
[12] AP Diary 1909. We do not know who Cully, Edith, Dora, Dim, Nellie and Rose were.
[13] AP Diary 1912 passim.
[14] AP Diary 7 May 1920.
[15] AP Diary 1919 and 1920 passim.
[16] Letter to Mother dated 20 June 1909 from Wadamago.

[17] Sharpe, Manning, Smith, Bowring, Thomas, Young, Kittermaster, McKenzie-Kennedy and Richards. Johnston was Commissioner and not Governor, from 1891 to 1897.
[18] Colby.
[19] Armitage.
[20] Elizabeth Saunder to author 5 July 2002.
[21] Elizabeth Saunder interview with author 10 August 2002. The neighbouring farmer was Major David Henderson, formerly of the KAR.
[22] Beryl Groves to author 10 November 2002: Muriel Archer suffered from high blood pressure and had a series of strokes. She stayed at Naiwale for a while and then lived with her daughter Beryl at Domasi ten miles north of Zomba. When Beryl married, Muriel moved to Newlands Home in Limbe and later went to live with her daughter Rosemary in Salisbury, Southern Rhodesia, where she died and was cremated. Her ashes were flown back to Zomba and interred next to her husband and close to their baby daughter. The epitaph that she selected to be inscribed on Jack's headstone is from Rudyard Kipling's 'Mowgli's Brothers' in *The Jungle Book* (London: The Reprint Society, 1955), p.20, first published in 1894. He also used the words 'man among men' in *Wressley of the Foreign Office, The Bridgebuilders,* and *A Wayside Comedy.*

ACKNOWLEDGEMENTS

Jack Archer's biography could not have been written without the help of four ladies: Sheila Bowden for – albeit inadvertently – first stimulating my interest in her uncle, Jack; and his daughters, Elizabeth, Rosemary and Beryl, for lending me their father's papers and photographs, and for their care and patience in answering my many questions. I am grateful to them.

I am grateful, too, to three special colleagues at the University of Glamorgan: Catherine Evans and Michael Davies for expert technical help with processing the photographs and producing the graphics; and Lucy Thomas for patient and skilful help with guidance on the more intricate aspects of word processing. Their help, always most readily given, is deeply appreciated.